MMPI: Research Developments and Clinical Applications

McGraw Hill Series in Psychology

Consulting Editors

Norman Garmezy
Harry F. Harlow
Lyle V. Jones
Harold W. Stevenson

Adams Human Memory
Beach, Hebb, Morgan, and Nissen The Neuropsychology of Lashley
Von Békésy Experiments in Hearing
Berkowitz Aggression: A Social Psychological Analysis
Berlyne Conflict, Arousal, and Curiosity
Blum Psychoanalytic Theories of Personality
Brown The Motivation of Behavior
Brown and Ghiselli Scientific Method in Psychology
Buckner and McGrath Vigilance: A Symposium
Butcher MMPI: Research Developments and Clinical Applications
Cofer Verbal Learning and Verbal Behavior
Cofer and Musgrave Verbal Behavior and Learning: Problems and Processes
Crafts, Schneirla, Robinson, and Gilbert Recent Experiments in Psychology
Crites Vocational Psychology
Davitz The Communication of Emotional Meaning
Deese and Hulse The Psychology of Learning
Dollard and Miller Personality and Psychotherapy
Ellis Handbook of Mental Deficiency
Epstein Varieties of Perceptual Learning
Ferguson Statistical Analysis in Psychology and Education
Forgus Perception: The Basic Process in Cognitive Development
Franks Behavior Therapy: Appraisal and Status
Ghiselli Theory of Psychological Measurement
Ghiselli and Brown Personnel and Industrial Psychology
Gilmer Industrial Psychology
Gray Psychology Applied to Human Affairs
Guilford Fundamental Statistics in Psychology and Education
Guilford The Nature of Human Intelligence
Guilford Personality
Guilford Psychometric Methods
Guion Personnel Testing
Haire Psychology in Management
Hirsch Behavior-genetic Analysis
Hirsh The Measurement of Hearing

Hurlock Adolescent Development
Hurlock Child Development
Hurlock Development Psychology
Jackson and Messick Problems in Human Assessment
Karn and Gilmer Readings in Industrial and Business Psychology
Krech, Crutchfield, and Ballachey Individual in Society
Lazarus Patterns of Adjustment and Human Effectiveness
Lazarus Psychological Stress and the Coping Process
Lewin A Dynamic Theory of Personality
Lewin Principles of Topological Psychology
Maher Principles of Psychopathology
Marx and Hillix Systems and Theories in Psychology
Messick and Brayfield Decision and Choice: Contributions of Sidney Siegel
Miller Language and Communication
Morgan Physiological Psychology
Nunnally Psychometric Theory
Rethlingshafer Motivation as Related to Personality
Robinson and Robinson The Mentally Retarded Child
Scherer and Wertheimer A Psycholinguistic Experiment on Foreign Language Teaching
Shaw and Wright Scales for the Measurement of Attitudes
Sidowski Experimental Methods and Instrumentation in Psychology
Siegel Nonparametric Statistics for the Behavioral Sciences
Stagner Psychology of Personality
Townsend Introduction to Experimental Methods for Psychology and the Social Sciences
Vinacke The Psychology of Thinking
Wallen Clinical Psychology: The Study of Persons
Warren and Akert The Frontal Granular Cortex and Behavior
Waters, Rethlingshafer, and Caldwell Principles of Comparative Psychology
Winer Statistical Principles in Experimental Design
Zubek and Solberg Human Development

MMPI:
Research Developments and Clinical Applications

EDITED BY

JAMES NEAL BUTCHER, PH.D.
ASSOCIATE PROFESSOR
UNIVERSITY OF MINNESOTA

McGraw-Hill Book Company
New York
St. Louis
San Francisco
London
Sydney
Toronto
Mexico
Panama

MMPI: Research Developments and Clinical Applications

Library of Congress Catalog Card Number 68-8660

07-009315-6

2 3 4 5 6 7 8 9 0 KPKP 7 9 8 7 6 5 4

PREFACE

This volume presents some of the recent research developments and clinical applications of the Minnesota Multiphasic Personality Inventory (MMPI). The stimulus for this volume came from the rapid and continuous growth in the use of the MMPI as a clinical assessment instrument, as an employment screening device in government and industry, and as a research instrument in a wide variety of areas.

The number of research publications dealing with the MMPI in recent years is overwhelming. During the years since 1959, just prior to the publication of Dahlstrom and Welsh's *MMPI Handbook* in 1960, more than 750 articles and books have been published. These publications are listed in Appendix D and have been classified for the reader's convenience into a number of broad areas according to title. An examination of the categories reveals a wide range of research activity as well as intensive research exploration in a number of areas. The scope of this volume does not permit the inclusion of articles representative of all these areas. However, the articles selected are representative of major trends in contemporary research.

The volume begins with Dahlstrom's presentation of a number of controversies which currently surround the use of the MMPI. He provides a comprehensive picture of the historical development of some of the more pervasive attacks on the MMPI and presents evidence from recent research revealing their untenability.

The next five chapters deal with several approaches to MMPI interpretation. In Chapter 2, Carson makes a strong case for the continuing need for the "clinician" and clinical MMPI profile interpretation despite the growing number of automated approaches to personality description. His very useful and widely circulated (unpublished) Manual on MMPI Interpretation is reproduced in Appendix A. The application of actuarial methods to personality assessment is a widely expanding area of interest. The MMPI, because of its psychometric properties and empirical research foundations, lends itself particularly well to this approach. Gilberstadt, in Chapter 3, compares the construction and application of three major "codebook" approaches to MMPI interpretation, while

Marks and Sines, in Chapter 4, discuss some of the problems in the development of an actuarial cookbook and suggest some remedies for them. In Chapter 5, Kleinmuntz presents evidence regarding the accuracy of computerized MMPI decisions of adjustment or maladjustment, and, in Chapter 6, Fowler gives a detailed description of the careful development and utility of the "computerized clinician" that is offered commercially by the Roche Laboratories.

In Chapter 7, Wiggins presents an extensive review of significant research directed toward the development of content scales for the MMPI. This work represents an approach to MMPI scale development which is quite different from the empirically based one on which most MMPI scales were developed.

The next five chapters exemplify some current applications of the MMPI in a number of contexts. In a large number of research studies parent personality characteristics associated with childhood disorders have been examined. Hafner, Butcher, Hall, and Quast, in Chapter 8, review the MMPI literature on parents and make a number of suggestions for future research. The reader interested in a more detailed presentation of the MMPI studies of parents is also referred to Appendix B in which all the studies conducted to date are presented in tabular form.

In Chapter 9 of this volume, Monachesi and Hathaway present a general summary of the personality patterns of delinquents that have emerged from their large-scale longitudinal research program, begun in 1947, aimed at identifying personality characteristics of delinquents.

In Chapter 10, Jacobson and Wirt present MMPI personality characteristics associated with group psychotherapy outcomes for prisoners. The MMPI results described here are only a part of the data collected in the seven-year research project conducted by Wirt. A comparison of "acceptable" and unacceptable" outcome groups on a large number of MMPI scales is presented in Appendix C.

The chapter by Tellegen, Gerrard, Gerrard, and Butcher (Chapter 11) provides an example of the information that can be gleaned from MMPI profiles despite the difficulties involved in subcultural group research. Their paper on serpent handlers, in addition to providing information pertinent to understanding a rather unique subcultural group, introduces some procedures for objectively analyzing MMPI profiles and quantifying clinical interpretations that could be applied effectively in other investigations.

Meier's contribution in Chapter 12 is the first comprehensive presentation of the effects of organic brain disorder on personality as measured by the MMPI. In the last chapter of this volume, Dahlstrom and Meehl present their views on various aspects of the "invasion of privacy" issue in an attempt to clarify the problems involved.

A number of individuals have helped me substantially in the organization and preparation of this volume. I owe a great deal to Mr. Fred Berger, Director of the Nolte Center for Continuing Education, who supported the Symposia on Recent Developments in the Use of the MMPI on which this volume is partially based. Auke Tellegen, Grant Dahlstrom, and Robert Wirt provided helpful suggestions in the early stages of this project. A number of persons have contributed to the preparation of the manuscript. Auke Tellegen and Beverly Kaemmer provided editorial assistance. Katherine Rouzer contributed significantly to the clerical task both in earlier drafts and in the final manuscript, and Mary Tosick made important contributions in organizing the final draft. Cathy Schagh and Ellen Heiting devoted a great deal of time and effort to preparing the final draft.

Acknowledgments must also go to my family—Nancy, Sherry, Jay, and Neal—for their patience throughout this project.

James Neal Butcher

CONTENTS

LIST OF CONTRIBUTORS

James Neal Butcher, Ph.D., Associate Professor, Department of Psychology, University of Minnesota

Robert C. Carson, Ph.D., Professor and Head, Division of Clinical Psychology, Duke Medical Center, Duke University

W. Grant Dahlstrom, Ph.D., Professor, Department of Psychology, University of North Carolina

Raymond D. Fowler, Jr., Ph.D., Associate Professor and Chairman, Department of Psychology, University of Alabama

Louise B. Gerrard. M.A., Research Analyst, West Virginia Department of Mental Health

Nathan L. Gerrard, Ph.D., Professor and Chairman, Department of Sociology, Morris Harvey College, Charleston, West Virginia

Harold Gilberstadt, Ph.D., Research Psychologist, Veterans Administration Hospital, Minneapolis, Minnesota

A. Jack Hafner, Ph.D., Associate Professor, Division of Clinical Psychology, University of Minnesota Medical Center

Marian D. Hall, Ph.D., Associate Professor, Institute of Child Development; Assistant Director, School Psychology Training Program, University of Minnesota

Starke R. Hathaway, Ph.D., Professor and Head, Division of Clinical Psychology, University of Minnesota Medical Center

James L. Jacobson, M.A., Research Fellow, Mayo Foundation for Education and Research, Rochester, Minnesota

Benjamin Kleinmuntz, Ph.D., Professor, Department of Psychology, Carnegie Institute of Technology, Pittsburg

Phillip A. Marks, Ph.D., Professor and Head, Division of Clinical Psychology, Department of Psychiatry, Ohio State University, Columbus

Paul E. Meehl, Ph.D., Professor, Department of Psychology, University of Minnesota

Manfred J. Meier, Ph.D., Professor, Department of Psychology and Department of Psychiatry and Neurology, University of Minnesota Medical Center

Elio D. Monachesi, Ph.D., Professor and Chairman, Department of Sociology, University of Minnesota

Wentworth Quast, Ph.D., Associate Professor, University of Minnesota Medical Center

Jacob O. Sines, Ph.D., Professor, Division of Psychology, University of Missouri Medical School, Columbia

Auke Tellegen, Ph.D., Professor, Department of Psychology, University of Minnesota

Jerry S. Wiggins, Ph.D., Professor, Department of Psychology, University of Illinois, Urbana

Robert D. Wirt, Ph.D., Professor and Director, Clinical Training Program, Department of Psychology, University of Minnesota

Chapter One
Recurrent Issues in the Development of the MMPI

W. Grant Dahlstrom
University of North Carolina

Rather than sketching the broad areas of application of the MMPI, this chapter takes up in detail some of the controversies in which the MMPI is currently embroiled. This decision is based not only on the belief that a careful examination of these criticisms can reveal the crucial attributes of this test but also on the fact that there are available several other means of gaining a broad overview of the recent MMPI developments. There is, for example, the excellent résumé of the MMPI written by Tellegen for the sixth volume of *Progress in Clinical Psychology* (1964). In that chapter, Tellegen reviews most of the books and monographs making up the core of the MMPI literature, discusses the issues involved in special scale construction versus pattern-analytic methods of solving differential diagnostic problems, and summarizes, economically and with insight, the extended debate over the role of response sets in the MMPI.

The reader can get further insight into recent MMPI developments by perusing the bibliography that Butcher gathered and organized into general content categories which appears at the end of this volume. It contains the references on the MMPI appearing in *Psychological Abstracts* since the publication of the Dahlstrom and Welsh *Handbook* in 1960. This bibliography documents the record of growth in the acceptance and use of the MMPI during the last eight or nine years and reflects its many new applications in psychology, sociology, anthropology, education, and related disciplines.

The papers in this volume provide a third, and even more satisfactory, means of gaining this broad overview of trends in MMPI usage. Here, the material given at the two Minnesota conferences is largely

Currently on leave as a special research fellow at the Menninger Foundation, Topeka, Kans., supported by National Institute of Mental Health Grant 1-F3-MH 35376.

preserved; in some cases, the editor has also seen fit to include material not available to the people attending those meetings. As a result, a great deal of valuable research and new ideas on the MMPI have been brought together in a handy and readable format.

All three of these sources providing a general overview of the MMPI developments not only reflect the growth and expansion of its applications but also point up the many heated controversies centering about the MMPI at this time. Some of these attacks are focused upon this particular test with varying degrees of relevance and cogency. There are some, however, which involve broader issues ranging beyond the MMPI to question the professional survival of this approach to personality assessment. Many of these controversies involve fundamental issues in psychometrics and personology. The responses to each of these attacks upon the MMPI and their success or failure in resolving the issues raised reveal many of the virtues of this approach to personality assessment as well as the ingenious and innovative solutions characteristic of the work on this instrument. A careful examination of these criticisms will indicate the possible limitations and weaknesses of this method of personality measurement, introduce several new developments in MMPI research, and reveal the role that the MMPI is coming to play in contemporary psychological theories and personality formulations. This is not to say that all the controversies that center about this instrument are equally cogent or relevant; many of these issues, upon examination, turn out to be old criticisms raised time and again under different guises but basically long repudiated. Since the history of clinical psychology has, until very recently (Reisman, 1966), been sadly neglected, each generation of psychologists has seemed destined to repeat the same round of disputes, arguments, and controversies. For this reason, it is well to begin this résumé with a brief examination of the criticisms that had been raised against personality questionnaires in general by the late 1930s when work on the MMPI was getting underway.

EARLY CRITICISMS OF QUESTIONNAIRES

A review of questionnaires available for personality assessment that was prepared by Ellis in 1946 provides a convenient means of summing up the many concerns voiced about this approach to personality testing around the time Hathaway and McKinley began their work on the multiphasic schedule. This review appeared a few years after the introduction of the MMPI, but the Minnesota developments had not yet had any appreciable impact upon the questionnaire field. (Ellis segregated his discussion of the MMPI in a separate section of his review.) The instruments inveighed against by the critics quoted by Ellis, and which were attacked by Ellis himself, were derivatives of the questionnaire devised by Woodworth and his associates under the pressure of screening demands in World War I. Ellis did not organize these criticisms into any carefully reasoned evaluation of the method or the instruments but merely listed them in a random order. The items varied a great deal in level of conceptualization and ranged widely over substantive, methodological, and psychometric issues. Table 1-1 gives his list of these alleged deficiencies and limitations of personality questionnaires.

Ever since questionnaires were first used systematically in psychological investigations by Galton (1883) and G. Stanley Hall (1883), they have encountered a steady and increasing barrage of criticism. The array of difficulties summarized in Table 1-1 relative to personality questionnaires is thus quite in keeping with the kinds of evaluations this approach has encountered throughout the fields of psychology in which it has been used. The general difficulty underlying these various uses of questionnaires lies in the strong temptation to accept the face validity of the component items. This temptation is almost irresistible, apparently; the error takes innumerable forms and variations, some of which will be traced here.

In Woodworth's Personal Data Sheet (1917) and its many civilian derivatives, the acceptance of face validity was explicit and deliberate. To use this device as a substitute for a much more expensive and time-consuming professional screening interview, the psychologist had to assume that the test subject would interpret and respond to the printed statements in essentially the same way that he would react if a professional interviewer asked him these same questions orally while seated across the desk from him in a private interview. Similarly, the assumption was made that the subject's marks in the answer column could be used in the same way that an assent or denial would be interpreted in the interview. Since these statements were restricted to various psychoneurotic experiences and difficulties, the additional assumption was also made that the more of these features that a subject endorsed as characteristic of himself, the more likely it was that he was indeed seriously psychoneurotic and, therefore, constituted poor potential for army service. This straightforward acceptance of the content of the test responses as descriptive of the subject's personality and behavior may be termed the first level of conceptualization about the validity of inventory item endorsements.

Table 1-1 The general case against the validity of personality questionnaires according to Ellis

1. They lack configurational meanings, give no whole, or organismic, picture of human behavior.
2. They may give an adequate picture of a group, but are rarely of use in individual diagnosis.
3. Personality cannot be described in terms of single traits, such as neuroticism; tests are really measuring a composite of several different traits.
4. They are sometimes unreliable, and so they cannot have a high validity.
5. They measure the same trait under two or more different names.
6. Cultural differences that cause persons to make different responses to tests may interfere with their validity.
7. Questions that are interpreted different ways by different people make test results suspect.
8. There is often a general overestimation, or self-halo, effect when normal persons take these tests.
9. Most subjects can easily falsify their answers and frequently choose to do so.
10. The motivations of respondents may vary in consequence of different conditions under which tests are administered, so true clinical rapport is not possible.
11. The manner in which the responses must be made to the test may influence validity.
12. A lack of internal consistency may invalidate a test; presence of such consistency will not necessarily validate it.
13. The manner in which the test directions are given may affect results.
14. The way in which questions are stated and the vocabulary range may cause misunderstanding and affect validity.
15. Testing is an artificial procedure which has little to do with real-life situations, so results are not very valid.
16. Validation is often against other instruments from which the component items were taken, rendering such validation spurious.
17. A respondent may lack insight into his true behavior or may unconsciously be quite different from the picture he draws of himself on the test.
18. Most of them consist of a potpourri of items of much or little or no significance, so that no one knows what their total scores really mean.
19. Chance plays a large factor in the way many tests are checked and scored.
20. Although neurotic scores on a test may mean something, nonneurotic scores may mean nothing at all or may indicate serious maladjustment.
21. They are often based upon armchair, rather than empirical, construction and evaluation of the test items.
22. Uncritical use of various statistical procedures adds a spurious reality to test data.
23. If no intermediate answers are allowed, the response form may

Table 1-1 The general case against the validity of personality questionnaires according to Ellis *(Continued)*

force inaccurate judgments on the respondents.

24. Tests that claim to measure the same traits may have low-intercorrelations with each other.
25. There are no statistical short-cuts to the understanding of human nature (such as involved factorial analyses).
26. When used for occupational purposes, tests give subjects incentives to overrate themselves and consequently are usually invalid.

Source: A. Ellis, The validity of personality questionnaires. *Psychological Bulletin,* 1946, **43,** 385–440.

After some pilot studies that led Woodworth and his associates to remove some ambiguous and faulty items from the Personal Data Sheet (professionally called the Psychoneurotic Inventory), the technique was employed with some success both in screening out inductees who were to be interviewed further by psychologists and psychiatrists and in making psychodiagnostic assessments in military hospitals. It is difficult to ascertain just how widespread any complete acceptance of questionnaires was at this first level of working assumptions. Actually, the Woodworth-type devices multiplied quickly and grew in number of applications in and out of the military service over the next decade or two. It is equally clear, however, that the evidence began to grow in the research literature that this naïve approach involved numerous problems. A series of studies by Joseph Zubin and his associates at the New York Psychiatric Institute was particularly telling (Landis, 1936; Landis, Zubin, & Katz, 1935; McNemar & Landis, 1935; Page, 1935; Page, Landis, & Katz, 1934).

These investigators systematically compared test answers obtained from various patients and from normal adults on standard published tests such as the Bernreuter (1933) and the Neymann-Kohlstedt (1929), with some questionnaires devised in their own setting. Zubin and his associates found a number of paradoxes: Many items scored for emotional disorder on these tests were actually answered in the significant direction more frequently by normal subjects than by the patients. Since there was no doubt at all about the psychiatric status of their patients and they were reasonably certain about the sound adjustment of their normal subjects, there was dismaying evidence that these test items were working backward.

In further studies, these investigators administered questionnaires to additional patients with various psychiatric difficulties and simultaneously made direct observations of their ward behavior, conducted interviews with these patients (and with knowledgeable informants) about their backgrounds and previous behavioral histories, and carefully examined the case records assembled on these individuals. Again, they found a number of contradictions between what the patients were doing, what they told interviewers about themselves, what was known about their previous behavior, and the ways that they described themselves on the questionnaire items. Some of the contradictions seemed to arise from deliberate lying; sometimes they covered up on the tests what they revealed in interviews, but often, just the reverse, they gave a more revealing self-portrayal on the test than in the interpersonal relationship of the psychiatric interview. Other contradictions seemed to be functions of poor self-insight, memory defects, or gross psychotic confusion. Although by no means all the self-depictions on the questionnaires were called into question by their findings, the work of Zubin et al. indicated serious difficulties in the dependability of test content and replies as a basis for a reconstruction of a patient's prior history, a summary of his previous experiences, or an appraisal of his current psychiatric status.

By the middle of the nineteen thirties, there was ample evidence that there were serious limitations in the use of questionnaires for personality appraisal based on simple face validity of the self-descriptions. A majority of the criticisms listed by Ellis concern this approach to questionnaire interpretation. (In Table 1-1, items 4, 5, 8, 9, 11 to 13, 16, 17, 19 to 24, and 26 are directly pertinent.)

As a consequence of these difficulties, many psychologists who continued to use these instruments shifted both their conceptualization of the questionnaire approach and their interpretation of item endorsements from their test subjects. If they could not always trust the self-descriptions to be accurate or isomorphic with some veridical fact about a person, they could at least accept the item endorsement itself as a behavioral datum. The fact that the person was willing to say that something was true or not true about himself provided the professional worker with additional material to be used in the assessment of that person. This new set of assumptions about the meaning of answers to test items constitutes a second level of conceptualization in the use of questionnaire data: Test responses are not always factual self-reports, but they are potentially useful expressions of self-attitudes.

Conceiving test item endorsements in this new way, many psychologists found this more sophisticated view of tests a very appealing and intriguing approach. It more closely approximates the way in which experienced interviewers judge the material obtained in clinical interviews. In both instances, the clinician does not accept what he is told at face value but generally considers it noteworthy that a given attribute is acknowledged or denied. It remains as a challenge for him to determine which, if any, of the client's assertions are factual and why he is presenting himself in just this particular way.

It is also important to note that this level of conceptualization about item answers and test scale scores characterizes a great deal of the factor-analytic research on personality questionnaires. These studies start from a set of intercorrelations, either among individual item answers or among scores on these items collected into scales, and seek order among these patterns of covariation. Interpretation of the reasons for certain items or scales clustering together is almost always sought by detailed examination of what the subjects are saying about themselves on the component items, the ways in which the test subjects are describing their own self-views. Judgments about the content of the items that are used to guide factor-analytic interpretations may occasionally reflect an acceptance of the actual face validity at the first level of conceptualization about test answers; but more frequently they reflect this more sophisticated second level, i.e., the reflection of attitudes toward the self.

Even this more advanced view of test behavior and its psychological significance came under close scrutiny and attack. The findings of Zubin and his associates had direct relevance to this approach, too. In addition to the difficulties arising from limitations in honesty, self-insight, or memory for emotionally charged experiences, they identified further problems stemming from limitations in the ability of their subjects to read and interpret the questionnaire statements. They found that some differences in interpretation of the test items came from unfamiliarity with the English language, from divergent connotations that various words, phrases, or idioms held for different individuals, from markedly different reactions to adverbial and adjectival modifiers, and from poor reading habits. Some patients were too tense to concentrate or too confused to grasp the content of what they were reading when they completed the test questionnaires. When interviewed later, they often retracted what they had endorsed and were puzzled as to why they had answered the way they did at the first test session.

From findings of this kind, Zubin and his colleagues raised serious doubts that questionnaires could be relied upon to give dependable samples of a person's self-attitudes. With the many areas in which interpretations of the test item content were known to diverge, in which gross differences in semantic inference could enter, the answers to personality questionnaires could not be a workable basis for reconstruction of a person's self-views. In Ellis's list, several criticisms seem especially relevant to this second level of conceptualization of test item endorsement (in Table 1-1, see items 6, 7, 10, 14, 18, and 25). Goldberg (1963) has developed a model of this kind of ambiguity in personality inventory items which also reflects this second level of conceptualization.

Many psychologists at this time in the development of clinical assessment methods abandoned their reliance upon personality inventories, switching their allegiance to other instruments, particularly the Rorschach and TAT, or relying upon personal interviewing exclusively in their clinical work. (Both these latter areas of personality assessment have claimed the attention of Zubin since this time. He and his associates—Zubin, Eron, and Schumer, 1965—have come to view the personality inventory as a rather degenerate form of the clinical interview in which the opportunity for observation of nonverbal behavior is virtually eliminated and in which the all-important interchange between interviewer and interviewee is all but deleted.)

At this point, against the general trend, Hathaway and McKinley (1940) took a third view of the potential utility of responses to test items. They considered that what is reflected about a test subject when he endorses an item as true or false as applied to himself is an open question—a question to be answered by empirical search. This approach to scale construction by the Minnesota group is simple, even obvious, perhaps, after it has been pointed out. To arrive at this view initially, however, the investigator has to be willing to confess ignorance. He has to look beyond the content of his items to the nontest information available on his test subjects. In the terminology of Florence Goodenough (1949), the empirical approach involves a shift from viewing the item replies as samples of self-attitude (which they may be for the person completing the test) to perceiving them as behavioral signs (which they can become for the psychodiagnostician). Even though the subject is being asked to describe his own history or present his own self-views, the psychologist accepts these endorsements as neither reflecting factual reality nor mirroring self-attitudes but as signs of something potentially important but not yet known.

The direction of search which Hathaway and McKinley took led them to seek these meanings within the major dimensions of psychiatric disturbance. Their choice of potential nontest correlates gave the MMPI a purchase on personality variables which determine a great many important real-life adjustments and adaptations. It also gave the test a strong coloration of psychopathology. As will be noted later, much of the subsequent work on the test has modified this initial restriction to the psychiatric domain and extended its application to nearly the whole range of personality manifestations; but over time, the importance of it empirical roots in these salient personality variables has become even clearer.

Simple as this shift to the third level of conceptualization may seem, it is surprising how often psychologists, clinicians, and psychometricians alike have failed to appreciate its significance. For example, some of the work of Hase and Goldberg (1967) at the Oregon Research Institute offers evidence that scales of several different derivations—factor-analytic, rational, or empirical—may perform criterion discriminations equally well as long as they all reflect the same sources of variance being sampled by an item pool. However, since the item pool that they used was the product of a great deal of prior empirical selection and refinement by Gough in building his California Psychological Inventory, their findings and conclusions may be quite circumscribed in generality.

Even now, many of the attacks on the MMPI are based upon the assumption that the MMPI is used in accordance with the first or second level of conceptualization described above. In Ellis's list, it is rather surprising to see how many of the early criticisms of questionnaires are vitiated by the systematic adoption of this third level of conceptualization; perhaps only items 1 to 3 and 15 (in Table 1-1) really remain relevant, hinging as they do upon the realities of empirical cross validation. Unfortunately, through ignorance or misunderstanding, many of these criticisms were applied to the MMPI when it appeared. Mixed in with them, however, were many relevant and important criticisms of the MMPI. Response to these constructive and cogent evaluations has led to new research that has strengthened the methods of test interpretation.

PROBLEMS OF NONCOMPLIANCE WITH INSTRUCTIONS

Many early critics, with only limited familiarity with the MMPI, mentioned the usual risks of poor cooperation, inefficient reading and clerical skills, poor mastery of English, or ignorance and confusion as reasons to reject this instrument along with all other questionnaires. These writers ignored the surprising effectiveness of the three original validity indicators—?, *L*, and *F*—in identifying protocols that were relatively useless samples of the appropriate self-descriptions that are needed to make the usual MMPI-based discriminations. Thus, gross misunderstanding or great resistance to taking the test often showed up as a large number of item omissions. Efforts to circumvent the instructions by failing to describe oneself and, instead, depicting some ideal adjustment or hypothetical person would appear as elevations on the Lie scale. Records from illiterate, psychotic, or completely uncooperative individuals which closely approached random responding were recognizable by a very high *F*-scale value and could be reliably segregated from dependable records. Subsequent research indicated (Dahlstrom & Welsh, 1960) that both validity scale patterns and clinical scale patterns were useful in this kind of discrimination.

More subtle forms of noncompliance with the test instructions embodied in various kinds of faking have also received a great deal of attention, both from MMPI critics and from MMPI investigators. It was early recognized by Hathaway and McKinley that these faking distortions will take several different forms either in the direction of greater adjustment or toward some type of emotional disorder. They provided the *L* (lie) and *F* (confusion) scales to evaluate gross and obvious efforts in these directions before the test was made available. Surprisingly, many quite sophisticated psychometric studies of test slanting in recent times have tended to emphasize one or the other of these faking dimensions to the exclusion of the other, failing to recognize that this kind of behavior is by no means unidimensional. In terms of MMPI variables, it should be obvious that the *L* scale is not just the obverse of the *F* scale. In terms of human personality processes, it is equally important to recognize the fact that styles of self-presentation cannot be adequately summarized by placing an individual somewhere along a single dimension ranging from faking bad, through accurate self-depiction, to faking good. All too often the clinician gets evidence that the subject is doing several different things simultaneously in his efforts to communicate about himself to the diagnostician or therapist.

Many studies, at Minnesota and elsewhere, were carried out on the effects of faking on MMPI profiles. The work at Minnesota led to the development of the *K* scale (Meehl & Hathaway, 1946) and to the statistical corrections it provided for five component scales in the clinical profile (McKinley, Hathaway, & Meehl, 1948). This refinement was an outgrowth of criticisms of the validity indicators and their limitations in identifying more subtle forms of slanting of answers to the test. In spite of these developments, and with little regard for or awareness of other work both scales—such as Gaugh's Dissimulation scale (1954), Cofer, Chance, and Judson's Positive Malingering scale (1949), or Meehl's Normality scale (1945)—and on patterns—

such as Gough's $F-K$ dissimulation index (1950)—a number of critics have recently advanced serious attacks on the validity of the test in terms of its susceptibility to "massive response set" distortions. These criticisms have taken three general forms: deviation response formulations, social favorability response formulations, and acquiesence response formulations.

THE DEVIATION RESPONSE FORMULATION

As originally enunciated by Berg and his students (Berg, 1955, 1957), the deviation response hypothesis was a rather bald statement that the value of any personality assessment procedure lay in its ability to provide an opportunity for the test subject to reveal his tendencies to deviate from some established norm. Although it has since been radically modified, its initial formulation had several unfortunate implications leading to some rather harsh judgments about the MMPI and similar instruments. One strong contention of this hypothesis was that there was really only one basic dimension in this tendency to deviate, only a single source of variance (Sechrest & Jackson, 1963). With this assumption, personality devices could be compared directly with one another in the degree to which they allowed this tendency to deviate (or to show abnormality) to appear in the responses or scores. Differences in content of the various devices could be ignored (Berg, 1959) in terms of what was being revealed, since all deviations were assumed to be reflecting a single basic attribute. Content differences, however, could be used to explain why some devices showed more or less of the desired variance. The MMPI came off poorly in such determinations. The implication was clearly drawn that subtle forms of response deviation were the most useful psychodiagnostically. The content of MMPI items was deemed to be too threatening and thus not permitting these more subtle degrees of response deviation to appear. (Compare this line of criticism with items 14 and 20 in Ellis's list in Table 1-1.)

Many difficulties in this deviation response formulation finally became apparent even to the proponents of this hypothesis. One of the first difficulties to appear when it was applied to the MMPI scales was that only deviations away from the endorsements of the majority of Minnesota normal subjects were taken into consideration by this formulation (the so-called plus items on the MMPI scales); the appreciable number of zero items, scored in the direction of the majority response, were completely overlooked. Hathaway and McKinley (1940) had identified useful items for membership on the component scales of the MMPI not only on the basis of excessive endorsements by clinical groups of the minority response but also on the basis of excessive conformity to the majority response. These zero items on the MMPI scales did not fit in with the simple form of the deviation response hypothesis.

Even more important, the data that were accumulating about MMPI configurations gave ample evidence that, on the MMPI at least, there were dependable differences among various abnormal subjects that could not be adequately summarized by any one tendency to deviate and that could not be ignored in any psychodiagnostic or therapeutic approach. As various modifications were made in the original statement of the deviation response hypothesis, it moved gradually back into a form that is in no way different from any other basic assessment approach (Berg, 1967), and thereby much of the catchy appeal it had in its radical form for some psychologists has been lost. Nevertheless, there are still some psychologists who tend to characterize the MMPI and kindred personality inventories as merely highly redundant devices for sampling, over and over again, the tendency to deviate from the social norm.

SOCIAL FAVORABILITY RESPONSE FORMULATIONS

Although conceptually quite similar, the formulations of Edwards and his followers (Edwards, 1957, 1962, 1964) have used social acceptability rather than sheer social conformity and deviation as the basis for explaining their view that the MMPI and other personality inventories are actually only measuring one major underlying dimension. Their position is that the MMPI is susceptible to the effect of an all-pervading response set to give the test administrator a self-flattering picture of oneself rather than a realistic one. A single source of variance, in this instance social desirability variance, is considered to be the major contribution to MMPI scores, while additional sources of variance, as from a tendency to acquiesce to the pressure to answer items in some one direction or from the tendency to answer honestly and factually, are given only a small role in determining the test scores. Figure 1-1 summarizes these views of Edwards and his associates. The basic measurement aim envisioned by the psychometric formulations within which Edwards's approach has been couched is to get the valid score variance in some scale (represented at the far right in Figure 1-1) to conform as closely as possible to the variance of

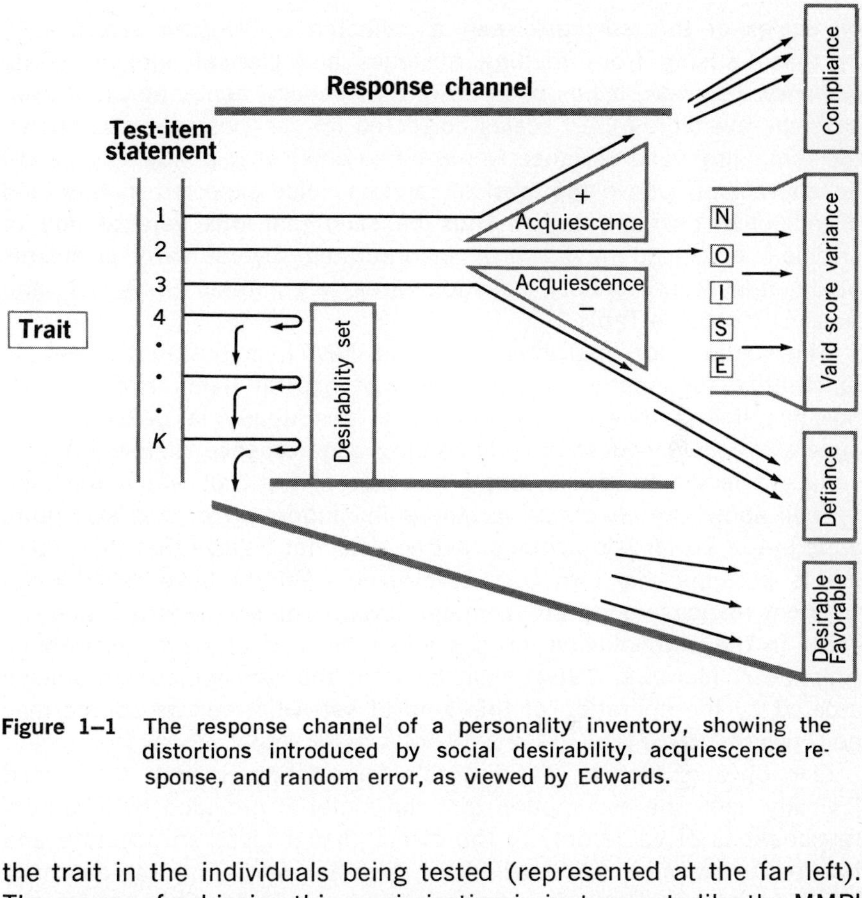

Figure 1–1 The response channel of a personality inventory, showing the distortions introduced by social desirability, acquiescence response, and random error, as viewed by Edwards.

the trait in the individuals being tested (represented at the far left). The means of achieving this maximization in instruments like the MMPI is by sampling responses of true or false to various items (1, 2, 3, 4, . . . through K); this is the response channel provided by personality inventories.

In Edwards's view then, this particular response channel is likely to be blocked by the controlling sets to respond in various erroneous ways. Most important of these sources of error is the tendency to give a stereotypic self-representation, so that the scores in the scale mostly reflect how much that subject wants to appear acceptable or worthy of positive regard and social approval; little of the accurate self-view comes through in the scale score summary. Answers to items neutral in their social import, and thus not markedly affected by social desirability slanting, may still be distorted by less important, but detectable, tendencies to acquiesce in answering one way or another in this true-false choice. The diagram also indicates that all scores on scales of this sort are seen as affected by random errors such as those arising from reading mistakes and clerical slips in filling out answer sheets. It has been Edwards's general contention that even were the available MMPI scales corrected for response set distortions, the remaining valid variance would be so small that it would not show up appreciably above the level of random noise expected in this kind of response channel. It can thus be seen that this general line of criticism advanced by Edwards incorporates several early criticisms made against personality questionnaires, e.g., items 8, 9, 19, and 26 in Ellis's list in Table 1-1.

The solution for instruments like the MMPI, in Edwards's view, is to identify sufficiently large numbers of neutral items (from the K possible items) that are free of social desirability influence and to generate a balanced scale (eliminating acquiescence distortion) with sufficient length to give a stable measure of the trait which will then be well above the effects of variations in random error. It is also quite apparent in Edwards's writings that he does not believe that this repair job is possible; his own test development efforts have relied upon different response and item formats. Edwards himself seems less interested in the psychological origins and processes of social desirability (Crowne & Marlowe, 1964) than he is in the psychometric problems created by the operation of this kind of set, whatever its source may be (Edwards, 1967).

One obvious feature of Edwards's formulation is that it is based logically upon the assumption that the material provided by inventory responses is of value only to the extent that it gives an accurate and true picture of a person's self-views. In other words, here is an entire approach to personality inventory responses that starts from the second level of conceptualization described above. The isomorphism that is sought is between a set of descriptions on the items (summarized in the scale score) and the trait as really viewed by the person being tested. From this point of view, any feature of the test—item statements, instruction answer sheet format, etc.—that gets in the way of an accurate self-revelation will be *by definition* a source of measurement error. Edwards's research has made this characterization all too clear; having demonstrated some influence of a particular response set in a test to his own satisfaction, he categorically labels that influence error. If that variance is large, it thereby damns the instrument and the approach. It can be shown, however, that this kind of interpretation does not hold for scale construction procedures that are based upon the third level of conceptualization of inventory data. Before examining any of this evidence, it would be helpful to present a description of the acquiescence response hypothesis by way of contrast to Edwards's formulations.

THE ACQUIESCENCE RESPONSE FORMULATION

The major proponents of the acquiescence response set as the most pervasive source of variance in MMPI scores are Messick and Jackson (1961; Jackson & Messick, 1962), although many other investigators

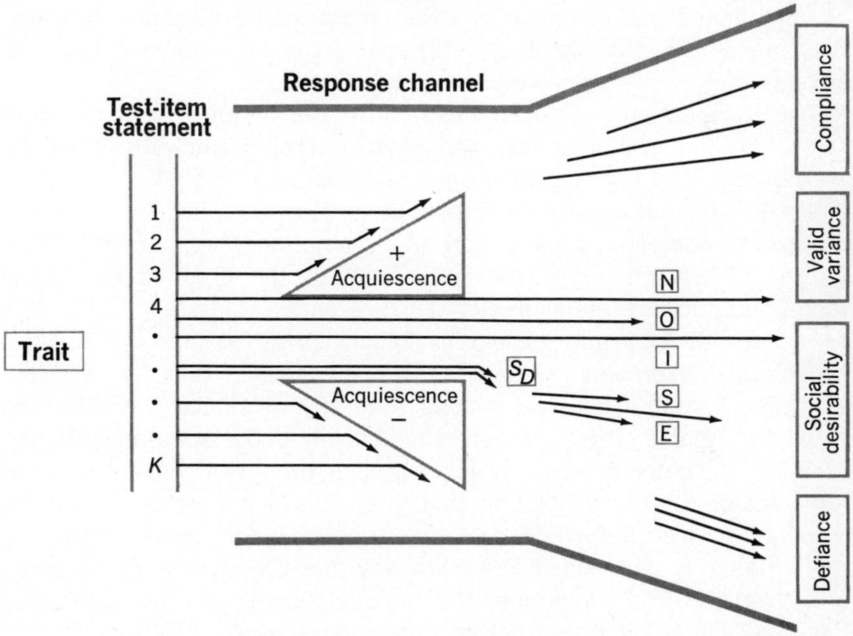

Figure 1–2 The response channel of a personality inventory, showing the distortions introduced by social desirability, acquiescence response, and random error, as viewed by Messick and Jackson.

have joined in the controversies over these issues. The psychometric issues and formulations in Messick and Jackson's criticisms of the MMPI are very similar to those advanced by Edwards, as Figure 1-2 shows. The maximization of correspondence between trait and scale score is again the goal; the response channel is viewed in the same way. The differences lie primarily in the proportions of variance assigned to acquiescence set and social desirability set. In their view, the MMPI, by its item formation and its item response format, generates a compelling tendency to go along with (or struggle against) an inclination to admit to all kinds of different emotional difficulties. (For comparison, see items 9, 11, 14, 19, and 23 in Table 1-1.) It is this orientation that test subjects are presumed to take; consequently, their answers on the scales do not reflect variations in the attributes being alluded to in the items but merely show in varying degrees how much they are influenced by the acquiescence set. Messick and Jackson have also made recommendations for changes in the basic MMPI scales: Reduce the preponderance of true or false keying of the component items in each scale to achieve a balance of compliance and defiance in these scores. Like Edwards, however, they are pessimistic that the MMPI scales can be reclaimed from the adverse effects of these various sources of error.

The formulations of social desirability and acquiescence response sets share more than a common psychometric framework: They are both based upon highly similar sources of data and modes of statistical analysis. The data come from test endorsements provided by single groups of subjects, usually normal in emotional adjustment (Dahlstrom, 1962). The approach involves both the creation of special scales to epitomize the source of variance under study (e.g., Edwards's *SD* scale, Messick and Jackson's *Dy* scales keyed also for acquiescence, or Fulkerson's *Aq* scale for acquiescence directly) and the analysis of intercorrelations among a variety of clinical, validity, and "stylistic" scales. The approach relies heavily upon factor-analytic partitioning of common factor variances; each proponent typically settles for a factor rotational solution that gives heaviest weights among the loadings to his preferred scale or variable. In all these endeavors, the variance is partitioned in such a way that the stylistic components are given maximal weighting, the residuals being left for estimating the "logical trait" variance in the substantive scales.

In this lengthy and acrimonious debate, the critics of the stylistic formulations of Edwards or Messick or Jackson have raised many kinds of evidence to refute the original contentions. These counterarguments have ranged widely from elegant logical analyses of the difficulties inherent in the kinds of data that are summed to compute social desirability values (Norman, 1967), through empirical demonstrations of the important differences between stereotyped social desirability ascriptions of a person and his own personal desirability views of item content (Wiggins, N., 1966), to deliberate manipulations of item content to plot the resulting changes in endorsement patterns (Rorer & Goldberg, 1965), to changes in test instructions to study the shifts in scale values that result (Wiggins, J. S., 1959, 1962). Perhaps the most compelling and forceful criticism of these views to date, however, has been the rebuttal by Block (1965).

Block accepted fully the challenge of response set formulations and carried out the suggested alterations and revisions of the component scales of the MMPI. First with the acquiescence formulation, then with the social desirability hypotheses, he modified the basic MMPI scales and carefully examined the resulting patterns of intercorrelation that they generated after such changes in item keying and favorability balancing. The factor-analytic data from which he worked came primarily from five sets of MMPI records of subjects who were studied at one time or another at the Institute for Personality Assessment and Research (IPAR), the University of California at Berkeley. Since the impact of these changes upon the factor loadings in his analyses was demonstrably weak for all these independent samples, he was able to show that these influences had been greatly overemphasized by their proponents. Using their own general approach and the same kinds of evidence, Block thus rejected both these formulations as misleading in ascribing to various stylistic sets massive amounts of variance in the basic MMPI scales.

Block's data were even more compelling, however, when he shifted from the internal analyses typical of Edwards's or Messick and Jackson's approaches and appealed to external evidence to clarify these issues. Block used the personality ratings and judgments that were made independently of test scores and placed on file for these subjects at IPAR. With these data he was able to explore nontest, external personality correlates of the sources of variance which Edwards and Messick and Jackson had been ascribing either to specific test biases or to circumscribed test-taking personality styles. The data on these subjects ranged widely over many traits, defenses, and mild psychopathological symptoms; in personality coverage, they contrasted rather markedly with the narrow range of personality data available for study prior to this time (McGee, 1962). Searching through these personality data in each of his research samples, Block identified a number of stable correlates of normal subjects who score at each end of the two general dimensions of personality variance that run through many of the basic clinical scales of the MMPI. Table 1-2 presents a few of these traits for each dimension (alpha and beta) and for each end of these dimensions (plus and minus).

In the course of Block's presentation, it becomes clear to workers who are familiar with previous factor studies of the MMPI that Edwards has been working with the variance previously identified with Welsh's factor A, while Messick and Jackson have been focusing on the variance identified quite well by Welsh's factor R (Welsh & Dahlstrom, 1956). Block's own research has led to somewhat different scales and slightly altered interpretations of these two major sources of vari-

Table 1-2 Traits associated with alpha or beta dimension

Minus-alpha traits

1. Feels a lack of personal meaning in life
2. Feels cheated and victimized by life; self-pitying
3. Thinks and associates to ideas in unusual ways; has unconventional thought processes
4. Tends to ruminate and have persistent, preoccupying thoughts

Plus-alpha traits

1. Is consciously unaware of self-concern; feels satisfied with self
2. Tends to arouse liking and acceptance in people
3. Is turned to for advice and reassurance
4. Is cheerful
5. Emphasizes being with others; gregarious
6. Judges self and others in conventional terms such as "popularity," "the correct thing to do," social pressures, etc.

Plus-beta traits

1. Is emotionally bland; has flattened affect
2. Favors conservative values in variety of areas
3. Tends toward overcontrol of needs and impulses
4. Is moralistic (regardless of the particular nature of the moral code)
5. Behaves in an ethically consistent manner; is consistent with own personal standards

Minus-beta traits

1. Is a talkative individual
2. Tends toward undercontrol of needs and impulses; unable to delay gratification
3. Is self-indulgent
4. Is self-dramatizing; histrionic
5. Tends to perceive many different contexts in sexual terms; eroticizes situations

Source: J. Block, *The challenge of response sets: Unconfounding meaning, acquiescence, and social desirability in the MMPI.* New York: Appleton-Century-Crofts, 1965.

ance common to MMPI scales; in his monograph he offered refinements of his scales and their personological implications. Block also prefers a characterological interpretation over the previous state or defense inferences. Thus, he named the first or alpha factor variance "ego resiliency," since so many of the empirical correlates among the independent ratings point up the resourcefulness, adaptability, and active engagement with the world of persons scoring high (plus) on his alpha factor scale. His scale for the beta factor is called "ego control." At the upper end it reflects important features of emotional constraint and distance from others; at the lower end, subjects are seen as showing excessive spontaneity, short-lived enthusiasms, and wide fluctuations in mood. (The reader is urged to read Block's monograph in order to follow in detail his reasoning and the powerful chain of evidence which he marshalls for his point of view.)

The import of Block's findings is crucial: Evaluations of many criterion characteristics that the MMPI provides for the psychodiagnostician are generated by the way test subjects present themselves or orient themselves to the test. Rather than being sources of distortion, as they have been labeled by Edwards or Messick and Jackson, these sets or styles of response actually turn out to be the basis for some of the important trait discriminations. Thus, in the material depicted in Figures 1-1 and 1-2, the biases in the response channel must be equated with the trait itself rather than having an independent status as these formulations would insist. The investigations of the social desirability and acquiescence response proponents have rarely included any evidence about the correspondence of their test scores to nontest data on the traits. Hence, they lacked the information necessary to decide whether the variance that they arbitrarily assigned to one response set or another was in fact unrelated to trait variance. From Block's findings it is clear that were these kinds of data to be thrown out of all test scores, important variance would be lost to the clinician. The MMPI scales would be weakened in their discrimination in proportion to this purification.

Block's evidence has had some impact upon these investigators as well. In a recent presentation, Edwards (1967) has acknowledged some special psychometric difficulties in simple applications of the social desirability formulation to scales that are mixed in desirability composition and complex in item endorsement patterns such as those making up the MMPI clinical scale profile. Similarly, Messick (1967) and Jackson (1967) have recognized some limitations inherent in traditional factor-analytic models when applied to data having important nonlinear properties and have also offered acquiescence response set interpretations that posit several different sets in place of the single pervasive influence that they originally advanced. Nevertheless, their previous attacks have led many psychologists who are not informed in detail about tests like the MMPI to believe that these instruments are both unsound and unworkable for any clinical application. It is unfortunate that some of these more reasonable statements appearing now could not have appeared earlier in time to offset the many bitter polemics resulting from these criticisms.

METHOD VARIANCE VERSUS CONTENT VARIANCE

In what has proved to be a highly influential paper, Campbell and Fiske in 1959 proposed an approach to the evaluation of the efficacy of any psychometric instrument termed the multitrait-multimethod matrix for construct validation. In this paper, they also evaluated many personality instruments including the MMPI; almost all these tests were found seriously wanting in meeting their new standards of validation. In simple terms, what these writers say is that any instrument purporting to measure, say, trait A should provide evidence in its manual (or other descriptive résumés) not only that its scores correlate with that trait but that they are not related to some other traits, B, C, etc. To establish that this instrument in question does measure trait A, this trait must of course be evaluated on some other basis than the first instrument; these other methods of evaluating traits A, B, C, etc., are designated methods 2, 3, 4, etc., in contrast to the trait evaluation provided by the instrument in question (method 1). Thus, the Campbell-Fiske proposal embodies multiple methods (tests, devices, assessment approaches) and multiple traits (A, B, C, etc.) which are combined into a single intercorrelational matrix. This matrix simultaneously provides evidence on the extent to which the separate measures of a particular trait converge (the desired validity for that trait) and on how the measures of different traits provided by any one instrument or method diverge (the required differentiation of one trait from another). Thus, the Campbell-Fiske approach embodies points raised by items 5, 12, 16, and 24 in Ellis's list. Point 25, however, is also pertinent, as will be made clear below.

Figure 1-3 shows how four common approaches to personality assessment could be applied to the evaluation of some particular trait. The trait is represented at the center; each method offers different situational stimuli as a means of sampling different kinds of behavior and results in recorded behavioral products that are combined to provide a set of four different indices of the trait in question. To generate a full multitrait-multimethod matrix, these four approaches would be used to evaluate several traits in turn. A hypothetical multitrait-multimethod matrix from Campbell and Fiske (1959) is shown in Table 1-3. (This table shows only three methods and three traits, but the representation is otherwise appropriate.)

According to these proponents, their approach not only provides the convergent and divergent validational information needed to evaluate the efficacy of any one method but also enables the psychometrician to evaluate the extent to which any one method introduces some common variance into any trait scores derived from that approach. In terms of the exemplary assessment approaches in Figure 1-3, the extent to which the inventory scores correlate with assessments of the trait by the interview approach or by either of the projective techniques would provide only partial evidence of the validity of the inventory scale. Equally important validational evaluations, in this approach,

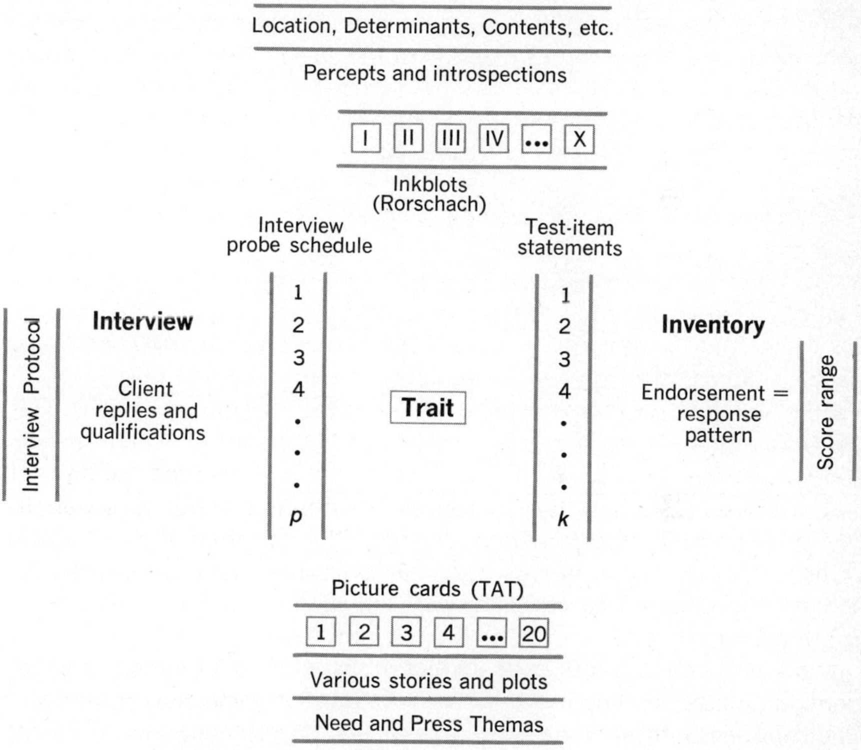

Figure 1–3 A representation of the stimuli, response modes, and products of four common assessment methods for evaluating a given trait.

are provided by the extent to which the inventory scores for this trait are independent of scores on that inventory for other traits. To the extent to which the various measures derived from the inventory all show significant levels of intercorrelation, these scores are judged to be influenced by factors common to the inventory method. These "method factors" are considered error factors to be either eliminated or minimized. Some method factors may, of course, extend beyond one particular approach: The subject's verbal fluency, for example,

Table 1-3 A synthetic multitrait-multimethod matrix

	Traits	Method 1			Method 2			Method 3		
		A_1	B_1	C_1	A_2	B_2	C_2	A_3	B_3	C_3
Method 1	A_1	(.89)								
	B_1	.51	(.89)							
	C_1	.38	.37	(.76)						
Method 2	A_2	*.57*	.22	.09	(.93)					
	B_2	.22	*.57*	.10	.68	(.94)				
	C_2	.11	.11	*.46*	.59	.58	(.84)			
Method 3	A_3	*.56*	.22	.11	*.67*	.42	.33	(.94)		
	B_3	.23	*.58*	.12	.43	*.66*	.34	.67	(.92)	
	C_3	.11	.11	*.45*	.34	.32	*.58*	.58	.60	(.85)

Note: The validity diagonals are the three sets of italicized values. The reliability diagonals are the three sets of values in parentheses. Each heterotrait-monomethod triangle is enclosed by a solid line. Each heterotrait-heteromethod triangle is enclosed by a broken line.
Source: D. T. Campbell and D. W. Fiske, Convergent and discriminant validation by the multitrait-multimethod matrix. *Psychological Bulletin,* 1959, **56,** 81–105.

would be expected to influence inkblot interpretations, thematic productions, and interview replies alike; and his level of verbal comprehension would be likely to pervade all four assessment methods shown in Figure 1-3.

The whole issue over response sets described above can conveniently be susumed under the general Campbell-Fske formulation in which response styles are seen as one form of method variance plaguing inventory approaches and as a serious source of test error (Wiggins, 1962; Wiggins & Lovell, 1965; also Wiggins's material in Chapter 7). Current discussions of response sets have often distinguished method variance of this sort from content variance that is presumed to embody the valid information to be derived from the scores about the criterion trait. The psychometric assumptions underlying this approach are in fact the same as those advanced for the response set formulations described earlier: A basic factor-analytic model is presumed to be the appropriate basis for score interpretation and personality inference. Idealized traits, completely independent of one another, are hypothesized; empirically determined intercorrelations among the scores from any one method, or across methods, are then used as a basis for estimating method variance and as a means of evaluating the superiority of one method over another in personality assessment. In Campbell and Fiske's survey of existing assessment instruments and the critique of the adequacy of the documentation of their convergent and discriminant validities, few devices were found to be either adequately documented (lacking as they do complete multitrait-multimethod matrices) or sufficiently valid for clinical use.

This formulation by Campbell and Fiske is attractive, logically compelling, and lucidly presented; their conclusions about current assessment approaches were quite devastating. Their formulation has been well received, with only a few dissenting voices raised, and they have had an impressive impact upon editors of journals in which basic assessment research is usually published. Yet there are serious problems in this approach when it is applied to the real-life data from personality assessment techniques which are derived within the imperfect models of personality structure and processes available today. Two examples from the MMPI literature demonstrate some of the difficulties in this approach and limitations in the geometric model of human nature that is its foundation.

One derivative from the Campbell-Fiske formulation is the strong dictum that two indices that purport to measure different things must be statistically independent; if these measures show too high an association, they are not really two measures but one, and one should be discarded. Precisely this kind of problem developed in the early stages of the construction of the MMPI when the *Hy* scale was derived by the usual method of empirically contrasting the item endorsements from cases of conversion hysteria and from Minnesota normal adults. McKinley and Hathaway (1944) found that the new *Hy* scale had a strong similarity to the previously developed scale for hypochondriasis, *H-CH* or *Hs* (McKinley & Hathaway, 1940). When they related both measures to diagnostic evaluations (method 2 in the Campbell-Fiske designation, as contrasted with the two inventory measures which represent method 1) of hypochondriasis (trait 1) and hysteria (trait 2), both the *Hs* and *Hy* scales gave excellent separations on both diagnostic dimensions. These investigators indicated that their initial temptation was to drop one or the other of these scales since on general psychiatric cases the two scales correlated .71. Yet careful examination of the clinical contributions of each of these scales led McKinley and Hathaway to retain both scales in the basic MMPI profile. It is important to note that these considerations do not have a place at all in the current version of the multitrait-multimethod formulation of construct validity. Several kinds of evidence were used (such as the fact that 32% of the cases of conversion hysteria had scores beyond the arbitrary cutting score on *Hy*, while being missed by the *Hs* scale), but the most compelling reasons for retaining both scales lay in their configural relationships. The way these scales related to each other and to the third scale in the neurotic triad, the *D* scale, provided clinically useful data in psychodiagnostic evaluations of anxiety, depression, and somatic reactions. Information provided by such indices as hit rates or summarized in nonlinear combinations of test scales is not adequately represented in tables of intercorrelations nor accurately preserved in factor-analytic solutions. The factor model underlying the Campbell-Fiske formulation does serious injustice to clinical assessment formulations that operate outside a narrow, geometrical view of human personality. There is no way to determine whether any particular set of traits under study should be completely independent or related in some particular configuration; the multitrait-multimethod formulation cannot be blindly applied to any arbitrary set of assessment data.

The obverse of the dictum derived from the multitrait-multimethod conceptualization of construct validity can also be shown to be seriously misleading. The expectation from this formulation is that test measures bearing upon the same trait discrimination will show increasing degrees of correlation the more highly perfected and developed they are for this purpose. A dramatic instance in which this expectation is not borne out, showing the limitations of this formulation as a guide to the development of clinically relevant personality measures, came to light in the continuing efforts to develop MMPI indices of clinical depression.

The initial work was, of course, by Hathaway and McKinley (1942) in which they reported their derivation of the *D* scale from item endorsements obtained from cases showing in their presenting complaints primarily significant levels of depression with little else of psychiatric interest. As usual, they contrasted these answers with those from Minnesota normal subjects and from samples of other normal and medically disabled individuals. The resulting *D* scale (now referred to as scale 2) proved to be sensitive to variations in depressive affect in many forms of psychiatric disturbance, not just to the depressive status of patients with a diagnosis of depressive reaction.

Later, for his doctoral dissertation, Albert Rosen (using a different approach to scale construction) tried to develop measures for a number of common psychiatric reaction patterns, including depressive reaction; after further work, Rosen published these new scales in a separate monograph (1962). Instead of comparing clinical cases in the various subgroups of interest with a reference group of normal sub-

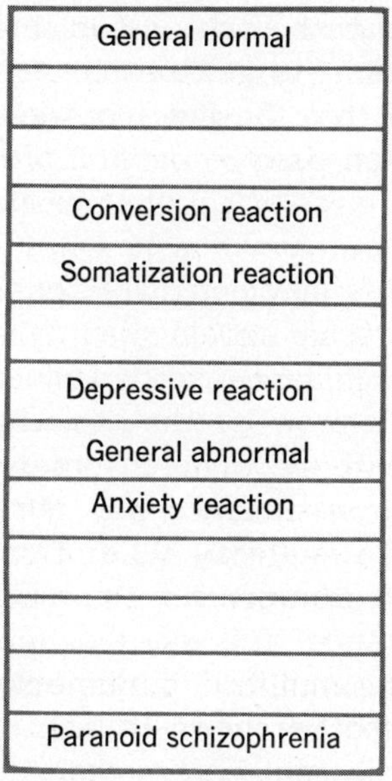

Figure 1–4 Representation of the psychological distance between various reference groups used in Rosen's study (1962).

jects, Rosen chose to contrast them to a sample of general psychiatric patients likely to be found in such a clinical setting. This shift in reference point can be shown in Figure 1-4 taken from Rosen's monograph. The scale developed by Hathaway and McKinley (scale 2) was based upon a contrast of the depressive group and the group of general normals at the far right-hand side of the scale; Rosen's scale for Depressive Reaction (*Dr*) was generated by the contrast of the depressive cases and the general abnormal group, slightly to the left of the center of this scale.

Contrary to the relationships expected from the Campbell-Fiske formulation about two measures converging upon the same criterion construct, the product-moment correlation between scale 2 and Rosen's *Dr* scale for a large sample of general psychiatric cases was found to be —.10. Although the two scales were derived from the same item pool, few of the items in one scale appear in the other; nearly one-half of these (3/7) are scored oppositely. Within the dictates of the Campbell-Fiske approach to construct validation, such an outcome would be considered a serious failure in the effort to get trait convergence. Nevertheless, Rosen provides evidence that the two measures of this important psychiatric manifestation, when used *conjointly*, provide improved clinical accuracy over that given by either scale separately.

Although the outcome of this work of Rosen's may not make sense in terms of standard notions of psychometric scale development, the results fit rather well current views of the psychiatric disorder under study. Important degrees of depression are shown by the majority of patients receiving inpatient treatment for acute emotional disorders. Those patients who show few other kinds of disturbance are likely to be categorized as having depressive reactions. They differ from normal adults in their depressive feelings and experiences; the main variance in scale 2 reflects this kind of difference. The way that this group of patients differs from other inpatient psychiatric cases, however, is not so much in their depressive affect as in their lack of other psychiatric disturbances. Rosen's *Dr* scale can be characterized as predominantly denial of a wide range of nondepressive psychiatric difficulties. When the two scales are used together, a person scoring high on both scales can be described as significantly depressed but showing few other psychiatrically significant features; this description would correspond to the current diagnostic summary of a depressive reaction.

To the extent that depression is a complex construct, it is not the sort of personality conception that is appropriate to the Campbell-Fiske approach to construct validation. The multitrait-multimethod formulation is defective in its lack of any specification about the kinds of traits to which it may legitimately be applied. Unfortunately, many journal editors seem to have adopted this formulation as the only legitimate basis for summarizing validational data on personality devices, applying these strictures indiscriminately to any and all kinds of personality constructs. It should be obvious that any personality construct, together with the scales proposed as measures of this construct, must be evaluated within the framework of the personality theory or diagnostic formulation of which it is an integral part. Only within such a context can meaningful distinctions be drawn between valid and appropriate degrees of correlation and inappropriate and misleading patterns of relationship. In the present form of the Campbell-Fiske formulation, however, psychometric considerations in generating the various statistical indices are weighted heavily, but personological considerations are ignored.

SCALE RELIABILITY AND CONTENT HOMOGENEITY

Similar care must be exercised in applying some of the other standard psychometric notions embodied in current test theory concerning the desirable attributes of scales of measurement. As can be seen in Table 1-3, the Campbell-Fiske formulation provides for estimates of the reliability of each measurement scale as part of the multitrait-multimethod matrix. These estimates are typically based upon methods of internal consistency as a means of estimating the inherent dependability of the scores provided by the scale in question. Occasionally they may be based upon retesting a group of subjects after some interval of time to measure the stability of the scores on the component scales. Either approach has serious limitations in providing estimates of score dependability on scales like those in the MMPI, although many psychometric theorists seem to overlook these difficulties in their reliance upon such reliability indices. All too often, serious objections to the MMPI have been based upon blind acceptance of these methods of estimating reliability and the traditional views of the alleged limitations that reliability values place upon potential validity. (See items 2, 4, 7, 9, 12, 18, and 19 in Ellis's list in Table 1-1.)

The limitations in the methods of reliability estimation based upon retest data can be readily discerned as they apply to instruments like the MMPI. The usual index of score stability is based upon the degree of correspondence between the ranking of subjects in a group on two different occasions, summarized in a correlation coefficient. To interpret such a correlation as a gauge of the dependability of the scores on some scale, it is necessary to assume that the rankings in the group from the first to the second testing should not change except through errors in the measurement of their positions. Since there is scarcely any scale on the MMPI for which this general assumption is tenable for any period of time longer than a day or two, the various estimates of scale stability published on the basic MMPI scales cannot be readily interpreted as indices of the inherent dependability of the scores from these scales obtained on any one occasion. Nonetheless, there are many adverse criticisms of MMPI scales which are based upon the assumption that the generally low score stabilities that are reported mean that the scores are not of any value.

In view of the great emphasis which psychometricians place upon retest characteristics of measurement scales, it is surprising to note how few studies in the test literature, either on the MMPI or on other devices, have employed the proper design for such an evaluation. The work of Endicott and Endicott (1963) on the implications of shifts, over a two-month interval, in the *Hs* scale for evaluating somatic preoccupation is one of the few empirical studies to use an appropriate research approach. They reported the relationships between *Hs* scores and independent clinical evaluations of overconcern with bodily functions that were made close in time to each MMPI testing. Although both sets of comparisons showed excellent correspondence, the agreement that was found between test scores and clinical ratings of these military personnel and their dependents was higher on the second occasion than on the first. It is unfortunate that there are so few studies of this kind; the important conclusion resulting from the Endicotts' work is that when the scale values of *Hs* change, there is likely to be an appropriate change in the personality status of the subjects as well. We need to know these properties of all our test scales.

Estimates of reliability based upon internal consistency measures, while varying widely in the way in which they are computed, all make a rather different set of assumptions about the desirable properties of a psychometrically acceptable scale. (See item 12 in Table 1-1 from Ellis's list.) Historically, these assumptions stem from work on scales developed in the ability domain; they appear to have been extended to apply to personality measures without adequate appreciation of the differences in the two behavioral areas. (In fact, reexamination of some of the traditional views by such psychometric theorists as Loevinger, 1965, has indicated that these long-accepted notions of scale properties may be quite inappropriate for some measurement problems in the ability domain itself, particularly for variables showing diphasic growth curves—milestone scales—or hiatuses such as those in Piaget's stages of mental development.) For the present purposes, perhaps, it is sufficient to examine two kinds of studies of interitem properties in scales like the MMPI and the ways in which the traditional assumptions fail to correspond to empirically determined characteristics of these scales.

The most familiar form of internal consistency evaluation of a scale is the index based upon a split-half correlation. Each item is assigned on some basis to one or the other of two halves of the scale, and these half scales are used to score the test records of a group of subjects. These half scores are correlated, and the coefficient (or some corrected value of the coefficient, is used as a basis for evaluating the inherent dependability of scores on the total scale. Early studies of the split-half reliabilities obtained on MMPI scales, such as the work of Gilliland and Colgin (1951) or Welsh (1952), reported some paradoxical findings: Many values of the split-half correlations were near chance level, and some coefficients were actually negative. Although some values were obtained within ranges that met the usual psychometric standards, the appearance of negative values for reliability estimates exceeded the tolerance of many psychometrically oriented critics!

Readers familiar with the distinction between obvious and subtle subscales of the MMPI (as introduced by Wiener, 1948; Wiener & Harmon, 1946) or the distinction between the admission and denial subscales of the *Hy* scale (Little & Fisher, 1958) can readily comprehend what was happening in some of these early studies of the internal consistency of the MMPI scales. If the method of splitting the scales happened to generate a half scale with a preponderance of obvious items, for example, leaving an excess of subtle items for the other half, and if the group of subjects used to generate the correlations was a heterogeneous one or one made up of largely well-adjusted individuals, then the halves would show low relationship to one another and might even give some negative values. The admission and denial components of the *Hy* scale would behave the same way in either a normal or a general psychiatric subject sample; for most people, these two kinds of self-description do not appear together very often. Persons prone to conversion reactions, on the other hand, are those interesting people who describe themselves in such a way as to obtain high scores on both subscales simultaneously. Correlations between these two halves of the *Hy* scale run considerably higher on a group of conversion reaction cases. The *Hy* scale, devised to help identify this personality characteristic, reflects both of these dependable features of their self-descriptions.

Although recently developed indices of internal consistency are more likely to be based upon interitem relationships rather than upon one large combination of scale items used for the split-half computations, the reasoning is largely the same. The assumption is made that a sound psychometric scale will be made up of items that bear a strong resemblance to one another in content; they will comprise a homogeneous set. Only in this way, it is reasoned, can the items work together to produce a scale that has a dependable metric underlying its score distribution. So compelling is this assumption in basic psychometric research that this criterion is typically employed to guide scale refinement efforts to the exclusion of evidence adduced from outside the test itself about how the scale relates to what it is supposed to be measuring.

As described above, whether an item is admitted into a scale is based upon its relationship to external criteria; the major concern is not so much whether it is strongly related to items already accepted into the scale but whether it adds new discriminating information not already reflected in the tentative scale. Soon after starting their scale development research, Hathaway and McKinley realized that most of the items in their research pool were multiphasic; that is, the MMPI items reflected several different characteristics of subjects that endorsed them. For a scale to evaluate any single personality aspect from items that are sensitive to many different personality attributes, one must collect items that operate collectively to maximize the desired separations and, at the same time, cancel out the other influences. Some of the early scales were found to be seriously confounded by sources of variance other than the criterion difference, and they were abandoned. Other scales were retained, even though they were found to be unduly sensitive to test-taking attitudes; these were later improved by various amounts of statistical correction by fractions of the K score. Still other scales (such as scale 2) had correction items added to them in an effort to reduce score variance that was judged to be inappropriate. In these efforts, however, it was the degree of relationship of an item with the external criteria that provided the determining evidence for accepting an item's membership in a scale under construction (Hathaway, 1965).

There are now sharp differences of opinion about the resulting heterogeneity of item content in the MMPI scales. The paper in this volume by Wiggins (Chapter 7) is devoted to research on how to get greater uniformity in the content of the scales to be used to generate personality scores. Although this work is directed toward several desirable purposes, such as further basic understanding about how empirically determined separations are actually generated by answers to personality inventories, the approach reflects some of the assumptions about internal consistency and face validity of the item endorsements that have been examined above.

A similar concern about what the test subject is communicating to the psychodiagnostician leads Carson in his paper (Chapter 2) to an interest in the component items of the scales and speculations about the messages buried in these item endorsements. This kind of inquiry, carried out simultaneously through clinical and psychometric approaches, should be very productive. The work should not be misled, however, by unwarranted assumptions about the apparent heterogeneity of content in these scales. At this stage of our ignorance about personality processes, it is premature to insist upon uniformity at any one arbitrary level of conceptualization in our measurement scales. The units that are in our present scales seem to be much more behavioral signs in a checklist than uniform intervals along scales of length or weight, such as those available to the physical sciences. In the same way that Meehl (1964) seems to have avoided any premature insistence that the items in his checklist for schizotypy operate at any one level of psychological abstraction (What is there in common between compulsion to sensory input and facial asymmetry?), any a priori purifications of our empirical scales of items that do not seem to belong would be unwarranted.

RECURRING PROBLEMS OF ACCURACY OF DISCRIMINATIONS

Most of the criticisms of the MMPI thus far considered stem either from misunderstanding or from seemingly unwarranted assumptions. It would be misleading to leave the impression, however, that the majority of questions raised about the MMPI are of this nature. As noted earlier, much of the critical response to the test has been legitimate and constructive, based upon careful considerations of the limitations in the efficacy of this device in meeting the demands of clinical practice. These questions continue to appear and continue to have a healthy impact upon the direction of research on this test.

One serious limitation which the empirical approach must always face is the fact that the criteria themselves are fallible. Many differences in opinion about the MMPI among present-day test users stem from preferences for one kind of criterion or another. These choices of criteria, in turn, are based upon the belief that one personality formulation is more economical, lawful, or sensible than another. Clinicians who work with less deviant clients than those used in the derivational work of the MMPI may reject the MMPI because it seems to be restricted to special psychiatric applications. The growth of research findings on more general personality features, less pathological in their referents, has led to an increasing acceptance of the test into contexts in which it previously was deemed wholly unsuitable. (In this connection, psychologists have recently stirred up some highly emotional controversies over the appropriateness of the instrument for some employment decisions, in and out of the government service, and the legitimacy of some of the items in the test—Brayfield, 1965. A discussion of some of these issues involved in the problem of invasion of privacy is included in Chapter 13.)

Although all the criteria against which the psychodiagnostician builds his measures are fallible to some extent, there are wide variations in the adequacy and dependability that they possess for research purposes. One instance of the way in which limitations in the criteria against which assessment instruments are evaluated can artificially restrict the level of correspondence found between the two sets of data is found in the study of Little and Shneidman (1959). These investigators include not only the MMPI but also the Rorschach, Thematic Apperception Test (TAT), and Make A Picture Story (MAPS) in their study of the accuracy of these instruments in the hands of well-known proponents of these assessment devices. Blind interpretations on 12 cases were obtained in the form of checklist completions, *Q* sortings, and formal diagnoses from these "experts" after they examined the test protocols. Their judgments were correlated with similar summaries of these cases prepared by judges who were familiar with the case histories. Little and Shneidman found generally poor correspondence between these test-based and history-based descriptions. They concluded that these experts were apt to be misled by the test data about both the degree of abnormality present (overemphasizing psychopathology) and the kinds of difficulties that these cases were manifesting. However, their conclusions must be tempered, more than they were willing to acknowledge, by the distinctly low levels of agreement that were found among the case history judges themselves. Since the people who best knew these cases were not able to agree on what each test subject was like, it is difficult to determine whether any test judge is accurate. The importance of this requirement in this instance can be seen in the generally more satisfactory levels of accuracy obtained by Golden (1964) using new test judges but employing those criterion data from Little and Schneidman's study which showed the most agreement among case history judges. Work by Graham (1967) along similar lines has also highlighted the importance of test relevance of criteria; judges can best match criterion information that is selected to correspond to the discriminations for which the particular diagnostic instrument has been constructed.

Another recurring problem in any effort to relate test attributes to external criteria that is inherent in multidimensional instruments is the choice of method to combine the component scores to maximize the criterion discriminations. An excellent case in point is furnished by the findings and conclusions of Fairweather, Simon, Gebhard, Weingarten, Holland, Sanders, Stone, and Reahl (1960). As part of their elaborate and ambitious study of different psychotherapeutic programs being used at Perry Point Veterans Administration Hospital, these investigators tested their inpatients on three different occasions: as they began the treatment to which they were assigned, at the end of six months of treatment prior to discharge or transfer, and eighteen months later. The MMPI data from these three testings were analyzed by means of complex analyses of variance across the various therapy groups; the authors concluded that the MMPI was unrelated to either the treatment or the subsequent course of these patients from the end of their treatment to follow-up. This set of findings about the MMPI's lack of relationship to treatment and posthospital adjustment was quite out of keeping with the large literature on the test in treatment evaluations and prognosis (Dahlstrom & Welsh, 1960); this apparent failure was indeed puzzling. Fortunately, Forsyth (1965) was in a position to reanalyze these data, employing pattern-analytic methods and statistical analyses more appropriate to the problem. His findings indicate that many important MMPI configurations (and special interactions with nontest parameters as well) had been washed out by the particular analysis of variance procedures employed in the original investigation.

A similar reversal of empirical findings can be cited in the reanalyses of the Meehl-Dahlstrom data on psychotic and neurotic discriminations by means of configural rules (Meehl & Dahlstrom, 1960) that was carried out by Goldberg (1965). The original conclusion that the empirically determined configural rules discriminated these two psychiatric groups better than a linear combination of basic MMPI scale scores was refuted by Goldberg after he identified a new linear formula through painstaking application of high-speed computer programs for both linear and configural solutions to this discrimination.

The development mentioned above in discussing Forsyth's findings in which nontest variables are combined with MMPI scores to enhance empirical separations on various clinical criteria is noteworthy. In his reanalysis of the Perry Point data, Forsyth found it useful to make his pattern discriminations within subgroups of patients that were formed on the basis of both their general psychiatric status (psychotic versus nonpsychotic) and the length of their illness (short-term versus chronic). In many other studies, however, these distinctions are used as criteria themselves for MMPI-based discriminations. At this stage of the development of psychodiagnostic methods, clinicians will have to be flexible in the way that they employ different variables; the status of many familiar variables will be shifting from criteria, to moderator variables, to predictor variables. As demonstrated by Rempel (1958), some nontest information, such as school attendance records and course grades, may be merely reflecting the same kinds of data already available in such scales of the test as F or Pd. On the other hand, judging by the work of Heilbrun (1961) on the K scale, the proper personological interpretations of this scale, either as evidence of poor insight or as a sign of sound psychological functioning, will depend upon knowledge of the status of the subject and his need for psychotherapy which come from extra-MMPI data.

Since sound clinical practice involves a deliberate effort on the part of the psychodiagnostician to fit the test and nontest findings into a coherent clinical assessment of each subject, it is important that the research on instruments like the MMPI give much more attention to the role of nontest parameters in sharpening the test-based discriminations. Preliminary work, such as that of Gorman (1965), has shown that, in spite of the larger sample sizes required and the inherent errors characteristic of many case history items, significant improvement in clinical accuracy can be achieved by introducing demographic data as moderator variables for MMPI patterns. The cookbooks and computer-based interpretative systems of the future will also probably have to incorporate such variables in their basic structure.

Similar considerations will also enter into the choice of appropriate norms for the basic scale values. A great deal of additional research will be needed to determine whether separate norms should be used for subjects from different age levels, socioeconomic classes, ethnic groups, or geographic regions. This will be difficult research to carry out, since the work must be taken beyond the sheer demonstration that a particular group membership affects MMPI score values. There must be clear evidence that the inferential discriminations are improved and not weakened by the normative transformations performed on the scores. There have been serious concerns voiced that instruments like the MMPI are sensitive to biases arising from minority-group status or educational deficiencies (Brayfield, 1965). The validity of such complaints must be carefully evaluated. Unfortunately, the amount of work needed to elucidate this problem is prodigious; we seem to be in no position at this time to give a clear answer one way or another. The question of differences between Negro and white subjects is getting increasing attention, however, in the MMPI literature. This volume contains an important contribution on another cultural subgroup, a deviant religious cult, in the report of Tellegen et al. (Chapter 11). In all these inquiries, the basic question comes down to whether the observed differences in MMPI patterns are valid reflections of personological processes or unfortunate errors and biases to be removed by normative transformations.

In addition to the concern about its allegedly narrow psychiatric orientation, the MMPI has also encountered objections from clinicians who feel that the whole pattern of psychodiagnostic assessment today is based upon faulty premises. These objections are derived from assumptions about the nature of personality assessment itself (Goldberg & Rorer, 1965; Rorer, 1965), the nature of the relationship between client and therapist (Rogers, 1951), or the nature of behavioral disorders and the appropriate ways to alleviate them (Kanfer & Saslow, 1965). These objections characterize current personality assessment approaches as unworkable, unnecessary, or actually undesirable and potentially damaging to the treatment effort. Judging by past history, the only way in which objections of this kind can be met is to marshall new and convincing evidence. It is quite likely, however, that the pessimism will prove to be an overreaction to current test failures, that the dismissal of the need for any assessment at all will turn out to be actually a case of substitution of one conceptual scheme for another, and that the alleged adverse effects of pretreatment assessment upon the course of therapy will be found to depend more upon the therapist's own attitudes than upon any actual impact on the client. These new challenges will require the same careful study and examination of the evidence that has been typical of the way that workers with the MMPI have risen to the many challenges of the past.

REFERENCES

Berg, I. A. Response bias and personality: The deviation hypothesis. *Journal of Psychology*, 1955, **40**, 61–72.

Berg, I. A. Deviant responses and deviant people: The formulation of the deviation hypothesis. *Journal of Counseling Psychology*, 1957, **4**, 154–161.

Berg, I. A. The unimportance of test item content. In B. M. Bass and I. A. Berg (Ed.), *Objective approaches to personality assessment*. Princeton: Van Nostrand, 1959.

Berg, I. A. The deviation hypothesis: A broad statement of its assumptions and postulates. In I. A. Berg (Ed.), *Response set in personality assessment*. Chicago: Aldine, 1967.

Bernreuter, R. G. Theory and construction of the personality inventory. *Journal of Social Psychology*, 1933, **4**, 387–405.

Block, J. *The challenge of response sets: Unconfounding meaning, acquiescence, and social desirability in the MMPI.* New York: Appleton-Century-Crofts, 1965.

Brayfield, A. H. (Ed.), Special issue: Testing and public policy. *American Psychologist,* 1965, **20,** 857–1005.

Campbell, D. T., and Fiske, D. W. Convergent and discriminant validation by the multitrait-multimethod matrix. *Psychological Bulletin,* 1959, **56,** 81–105.

Cofer, C. N., Chance, J. E., and Judson, A. J. A study of malingering on the MMPI. *Journal of Psychology,* 1949, **27,** 491–499.

Crowne, D. P., and Marlowe, D. *The approval motive.* New York: Wiley, 1964.

Dahlstrom, W. G. Commentary: The roles of social desirability and acquiescence in responses to the MMPI. In S. Messick and J. Ross (Eds.), *Measurement in personality and in cognition.* New York: Wiley, 1962.

Dahlstrom, W. G., and Welsh, G. S. *An MMPI handbook: A guide to use in clinical practice and research.* Minneapolis: University of Minnesota Press, 1960.

Edwards, A. L. *The social desirability variable in personality assessment and research.* New York: Dryden Press, 1957.

Edwards, A. L. The social desirability hypothesis: Theoretical implications for personality measurement. In S. Messsick and J. Ross (Eds.), *Measurement in personality and cognition.* New York: Wiley, 1962.

Edwards, A. L. Social desirability and performance on the MMPI. *Psychometrika,* 1964, **29,** 295–308.

Edwards, A. L. The social desirability variable: A broad statement. In I. A. Berg (Ed.), *Response set in personality assessment.* Chicago: Aldine, 1967.

Ellis, A. The validity of personality questionnaires. *Psychological Bulletin,* 1946, **43,** 385–440.

Endicott, N. A., and Endicott, J. Objective measures of somatic preoccupation. *Journal of Nervous and Mental Disease,* 1963, **137,** 427–437.

Fairweather, G. W., Simon, R., Gebhard, M. E., Weingarten, W., Holland, J. L., Sanders, R., Stone, C. D., and Reahl, J. E. A multi-criteria comparison of the relative efficiency of four psychotherapeutic programs for three different patient groups. *Psychological Monographs,* 1960, **74** (5, Whole No. 492).

Forsyth, R. P. MMPI and demographic correlates of post-hospital adjustment in neuropsychiatric patients. *Psychological Reports,* 1965, **16,** 355–366.

Galton, F. *Inquiries into human faculty and its development.* London: Macmillan, 1883.

Gilliland, A. R., and Colgin, R. Norms, reliability, and forms of the MMPI. *Journal of Consulting Psychology,* 1951, **15,** 435–438.

Goldberg, L. R. A model of item ambiguity in personality assessment. *Educational and Psychological Measurement,* 1963, **23,** 467–492.

Goldberg, L. R. Diagnosticians vs. diagnostic signs: The diagnosis of psychosis vs. neurosis from the MMPI. *Psychological Monographs,* 1965, **79** (9, Whole No. 602).

Goldberg, L. R., and Rorer, L. G. Learning clinical inferences: The results of intensive training on clinicians' ability to diagnose psychosis vs. neurosis from the MMPI. *American Psychologist,* 1965, **20,** 736.

Golden, M. Some effects of combining psychological tests on clinical inferences. *Journal of Consulting Psychology,* 1964, **28,** 440–446.

Goodenough, F. L. *Mental testing: Its history, principles, and applications.* New York: Rinehart, 1949.

Gorman, J. A. MMPI and demographic patterns for discriminating abnormal behavior. *Dissertation Abstracts,* 1965, **25,** 6759.

Gough, H. G. The *F* minus *K* dissimulation index for the MMPI. *Journal of Consulting Psychology,* 1950, **14,** 408–413. (Also in Welsh & Dahlstrom, *Readings.*)

Gough, H. G. Some common misconceptions about neuroticism. *Journal of Consulting Psychology,* 1954, **18,** 287–292. (Also in Welsh & Dahlstrom *Readings.*)

Graham, J. R. A *Q*-sort study of the accuracy of clinical descriptions based on the MMPI. *Journal of Psychiatric Research,* 1967, **5,** 297–305.

Hall, G. S. The contents of children's minds. *Princeton Review,* 1883, **12,** 249–272.

Hase, H. D., and Goldberg, L. R. Comparative validity of different strategies of constructing personality inventory scales. *Psychological Bulletin,* 1967, **67,** 231–248.

Hathaway, S. R. Personality inventories. In B. B. Wolman (Ed.), *Handbook of clinical psychology.* New York: McGraw-Hill, 1965.

Hathaway, S. R., and McKinley, J. C. A multiphasic personality schedule (Minnesota): I. Construction of the schedule. *Journal of Psychology,* 1940, **10,** 249–254. (Also in Welsh & Dahlstrom, *Readings.*)

Hathaway, S. R., and McKinley, J. C. A multiphasic personality schedule (Minnesota): III. The measurement of symptomatic depression. *Journal of Psychology,* 1942, **14,** 73–84. (Also in Welsh & Dahlstrom, *Readings.*)

Heilbrun, A. B., Jr. The psychological significance of the MMPI *K* scale in a normal population. *Journal of Consulting Psychology,* 1961, **25,** 486–491.

Jackson, D. N. Acquiescence response styles: Problems of identification and control. In I. A. Berg (Ed.), *Response set in personality assessment.* Chicago: Aldine, 1967.

Jackson, D. N., and Messick, S. Response styles and the assessment of psychopathology. In S. Messick and J. Ross (Eds.), *Measurement of personality and cognition.* New York: Wiley, 1962.

Kanfer, F. H., and Saslow, G. Behavioral analysis: An alternative to diagnostic classification. *Archives of General Psychiatry,* 1965, **12,** 529–538.

Landis, C. Questionnaires and the study of personality. *Journal of Nervous and Mental Disease,* 1936, **83,** 125–134.

Landis, C., Zubin, J., and Katz, S. E. Empirical evaluation of three personality adjustment inventories. *Journal of Educational Psychology,* 1935, **26,** 321–330.

Little, K. B., and Fisher, J. Two new experimental scales of the MMPI. *Journal of Consulting Psychology,* 1958, **22,** 305–306.

Little, K. B., and Shneidman, E. S. Congruencies among interpretations of psychological test and anamnestic data. *Psychological Monographs,* 1959, **73** (6, Whole No. 476).

Loevinger, J. Measurement in clinical research. In B. B. Wolman (Ed.), *Handbook of clinical psychology.* New York: McGraw-Hill, 1965.

McGee, R. K. Response style as a personality variable: By what criterion? *Psychological Bulletin,* 1962, **59,** 284–295.

McKinley, J. C., and Hathaway, S. R. A multiphasic personality schedule (Minnesota): II. A differential study of hypochondriasis. *Journal of Psychology,* 1940, **10,** 255–268. (Also in Welsh & Dahlstrom, *Readings.*)

McKinley, J. C., and Hathaway, S. R. The MMPI: V. Hysteria, hypomania, and psychopathic deviate. *Journal of Applied Psychology,* 1944, **28,** 153–174. (Also in Welsh & Dahlstrom, *Readings.*)

McKinley, J. C., Hathaway, S. R., and Meehl, P. E. The MMPI: VI. The *K* scale. *Journal of Consulting Psychology,* 1948, **12,** 20–30. (Also in Welsh & Dahlstrom, *Readings.*)

McNemar, O. W., and Landis, C. Childhood disease and emotional maturity in the psychopathic woman. *Journal of Abnormal and Social Psychology,* 1935, **30,** 314–319.

Meehl, P. E. An investigation of a general normality or control factor in personality testing. *Psychological Monographs,* 1945, **59** (4, Whole No. 274).

Meehl, P. E. Manual for use with the checklist of schizotypic signs. Minneapolis: Psychiatric Research Unit, University of Minnesota Medical School, 1964. (Mimeographed)

Meehl, P. E., and Dahlstrom, W. G. Objective configural rules for discriminating psychotic from neurotic MMPI profiles. *Journal of Consulting Psychology,* 1960, **24,** 375–387. (Also in Appendix J, Dahlstrom & Welsh, *MMPI Handbook.*)

Meehl, P. E., and Hathaway, S. R. The *K* factor as a suppressor variable in the MMPI. *Journal of Applied Psychology,* 1946, **30,** 525–564. (Also in Welsh & Dahlstrom, *Readings.*)

Messick, S. J. The psychology of acquiescence: An interpretation of research evidence. In I. A. Berg (Ed.), *Response set in personality assessment.* Chicago: Aldine, 1967.

Messick, S., and Jackson, D. N. Acquiescence and the factorial interpretation of the MMPI. *Psychological Bulletin,* 1961, **58,** 299–304.

Neymann, C. A., and Kohlstedt, K. D. A new diagnostic test for introversion-extroversion. *Journal of Abnormal and Social Psychology,* 1929, **23,** 482–487.

Norman, W. T. On estimating psychological relationships: Social desirability and self-report. *Psychological Bulletin,* 1967, **67,** 273–293.

Page, J. Superstition and personality. *Journal of Educational Psychology,* 1935, **26,** 59–64.

Page, J., Landis, C., and Katz, S. E. Schizophrenic traits in the functional psychoses and in normal individuals. *American Journal of Psychiatry,* 1934, **13,** 1213–1225.

Reisman, J. M. *The development of clinical psychology.* New York: Appleton-Century-Crofts, 1966.

Rempel, P. B. The use of multivariate statistical analysis of the MMPI scores in classification of delinquent and nondelinquent high school boys. *Journal of Consulting Psychology,* 1958, **22,** 17–23.

Rogers, C. R. *Client-centered therapy.* Boston: Houghton-Mifflin, 1951.

Rorer, L. G. The proper domain of prediction. *American Psychologist,* 1965, **20,** 735.

Rorer, L. G., and Goldberg, L. R. Acquiescence in the MMPI? *Educational and Psychological Measurement,* 1965, **25,** 801–817.

Rosen, A. Development of MMPI scales based on a reference group of psychiatric patients. *Psychological Monographs,* 1962, **76** (8, Whole No. 527).

Sechrest, L., and Jackson, D. N. Deviant response tendencies: Their measurement and interpretation. *Educational and Psychological Measurement,* 1963, **23,** 33–53.

Tellegen, A. The Minnesota Multiphasic Personality Inventory. Chapter 2 in L. E. Abt and B. F. Riess (Eds.), *Progress in clinical psychology.* New York: Grune & Stratton, 1964.

Welsh, G. S. A factor study of the MMPI using scales with item overlap eliminated. *American Psychologist,* 1952, **7,** 341. (Also in Appendix K, Dahlstrom & Welsh, *MMPI Handbook.*)

Welsh, G. S., and Dahlstrom, W. G. (Eds.) *Basic readings on the MMPI in psychology and medicine.* Minneapolis: University of Minnesota Press, 1956.

Wiener, D. N. Subtle and obvious keys for the MMPI. *Journal of Consulting Psychology,* 1948, **12,** 164–170. (Also in Welsh & Dahlstrom, *Readings.*)

Wiener, D. N., and Harmon, L. R. Subtle and obvious keys for the MMPI: Their development. Advisement Bulletin No. 16, Regional Veterans Administration office, Minneapolis, 1946. (Also in Appendix I, Dahlstrom & Welsh, *MMPI Handbook.*)

Wiggins, J. S. Interrelationships among MMPI measures of dissimulation under standard and social desirability instructions. *Journal of Consulting Psychology,* 1959, **23,** 419–427.

Wiggins, J. S. Strategic, method, and stylistic variance in the MMPI. *Psychological Bulletin,* 1962, **59,** 224–242.

Wiggins, J. S., and Lovell, V. R. Communality and favorability as sources of method variance in the MMPI. *Educational and Psychological Measurement,* 1965, **25,** 399-412.

Wiggins, N. Individual viewpoints of social desirability. *Psychological Bulletin,* 1966, **66,** 68–77.

Woodworth, R. S. *Personal data sheet.* Chicago: Stoelting, 1917.

Zubin, J., Eron, L. D., and Schumer, F. *An experimental approach to projective techniques.* New York: Wiley, 1965.

Chapter Two
Issues in the Teaching of Clinical MMPI Interpretation

Robert C. Carson
Duke University

Stated simply, the pedagogical problem is to train clinical students to be able to infer from any particular set of MMPI responses, ordered in whatever manner is available or suitable, the maximum amount of correct information attainable about the person providing those responses. This is the task that is set for anyone aspiring to full competence in MMPI interpretation. The fact that in a given practical situation much of the reliable information contained in MMPI responses is superfluous or irrelevant is not, from this perspective, pedagogically important. Although the goal can thus be simply stated, the complexity and difficulty involved in its realization is underestimated by many people, especially by beginning students. Prior to all of the success and ballyhoo of the actuarial or mechanical methods of MMPI interpretation, clinicians were well aware that, if they wished to become skilled interpreters, they would have to spend many hours learning the basic lore from a master, and many additional hours sharpening their skills by informally monitoring their "hit" rates with the patients they evaluated and correcting their notions about the MMPI scales as they gained experience with them. Not infrequently, aspirants would begin to view patients with whom they came in contact in terms of their imagined MMPI profiles, and some developed to a fine art the striking skill of postdicting with essentially no error an undisclosed MMPI profile on the basis of a paragraph of case history. In the course of a few years, a very great deal of knowledge about the MMPI and its scales, much of it undoubtedly implicit, could be acquired in this intensely dedicated manner. The reader may know of cases of quite astonishing interpretative skill acquired in this manner. This type of skill is presently in danger of becoming a lost art; the loss is premature, since such a skill will be necessary for some time to come. Why should this loss occur? Hunt (1951) may have suggested a major reason a number of years ago when he wrote:

> The development of objective knowledge applicable to the prediction and control of natural events occurs somewhat as follows. Science is basically empirical. It begins with individual experience which is assessed and then applied to the solution of some problem. Such primitive empiricism is fun, but it is seldom clean. Its rough use of experience is soon seen to have its shortcomings; then certain ground rules develop for its improvement. The individual checks his experience with that of other individuals (the anecdotal method) and adopts certain standard ways of assessing it (logic, mathematics, etc.). Finally he conceives the idea of checking his predictions in advance of their practical application, and at this point the experimental method is born. This highly sophisticated empiricism is eminently clean, but it is seldom fun [p. 683].

One can hardly be surprised if bright graduate students do not seem to enjoy looking up probabilities in a prediction table and transferring them, preferably thoughtlessly, to a "clinical report." This picture is being presented in an unduly stark way, and I am quite aware that even the most enthusiastic actuarialists do not advocate this as the model for the clinical psychologist of the future. On the other hand, students do perceive somehow that the clinical method is dead and that they, therefore, should not think very much about their patients' problems except perhaps in therapy.

We are living in an age of efficiency, of high-speed functioning, and of great and increasing social complexity. We are quite properly enamored of devices, preprogrammed to make our decisions and calculations automatically without the necessity of thought, whose peculiar limitations are exceeded by the immediacy and intricacy of many contemporary decision-demanding situations. The students we hope to train are, of course, not unaffected by this aspect of the cultural milieu; and they are encouraged by positivist-behaviorist propaganda and the general bandwagon effect to believe that it is unecessary—indeed archaic and unscientific—to think about MMPI profiles and the patients who produce them. They, therefore, conclude before getting to know the full potential of the MMPI that it is, after all, a simple-minded instrument unworthy of more than technical study. This is only one step removed from seeing patients as mere collections of probabilistic reaction tendencies. This set on the part of students is the major roadblock to teaching them about the MMPI and, indirectly, about what people are like, since these two issues are not realistically separable. In a teaching situation, this problem has to be engaged directly from the start. Students must be told quite explicitly that, although good research of the past few years has made the task of learning how to interpret the MMPI much more efficient, it is still, at best, a demanding, time-consuming process. It can be fun, but, much as one might prefer it otherwise, there is no easy way to develop general professional competence with the instrument.

VARIETIES OF PSYCHOLOGICAL ASSESSMENT

Much of the students' confusion about the stance they should take concerning MMPI interpretation results from the frequent failure of authors in this area to specify the assessment context within which their observations apply. The only justification for this failure would be that context is irrelevant—a conclusion which is unsupportable. Consider, for example, the distinction between behavior prediction and personality description. In the abstract, this distinction is a rather arbitrary one. In the concrete practice of psychological assessment, however, there may be crucial operational differences distinguishing between, and even within, these types of assessment problems. Part of the educational task is to teach students how to make discriminations at this level.

Without attempting to be exhaustive, let us consider some of the varieties of assessment problems for which the MMPI is allegedly an appropriate instrument. For the sake of communicative efficiency, I shall state at the outset that I am completely convinced that a strictly mechanical, actuarial approach to MMPI interpretation cannot be exceeded in accuracy or efficiency when the assessment problem is confined to predicting specific, definable events under given conditions and when the reference data pool is statistically adequate for the task at hand. This latter phrase is, of course, the key one, the former being, in the main at least, a kind of pragmatic corollary. I should like to consider the various kinds of assessment situations from this perspective.

First, there is a very large class of assessment problems which is purely administrative in nature; these problems are concerned with making decisions among possible specified courses of action. This would include most types of routine screening, prediction of behavioral adequacy under circumstances having given demand characteristics, and prediction of behavioral outcomes resulting from various types of possible input manipulations. For any given level of attainable criterion specification and measurement and for any given level of statistical experience, it seems unquestionable that, with this class of problems, an adequate actuarial approach will, in the long run, yield less error than the actuarially unaided professional judgments of a clinician. One may note in passing, however, that in these circumstances the MMPI profile, as such, is an inefficient and "noisy" way of ordering the data. Of course, it frequently happens that adequate statistics are not yet available in a given decision-making situation, in which case I would be willing, even with this kind of assessment problem, to rely upon the considered judgment of a skilled clinician; I think I would urge him, however, to begin collecting the necessary data.

There is one special subclass of administrative uses of the MMPI which deserves some additional comment, if only because it has recently attained a certain public notoriety. I am referring to those situations in which the instrument may be employed for the purpose of extracting covert or concealed information about a person against his will, so to speak—for example, to discover whether a patient may be secretly contemplating suicide or whether a candidate for a "sensitive" position in the government may be homosexually inclined. Apart from questions of ethics and appropriateness, there are serious practical limitations which would impede the development of adequate actuarial models for use in diagnosing from the MMPI many such concealed and/or low base rate phenomena. In many instances, therefore, the use of clinical inference and judgment may be the only rational alternative available. I do not want to give the impression, however, that I think it would be very successful—probably in most cases one would do as well or better to play the base rates. As I shall attempt to spell out in greater detail later, people do not *inadvertently* reveal as much as we generally like to think they do in producing an MMPI profile.

Up to this point in our discussion of assessment situations, we have considered mainly cases in which the consequences of decisions in particular circumstances have, at least potentially, a high degree of a priori estimatability by virtue of a systematically ordered prior experience with the same or highly similar variables. Under such conditions, the teacher of MMPI interpretation would be well advised to urge his students to consider seriously the development and the use of a judgment-free actuarial system. There are, however, other uses of the MMPI which do not have the characteristics mentioned, of which one large class is that associated with clinical, nonadministrative assessment. In the main, this type of assessment is concerned with those processes suggested by the expression "understanding the patient." In the remainder of this paper, I shall discuss certain limitations of the actuarial method as it applies in this context and shall suggest the general outlines of a framework that I have found useful in teaching clinical MMPI interpretation.

LIMITATIONS OF THE ACTUARIAL METHOD

In discussing the limitations of the actuarial method in clinical work, my comments will be mainly directed, for heuristic purposes, to the material contained in the Marks and Seeman (1963) *Atlas*. The excellence of the conception and execution of the research described in this volume makes it well suited to my purpose of highlighting limitations of the actuarial method.

The basic point I want to emphasize is not that the actuarial approach has no place in the clinical assessment of individual patients but rather that for maximum general effectiveness it must be supplemented by clinical inference and judgment. Speaking very generally, there are two principal varieties of constraint on the effectiveness of actuarial methods: One of them is purely pragmatic and, therefore, at least conceivably temporary; the other, however, appears to be more substantive in character and may never be overcome within an actuarial framework. Let us consider each of these issues in turn. The first type of constraint relates to the fundamental fact that the construction of an actuarial table assumes prior experience of some considerable order of magnitude with the specific variables whose degree of relationship one wishes to assess. Moreover, there is no assurance that any such relationship established in one context will hold for any particular other. We are confronted, then, with the possibility that the astronomical dimensions of the statistical task will overwhelm us. A closer look at Marks and Seeman may be instructive in relation to this point.

After several years of data collection and analysis, Marks and Seeman were able to identify 16 profile types that permitted classification of 80% of their patients. The achievement of this not unimpressive classification scheme was dependent upon discarding a considerable amount of profile information that a clinician would use, e.g., low-point scales; and, as they explain, transport of the system to another setting would almost certainly reduce the proportion of patients who are classifiable. It might be noted, then, that even at the test data side of the equation rather severe compromises were necessary in order to get the problem scaled down to manageable limits; what emerges from this truly heroic effort is a rather coarse prediction screen with somewhat indeterminate limits of applicability.

The ultimate proof of the system, however, should rest with what it can accomplish in the task the authors set for themselves, that is, the description of abnormal personality. How well, in and of itself, does it do? Here again, the inexorable limits of human endurance have inevitably forced compromises. In large measure the system predicts, or perhaps I should say postdicts, in a decidedly imperfect and probabilistic manner patient characteristics concerning which information is readily obtainable from more direct and reliable sources. Thus, if one were really interested in a patient's *IQ,* one would be inclined to give him an intelligence test; or if one were really interested in some factual case history material, one would ask him or his relatives about it. Ignoring for the moment the *Q*-sort material, it is not unfair to say that the uniquely valuable item of information provided in these descriptions, from the point of view of individual diagnosis, is the response to treatment data. In many ways these materials tell us more about the meaning of MMPI scales and their interaction than they do about individual patients. I would be among the last to disparage such information; but it is important to make this discrimination, particularly for students.

The *Q*-sort data provided by Marks and Seeman are more difficult to evaluate. One may note the artificial constraints imposed by the use of any particular set of *Q* items of any particular number (in this case 108) and the inherent unclarity of an ipsative, rather than a normative, metric. On the whole, however, this is a very valuable, if rather circumscribed, source of information about the personality characteristics of individual patients. It is certainly something with which serious students of MMPI interpretation have an obligation to familiarize themselves; my point is that they will need much more for at least the foreseeable future. I am here simply restating Holt's (1958) well-known argument concerning the desirability of a sophisticated combination of the actuarial and the clinical. Marks and Seeman understand and acknowledge the issue; but students sometimes do not, even after they have repeatedly had the experience of discovering that questions of crucial significance in the assessment of a given patient are not explicitly answered for them in the Marks and Seeman data.

It is to be expected that, over time, we shall develop increasingly adequate actuarial data for use with the MMPI. Although the magnitude of the task at this point seems monumental, one can imagine a state of affairs in which very discriminating and detailed trait descriptions may be generated from any set of MMPI data in a wholly automatic manner. Would we then have reached the zenith of perfection in MMPI personality diagnosis? I am not at all sure that we would, and this brings me to the second and possibly more enduring limitation of the actuarial method. Let me begin by quoting Marks and Seeman (1963): "The *Atlas* was conceived with the idea that one of the most important of the clinician's objectives—perhaps the most important—is that of forming a conception of the individual patient."

I am in complete agreement with this statement of the clinician's objectives, and I also believe that such works as the *Atlas* can be a very substantial aid to their attainment. It is somewhat misleading, however, to suggest, as Marks and Seeman seem to, that the inclusion of "dynamic" or "genotypic" language in a sample of descriptive actuarial statements will render the objective more attainable. The labeling of a patient with some finite number of such statements, even when it can be done with a high degree of statistical and consensual certainty, does not constitute a complete understanding of him. The latter requires a rather complicated array of cognitive apparatus by means of which various items of information about the patient are filtered, modulated, and otherwise processed. It may be objected that at this point we are no longer talking about the MMPI but rather about a more general kind of knowledge. In part this is so, but I have never been able to teach MMPI interpretation satisfactorily without simultaneously teaching something of this other "extraneous" material. Somewhat happily, and possibly not accidentally, my own evolving ideas about people and how they function are congruent with the kinds of information provided in an MMPI profile. I should like to sketch the main outlines of these ideas, making it clear that I regard them as merely one of perhaps many fruitful approaches to personality diagnosis and MMPI interpretation.

A CONCEPTUAL PERSPECTIVE

I should like to begin by asking the question, What is the patient attempting to accomplish in providing for us a particular constellation of true or false responses to the MMPI item pool? Or, to put it another way, What is his strategy? If we can understand this, we can understand a very great deal about the patient's extratest behavior—the manner in which he deals with his problems. The MMPI is particularly well suited for the adoption of this sort of analytical orientation, provided only that one shift his perspective slightly so as to view the responses of the patient as a somewhat structured form of self-presentation—using that term in approximately the same manner as Goffman (1956). Let us consider briefly whether such a perspective is justified or legitimate.

If one considers from the patient's point of view the situation of being confronted with the MMPI item pool and being instructed to answer each item "True" or "False," it does not seem farfetched to assume that the typical patient views this as an opportunity to communicate certain messages concerning himself to whoever he believes will be the recipient of these data. This is the most parsimonious and compelling assumption that one might make about the orientation of the patient in the examination situation. In a basic sense, the patient tells us something that he wishes us to believe about him on each occasion that he responds to an item. Thus, if a person tells us via the MMPI that he believes he is being plotted against and if we may assume that he has read the item correctly, there are essentially two possibilities: (1) He thinks he is being plotted against, and he wishes us to know that he does; or (2) he does not think that he is being plotted against, but he wishes us to believe that he thinks so. In either case, he has made a (perhaps implicit) decision to present himself to us as a person who thinks he is being plotted against; and this is the only information contained in his unprocessed response to that particular item. In a sense, it does not matter whether he, in fact, believes he is being plotted against—such information is neither accessible nor usable for diagnostic purposes with respect to the MMPI and possibly not with respect to any other conceivable diagnostic technique.

The situation is no different in regard to so-called subtle items. Consider the item, "What others think of me does not bother me," which is regarded as a subtle item, keyed False, in both the *Hy* and *Pd* scales. Although it is evidently statistically true that conversion hysteric and psychopathic subjects both tend to claim this type of social sensitivity and that we can, therefore, glean diagnostic information from the item independent of its semantic content or the objective truth of the response to it, we may lose something by letting it go at that. It is important in understanding the patient to know that he does or does not portray himself as sensitive to others' opinions of him; and this is also independent of the veridicality of the response. The magnificent success of the empirical method and the persuasiveness of certain classic arguments advanced by Meehl (1945) and others have contributed to the development of rather stereotyped notions about the significance of the content of MMPI items. Thus, although it is indeed true, in one sense, that item content is a very unreliable index for discovering anything factual about a patient who responds one way or the other to that content, this conclusion rests upon a limited and somewhat naïve view of test-taking attitudes. Have we not, in fact, tended to think of the strategic considerations involved in taking the MMPI in an overly simple way in terms of our trichotomy of "faking good," "faking bad," and "not faking"?

It is, of course, conceivable that many—or perhaps even most—patients in a clinical situation adopt a conscious strategy of complete honesty in taking the MMPI—that is, they answer the items entirely in accord with what is *subjectively* true about them. It is commonly believed, in fact, that just this assumption must be met if the results of the test are to be considered valid; and the so-called validity scales based on the rather simple view of the test-taking attitude noted above were originally devised in the main as a check on this assumption. Let us take again the case of the person who asserts on the test that he believes he is being plotted against, and let us say that he also asserts a number of other things of roughly comparable quality. He will, thereby, surely obtain a high score on the *Pa* scale; but this will happen whether or not he *really believes* all those "crazy" assertions. He amasses points on the *Pa* scale not for anything he really believes but rather because he makes assertions that are similar to those made by a certain class of other people, who, by the way, gained their admission to that class not because of anything they really believed either. At a basic level, of course, this argument raises the whole question of the nature of paranoia and, by implication, of the nature of psychological disorders in general. It is a very important question, which, unfortunately, cannot now be answered. From a purely psychometric standpoint, however, it is irrelevant. What to work with in the MMPI and similar instruments is what people *say* about themselves, not what they subjectively believe to be true. The validity of conclusions drawn from responses to the MMPI is *not* dependent upon any requirement of subjective veridicality. To my knowledge, none of the vast amount of well-established findings emanating from research on the MMPI would constitute a serious challenge to this conclusion, and some can be interpreted to support it.

One could grant all the above and yet remain uncomfortable with what seems to be an unduly cynical view of the human condition or, at any rate, that aspect of it which may emerge under test-taking conditions. Although it may not be the most parsimonious assumption to make, it may yet be the case that most people, including most psychiatric patients, give subjectively honest answers to most of the

MMPI items. As a matter of fact, in a sense, they do; and I have oversimplified some very complex matters in order to establish a frame of reference for my not altogether orthodox approach to MMPI interpretation. The issue I have raised is probably an insoluble one, and a full discussion of it would involve us in very complicated problems of the meaning of subjective truthfulness, levels and modes of communication, motivational overdetermination, and a host of other rather philosophical considerations which it is not my purpose to explore. I shall be satisfied if I have made the point that considerations of self-presentation and purposeful strategy are probably extremely important determiners of test responding and, in this connection, that the distinction between "validity" and clinical scales of the MMPI is in many ways an arbitrary one. The implications of this analysis are perhaps especially relevant to the assessment of psychiatric patients whose capacity for objective self-appraisal is, in general, less than impressive and whose penchant for interpersonal game playing has been rather convincingly noted and described by a number of contemporary observers, notably Berne (1964), Haley (1963, 1965), Leary (1957), and Szasz (1961).

Because I am aware that my viewpoint represents for many a rather radical departure from their conception of the nature of the processes measured by the MMPI scales, I should like, at the risk of overstating the case, to make a few additional and, I hope, clarifying remarks about the development and essential character of these scales. It will suffice for our purposes to consider a single scale (*Hy*) as representative.

As is well known, this scale, like most of the others, was developed basically by isolating items which differentiated (in terms of true or false response frequencies) a normal from a criterion group—in this case a group of 50 patients diagnosed as manifesting so-called conversion reactions. The criterion group for the *Hy* scale, then, consisted of 50 persons who complained of and/or exhibited various approximations to true physical disorders when in fact no such disorders existed or could be proved. The degree to which these persons may have been calculated impostors (Szasz, 1961) is a moot question; but there is essentially no question at all that they did not, in fact, have the kinds of disorders their "symptoms" superficially suggested. These criterion groups were formed on the basis of shared *phenotypic* characteristics, that is, on the basis of the behavior they *displayed*.

To return to our criterion group of hysteric subjects, it is not surprising that a large proportion of the items which differentiated them from the standardization normals refers to physical infirmities of one kind or another, the range and variety being truly impressive. The descriptions of their alleged illnesses on the MMPI item pool, in other words, were entirely consistent with the descriptions they had offered in prior clinical evaluation situations. As with several of the other MMPI criterion groups, however, a considerable proportion of the items discovered to be discriminating for the hysteric subjects contains content that could not readily have been predicted. These are commonly called subtle items, and a certain amount of magical thinking concerning them has appeared from time to time in the MMPI literature. Let us examine the subtle items of the *Hy* scale in somewhat greater detail.

In general, as has often been observed, these items, keyed in the *Hy* direction, constitute a rather insistent claim of social adjustment, confidence, and poise. A surprisingly numerous subset of these items asserts essentially that people are decidedly sincere, unmanipulative, and trustworthy. Thus, paraphrasing to some degree, we are told that the subject is not given to wondering about the motives of someone who has been nice to him, he does not resent being taken in, he does not believe it is safer to trust no one, he does not believe it takes a lot of argument to convince people of the truth, he does not think many people exaggerate their misfortunes to gain sympathy, he does not think most people would lie to get ahead, he does not think that some people are so bossy that he is inclined to rebel, and he does not think that most people would use unfair means to gain profit or an advantage. In summary, this group of carefully selected cases of conversion hysteria distinguished themselves from normals on the MMPI items chiefly by asserting an extraordinary amount of physical disability and social facility and by protesting rather vigorously that people in general are not opportunistic con artists. As a consequence, it is one's stated position on these issues which will largely determine his score on the *Hy* scale.

It is rather hazardous to assume that a person who responds to MMPI items in a manner that bears some degree of similarity to the responses of a criterion group will be proportionally similar to that group in other respects, especially when this assumption becomes transformed into the notion of an underlying, unitary trait dimension. If the logic is less than compelling, however, I must admit that available empirical findings do not present a severe challenge to this thinking. In any case, one is not, at this point in time, logically or empirically constrained to interpret scores on the *Hy* scale in terms of the characteristics, whatever they may in fact have been, of the original hysterical criterion group. For one thing, there is available an extensive array of empirical findings regarding the correlates of the *Hy* scale; and for another, there is a variety of rather direct inferences which can be made from the content of the *Hy* scale considered as an opportunity for a certain, not unfamiliar, type of self-presentation. In regard to the latter, I would be inclined to ask my students what sort of adaptational sense they could make out of a patient's self-presentation as a person who (1) has multiple, improbable combinations of physical infirmities, (2) is markedly friendly, well adjusted, and sure of himself in the interpersonal sphere, and (3) vehemently insists that there is very little deviousness, opportunism, or exploitation to be found among people generally. This is an oversimplified example based on a single scale, but few readers would be unable to generate with some confidence various ideas about the adaptational style of such a hypothetical patient. It is not entirely happy coincidence that these ideas will very likely be highly consistent with what we know to be characteristic, in fact, of the behavior of persons with a high *Hy* score. My point is that there is a great deal of *pedagogical* merit in the adoption of this approach to profile interpretation. It does not, of course, preclude the simultaneous use of other interpretative frameworks.

In summary, contemporary students of clinical interpretation are in the fortunate position of having access to an almost incredibly rich store of reliable information on various correlates of MMPI scales, taken singly or in various combinations. Moreover, suitable research designs exist for establishing almost any such additional information as may be required for special, circumscribed purposes. In terms of the many quasi-administrative purposes for which the MMPI is an appropriate assessment instrument, nothing further is needed. In many *clinical* assessment situations, however, when the task is to gain as full an understanding of the patient's life as possible, an additional component of clinical inference and judgment is needed in order to integrate the various items and kinds of information available. To do this effectively, the interpreter must have an adequate interpretative framework according to which the data at his disposal may be organized into a comprehensive, coherent conception of the personality of the patient. The MMPI is perhaps peculiarly suited to a framework that is organized around the concepts of self-presentation and interpersonal strategy, and this framework provides a useful and potentially very effective intellectual tool for understanding personality disturbance as reflected in the MMPI.

My primary approach to MMPI interpretation, then, revolves around a fundamental question that may be restated somewhat as follows: What effects upon the environment is the patient attempting to accomplish, consciously or unconsciously, by presenting himself in the manner in which he does? If we can understand the adaptational objectives of the patient from this standpoint, we will understand the core of what we, as clinicians, need to know about him. Needless to say, the answer to the question is usually an exceedingly complicated one. At the level of raw data, each MMPI response could conceivably contain at least some information on differing aspects of the patient's adaptational purposes in relation to the particular circumstances of his being examined. Organizing the patient's responses in terms of the various classic MMPI scales represents a particular way of ordering these self-representations. It has, as an organizing scheme, several advantages, chief among which perhaps is that it relates general self-representational tendencies to the particular classifications of behavior with which we, as clinicians, are professionally familiar. Looked at in this way, however, the scales of the standard MMPI profile, together with their empirically established correlates, take on an added and illuminating dimension. In addition, it can be fun to think about MMPI profiles in this way.

REFERENCES

Berne, E. *Games people play.* New York: Grove, 1964.

Goffman, E. *The presentation of self in everyday life.* Edinburgh: University of Edinburgh, 1956.

Haley, J. *Strategies of psychotherapy.* New York: Grune and Stratton, 1963.

Haley, J. The art of being schizophrenic. *Voices,* 1965, **1,** 133–147.

Holt, R. R. Clinical and statistical prediction: A reformulation and some new data. *Journal of Abnormal and Social Psychology,* 1958, **56,** 1–12.

Hunt, W. A. Clinical psychology—science or superstition. *American Psychologist.* 1951, **6,** 683–687.

Leary, T. *Interpersonal diagnosis of personality.* New York: Ronald Press, 1957.

Marks, P. A., and Seeman, W. *The actuarial description of abnormal personality: An atlas for use with the MMPI.* Baltimore: Williams & Wilkins, 1963.

Meehl, P. E. The dynamics of "structured" personality tests. *Journal of Clinical Psychology,* 1945, **1,** 296–303.

Meehl, P. E. *Clinical vs. statistical prediction.* Minneapolis: University of Minnesota Press, 1954.

Szasz, T. S. *The myth of mental illness.* New York: Hoeber-Harper, 1961.

Chapter Three
Construction and Application of MMPI Codebooks

Harold Gilberstadt
Minneapolis Veterans Administration Hospital

Given unlimited funds and unrestricted access to suitable samples, would it be possible to construct an ideal clinical codebook based on the MMPI, or would there be serious limitations imposed by imperfections in the present system of nosology and deficiencies in the present MMPI? There tend to be differences of opinion about this difficult question, but the specter of it haunts the atmosphere of discussion about current codebook procedures.

The MMPI was constructed by Hathaway and McKinley to satisfy the need for a practical, valid psychometric device for diagnosis and assessment partially based on the standard psychiatric diagnostic system. The choice by Hathaway and McKinley of the personality-inventory, self-report type of test was typical of the times. The inventory method had evolved from the World War I Woodworth Personal Data Sheet through the face-valid Bernreuter and Bell tests and the rational-empirical Humm-Wadsworth test, all of which had proved to be unsatisfactory psychiatric assessment instruments (Hathaway, 1965). Hathaway and McKinley tried to improve methodology by adopting a completely empirical approach to scale construction. Evidence abounds indicating that they succeeded in building a superior diagnostic device; but, on the other hand, there does not appear to be any rigorous means to evaluate the adequacy of the present MMPI. Opinions range from those of enthusiasts who view the present test as quite satisfactory for the purposes to which it is properly directed to those of critics who find what they consider to be serious defects in the item pool, scoring methods, and modes of interpretation (Goldberg, 1965). Although there is general agreement that the present MMPI has demonstrated practical worth as a clinical, diagnostic, and research instrument, many people feel that an improved version of the test could be designed.

The MMPI was built by psychometric principles, but the basic frame of reference was the descriptive psychiatry of the pre–World War II era. Even at that time, the taxonomic systems for classifying abnormal behavior were generally considered to be unsatisfactory (Strecker, Ebaugh, & Ewalt, 1947). It was felt that there were too many competing diagnostic systems and that diagnostic labeling was too static. Some authorities also believed that psychiatry lacked the breadth and depth of knowledge to classify behavioral disorders as adequately as other branches of medicine had developed a classification for physical disorders. On the other hand, the descriptive psychiatry stemming from that recent period does contain rich and valuable constructs. Many of the formulations were refined through years of observation by clinicians who were both highly sensitive and gifted. But there was a weakness inherent in the richness and surplus of meaning which characterized these clinical constructs. Ordinary clinicians were unable to incorporate the complex formulations in order to apply them in a uniform, objective, and reliable manner. The naturalistic, biological point of view which spawned many of the constructs contained the assumption that, once painstaking classification had revealed the true order of nature, the significant principles regarding etiology, pathology, and therapy would be discovered. Such did not prove to be the case or, at least, progress has not been fast enough. Much of the present dissatisfaction with psychiatric diagnosis is based not only on questions of reliability (which frequently are misconstrued) but even more on the lack of established connections between the "What is it?" questions of description and the "What to do about it?" considerations of therapy.

It is against this backdrop that the discussion of the construction and application of MMPI codebooks should be viewed. Even those MMPI interpretative systems which attempt to skirt the problem by ignoring diagnostic formulations and focusing on descriptive statement or trait predictions are not immune from any underlying weaknesses in the theoretical system and in the test instrument. Such concerns might be less significant were not computer-based MMPI interpretative systems already being established which conceivably, although not necessarily, could introduce an undesirable kind of rigidity into the field of diagnostic testing.

CONSTRUCTION OF CODEBOOKS

In the discussion of MMPI codebook construction, the techniques of Gilberstadt and Duker (1965), Marks and Seeman (1963), and Fowler

(1965) will be used as examples for comparison. The reader should be aware of possible favorable biases the author may show toward his own work. There will be some attempt to examine critically the other two codebook approaches which are given here as examples because they are representative of the best that has been achieved in the field of codebook construction. It should be noted in passing that the term "codebook" is being substituted for the more popular term "cookbook." The latter was intended as a catchword, and its continued use as a blanket term for MMPI code-type interpretative systems seems neither accurately descriptive nor scientifically desirable. Comparisons of the three approaches to codebook construction will be based on (1) identification and specification of profile types, (2) kinds of intermediate processing in the derivation of profile correlates, and (3) types of codebook output.

The Identification and Specification of Profiles

Gilberstadt and Duker began with the aim of studying certain profile types which had appeared to be related to significant clinical constructs. Originally, the profiles of male veteran inpatients were specified impressionistically from experience. They had been noticed either because they seemed to represent cardinal types or because they occurred with high frequency. Contingency rules were devised which specified the shape and elevation of the profiles so that profiles of a given type would be included and all other profiles would be excluded. Only profiles obtained close to the time of hospital admission were used in an attempt to control for test-taking set. Initially, the focus of interest was on the particular profile types which had been previously noted and not on the study of the incidence of various types of profiles in the population.

Marks and Seeman started with a different emphasis from that of Gilberstadt and Duker. They examined an entire set of profiles obtained during the course of a year, and from this set they selected several two- and three-digit code types. They obtained a second sample during the course of the next year, and with the added sample they picked out several additional code types. Thus, frequency seems to have played a large part in their initial selection of profile types for study. Marks and Seeman used contingency rules similar to those of Gilberstadt and Duker to specify their profile types.

Fowler developed his system in a different way. He observed, during the course of his work as a consultant to alcoholism clinics, that he was obtaining recurring profile patterns and repetitively writing highly similar reports for given profiles. He reasoned that time and effort could be spared if the profile characteristics were defined so that, when a given profile appeared, the report that previously had been written for similar profiles could be used. Like the other investigators, Fowler relied on frequency and clinical experience for selection of profile patterns; but, rather than using inclusion rules for complete profiles, his specifications consisted of two-digit high points. Some of these were culled from the literature. Thus, rather than investigating profile-type constructs, as Gilberstadt and Duker started out to do, or specifying more or less completely the most frequent profiles from a population of patients, as Marks and Seeman did, Fowler started with an attempt to obtain a set of clinically meaningful two-digit profile elevations from which interpretations could be made.

In one sense, it is somewhat of an academic exercise to describe the origins of the several approaches to codebook construction, since they all ultimately converged toward the similar aim of being as complete in coverage as possible. But, in another sense, close examination could help to clarify differences in approach which might be helpful in future attempts to construct codebooks as well as to suggest strengths and weaknesses in the approaches to the development of the presently discussed codebooks.

Kinds of Intermediate Processing in Codebook Development

Gilberstadt and Duker successively refined the clinical conception of each of their profile-type constructs and the corresponding contingency rules. This was accomplished by rating cases selected by the rules at each point in the refinement process for goodness of fit to the nascent conception of the profile type. Ratings were based on the psychiatric social case work histories and discharge summaries for each case. The refinement process reduced the size of the sample for each of the profile types so that a file of several thousand cases was required to produce minimally acceptable numbers for statistical analysis. Statistical comparisons were made with a control group that was a representative sample of the hospital's psychiatric patients. Comparisons were based on a checklist built empirically to provide an exhaustive list of symptoms, trait names, and psychiatric descriptive terms in common usage in the department's discharge summaries. This ensured that the domain of sublanguage in actual use in the setting was covered adequately. Life history items and psychiatric discharge diagnoses also were included in the checklist.

Marks and Seeman had a diversified sample of both male and female patients admitted to the University of Kansas Medical Center Psychiatry Service. Using a carefully chosen Q array of 108 phenotypic and genotypic statements and a group of 19 clinicians, they obtained Q sorts on the patients in their samples. Employing an analysis that was based on pairwise intercorrelations of Q sorts for each profile type, they selected the five patients who were most representative of the profile-type group. The average Q-item placements of the three most typical and three least typical Q items of the selected patients became the personality descriptions to be predicted actuarially. Frequency on a 225-item checklist of life history and clinical variables was calculated for each profile type. Characteristic intelligence test scores and psychometric data, including average discharge MMPI profiles, were also computed for each of the profile-type groups.

Fowler proceeded by writing descriptive statements based on his judgment and clinical experience for each of his two-point code patterns. This part of his process was not strictly actuarially based. He subsequently refined his program by adding descriptive statements that were based on empirical research findings for scale elevations, but he kept the two-digit code at the heart of his system. Fowler's program took into account the configuration of the validity scales as well as age, marital status, etc. It included the scoring of more than 200 special MMPI scales such as Welsh's *A* scale and Barron's Ego Strength Scale and the reporting of results on about 20 of these. Finally, he formulated diagnostic statements based on the actuarially derived Taulbee-Sisson scale pairs and the Peterson signs for subclinical schizophrenia.

Type of Output

Gilberstadt and Duker derived two types of diagnostic statements to be predicted from each profile type. First they determined, ex post facto, the diagnosis, based on the APA diagnostic nomenclature, that appeared to best characterize the profile type in its refined, crystallized conception which became apparent to them in retrospect. This diagnostic classification was not determined on a strict, actuarial basis but relied on the clinical sophistication that accrued in the process of codebook construction. In addition, they determined diagnostic alternatives that were based on the actual diagnoses assigned to the cases of a profile type in the psychiatric discharge summaries. Second, for each profile type they presented a capsule, narrative summary of the personality description that most succinctly characterizes the profile type. This summary is both actuarially derived—it represents a distillation of the set of psychiatric and social service case descriptions that were empirically found among the profile-type cases—and nonactuarially derived—clinical judgment was employed in the selection and implicit weighting of the narrative statements that were included in the capsule summary. To broaden coverage to profiles that would not meet specifications for any one of their 19 profile types, Gilberstadt and Duker included a set of interpretative statements based on configurations of two and three scale elevations that were empirically derived from a complete one-year sample of admissions to the inpatient psychiatric service. They also presented a set of empirically derived contingency rules for diagnosing the clinical states of depression, anxiety, agitation, and mania.

Marks and Seeman provided a rich assortment of demographic, case history, and psychometric data about each of their profile types; but, in the experimental, computerized MMPI reports that they developed at the University of Kansas, the bulk of the output consisted of the most and least descriptive personality characteristics in terms of the *Q* statements. In these experimental reports, they also included a diagnosis and recommendation for administrative decision making.

Fowler, from the outset of his project, had a primary concern about the nature of his reports. He considered, and rejected, the possibility of writing complete sentences of interpretation for various two-point codes and then combining such sentences into narrative paragraphs which had been suggested by the work of others. He felt that this procedure was too complex for his purposes. He decided instead to write simple interpretative statements of the kind he ordinarily produced in his clinical reports. Fowler's computer-generated reports contain scores on the MMPI clinical scales, scores on many of the special scales, results of the analysis by the diagnostic sign rules, the "critical items" endorsed in the patient's test responses, and a psychological narrative report which, although based on the library of simple interpretative statements, is organized into paragraphs and to the reader resembles an individual case assessment report written by a clinician.

THE APPLICATION OF CODEBOOKS

In current practice, the terms "automated" and "nonautomated," as applied to MMPI processing, are equivalent to the terms "computerized" and "noncomputerized." The term "actuarial" means, broadly, that the various nontest clinical or case history correlates of profile types have been determined empirically. By contrast, the term "nonactuarial" signifies that the construction of a statement library of presumed correlates of profile characteristics is based upon the codebook builder's clinical skill and experience. The present discussion will consider (1) nonautomated actuarial systems as represented by Gilberstadt and Duker; (2) automated actuarial systems as represented by Marks and Seeman; and (3) automated nonactuarial systems as represented by Fowler.

Nonautomated Actuarial Systems

The Gilberstadt and Duker codebook is an example of a nonautomated codebook that is basically, but not completely, actuarial. No provision has been made as yet and no program has been published to date for computer scoring and interpretation of their codebook. Any of several of the individual or group forms of the test can be administered, depending upon the needs of the patient. Administration, scoring, and interpretation all are done by clerks using codebook instructions. All results are passed on to a psychologist who may communicate them without change if he considers them to be adequate, supplement them if he feels they are incomplete, or revise them if he has additional information that suggests to him a need for modifications of any kind. The Gilberstadt and Duker codebook can have limitations in scope. They state that, within the limits of the error of measurement, profiles which meet specifications for a profile type can be interpreted according to their codebook regardless of contingencies, such as sex, which are not explicitly enumerated in their inclusion or exclusion rules. Because of the restricted range of the samples on which their codebook was developed, however, profile types that are significant in other samples may be missing from their codebook. For example, profile types commonly found in groups of acutely disturbed female psychiatric inpatients may not be included in their codebook. The best current estimate, based on cross-validation of samples of psychiatric inpatients of diverse types, is that if the codebook rules are relaxed so that only one contingency rule from each of the sets of profile-type contingency rules is ignored, approximately 60% of the obtained profiles will be covered by the 19 profile types in the codebook (Wiggins, 1965).

The Gilberstadt and Duker codebook represents, in itself, the outcome of research intended to validate the MMPI for psychiatric screening and personality description. The results for the 278 profile type already serve as cross-validation of a similar, earlier study. Throughout their book, Gilberstadt and Duker cite earlier studies that are supported or not supported by their results. Because of the profile-type construct approach, interpretations made from the Gilberstadt and Duker codebook lend themselves to evaluation as either total hits or misses, if minor exceptions are allowed for various specific details.

Automated Actuarial Systems

This type of system is similar to the automated nonactuarial system except that the output and profile-type correlates have been determined empirically rather than impressionistically. The details of the Marks and Seeman experiment in which they programmed their codebook for computer processing have not been published. They used a mark-sensing machine to score MMPI answer sheets and transferred the data to punch cards which then were fed into a computer. The program was devised so that the output consisted of *Q* statements which were typed out in the form of a narrative paragraph. The diagnosis and any administrative recommendations were included also. The profile was graphed, and the overall format of the output was of the usual type produced by computer systems.

The Marks and Seeman codebook has limitations of scope similar to those of the Gilberstadt and Duker book largely because it, too, is actuarially based on a sample of limited scope. Although there are several profile types included in the Marks and Seeman codebook which are not found in the Gilberstadt and Duker codebook, when their codebook was applied to the same sample on which the Gilberstadt and Duker codebook was cross-validated, there was an almost identical rate of coverage of about 60% (Wiggins, 1965).

Marks and Seeman, in their book, report a validation experiment using actuarially derived *Q*-statement descriptions versus psychotherapist's *Q*-statement descriptions of eight patients. For the actuarial descriptions the validity coefficients ranged from .36 to .88, and for the clinical descriptions the validities ranged from .29 to .75. There was a clear superiority for the actuarial over the clinical descriptions. There have been criticisms and objections on theoretical grounds about the use of *Q* technique for personality assessment (Holt, 1965), but in clinical applications such as the Marks and Seeman codebook it would seem that the user must make his own judgment about the desirability of this form of personality description.

Automated Nonactuarial Systems

Fowler's program is an example of an automated MMPI interpretative system that, at least in its origins, was largely nonactuarial. Fowler continues to revise his computer program and may have added empirically derived actuarial data. The MMPI interpretation service based on Fowler's program is offered through the Roche Psychiatric Service Institute. Users who request the service are supplied with specially designed booklets and answer sheets. The completed answer sheets are mailed to New Jersey for processing, and test results are then relayed to a large computer in Huntsville, Alabama, by means of a data line. The computer relays back the test output which is then mailed to the user from the Newark office. The nature of the output from Fowler's system has been described above. The computer prints out one page of narrative report, a page containing scores on the MMPI clinical scales and on a number of special scales, plus a printout of the "critical items," and a page on which the profile is graphed.

The Fowler program is based on the relationship between profile characteristics and items in the statement library. Every profile is analyzed and interpreted according to this program so that there will be 100% coverage. The degree to which these interpretations "fit" or are valid still appears to rest on clinical judgment. Neither formal validational studies nor the detailed data that would permit such studies have yet been published. Any attempt to validate the procedures would seem to involve the same methods and problems that are associated in the validation of any kind of clinical judgment.

Ultimately, it would seem likely that automated systems will show an advantage in the area of cost of processing compared to clerical systems. However, computer approaches do not as yet have clear-cut superiority in terms of either cost or scoring reliability. It should be apparent from the preceding discussion that applications of the MMPI codebook approach should still be considered to be in an experimental stage. Although the commercial availability of professionally approved MMPI scoring and interpretation services is evidence of the practical value of such services, it should not be concluded that the ultimate in technology has been approached.

The Use of Codebooks with Descriptive Handbooks

Both Gilberstadt and Duker and Marks and Seeman supplement their actuarial codebooks with large amounts of descriptive data, and both include much clinical and case history data. Gilberstadt and Duker also present selective references from the psychiatric and psychological personality theory literature which tie into their profile-type constructs. Marks and Seeman provide supplementary psychometric data. Neither of these handbook supplements are of the scope of the encyclopedic Dahlstrom and Welsh *MMPI Handbook* (1960), nor are they intended to be. They represent specialized handbooks of data directly related to the actuarial codebooks that they accompany. Both of them present the frequency data for symptoms, traits, complaints, and other clinical characteristics of their samples. These data may be valuable for future research purposes; they provide teaching material for the training of clinicians and give the diagnostician data on which to base his own understanding and enrichment of the profile-type constructs presented in the codebooks. The latter consideration raises the question of the relationship between clinical and actuarial personality descriptions.

For the case of a determinate trait domain and a specified clinical population when the aim is to predict diagnosis or personality description on a finite set of traits, there seems to be little doubt that the clinician is superfluous once the empirical correlations have been established. In their zeal to make a case for the actuarial approach, the advocates of this strategy, despite the clear admonitions to the contrary by authorities such as Meehl (1959), are often led astray by a kind of fallacious, reductionistic reasoning which also often characterizes their critics. The latter frequently base their objections to the actuarial approach on the "mechanistic" procedures that rob subjects of their individuality by employing stereotypes. Such indeed might be a valid criticism if proponents of actuarial MMPI prediction argued that once an actual personality diagnosis or description is produced there remain no individual differences of importance or significance to life adjustment or life strivings. Although this proposition is obviously false, it may be worthwhile to examine its weaknesses briefly.

Because we are able to narrow the range of variables over which individual differences exist between persons by assigning them to test-derived classes based on variables of clinical significance, it does not hold that there remain no other significant personality or life adjustment variables in terms of which individuals in the test-defined classes may differ. It is true that, if sorting is done on the basis of powerful source traits, it should be possible to predict limits beyond which individuals highly deviant with respect to the traits are unlikely to vary in relevant aspects of behavior. Just as the individual of test-defined borderline intellect is unlikely to become a successful graduate of a standard liberal arts college, so a test-defined pseudoneurotic schizophrenic is unlikely to become anxiety-free, warm and flexible in emotional give-and-take with a spouse, and completely free of slips in logical thinking. However, some energetic, shrewd individuals of borderline intellect become millionaires through success in business even though on test performance they could not be discriminated from others in their deviant category who become chronic public charges; test-defined pseudoneurotic schizophrenics become writers, philosophers, and public figures of great importance even though on test performance they cannot be differentiated from their chronically unproductive hospitalized counterparts.

In the context of concurrent validity, a large sample of Rorschachs from individuals whose MMPI profiles meet the contingency rules for the 278 MMPI profile type might be expected to show less variability than a sample from a representative group of patients or normals; but few or no Rorschachs from such a group would be expected to be identical. Beyond any statistical considerations, many students of personality would have an implicit interest as observers of behavior in those responses which might emerge during the administration of a test such as the Rorschach which could be presumed to be unique to the individual and reflective of his cognitive processes, modes of symbolization, and approaches to task mastery rather than of significance because they tended to be common to members of a diagnostic class.

At the level of a trait, many individuals of the 278 MMPI profile type have strong religious interests; but it would not be inconsistent with the profile-type construct to find one individual who was a seminary student preoccupied with formal religious philosophy and another who was a Greenwich Village hippie dedicated to peace movements. Not only would the differences in value orientation between two such individuals be of importance in any clinical appraisal of them but also the total matrix of relationships between them and cultural, environmental, and situational realities. Those areas of an individual's life encompassed by psychiatric personality evaluation might be of considerably less importance than other aspects of the life as it was being lived. This would make it no less desirable, it would seem, for personality diagnosis to be as scientific and free from distortion as possible. It might be argued that this statement implies a very narrow view of the goal of personality diagnosis and description. The results of any actuarial diagnostic procedure are merely one facet of the total formulation and management of a case. These results must be utilized by a clinician if they are to have any pragmatic significance. The consensus emerging from the arguments about actuarial versus clinical prediction seems to be that the role of fitting personality diagnosis into the broader clinical context should be assigned to the clinician, while the more narrow task of normative prediction should be done by the actuary whenever possible.

Research Applications

MMPI profile-type constructs lay the groundwork for a wide variety of research approaches because the profile-type specifications, such as those given by Gilberstadt and Duker or Marks and Seeman, ensure that within tolerable limits classification will be uniform. This was one of the purposes for which the MMPI was constructed originally. At the time of the construction, it was intended that single scales should serve as measures of the diagnostic categories. The scales were named according to the diagnostic groups on which they were standardized (e.g., Hypochondriasis, Depression, Hysteria). It soon became apparent that there was not always a close correspondence between scale elevations and corresponding diagnostic constructs, even though single MMPI scales treated separately did yield useful trait descriptions. Consequently, a convention was established of referring to scales by their respective numbers (according to the order on the standard profile sheets). Also, it became apparent in clinical experience with the MMPI that the most powerful use of the test lay in the interpretation of profile patterns rather than of single scales. Clinicians noted that certain scale combinations were regularly associated with certain symptom syndromes. Many profile types that appeared to be diagnostic signs of high probability with respect to various psychiatric syndromes were gradually accumulated. It should be noted that, rightly or wrongly, there was not a planned, systematic attempt to match the range of psychiatric diagnostic constructs by corresponding profile types. Rather, some profile types began to stand out in the course of ordinary clinical usage as being especially powerful and significant in clinical construct terms. At this stage, even among clinicians who shared knowledge about the profile-type constructs, there were large differences in how much was interpreted from the profiles and in the amount of time and effort they invested in the process of interpretation and communication of results.

Meehl's papers on clinical versus actuarial interpretation (1956, 1957) served to clarify this state of affairs. As a result, great impetus was provided for the construction of codebooks based on MMPI pattern research. Even before this stage in the evolution of codebooks, Hathaway and Meehl (1951) had pioneered in the code-type approach by the publication of their clinical atlas for the MMPI.

Once profile patterns became easily recognizable through experience, it still was necessary to accumulate samples of thousands of cases to provide sufficient numbers of classical cases of a given type to assure, in the absence of an acceptable statistical criterion, that maximal homogeneity obtained among cases of a type.

Profile Types as Constructs

Research potentialities of profile-type constructs will be illustrated by the example of the Gilberstadt-Duker 49 profile type. The personality descriptions abstracted from the case history correlates of the 49 profile type matches the APA diagnostic manual description of the sociopath more closely than does any other profile type with sufficient similarity so that there can be little doubt about the congruence of the two descriptions. However, there may not be perfect predictive validity from the profile type to the APA diagnosis. Clinical experience has shown that, even as specified in the Gilberstadt-Duker codebook, this profile type can be produced by some small, as yet undetermined, percentage of patients who are not sociopaths but who are, for example, schizophrenics with psychopathic character traits whose schizophrenia is in some degree of remission at the time of testing. It might be estimated, however, that at least 90% of the patients who obtain the 49 profile on admission to a psychiatric service will be diagnosable sociopaths.

The clinical and life history data associated with the 49 profile type contain numerous suggestions about variables of etiologic and psychodynamic significance. First, there clearly are indications that body build is, with very high frequency, of the Sheldon mesomorphic type. In the majority of cases, it is observed that these individuals are well built and have corresponding athletic interests. Second, frequency appears to be high enough to predict for any case that learning history will show a doting mother who was a critical, unaffectionate, possibly subversive wife and a father who was a weak symbol of authority and an inadequate source of external control. This hypothesis ties in with recurrent observations reported from samples differing widely in time and place (Aichhorn, 1935; Cleckley, 1955). Precise comparisons of such reports have been hindered greatly in the past by the lack of techniques for objectively defining cases. This definition can be facilitated by the use of the MMPI profile type. A more speculative kind of hypothesis is the notion that there may be in the highly active, athletic 49 profile type an innately weak potential, relative to other personality types, for the emission of those physiological and psychological responses which are major components of the kinds of relationships described as "loving" that exist between, for example, children and parents or between spouses. From this standpoint sociopathy might be viewed, in part, as a deficiency disorder for which restitutive measures would be sought. The 49 profile-type construct appears to overlap a great deal with Freud's description of the normally occurring narcissistic personality type. This typology of Freud's has been criticized by Fenichel (1945) on the grounds that it lacks an etiological and psychopathological framework. It would appear that research with the profile-type construct would help to supply some of the missing supports for the Freudian typology. Last, but not of least importance in the present context, is the hypothesis that a major determinant of the 49 profile type is active temperament which is largely of genetic origins. There are suggestions in the case histories of the codebook cases of this profile type that other family members shared the temperamental characteristics of the patients which is why, for example, fathers frequently were too active outside the home to invest themselves sufficiently in the sedentary aspects of parenthood. The Gilberstadt-Duker handbook also contains hypotheses about precipitating factors. In the 49 profile-type cases, decisive encounters with authority or unpredictable failures in competitive strivings appeared to add chance factors of importance in determining which potential sociopaths embark on the typical, continual downhill course that characterizes those unsuccessful psychopaths who become 49 profile-type sociopathic patients.

The major problem in validating the 49, or any of the profile-type constructs, would appear to be the difficulty in accumulating sufficiently large samples of cases when and where they would be needed. Large-scale methods for collecting cases probably would be required, and elaborate validational procedures would need to be applied. This might require a high level of organization of cooperative research facilities.

One more research implication of the Gilberstadt-Duker data is the hypothesis that cutting across the profiles, which have been identified, are a set of higher-order variables which may or may not be exhaustive as presently perceived but which nonetheless can point the way toward areas in which attempts might be made to develop quantitative measurement by techniques which are more precise and experimentally manipulatable than the present self-report inventory measures. These variables include autonomic nervous system reactivity (reflected by MMPI 123 scale elevations), anxiety (indicated by elevations on scale 7 and the correlated elevations of scale 2), aggressive temperament (reflected in 49 scale elevations), a passivity-repression-denial-physiological instability dimension (indicated by 13 scale elevations), a cognitive-affective deficiency dimension (indicated by scale 8 elevations), and a deficiency in arousal or activation regulation (indicated by scale 9 elevations). Assuming that these more or less crude conceptions can be tightened, the first task of research would appear to be the development of methods and measurements of physiological, psychometric, and other areas that could provide quantification. The implicit hypothesis is that these variables are among the ingredients of every personality and that their balance or deviation defines, in large part, the personality constructs represented in the formulations of abnormal psychology and psychiatry.

It has been realized for some time now that relative to personality theory we still are in a stage which is primitive and has been described as "preclassificatory." Actuarial personality diagnosis appears to be a step in the right direction from a pragmatic point of view. If we are to make strides in the development of personality theory, we must first sharpen our constructs and then engage in taxonomic efforts to identify basic variables. It would appear that MMPI techniques can contribute to progress in both the applied and the theoretical aspects of this quest.

REFERENCES

Aichhorn, A. *Wayward youth.* New York: Viking Press, 1935.

Cleckley, H. *The mask of sanity.* St. Louis: Mosby, 1955.

Dahlstrom, W. G., and Welsh, G. S. *An MMPI handbook: A guide to use in clinical practice and research.* Minneapolis: University of Minnesota Press, 1960.

Fenichel, O. *The psychoanalytic theory of neurosis.* New York: Norton, 1945.

Fowler, R. D. Purposes and usefulness of the Alabama program. In Three approaches to the automatic interpretation of the MMPI. Symposium presented at the American Psychological Association, Chicago, September 5, 1965.

Gilberstadt, H., and Duker, J. *A handbook for clinical and actuarial MMPI interpretation.* Philadelphia: Saunders, 1965.

Goldberg, L. R. Still wanted—a good cookbook. In Three approaches to the automatic interpretation of the MMPI. Symposium presented at the American Psychological Association, Chicago, September 5, 1965.

Hathaway, S. R. Personality inventories. In B. B. Wolman (Ed.), *Handbook of clinical psychology*. New York: McGraw-Hill, 1965.

Hathaway, S. R., and Meehl, P. E. *Atlas of clinical interpretation of the MMPI*. Minneapolis: University of Minnesota Press, 1951.

Holt, R. R. Experimental methods in clinical psychology. In B. B. Wolman (Ed.), *Handbook of clinical psychology*. New York: McGraw-Hill, 1965.

Marks, P., and Seeman, W. *The actuarial description of abnormal personality: An atlas for use with the MMPI*. Baltimore: Williams & Wilkins, 1963.

Meehl, P. E. Wanted—a good cookbook. *American Psychologist,* 1956, **11,** 263–272.

Meehl, P. E. When shall we use our heads instead of the formula? *Journal of Consulting Psychology,* 1957, **4,** 268–273.

Meehl, P. E. Some ruminations on the validation of clinical procedures. *Canadian Journal of Psychology,* 1959, **13,** 102–128.

Strecker, E. A., Ebaugh, F. G., and Ewalt, J. R. *Practical clinical psychiatry*. Philadelphia: Blakiston, 1947.

Wiggins, J. S. Personal communication, 1965.

Chapter Four
Methodological Problems of Cookbook Construction

Philip A. Marks
The Ohio State University
and
Jacob O. Sines
University of Missouri

Attempts to develop cookbook interpretations of psychological tests are based on the deceptively simple hypothesis that there are statistically reliable and clinically significant regularities between certain features of the tests on the input side and other more interesting, nontest personality characteristics on the output side. The variety of ways in which the components of these presumed regularities may be sought, classified, combined, and reported offer the investigator a number of methodological options, each requiring a set of decisions that will profoundly affect not only the validity and utility of the cookbook but its acceptability as well.

It is our purpose here to discuss several of the methodological issues that should be considered by the cookbook constructor. Our decision to deal with only five of these does not imply that other equally challenging and stimulating issues do not exist—they do, and they require careful attention (e.g., see Briggs, Taylor, & Tellegen, 1966; Finney, 1967; Seeman, 1964). We shall, however, restrict this discussion to the following problems: (1) the selection of input data, (2) the selection of predictors, (3) the selection and specification of descriptors, (4) determining predictor-descriptor relationships, and (5) the validity and utility of cookbooks.

It is obvious that our topical distinctions are somewhat arbitrary. In actually constructing a cookbook, these several points cannot easily be separated because a decision concerning any one of them will materially affect, if not completely determine, a decision concerning a subsequent one.

Before continuing, we wish to point out that "cookbook" is a much more inclusive term than "actuarial." Although we shall draw a distinction between actuarial methods such as those employed by Gilberstadt and Duker (1965, pp. 101–105), Marks and Seeman (1963), and Sines (1966) on the one hand and nonactuarial mechanical methods such as those found in the work of Finney (1966, 1967), Fowler (1964), Glueck (1966), Hovey and Lewis (1967), Pearson, Swenson, Rome, Mataya, and Brannick (1964), and Piotrowski (1964) on the other, both approaches are "cookbook methods." But, recognizing that such distinctions are another matter, we wish only to suggest now that the term "cookbook" be used to refer to any set of rules that specifies a set of descriptors (interpretative statements) that follow in an automatic fashion from some specified information about a person. Such information most often is, although it need not be, a test score or pattern, or configuration, of test scores. In contrast to the constraints imposed on the use of the term "actuarial," the cookbook approach implies only that there be a set of rules by means of which one automatically assigns certain attributes to persons who generate certain test scores, regardless of the way in which the attributes were derived or the way in which their association with features of the test may be determined.

THE SELECTION OF INPUT DATA

There are at least 12 cookbooks currently available or being developed (Drake & Oetting, 1959; Eber, 1964; Finney, 1965; Fowler, 1964; Gilberstadt & Duker, 1965; Glueck, 1966; Hovey & Lewis, 1967; Marks, 1967; Marks & Seeman, 1963; Piotrowski, 1964; Rome, Swenson, Mataya, McCarthy, Pearson, Keating, & Hathaway, 1962; and Sines, 1966). All these require input data that are in quantifiable form, and all but one employ objective tests (nine use only the MMPI)—tests that are relatively inexpensive to administer and score. This is particularly significant in view of the discussions by a number of writers indicating that the utility of any assessment device be judged not only in terms of its conventional validity but in terms of its cost as well (Cronbach & Gleser, 1965; Gough, 1962; Hathaway, 1959; Marks & Kangas, 1968; Meehl, 1956a, 1956b, 1959b, 1960, 1963; Sawyer, 1966; Sechrest, 1963).

As Meehl (1954a, 1954b) pointed out earlier, the input information may consist of either psychometric or nonpsychometric data or of some combination of these. Moreover, Hathaway and Monachesi (1963) have suggested that input can also derive from social data which emphasize one or more aspects of the environment. A detailed consideration of the issues related to the choice of test or nontest input and to the modes of collecting data would require an examination of the rationale for the use of tests (or clinicians!) in general and is not appropriate here (see Sawyer, 1966; also Lyons, on "primary and meta-data," 1967, pp. 12–14). It should be made clear, however, that even though existing cookbooks in psychology and psychiatry do employ psychometric sources of input, they are not an essential feature of the general approach (e.g., see Rosenberg, Glueck, & Bennett, 1967).

THE SELECTION OF PREDICTORS

Whatever choice is made concerning the type of input data that is going to be used, one is still faced with the necessity of specifying the units from which he wishes to classify or predict. Here one may focus on bits, or parts, of the input data, or one may identify patterns and interrelationships that take a number of components into account at one time.

We should like to define a continuum of complexity of the predictor units that has been used in cookbooks thus far. This continuum does not refer to complexity of the psychological processes that may be presumed to determine the test score or predictor but rather to the number and elaborateness of the interrelationships between the bits of input information that are taken into account in arriving at, or in defining, a predictor unit. In these terms, one might consider each of several different levels of scores on many different MMPI scales as predictor units and attend not at all to their configurational relationships (Drake & Oetting, 1959; Hovey & Lewis, 1967; Sines, 1966). Most investigators would agree that, although there could be an impressively large number of such predictor units to consider, the level of their complexity would be quite low. At the other end of this continuum are several attempts to define and use as predictor units some specified configuration, or pattern, of scores on a number of MMPI scales (cf., Gilberstadt & Duker, 1965; Kleinmuntz, 1963; Marks & Seeman, 1963; Meehl & Dahlstrom, 1960) and the more recent suggestions by Briggs et al. (1966) and Dahlstrom (see Chapter 1) to include additional nontest variables such as sex, age, or intelligence, as "part of the profile" defining the predictor. Although to our knowledge there are only a few successful attempts to use isolated MMPI scales, subscale scores, or individual items as predictors, it is nonetheless true that in most approaches to the development of cookbooks the basic predictor is but a portion of the total test profile.

The fact that the significance of a specific portion of the test protocol is dependent upon or is moderated by the presence or absence of other test (or nontest) components and their interrelationships (see Saunders, 1956) is reflected in the efforts of Finney (1967), Fowler (1964), and Pearson et al. (1964) to deal with a variety of configural relationships between MMPI scores and by Piotrowski's (1964) use of complex combinational rules for Rorschach interpretation. Gilberstadt and Duker (1965), Marks and Seeman (1963), and Sines (1966), on the other hand, use individual test scores very little, if at all, and define the predictor unit in terms of the overall pattern of scores on 13 MMPI scales.

The complexity of the predictor unit chosen has considerable practical importance. A single-scale analysis of the test protocol is much more flexible than a multiscale approach in that the former permits the programming of interpretative statements about almost all test profiles. Thus, in the cookbooks developed by Finney (1967), Fowler (1964), Hovey and Lewis (1967), and Pearson et al. (1964), essentially all MMPI profiles can be interpreted. This may be contrasted with the fact that the cookbooks developed by Gilberstadt and Duker (1965) and by Marks and Seeman (1963) accommodated only about 80% of the profiles in the derivation sample; and, when applied to appropriate samples of profiles obtained from other clinical settings, the coverage afforded by the latter was reduced to 20 to 55% (Briggs et al., 1966; Glueck, 1966; Pauker, 1966; Sines, 1966). (Both Briggs et al. and Pauker also found, however, that by allowing a one-rule violation in the Marks and Seeman system the classification rate increased from 20 to 70%.)

If the decision is made to use combinations of test scores as predictors, a number of methods may be considered for identifying homogeneous profile patterns (Gaier & Lee, 1953; Goldberg, 1965; Helmstadler, 1957; Lykken, 1956, 1963; McHugh & Apostolakos, 1959; Meehl, 1959a; Meehl & Dahlstrom, 1960; Mosel & Roberts, 1954; Muldoon & Ray, 1958; Sawrey, Keller, & Conger, 1960). It should be pointed out, however, that whether one uses a set of configural rules, a geometric index of profile similarity, or some other method, he must decide, often quite arbitrarily, how much variability is to be allowed within a group of "similar" but nonidentical profiles (the within-class heterogeneity of a predictor). In commenting on the problem, Meehl (1963) states:

> At present there is no rigorous, straightforward actuarial "searching" technique available for grouping similar but nonidentical MMPI profiles into coarser classes or "types" so as to com-

> bine the desiderata of stable sample size, high psychological homogeneity, easy identifiability for routine clinical entrance, and quasi-complete coverage of the range of patterns empirically found [p. viii].

Again, although there are no empirical data to rely on, it seems obvious that the validity (though not necessarily the utility or acceptability) of the output will be inversely related to the intragroup variability of the subtest scores.

The lack of guidelines for use in establishing classes of persons on the basis of input data results in an arbitrariness that was discussed by Gleser (1965), Greenhouse (1965), and Torgerson (1965), among others, at a recent conference on "The Role and Methodology of Classification in Psychiatry and Psychopathology." Without going into great detail at this time, we may reasonably state that a satisfactory representation of patterns of input data requires considerable familiarity with the frequency or incidence of values (base rates) of each of the input variables encountered in the populations for which cookbook descriptions are to be developed. Validity and utility considerations aside, whether a cookbook accommodates every profile or only a subset of profiles and whether it yields mechanical descriptions for every patient or only for some are issues that may significantly affect the reception given the cookbook by the clinician and the administrator. In a later section we shall discuss some of the problems involved in evaluating the validity and utility of cookbooks. Suffice it to say at this point that these problems are considerable, and attempts to deal with them have only begun.

THE SELECTION AND SPECIFICATION OF DESCRIPTORS

There is a great deal of variability in the ways in which descriptors have been chosen in the development of the cookbooks that are now available. We shall discuss two dimensions of descriptor choice: content and level of discrimination.

Content

In view of the prevailing notion that the proper function of psychological assessment is to elucidate a patient's underlying behavior-determining drives, traits, motives, and defenses, a cookbook's acceptability by most practicing clinicians will often depend in large part on the degree to which the descriptors consist of *genotypic* (psychodynamic) content. Since the most easily obtainable criterion information concerning a person is characteristically judgmental, one indicator of descriptor validity is necessarily dependent upon the interjudge agreement in determining the presence or absence or the degree of presence of an attribute (Koch, 1964). It should be noted that the available literature has clearly documented, without significant exception, greater validity for judgments of *phenotypic* (observable) attributes than for genotypic ones when concurrent agreement indicated by interjudge reliability is the criterion. Thus both the validity and the acceptability of a cookbook will be influenced to a large extent by the content of the descriptors. But it may be that a choice here that maximizes one of these variables may reduce the other.

Numerous descriptor sources have been examined in an attempt to obtain comprehensive coverage of content in the personality domain. Among these are institutional records, case histories, psychological reports, discharge summaries, clinical experience and observation, research reports, published personality and interest tests, school and legal records, court reports, adjective checklists, behavior rating forms, essays and research papers on personality, doctoral dissertations, clinical examination forms, checklists of symptoms and complaints, comments of informants, lexicographic compilations of trait names, and textbooks in psychiatry, clinical psychology, abnormal psychology, and personality. Additional suggestions are found in several sources dealing specifically with the content of psychological reports (e.g., Foster, 1951; Hammond & Allen, 1953; Klopfer, 1960).

Above all else, however, the decision made regarding the use of *observable* (phenotypic) or *inferential* (genotypic) descriptors will greatly influence the rate with which the cookbook can and will be subjected to empirical validation. In view of the consistent finding that genotypic judgments are made less reliably than phenotypic ones, it seems likely that cookbooks whose output consists of statements about observable behaviors will stand the greater chance of being validated. As mentioned above, however, the degree to which a cookbook's validity is upheld may be related in a negative way to the acceptability of its content to many clinicians.

Level of Discrimination

The types of output statements that are available in the several cookbooks vary in level of discrimination. At one end of the continuum are statements, either phenotypic or genotypic, that are descriptive of people in general—statements of the P. T. Barnum sort (Marks &

Seeman, 1962b). Further along the continuum are statements that tend to discriminate some major subgroup of persons (such as medical patients or psychiatric patients) from the general population, and toward finer discrimination are statements that distinguish subclasses of psychiatric patients or medical patients who do and do not express psychosomatic complaints.

Depending upon the investigator's purpose in constructing a cookbook, he may appropriately choose descriptors that serve only to discriminate persons into large classes with a base rate for a given attribute that differs from the base rate for that attribute in the general population, or he may choose descriptors that permit the finer discriminations involved, for instance, in differential diagnosis within a psychiatric population. The legitimacy of both ventures is unquestioned, but the descriptors selected with one intended goal may yield spurious results if applied or tested in another context. Several examples of the procedures used in the selection of descriptors may illustrate this point.

One of the earliest reported cookbook systems is that developed by and being used at the Mayo Clinic (see Pearson & Swenson in Rome et al., 1962). In their discussion of the selection of their descriptors, Pearson and Swenson note that the descriptive statements reflect their clinical experience with the "core of similarity" that characterizes various groups of individuals, in this case patients seen in the medicine sections of the Mayo Clinic. Examination of the Mayo descriptors suggests that they are intended to distinguish between subgroups of medical patients who do or do not show a degree of psychological abnormality that might significantly affect their medical diagnosis and treatment. If placed on the above continuum, the Mayo descriptors would certainly cluster somewhere toward the less discriminating end. It may be inappropriate, however, to attempt to specify personality characteristics in greater detail if the evaluation is to be used in screening general medical patients, as it is at the Mayo Clinic.

Marks and Seeman (1963) have developed their *Atlas* for discriminating among subclasses of patients seen in a general psychiatric setting. Clearly, more specific descriptors reflecting the essential distinctions are required for such a purpose. In this regard, Marks and Seeman reported that their *Q*-sort items were originally selected for their representative coverage of the personality domain and then empirically screened for applicability to both sexes, for clinical pertinence, for ratability, and for interpatient variability. The descriptors obtained from case histories met two criteria: (1) sufficient data for ratability and (2) sufficient agreement (among raters) for reliability of rating.

Gilberstadt and Duker (1965) and Sines (1966) examined both the absolute frequency of attributes within their general patient groups and the frequency of occurrence of these attributes within specified subclasses of patients. Thus descriptors that are characteristic of psychiatric patients in general, as well as descriptors that occur rarely among general psychiatric patients but may frequently occur among a subgroup of such patients, may be identified and treated differently or used in reports with quite different purposes.

The level of discrimination to be sought in the descriptive content of a cookbook will critically affect the apparent validity, as we shall note later. It has, at the same time, important implications for ethics in the use and dissemination of the cookbook output.

DETERMINING PREDICTOR-DESCRIPTOR RELATIONSHIPS

There are several distinctions here that warrant explicit recognition. First it is necessary to recognize that the whole notion of automation is quite unessential in the development and use of cookbooks. As Gilberstadt and Duker (1965) and Marks and Seeman (1963) have indicated, their cookbooks may be readily adapted to automation techniques. Quite independently of the procedures involved in recognizing predictor units and in assigning descriptors to them, the cookbooks offered by Fowler (1966) and Pearson et al. (1964) are both automated but obviously could be employed, albeit much more laboriously, by the clinician without recourse to a computer. It would be unfortunate if anyone were to have the impression that automation as a delivery technique were essential to the development or use of cookbooks as we have defined them earlier in this discussion. The use of computer technology in relation to cookbooks provides a means by which they may be disseminated widely. Thus automation of any cookbook should be recognized as a logical extension of the method, but it should not be viewed as essential to the cookbook approach.

A second source of misunderstanding which still occurs in the literature is the confusing of actuarial with psychometric or normative, and empirical with actuarial. Thus Hilgard (1962) in commenting on Meehl's 1954 survey notes,

> In all but one of the studies the statistical predictions based on the formula were equal or superior to the predictions made by clinicians. . . . This support for *tests* (which permit arriving at scores that can be entered into formulas) must not be taken as an indictment of the clinical method [pp. 465–466, italics added].

More recently, Shontz (1965) has stated,

> Even factor analytic approaches, like Cattell's, are usually directed toward the construction of measuring instruments for evaluating the patterning of relevant forces or qualities that characterize particular persons. The same is true of actuarial devices, such as the MMPI [p. 8]. (See also Hunt, 1959, p. 175.)

As we have noted elsewhere, the MMPI is a psychometric instrument that may or may not be used in an actuarial or in a cookbook fashion. Its empirical development does not constitute an actuarial procedure in the sense that that term is used here. Although it is true that the MMPI fulfills the input requirement of the actuarial approach—viz., scores or signs explicitly expressed—the *essential* feature of the approach in cookbook construction is that the association between these scores (predictor units) and their meaning (descriptor statements) is empirically determined and explicitly stated by a number (*Q*-sort placement, correlation coefficient, frequency of attribution, etc.). The transition from predictor to descriptor is an automatic, mechanical, clerical task, proceeding by the application of rules set forth in the cookbook. If the predictor-descriptor relationship is mediated by an individual's judgment and reflection, the cookbook is nonactuarial by our present definition.

The empirical relating of predictors to descriptors in developing an actuarial cookbook may follow along either *typological* or *dimensional* lines. In the typological approach, as exemplified by the work of Gilberstadt and Duker (1965) and Marks and Seeman (1963), profiles are grouped into classes or types, and class characteristics in the form of descriptors are recorded for members of each class. This approach involves no restrictive assumptions about the form of the distribution of profile scores, nor does it involve any assumption about the psychological relevance of the scores throughout their range. Its practical disadvantage, however, is that it requires a large number of members for each class, as we shall note later.

The dimensional approach, which may take the form of a simple linear (additive) model or a more complex nonlinear configural model, is best illustrated in the work of Goldberg (1965). Goldberg examined the relative accuracy of simple linear combinations of MMPI scores and complex nonlinear configural procedures in diagnosing neurosis versus psychosis. Although he found that a linear combination of five scales outperformed even the most complex configural rules, to our knowledge this approach has not been explored in relation to *personality description*. One major difficulty of dimensional procedures in developing an actuarial cookbook is the enormous amount of labor involved in relating the predictors to each of the many descriptors that are of clinical or social interest and importance.

The nonactuarial cookbook approach is exemplified by the work of Finney (1966, 1967), Fowler (1964), Glueck (1966), Hovey and Lewis (1967), Pearson et al. (1964), and Piotrowski (1964). These investigators have developed cookbooks in which test data are interpreted on the basis of contingencies which have been reported in the literature or which reflect their own or other expert opinion and experience. It is reasonable to expect that the validity of such cookbooks will be greater than that of individually interpreted test data to the extent that they are based on the distilled interpretations of experts and/or research findings that may have accumulated (although the expertise of "experts" is itself an empirical judgment, of course). Piotrowski's description (1964) of the laborious validation required using this approach with the Rorschach strongly suggests that little if any savings in overall effort can be achieved, however, by the initial use of such "ready-made" descriptors.

Unfortunately there are no relevant data on which to evaluate the merits of these two methods of relating the descriptive or interpretative material to the input data. In view of the frailty of logic-based predictions and the lack of empirical data, we must admit that the method used remains purely a matter of choice at this time. It is by no means certain that these two different methods of relating descriptors and predictors will yield similar results. There are no published data yet available, for instance, comparing the output from cookbook interpretations of an MMPI profile generated by Fowler's program and by Marks and Seeman's *Atlas*, although one of us (PAM) is pursuing a study along this line. Even so, we would predict that the validity and the utility of interpretations based on actuarially derived cookbooks will be significantly greater than interpretations based on mechanical, nonactuarial predictor-descriptor relationships.

Whatever means are employed to relate a set of descriptors to the one of several predictor units employed, there are still important decisions to be made concerning the format in which the descriptive material will be reported. Although admittedly the format will be determined in part by the content of the descriptors, clinicians of all disciplines are accustomed to viewing a psychological report that is in sequential narrative form. The data reported by Marks and Seeman (1963) are presented as an array of disconnected statements with their rates of occurrence; their palatability depends upon their being processed further. Gilberstadt and Duker (1965) note that the use of their actuarially derived interpretative data requires essentially the same combinatorial processing used in the preparation of the traditional psychological report.

Both Finney (1967) and Fowler (1966) have explicitly addressed themselves to this issue. Their programs provide a series of interpretative statements that have been carefully constructed to yield a comprehensive narrative report. Finney not only has programmed his report for a specific audience (psychiatrists and clinical psychologists) but has organized it on the basis of certain theoretical assumptions, reducing as much as possible any redundancies or contradictions in content. There are, as Fowler indicates, formidable problems entailed in any attempt to evaluate the validity of a narrative report. There is little doubt, however, that the acceptability of a cookbook will be significantly influenced by the format of the output report. The average consumer of the psychological report expects a practical product that requires little, if any, additional processing prior to use.

THE VALIDITY AND UTILITY OF COOKBOOKS

The development of cookbooks and the construction of actuarial programs for the interpretation of psychological tests have involved an enormous amount of work aimed at formalizing and routinizing a number of procedures that have evolved over many years. They reflect, to be sure, an advance in our ways of thinking about personality appraisal. To us they represent an inevitable step forward in the technology of assessment. Their development requires no new raw materials or radical departures from conventional procedures.

The fact that it is now possible to make assessments much more quickly and in much greater numbers certainly promises to lessen the growing discrepancy between clinical psychology's available manpower and the expressed demand for psychological assessment. But the fact that test interpretations are now automated and readily available makes the evaluation of them from several points of view even more critical than it has been in the past. And yet the evaluation of such procedures appears not to have evolved nearly as rapidly as the concepts and methods for producing them, even though new standards for computer-based test interpretation have been proposed (American Psychological Association, 1966).

The questions of cost and coverage are no longer barriers to the use of the MMPI, at least in the office practice of psychiatry and clinical psychology. Problems of cost and coverage within institutional practice will shortly be overcome as well. Although the resistance to the use of cookbooks, in principle, continues in some areas, it is rapidly becoming a minor issue. Having overcome these problems, for all practical purposes, we must now face more directly the crucial issues concerning psychological assessment itself—issues that have remained unresolved for some time. It is in this connection that we may consider several determinants of the value of cookbooks.

Validity

There are no known published reports of systematic attempts to cross-validate or assess the generalizable validity of any of the currently available cookbooks, although the recent findings of Pope and Scott (1967) would suggest rather promising results (pp. 99–110). This, in part, is attributable to the fact that cookbooks have appeared only recently. In Chapter 6 of this volume Fowler refers to the first known validation study, and that is still in progress. In the same connection, Fowler refers to two quite different aspects of the question of validity. He indicates that evidence for the validity of individual descriptors can be cited, but means for determining the global accuracy of the integrated psychological report have not yet been developed. Fowler's own work in comparing the similarity of the clinician's inferences based on a cookbook description with those based on a case history is an important step in this direction. Thus we are faced with at least two levels of validity—the validity of the individual descriptor and the validity of the total report. It is much easier to deal with the individual descriptors.

The usual indication of validity, the detectable presence of a predicted attribute, is markedly influenced by the choice of the predictors, the descriptors, and the way in which their relationship is determined. The complexity and the within-class heterogeneity of the predictors will directly affect validity in several ways. As one increases the complexity of the predictor unit, one successively defines groups of persons for whom the base rates of certain attributes (attributes with low base rates in the general population) are increasingly differentiated from their frequency in the general population, a procedure recommended by Meehl and Rosen (1955) some years ago. In view of the often low validities of most test components, it should thus be possible, in principle, to find some degree of complexity with any given test beyond which greater complexity or attention to configural relationships would yield no further increase in validity, regardless of the discrimination level of the descriptors used. It should be pointed out again, however, that no empirical data relevant to this issue are yet available.

The significance of the within-class variance of the predictor for the validity of a cookbook seems obvious. Some of its implications can best be discussed in relation to the findings reported by Gilberstadt and Duker (1965), Marks and Seeman (1963), and Sines (1966). In another discussion of methods for identifying MMPI profile patterns, Sines (1964) presented the means and standard deviations for groups of profiles selected by the rules offered by Gilberstadt and Duker, by those developed by Marks and Seeman, and also by his use of the D^2 statistic. Using either set of configural rules, the scale variances within the several groups of profiles were greater than the variance within groups of profiles identified by means of the D^2. Before continuing, it should be emphasized that the use of configural rules does not necessarily result in larger variances, nor does the use of the D^2 statistic necessarily result in a profile pattern with smaller intragroup variances. It is a simple procedure to shift any of a number of parameters in either method in order to increase or decrease the resulting intragroup variability. Within limits, it would appear that the rate of occurrence of an attribute within a group may vary directly with the precision with which that group is specified. If the target group is identified by means of imperfect measures (a presently inescapable state of affairs) and if the definition of that group is so broad that nonmembers are included, error is introduced in the cookbook from both these sources.

It would, therefore, seem appropriate to reduce the within-class heterogeneity of the predictor units as much as possible even though there are practical limits whose effects are readily apparent. First, the possibility of locating a group of any given size decreases rapidly as the inclusion rules are made more strict. Similarly, the number of groups that are distinguishable in terms of the predictor increases rapidly; therefore the labor involved in collecting the descriptive data increases at least proportionately. It is on precisely this issue that Meehl (1959b) has written:

> A tough practical problem in the validation of multivariate instruments is that of utilizing higher order interaction effects among the test variables. The qualitative merits of the independent construct variable estimates should be excellent, . . . otherwise we are wasting our time. This usually means that the patients have been subjected to intense scrutiny by judges of a high level of clinical competence. On the other hand, the capitalization of

> random sampling errors increases horrendously as patterning effects are taken into consideration, so that the determination of a function and the assignment of optimal weights requires a large sample. In other branches of applied psychology or even in clinical psychology where predictive validity is really the problem, it often suffices to know a very little bit about a large number of persons; for other purposes, as in carrying out individual psychotherapy, it suffices to know a very great deal at a deep level about a single person. In validating the configural indicators of a multivariate test, we find ourselves in the unhappy position of requiring to know a *great* deal about a *large* number of persons [p. 270].

The aforementioned consequences of limiting the within-class heterogeneity require that decisions here must take into consideration other issues relating to the descriptors used, the coverage desired, and the purpose for which the cookbook is designed.

The degree to which the cookbook's descriptors are directly observable or must be inferred would seem to have an unavoidable influence on attempts to validate a cookbook report. Genotypic descriptors introduce several practical problems. For example, if the cookbook descriptors are genotypic statements, is the judge's task that of inferring other genotypic attributes, or is he to predict the patient's observable behavior? If the cookbook report consists of statements about the patient's phenotypic behavior, does the judge attempt to infer the patient's dynamics or other specific behaviors that may covary with those noted in the report? The answers to these questions bear directly on the utility of the psychological report and on the choice of descriptors that may be used to maximize that utility. Local clinical practice will probably determine the choices to be made here for some time. It would be unfortunate, however, if actuarial or cookbook development were to deteriorate into the class of psychological research that Meehl and Rosen (1955) label the "so-what-type" simply because of an unpopular choice of form or content of the psychological report.

It seems reasonable to expect a spuriously high degree of validity—reproducibility—for a set of descriptors if it consists of general statements that are not highly discriminating by our definition. In view of this, it will be critically important for studies designed to validate existing cookbooks to use samples that are chosen with great care. It would be most appropriate, therefore, to attempt to validate the Mayo cookbook by determining the degree to which it discriminates medical outpatients who do and do not show psychological or psychiatric symptoms severe enough to affect their medical diagnosis and treatment.

Although it has no bearing on external validity, Table 4-1 presents some hitherto unpublished data on typological relationships of the Marks-Seeman *Atlas*. The Q correlations were computed between average sorts of the 16 code types (Marks & Seeman, 1963, pp. 221–224) and average sorts of four stereotypic descriptions: Nor (normal), Pso (psychotic), Psn (psychoneurotic), and PD (personality disorder). Each stereotype was derived from the five most highly intercorrelated sorts of nine skilled clinicians—five psychologists and four psychiatrists (Marks & Seeman, 1962a, 1962b).

It is of some interest that the code types with the highest incidence of a psychotic clinical diagnosis (8-6, 8-9, 9-6) correlate most highly with the psychotic stereotype (rs = .83, .77, and .75, respectively). Similarly, the code types having the highest incidence of neurotic membership (2-3-1, 2-7, 3-1) show the same relationship to the neurotic stereotype (rs = .68, .71, and .66, respectively). And essentially the same correlations obtain for the personality disorder stereotype and the codes with personality disorder as the primary clinical diagnosis (4-6, $r = .56$; 4-9, $r = .64$). Of greater interest, however, is the magnitude of intercorrelations for common families of codes (e.g., see 4-6 versus 4-8-2, 4-6-2, and 4-9; also 2-3-1 versus 2-7, 2-7-4, and 2-8). Other relationships, such as those between code types having no common scale elevations (e.g., 3-1 versus 4-6, $r = .16$; 2-7 versus 8-9, $r = .01$), provide evidence of between-type distinctiveness or discriminant validation for these constructs.

Whether any or all of the descriptors provided in the Marks and Seeman *Atlas* are valid when tested in an outpatient medical setting, or those of Gilberstadt and Duker when tested in other than a VA inpatient setting, is unknown. The decision to use or not to use these cookbooks with patients in different settings involves, in addition to the question of generalizable validity, certain ethical and practical issues as well.

Generalizability

Although it is essential that a cookbook first survive cross-validation (i.e., be valid if used with nonderivation samples of the same population), the value of a cookbook would certainly be enhanced if its validity generalized to other populations (i.e., if the descriptors were dependably present in groups that differed from the derivation sample). Lindzey (1965) has reported one instance in which such generalization was not possible. Gilberstadt and Duker suggest, on the other hand,

Table 4-1 *Q*-sort intercorrelations of Marks-Seeman 16 code types* and 4 stereotype personality descriptions†

	27	274	278	28	31	321	46	462	482	49	83	86	89	96	*K*+	Nor	Pso	Psn	PD
2-3-1	62	64	37	61	72	49	12	12	06	22	33	09	−01	27	28	−17	15	68	−15
2-7		39	62	50	52	55	−15	−15	04	−33	45	14	01	41	44	−21	26	71	−51
2-7-4			57	69	52	58	44	50	44	50	44	40	37	51	34	−47	44	53	15
2-7-8				68	25	84	23	20	54	14	78	69	60	79	66	−74	80	53	−24
2-8					49	70	42	32	46	28	59	54	38	56	58	−49	55	57	01
3-1						36	16	20	06	21	17	−02	−16	18	23	01	01	66	−08
3-2-1							33	29	56	24	73	62	51	66	66	−67	72	48	−12
4-6								66	68	57	36	48	45	43	35	−26	37	07	56
4-6-2									62	79	25	31	39	36	06	−27	29	04	61
4-8-2										49	59	72	72	47	59	−49	65	05	41
4-9											15	16	32	25	02	−26	20	08	64
8-3												70	67	79	60	−62	74	32	−12
8-6													80	61	71	−69	83	12	12
8-9														71	54	−62	77	03	20
9-6															65	−63	75	38	−06
K+																−43	59	38	−11
Normal																	−77	−21	12
Psychotic																		21	−09
Neurotic																			−33
Personality Disorder																			

* Average sort of five most homogeneous (i.e., highly intercorrelated) descriptions (P. A. Marks and W. Seeman, *The actuarial description of abnormal personality: An atlas for use with the MMPI.* Baltimore: Williams & Wilkins, 1963, pp. 221–224).

† Average sort of five most homogeneous (of nine) stereotype descriptions (P. A. Marks and W. Seeman, The heterogeneity of some common psychiatric stereotypes. *Journal of Clinical Psychology,* 1962, **18,** 266–270; On the Barnum effect. *Psychological Record,* 1962, **12,** 203–208.)

that the descriptors in their cookbook will probably apply to their specified MMPI profile patterns regardless of the setting from which the test data are gathered.

The only information available relating to this point concerns an MMPI profile type described by Sines (1966). The profile is a 4′3 for males, derived originally from a sample of 500 state hospital inpatients. The descriptors found to apply to the state hospital's 4′3 patients were essentially the same as those applied to penitentiary inmates and to psychiatry outpatients who generated that profile pattern.

We should note, however, the paucity of empirical data on this issue. Theoretical analyses of generalizability have little value here. It is hoped that eventually a set of general principles can be developed to explain the occurrence of whatever generalization may be found and to point toward other conditions to which cookbook recipes probably will and will not be generalizable.

Utility

A cookbook may be quite valid, it may generalize widely, and yet it may be worthless to apply. The determination of the utility of any procedure requires that the costs be weighed against the payoff. These concepts seem at first glance contrary to the values of many clinicians, but they would appear to be related to the often nonspecific but pervasive disenchantment with psychological assessment that is acknowledged by large numbers of clinicians. The utility of the psychological report will depend, apart from its cost, on whether the information it provides will have any discernible effect on what is subsequently done to or about the tested person. The pragmatics of psychological test interpretation (cookbook or otherwise) have to date been neither adequately studied nor clearly understood. Presumably the major use of (and justification for) personality tests is to acquire advance information about the kind of person the patient is. If, as Meehl says, "a psychotherapist knows by the tenth session something he didn't know by the fifth but which our test could have told him pre-therapy, this might still be comparatively unimportant in a clinical setting where most patients are seen 25 or more times." But in settings in which there is a shortage of therapists or when shorter-term treatment is the goal, such advance information could be of crucial importance.

Figure 4-1 shows some relevant data based on the Marks-Seeman 108 Q-item pool. Plotted are the average Q correlations between sorts (on 18 patients) after the twentieth hour, pre-therapy stereotype sorts (S), and successive sorts after the first, second, third, fifth, seventh, tenth, and fifteenth therapeutic interview. The therapists are seven third-year clinical psychology interns. It would appear that with this mixed phenotypic-genotypic descriptor pool the therapists' image of their patients crystallized somewhere between the tenth and fifteenth therapeutic hour. Although these findings do not correspond directly

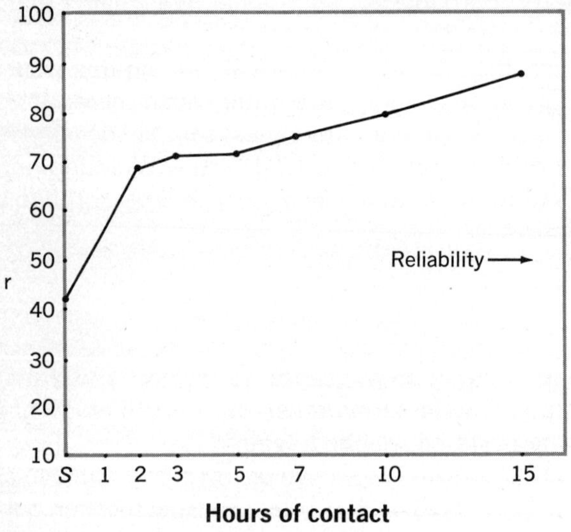

Figure 4–1 Average Q correlations between seven therapists' (clinical psychology interns) sorts after 20 hours and earlier sorts. (Mixed 108-item genotypic-phenotypic pool; $N = 18$ patients.)

with Meehl's (1960), they still question the expenditure of considerable time in traditional testing endeavors. Not only the validity but the practical effects of descriptors must be assessed. At this point it would appear that, given equal validity, a statement about a patient's observable behavior would stimulate more action than a statement about an intrapsychic disposition, the behavioral expression of which may be moderated by other factors not yet specifiable or understood. In essence we are saying that our current theories of behavior possess such low-order predictive power that the utility of the psychological report may be greatest if we stay fairly close to observable behavior.

ETHICAL CONSIDERATION

The ready availability of cookbook descriptions of personality characteristics and socially significant behaviors intensifies the need for careful attention to a number of ethical issues that have essentially been ignored in the past. A detailed reading of the APA policy statement (1966, see also Chapter 6 by Fowler) concerning automated test interpretations is essential, and we shall touch on only two of the issues here.

First, the widespread dissemination of highly personal information increases the risk that the patient's confidence may be violated. The exemplary control mechanisms employed by the Roche Psychiatric Service Institute in processing Fowler's MMPI program are designed to maintain far more than just reasonable care to ensure the confidentiality of the test results, to determine the qualifications of persons to whom the reports are transmitted, and to apply the cookbook descriptions to the class of subjects for which they were designed.

As cookbook descriptions are developed that include highly specific statements concerning the probabilities of such behavior as suicide, homicide, excessive drinking, and illegal sexual practices, we shall be compelled to make decisions for which only very general guidelines are noted in the APA policy statement.

We may anticipate the time when a person who is tested for some relatively benign administrative purpose generates a test pattern with high-probability behavioral correlates that are of critical social importance. The APA statement touches on this possibility, but the evolution of actual practices will be a difficult process. Although it is premature to expect a precise set of guidelines at this time, we should be prepared to develop such guidelines in the not-too-distant future.

SOME GENERAL RUMINATIONS

The initial appearance of the cookbook notion was at variance with the practice of clinical psychological assessment in 1956, and for most psychologists it posed a greater threat than a promise. This original resistance has been reduced somewhat by the concrete application of this notion in the form of cookbooks. However, the full practical implications of Meehl's conception of the actuary-clinician are still not completely accepted by some professionals and are not even accorded historical importance by others (e.g., Reisman, 1966).

Although none of the cookbooks that are currently available or are being developed are completely adequate, each of them makes some particularly valuable contribution to the solution of one or more of the numerous methodological problems that must be overcome if we are to realize the full potential of the actuarial description and prediction of human behavior.

The following summary of our bias provides an overview of the major contributions offering solutions to the problems inherent in the actuarial approach. It is hoped that others will follow Eber and Piotrowski in attempting to formalize the interpretation of tests other than the MMPI. As we have both noted elsewhere, it is highly probable that some other test or nontest data may prove more useful than the MMPI in describing or predicting important aspects of human behavior.

The full development of an actuarial cookbook requires a system for rapidly processing and interpreting test data. Even though disconnected parts of such a system have been in use for some years, first the Mayo group and now Fowler and Glueck have begun to put those pieces together.

A number of methods of defining the predictor units to be used in cookbooks will necessarily have to be studied, and many will doubtlessly be discarded. The systems employed by the Mayo group, by Fowler, by Gilberstadt and Duker, by Glueck, by Marks and Seeman, and by Sines provide a broad range; and each offers advantages and entails disadvantages of one type or another.

The "best" or even the most appropriate source and type of descriptors to use in any particular setting have not yet been identified. The Mayo program, Fowler's cookbook, and Piotrowski's work with the Rorschach demonstrate that acceptable descriptors need not be empirically determined in every case. Marks and Seeman demonstrate the value of formalizing the clinician's observation and, together with Gilberstadt and Duker and Sines, further demonstrate the feasibility of going beyond the clinician for usable descriptors.

There is no evidence to indicate that the predictor-descriptor contingencies can most accurately be determined by the experienced clinician or by a study of each different predictor unit. Increased attention should be directed to this issue.

Only Finney, Fowler, and Eber, to our knowledge, have ventured to produce cookbook reports in narrative form. The fact that the output of the other cookbooks consists of fragmentary and disconnected statements will, we hope, direct much-needed attention to the processes involved in the production of an integrated psychological report. So far these processes continue to be frustratingly elusive.

To our knowledge there have been no formal attempts either to cross-validate or to determine the validity generalization of the descriptors reported in cookbooks. Such formal attempts we deem imperative.

The virtual elimination of cost and delay as factors to consider in determining the utility value of psychological assessment will quite likely stimulate the more detailed examination of some of the hitherto implicit assumptions and expectations held by a number of clinicians relative to tests and testing in particular and diagnosis in general (see e.g., Piotrowski, 1967; Towbin, 1960; Wyatt, 1967).

Finally, the fact that cookbooks have dramatically increased the availability of test-based information which concerns itself with socially significant behavior has already encouraged a substantial number of responsible laymen and psychologists to examine critically our activities in relation to both the rights and responsibilities of society and the individual. In considering this fact, we are inclined to concur with the conclusion of Shontz (1965) that "the supreme test of a method is its degree of success or efficiency in predicting events in applied situations. . . . By this criterion the actuarial approach has already demonstrated its superiority to personality theory [p. 99]." It does not seem unreasonable to expect that the level of activity finally provoked by Meehl's statements of over a dozen years ago will soon result in significant advances in our knowledge as well as in our ability to apply that knowledge to the solution of problems in daily clinical work.

REFERENCES

American Psychological Association. Interim standards for interpretations of clinical psychological measurement instruments. Washington, D.C.: APA, 1966.

Briggs, P. F., Taylor, M., and Tellegen, A. A study of the Marks and Seeman MMPI profile types as applied to a sample of 2,875 psychiatric patients. Research Laboratories Report No. PR-66-5, University of Minnesota, 1966.

Cronbach, L. J., and Gleser, G. C. Assessing similarity between profiles. *Psychological Bulletin*, 1963, **30**, 456–473.

Cronbach, L. J., and Gleser, G. C. *Psychological tests and personnel decisions*. Urbana: University of Illinois Press, 1965.

Dahlstrom, W. G. Recurrent issues in the development of the MMPI. In J. Butcher (Ed.), *MMPI: Research developments and clinical appli-Cations*. New York: McGraw-Hill, 1969.

Drake, L. E., and Oetting, E. R. *An MMPI codebook for counselors*. Minneapolis: University of Minnesota Press, 1959.

Eber, H. W. Computer reporting of 16PF data. In Computer processing and reporting of personality test data. Symposium presented at the American Psychological Association, Los Angeles, September 1964.

Finney, J. C. Purposes and usefulness of the Kentucky program for the automatic interpretation of the MMPI. Paper presented at the meeting of the American Psychological Association, Chicago, September 1965.

Finney, J. C. A programmed interpretation of the MMPI and the CPI. *Archives of General Psychiatry*, 1966, **15**, 75–81.

Finney, J. C. Methodological problems in programmed composition of psychological test reports. *Behavioral Science*, 1967, **12**, 142–152.

Foster, A. Writing psychological reports. *Journal of Clinical Psychology*, 1951, **7**, 195.

Fowler, R. D. The automated cookbook. In Computer processing and reporting of personality test data. Symposium presented at the American Psychological Association, Los Angeles, September 1964.

Fowler, R. D. *The MMPI notebook: A guide to the clinical use of the automated MMPI*. Nutley, N.J.: Hoffmann-LaRoche, 1966.

Gaier, E. L., and Lee, M. C. Pattern analysis: The configural approach to predictive measurement. *Psychological Bulletin*, 1953, **50**, 140–148.

Gilberstadt, H., and Duker, J. *A handbook for clinical and actuarial MMPI interpretation*. Philadelphia: Saunders, 1965.

Gleser, G. C. Quantifying similarity between people. Paper presented at the Conference on the Role and Methodology of Classification in Psychiatry and Psychopathology, Washington, D.C., November 1965.

Glueck, B. C. Current personality assessment research. *International Psychiatry Clinics*, 1966, **3**, 205–222.

Goldberg, L. R. Diagnosticians vs. diagnostic signs: The diagnosis of psychosis vs. neurosis from the MMPI. *Psychological Monographs*, 1965, **79** (9, Whole No. 602).

Gough, H. G. Clinical versus statistical prediction in psychology. In L. Postman (Ed.), *Psychology in the making*. New York: Knopf, 1962.

Greenhouse, S. W. On the meaning of discrimination, classification, mixture, and clustering in statistics. Paper presented at the Conference on the Role and Methodology of Classification in Psychiatry and Psychopathology, Washington, D.C., November 1965.

Hammond, K. R., and Allen, J. M. *Writing clinical reports*. Englewood Cliffs, N.J.: Prentice-Hall, 1953.

Hathaway, S. R. Increasing clinical efficiency. In B. M. Bass and I. A. Berg (Eds.), *Objective approaches to personality assessment*. Princeton: Van Nostrand, 1959. Pp. 192–203.

Hathaway, S. R., and Monachesi, E. D. *Adolescent personality and behavior*. Minneapolis: University of Minnesota Press, 1963.

Helmstadler, G. C. An empirical comparison of methods for estimating profile similarity. *Educational and Psychological Measurement*, 1957, **17**, 17–82.

Hilgard, E. R. *Introduction to psychology.* New York: Harcourt, Brace & World, 1962.

Hovey, H. B., and Lewis, E. G. Semiautomatic interpretation of the MMPI. *Journal of Clinical Psychology,* 1967, **23** (Monogr. Suppl.) 15, 123–134.

Hunt, W. A. An actuarial approach to clinical judgment. In B. M. Bass and I. A. Berg (Eds.), *Objective approaches to personality assessment.* Princeton: Van Nostrand, 1959.

Kleinmuntz, B. MMPI decision rules for the identification of college maladjustment: A digital computer approach. *Psychological Monographs,* 1963, **77** (14 Whole No. 577).

Klopfer, W. G. *The psychological report.* New York: Grune & Stratton, 1960.

Koch, S. Psychology and emerging conceptions of knowledge as unitary. In T. W. Wann (Ed.), *Behaviorism and phenomenology.* Chicago: University of Chicago Press, 1964.

Lindzey, G. Seer versus sign. *Journal of Experimental Research in Personality,* 1965, **1,** 17–26.

Lykken, D. T. A method of actuarial pattern analysis. *Psychological Bulletin,* 1956, **53,** 102–107.

Lykken, D. T., and Rose, R. Psychological prediction from actuarial tables. *Journal of Clinical Psychology,* 1963, **19,** 139–151.

Lyons, J. Whose experience? Symposium: The role of experiential data in personality assessment. *Journal of Projective Techniques and Personality Assessment,* 1967, **31,** 11–16.

Mark, H. J. Automatic interpretation of children's psychological test results. Personal communication, 1967.

Marks, P. A. An assessment of the diagnostic process in a child guidance setting. *Psychological Monographs,* 1961, **75** (3, Whole No. 507).

Marks, P. A. Progress on a cookbook of personality descriptions of emotionally disturbed youth. In J. Butcher (Chm.), Second Annual Conference on Recent Developments in the Use of the MMPI, Minneapolis, March, 1967.

Marks, P. A., and Kangas, J. O. Psychological tests. In I. Gregory, *Fundamentals of psychiatry.* (2nd ed.) Philadelphia: Saunders, 1968.

Marks, P. A., and Seeman, W. The heterogeneity of some common psychiatric stereotypes. *Journal of Clinical Psychology,* 1962, **18,** 266–270. (a)

Marks, P. A., and Seeman, W. On the Barnum effect. *Psychological Record,* 1962, **12,** 203–208. (b)

Marks, P. A., and Seeman, W. A study of change in stereotype conceptions of psychological disorders. *Journal of Clinical Psychology,* 1962, **18,** 507–510. (c)

Marks, P. A., and Seeman, W. *The actuarial description of abnormal personality: An atlas for use with the MMPI.* Baltimore: Williams & Wilkins, 1963.

McHugh, R. B., and Apostolakos, P. Methodology for the comparison of clinical with actuarial predictions. *Psychological Bulletin,* 1959, **56,** 301–308.

Meehl, P. E. *Clinical versus statistical prediction: A theoretical analysis and a review of the evidence.* Minneapolis: University of Minnesota Press, 1954. (a)

Meehl, P. E. Comments on analyzing the clinical process. *Journal of Counseling Psychology,* 1954, **1,** 207–208. (b)

Meehl, P. E. Wanted—a good cookbook. *American Psychologist,* 1956, **11,** 263–272. (a)

Meehl, P. E. When shall we use our heads instead of the formula? *American Psychologist,* 1956, **11,** 368. (b)

Meehl, P. E. A comparison of clinicians with five statistical methods of identifying psychotic MMPI profiles. *Journal of Counseling Psychology,* 1959, **6,** 102–109. (a)

Meehl, P. E. Structured and projective tests: Some common problems in validation. *Journal of Projective Techniques,* 1959, **23,** 270. (b)

Meehl, P. E. What can the clinician do well? In Clinical skills revisited. Symposium presented at the American Psychological Association, Cincinnati, 1959. (c)

Meehl, P. E. The cognitive activity of the clinician. *American Psychologist,* 1960, **15,** 19–27.

Meehl, P. E. Logic for the clinician (Review). *Contemporary Psychology,* 1961, **6,** 389–391.

Meehl, P. E. Foreword. In P. A. Marks and W. Seeman, *The actuarial description of abnormal personality.* Baltimore: Williams & Wilkins, 1963.

Meehl, P. E., and Dahlstrom, W. G. Objective configural rules for discriminating psychotic from neurotic MMPI profiles. *Journal of Consulting Psychology,* 1960, **24,** 375.

Meehl, P. E., and Rosen, A. Antecedent probability and the efficiency of psychometric signs, patterns, or cutting scores. *Psychological Bulletin,* 1955, **52,** 194–216.

Mosel, J. N., and Roberts, J. B. The comparability of measures of profile similarity: An empirical study. *Journal of Consulting Psychology,* 1954, **18,** 61–66.

Muldoon, J. F., and Ray, O. S. A comparison of pattern similarity as measured by six statistical techniques and eleven clinicians. *Educational and Psychological Measurement,* 1958, **18,** 775–781.

Pauker, J. D. Identification of MMPI profile types in a female, inpatient, psychiatric setting using the Marks and Seeman rules. *Journal of Consulting Psychology,* 1966, **30,** 90.

Pearson, J. S., Swenson, W. M., Rome, H. P., Mataya, P., and Brannick, T. L. Further experience with the automated MMPI. *Proceedings of the Mayo Clinic,* 1964, **39,** 823–829.

Piotrowski, Z. A. Digital-computer interpretation of inkblot test data. *Psychiatric Quarterly*, 1964, **38**, 1–26.

Piotrowski, Z. A. Psychological testing of intelligence and personality. In A. M. Freedman and H. I. Kaplan (Eds.), *Comprehensive textbook of psychiatry*. Baltimore: Williams & Wilkins, 1967.

Pope, B., and Scott, W. H. *Psychological diagnosis in clinical practice*. New York: Oxford University Press, 1967.

Reisman, J. M. *The development of clinical psychology*. New York: Appleton-Century-Crofts, 1966.

Rome, H. P., Swenson, W. M., Mataya, P., McCarthy, C. E., Pearson, J. S., Keating, R. F., and Hathaway, S. R. Symposium on automation techniques in personality assessment. *Proceedings of the Mayo Clinic*, 1962, **37**, 61-82.

Rosenberg, M., Glueck, B. C., and Bennett, W. L. Automation of behavioral observations on hospitalized psychiatric patients. *American Journal of Psychiatry*, 1967, **123**, 926–929.

Saunders, D. R. Moderator variables in prediction. *Educational and Psychological Measurement*, 1956, **16**, 209–222.

Sawrey, W. L., Keller, L., and Conger, J. J. An objective method of grouping profiles by distance functions and its relation to factor analysis. *Educational and Psychological Measurement*, 1960, **20**, 651–673.

Sawyer, J. Measurement *and* prediction, clinical *and* statistical. *Psychological Bulletin*, 1966, **66**, 178–200.

Sechrest, L. Incremental validity: A recommendation. *Educational and Psychological Measurement*, 1963, **23**, 153–158.

Seeman, W. Some persistent misconceptions about actuarial (statistical) description of personality. Paper presented at the meeting of the Midwestern Psychological Association, St. Louis, May, 1964.

Shontz, F. C. *Research methods in personality*. New York: Appleton-Century-Crofts, 1965.

Sines, J. O. Actuarial methods as appropriate strategy for the validation of diagnostic tests. *Psychological Review*, 1964, **71**, 517–523.

Sines, J. O. Actuarial methods in personality assessment. In B. A. Maher (Ed.), *Progress in experimental personality research*. New York: Academic Press, 1966, pp. 133–193.

Swenson, W. M., and Pearson, J. S. Automated techniques for personality assessment. Paper presented at the meetings of the Midwestern Psychological Association, St. Louis, May, 1964.

Torgerson, W. S. Multidimensional representation of similarity structures. Paper presented at the Conference on the Role and Methodology of Classification in Psychiatry and Psychopathology, Washington, D.C., November, 1965.

Towbin, A. P. When are cookbooks useful? *American Psychologist*, 1960, **15**, 119–123.

Wyatt, F. How objective is objectivity? *Journal of Projective Techniques and Personality Assessment*, 1967, **31**, 3–19.

Chapter Five
Personality Test Interpretation by Computer and Clinician

Benjamin Kleinmuntz
Carnegie-Mellon University

BACKGROUND OF THE STUDY

Psychologists are essentially in agreement about the usefulness of statistical aids in scoring and plotting personality test profiles. They are not agreed, however, about the best way to combine observations and test scores in order to arrive at decisions about patients or predictions about their future behavior. This lack of agreement has occasioned considerable controversy as to whether information processing is best accomplished by combining data in a subjective, intuitive, or clinical manner or whether it would be more efficiently processed by formal, mechanical, or statistical means.

This issue has frequently been referred to as the clinical versus actuarial controversy. Paul E. Meehl (1954), in his now classic *Clinical versus Statistical Prediction,* addressed himself to the question of whether more accurate predictions could be made by the use of a formula (e.g., statistical equation, set of rules, or reference to an actuarial table) or by more subjective methods (e.g., formulating hypotheses, clinical impressions, or intuitive judgments). The present paper is aimed at this controversy, and its purpose is to demonstrate that there is a set of decision-making tasks in which formal rules perform at least as well as, and perhaps better than, clinicians' judgments.

The present study is an extension of earlier work (Kleinmuntz, 1963a, 1963b) in which a set of decision rules was devised for interpreting profile patterns of the Minnesota Multiphasic Personality Inventory of maladjusted and adjusted college students. In the earlier study, the procedure used was the computer programming of the "maladjusted" versus "adjusted"'decisions of an expert test interpreter.

This research was supported in part by a grant from the Maurice Falk Medical Fund for which the author expresses his gratitude.

Specifically, in the earlier study, several experienced MMPI interpreters were instructed to sort 126 MMPI profile sheets along a prescribed 14-step forced normal distribution. The MMPI expert who achieved the highest hit percentage in predicting the criteria of "most" and "least" adjusted was selected for intensive study. He was instructed to think aloud while performing his task of sorting MMPIs and was encouraged to elaborate his precise reasons for classifying each profile into one or the other category. His performance was tape-recorded. For illustrative purposes, the expert's verbalizations and each corresponding decision rule, phrased in more formal language, are presented in Table 5-1. It was from this expert's protocol that a set of decision rules was finally devised. These rules were further formalized for the computer and, after numerous refinements, were used

Table 5-1 MMPI decision rules and tape-recorded protocol

Rule	Protocol
1. If four or more clinical scales $\geq$ *T* score 70, call maladjusted.	1. "Now I'm going to divide these into two piles . . . on the left [least adjusted] I'm throwing all Mults with at least four scales primed."
2. If scales *Hs, D, Hy, Pd, Mf, Pa, Pt, Sc,* and *Si* are ≤ 60 and if *Ma* ≤ 80 and *Mt* $\leq 10_R$, then call adjusted.	2. "I'll throw all Mults to the right [most adjusted] if there's no clinical scale above a *T* score of 60 . . . I'll let *Ma* go up as high as 80 . . . maybe a raw score of 10 on *Mt* would be playing it safe . . . so I'm looking at three things now and sorting according to these conditions."
3. If the first two scales in the Hathaway code include *Pd, Pa,* or *Sc,* and at least one of these is ≥ 70, then call maladjusted. (If *Mf* is among the first two scales, then examine the first three in the Hathaway code.)	3. "If either *Pd, Pa,* or *Sc* is primed I'm putting it on the left side [least adjusted] . . . it would also be nice to have all of these scales slightly more elevated than the others."
4. If *Pa* or *Sc* ≥ 70 and *Pa, Pt,* or *Sc* $\geq$ *Hs, D,* or *Hy,* call maladjusted.	4. "If the elevations are lopsided to the right with the left side of the profile fairly low, I'm throwing the Mults to the left [least adjusted]."

Table 5-1 MMPI decision rules and tape-recorded protocol *(Continued)*

Rule	Protocol
5. Call maladjusted if *Pa* $\geq$ 70 unless *Mt* $\leq 6_R$ and *K* $\geq$ 65.	5. "Here's a paranoid character . . . I wish his *K* score were not quite so high . . . and he could use more *Mt* . . . when that *Mt* score is less than 10, I figure something must be stabilizing him . . . I like an inverted V with *F* high on the validity scales."
6. If *Mt* $\leq 6_R$, call adjusted.	6. "Boy, I don't know—that *Mt* is too low to call her maladjusted . . . I'll settle for calling them adjusted if *Mt* is at a raw score of 6 or lower."
7. Call maladjusted if ($Pa + Sc - 2 \cdot Pt$) $\geq$ 20 and *Pa* or *Sc* $\geq$ 65.	7. "Here's a nice valley between scales 6 and 8 and both 6 and 8 are high . . . I'll call this one maladjusted."
8. If *D* or *Pt* are the primary elevations and *Es* $\geq 45_R$, call adjusted.	8. "These 27 profiles are giving me a pain . . . if 2 or 7 is too elevated, like, say, higher than a *T* score of 80, and if the *Es* scale is approaching a raw score of 50 . . . I'll call it adjusted."
9. If *Pd* $\geq$ 70 and (a) male: *Mt* $\geq 15_R$ or (b) female: *Mt* $\geq 17_R$, call maladjusted.	9. "A primed *Pd* and an *Mt* raw score of 15 or more is going over to the left pile (least adjusted) . . . I guess on a male profile an *Mt* of 15 or more will do . . . and an *Mt* of 17 or more on a female profile."
10. If *Mt* $\geq 23_R$ and *Es* $\leq 45_R$, call maladjusted.	10. "With *Mt* high and *Es* low, I'll call maladjusted at this stage of the game."
11. If five or more clinical scales $\geq$ 65 and if either Pa or Sc $\geq$ 65, call maladjusted.	11. "Everything's up on this girl's MMPI . . . I'm especially bothered by the high *Pa* . . . here's a high *Sc* . . . everything else is up too . . . over to the left [least adjusted]."

Table 5-1 MMPI decision rules and tape-recorded protocol *(Continued)*

Rule	Protocol
12. Call adjusted if at least five clinical scales are between 40 and 60 and $Es \geq 45_R$.	12. "Here are a couple of nice, normal-looking Mults . . . all scales hugging a *T* score of 50, and *Es* is nice and high . . . over to the right [most adjusted]."
13. Call maladjusted if the profile is male and $Mf \geq 70$ and $Sc \geq Pt$ and $Sc \geq 60$.	13. An elevated *Mf* is pretty common for boys around colleges, but when it's primed and when *Sc* is up and is higher than *Pt*, I'll throw it to the left [least adjusted]."
14. If $Si \geq 60$ and $Pa \geq 60$ or $Sc \geq 70$, call maladjusted.	14. "That's a fairly high *Si* . . . and *Pa* is up; I'll call it maladjusted . . . here's one with a high *Si*, and *Sc* is also up; I'll call this maladjusted."
15. Call maladjusted if $Es \leq 35_R$.	15. "Here's a pretty good-looking MMPI, but that low *Es* makes me think something might be wrong . . . to the left [least adjusted]."
16. Call adjusted if $Mt \leq 10_R$.	16. "These are all pretty bad-looking Mults . . . I'll call adjusted if the *Mt* is lower than 10."

to interpret the MMPIs of the criterion sample and of several cross-validation samples. On the basis of such preliminary evidence, the decision rules were demonstrated to be adequate.

Carnegie Institute of Technology students were accepted into either a "maladjusted" or "adjusted" group on the basis of a number of criteria. These were (1) two counselors' judgments of 65 students who contacted Carnegie Institute's Counseling Center. The counselors were asked to judge whether the students' problems were of the academic-vocational variety (adjusted) or of the emotional-personal type (maladjusted). (2) All fraternities and sororities were asked to nominate, from a roster, those of their brothers or sisters who were most and least adjusted. Students were accepted into the most-adjusted ($N = 14$) and least-adjusted ($N = 17$) categories if at least 60% of their peers nominated them as such. And, finally, (3) a group of normal ($N = 30$) MMPIs was randomly selected from the files of 825 entering freshmen and then was called adjusted simply on the basis of having found no evidence to the contrary—that is to say, there was no record of contact with a counselor and no votes by their peers putting them in the maladjusted category.

THE STUDY

We now report a study that compares the relative superiority of the computer-programmed rules and eight test interpreters. The purpose of this study was to determine whether a set of formal rules could equal or surpass clinicians' judgments for the particular prediction problem under consideration.

The subjects for this study were a group of eight MMPI interpreters with varying lengths of clinical experience but with substantial reputations for their interpretative skills with the MMPI. They were solicited by mail to preform the required task and were not paid for their services. Also they were assured of the confidentiality of their identities and the outcome of their participation. Of the total number of persons contacted, four did not respond.

Five samples of MMPI profiles were prepared for *Q* sorting (by cutting the profile graphs away from the entire sheet). The MMPIs were identified only by code numbers. A total of 16 MMPI scales were included in each profile. These were the four validity scales, ?, *L*, *F*, and *K*, and the clinical scales, *Hs, D, Hy, Pd, Mf, Pa, Pt, Sc, Ma, Si, Es*, and *Mt* (Kleinmuntz, 1960). The last of these scales, *Mt*, is a 43-item maladjustment scale developed by an item analysis of MMPI protocols of adjusted and maladjusted college students.

The samples were drawn from Brigham Young University (N = 100), the University of Nebraska (N = 116), the University of Iowa (N = 155), the University of Missouri (N = 198), Bucknell University (N = 151), and Carnegie Institute of Technology (N = 126). The students from the last school served as the criterion subjects for the original development of the computer-programmed rules; therefore, their MMPIs were not used in the comparison between computer and clinician. With the exception of the Carnegie Tech sample, MMPIs were administered when the students sought counseling, and the criterion of maladustment or adjustment was based on the consulted counselors' judgments. In all, among the non-Carnegie Tech samples there were 355 maladjusted and 365 adjusted students.

Each of the eight MMPI interpreters was instructed to *Q*-sort the profiles of the five samples (i.e., all groups except Carnegie Tech) along a prescribed continuum from most to least adjusted and to record his sortings on specially prepared coding sheets. The number of piles (i.e., discrete steps along the continuum) to be sorted varied from a 10-step continuum for the smallest sample ($N = 100$) to a 16-step continuum for the largest sample ($N = 198$). Additionally, Q sorters were asked to draw a line at some point along the Q-sort distribution. They were told that this line demarcated that portion of their Q sort in which they had the greatest confidence about their maladjusted versus adjusted decisions. In our analyses of the data, each Q-sorter's line was used as the point at which his judgments were dichotomized into either the maladjusted or adjusted category.

No information was given the sorters about the criteria used to determine maladjustment or adjustment, nor were they given any description of the particular samples beyond the statement, "emotionally maladjusted and adjusted college students."

The results of the comparisons are summarized in Table 5-2. The differences in hit percentage between the computer and the best clinician among the eight (i.e., the clinician who achieved the highest overall success rate) are not statistically significant. Likewise, the differences in hit percentage between the computer-programmed rules and the average of the eight clinicians are not statistically significant. However, the direction of the differences between the computer and the average clinician are consistently (five out of five) in favor of the computer-programmed rules. These differences are statistically

Table 5-2 Hits and misses of computer-programmed rules and clinicians with five MMPI samples (In percent)

Sample	Computer		Best clinician		Average clinician	
	Hits	Misses	Hits	Misses	Hits	Misses
Brigham Young ($N = 100$)	72	28	68	32	63	37
Nebraska ($N = 116$)	86	14	78	22	74	26
Iowa ($N = 155$)	65	35	65	35	61	39
Missouri ($N = 198$)	71	29	75	25	70	30
Bucknell ($N = 151$)	62	38	65	35	60	40

significant at the .03 level according to the nonparametric "sign test" [Wilcoxon, 1949] for small samples.

For the most part, the results of this study indicate that for the prediction problem under consideration the computer does about as well as the best MMPI interpreter and surpasses the average clinician. Moreover, our results suggest that the overall hit percentage achieved by both the computer-programmed rules and the best of eight clinicians in all but one of the five samples (i.e., Nebraska) is not especially high.

IMPLICATIONS OF THE STUDY

The findings of this study have a threefold significance for future use of computers in screening decisions: (1) Since computers are more accessible than clinicians for the tedious data processing task that is entailed in MMPI profile interpretation, it may be well to assign this task to machines rather than to trained clinicians. (2) The computer has an advantage over the clinician for this type of screening assignment in that it can accept and utilize such programmed instructions as "Here comes an Iowa (or Minnesota, Yale, or Brigham Young) sample" and can be easily programmed to make proper normative adjustments in order to achieve maximal hit rates. The clinician, on the other hand, is severely limited by his experience with one or at most two types of samples. (3) Finally, the special power of the computer for the type of decision task presented in this study is its relatively greater consistency. Whereas the human being may apply certain hypotheses or rules of thumb occasionally, the computer, once it is programmed to contain these hypotheses or rules, will apply such rules consistently and, therefore, does not add "error variance" to its judgments. All these considerations lead to the speculation that the computer is potentially superior to the human being for this and similar types of prediction problems.

In terms of the clinical versus statistical prediction controversy, this paper does not just provide another tool for the statistical side of the argument. By attending directly to what the clinician does with the data, we do not assert that statistics are as good as clinicians but rather that the clinician himself is simply another variant of statistical predictor. This assertion is made in the form of a detailed description of what the clinician does and by a demonstration of approximately parallel competence between "statistics" (i.e., the computer) and the clinician.

REFERENCES

Kleinmuntz, B. Identification of maladjusted college students. *Journal of Counseling Psychology*, 1960, **7**, 209–211.

Kleinmuntz, B. MMPI decision rules for the identification of college maladjustment: A digital computer approach. *Psychological Monographs*, 1963, **77**, 1–22. (a)

Kleinmuntz, B. Personality test interpretation by digital computer. *Science* 1963, **139**, 416–418. (b)

Meehl, P. E. *Clinical versus statistical prediction.* Minneapolis: University of Minnesota Press, 1954.

Wilcoxon, F. *Some rapid approximate statistical procedures.* Stamford, Conn. American Cyanamid, 1949.

Chapter Six
Automated Interpretation of Personality Test Data

Raymond D. Fowler, Jr.
University of Alabama

AUTOMATION AND THE COMPUTER

The concept of automation is not a new one. Human ingenuity has devised new processes and new machines that have progressively replaced routine human functions. Various periods of history have been characterized by a man-to-machine shift resulting from technological developments such as the steam engine, electric power, rapid communication and transportation, and, particularly during the past decade, the computer. Those who are employed in industry face economic and social problems as industrial automation—principally the operation of complex machine systems by computers—increases production while employing fewer workers.

In the sciences, however, automation has become a partial solution to the reverse problem. A geometric increase in the scope and complexity of scientific and technological knowledge with no comparable increase in the number of qualified scientists has resulted in acute scientific manpower shortage. By virtue of their speed and accuracy and their ability to store and process large volumes of material, computers are freeing scientists from much of the labor of routine operations, thus permitting more rapid progress in scientific discovery and application.

AUTOMATION AND MENTAL HEALTH

In a world of automation and computer technology, the mental health field has been, until recently, one of the few important areas of endeavor that has not benefited from these time-saving developments. During the past five years, however, several significant advances have been made in the application of computer technology to the problems of mental illness. One important advance is found in the use of the computer in the clinical diagnostic process. It is a matter of critical concern to many in the field of mental health that the diagnostic process requires such a disproportionate amount of professional time. In mental health clinics alone, diagnosis occupies several hundred thousand hours of professional time yearly. In some facilities, 80% of the total number of professional hours is spent in the diagnostic process. With few highly trained professionals available, it is apparent that a reduction in the time consumed in diagnosis, with a consequent increase in the time available for other functions, would have an important impact upon the utilization of mental health manpower.

The diagnostic process is basically a method of classification. A number of characteristics are grouped together, weighed according to an assessment of the importance of each characteristic, and matched against an established nosology. The diagnostician utilizes many skills including some which are principally subjective. But the heart of the process is an ability to *memorize* the descriptive characteristics of each diagnostic group and to rapidly *recall* this material in order to match it with the characteristics of a specific clinical case. This process—memory and rapid recall—is one which the computer performs most outstandingly. With its vast storage capacity, the computer can record volumes of material about diagnostic groups and rapidly relate this material to new case data.

COMPUTER PROCESSING OF TEST DATA

The use of mechanical devices to process psychological test data is not a recent innovation. The phenomenal increase in testing in the fields of education, industry, and health has necessitated the development of increasingly efficient methods of handling the data. A progression from the simple hand-scoring stencil through a variety of "scoring machines" to the optical scanner-computer combination has made it possible to score large numbers of tests rapidly and economically.

Unfortunately, the efficiency of scoring machines, although freeing secretaries from laborious hand scoring, provided no relief to the test interpreter. Indeed, he began to be threatened with inundation by computer print-outs of scores and profiles, while his own efficiency in analyzing and reporting the results was unchanged.

To the extent that test interpretation is an objective process, the rules of which can be specified, it is possible for the experienced test interpreter to teach the rules to others. If a given score or combination of scores, however complex, is reliably associated with a given characteristic, behavior potential, or description, the relationship may be specified and communicated. If a score of over 50 on the Frisbee test is consistently associated with aphasia, the rule "If Frisbee $>$ 50, call aphasic" can be taught to a student, a clerk, or a computer.

It is possible to program a computer, or for that matter a clerk, to inspect test data according to a set of specified rules and to select from a store of previously compiled material the descriptive statements which are applicable. Although it is possible, in theory, to develop an automated interpretation system for any psychological test, it is no accident that the Minnesota Multiphasic Personality Inventory has received the most attention in this regard. The MMPI is the most widely used personality inventory, and the binary character of the responses makes it admirably suited for computer processing. Interpretation, scoring and administration of the projective tests has tended to be highly individualistic and dependent upon intuition, clinical experience, and internal norms. Thus it is difficult, although not impossible, to convert projective tests to the objective format necessary for computer processing.

The self-report inventories that have standard procedures for administration and scoring present fewer problems for computer processing. More important, the interpretation systems associated with the inventories have emphasized an objective, empirical approach.

AUTOMATED INTERPRETATION: ACTUARIAL AND CLINICAL

Although they share a philosophical kinship, the automated approach to personality test interpretation is not necessarily like the actuarial approach in nature. Conversely, actuarial methods of personality description do not require automation.

Automation, as used here, refers to the use of a computer to store descriptive statements and to assign them on the basis of formalized decision rules. The rules that determine which statements will be assigned on the occurrence of a particular test pattern may be drawn from actuarial tables, from published research, or from clinical experience. The procedure can be described as mechanical if the relationship between the test characteristic and the descriptive statement is specified so that the statement is automatically assigned without the intervention of human judgment whenever the test characteristic occurs. It is automated if the entire procedure, from the input of the test data to the output of the psychological report, is carried out by a computer.

Actuarial prediction or description refers to "the empirical determination of the regularities that may exist between specified psychological test data and equally clearly specified socially, clinically or theoretically significant non-test characteristics of the persons tested" (Sines, 1966). Meehl, in his paper entitled "Wanted—A Good Cookbook" (1956), stressed the need for a complete collection of test-defined code types with empirically derived descriptive data. In the years that have elapsed since Meehl's want ad, only three major attempts at actuarial description have been reported.

In their *Codebook for Counselors* (1959), Drake and Oetting present a large collection of actuarial data on the relation between specified behaviors of college students and their MMPI three-point codes. They were careful, however, to rule out the cookbook designation, preferring to see the various code descriptions used as preliminary hypotheses about a client which a counselor might confirm or reject on the basis of his clinical observations.

The first real cookbook was produced by Marks and Seeman and entitled *The Actuarial Description of Abnormal Personality* (1963). This cookbook, or actuarial atlas, served both as an exciting glimpse into the potential of actuarial description and as an illustration of the staggering amount of labor required to produce such an atlas even for a relatively homogeneous population in a highly particular institutional setting. The application and modification of their 16 recipes to fit other different groups is a worthwhile and vitally important task, but one which is not likely to inspire many because of the sheer labor required.

Gilberstadt and Duker, in *A Handbook for Clinical and Actuarial MMPI Interpretation* (1965), presented empirical descriptive data on 19 test-determined profile types. They argue for an approach that, although objective in input and output, permits subjective integration of the data on the basis of the clinician's experience and judgment.

Sines (1966) advocates a rigorously empirical approach that makes use of all patient-descriptive data found in hospital records to describe MMPI profile types that have been narrowly defined in terms of a mathematical index of similarity. His work is still in progress, and no actuarial data have been reported at the time of this writing.

THE AUTOMATED COOKBOOK

If a cookbook is to serve as the basis for an automated system of test interpretation, it should contain "recipes" for all cases. The disadvantage of an automated interpretation system based on an incomplete cookbook is obvious. When the computer encounters a case which fits none of the profile types for which data are available, the case cannot be interpreted.

Unfortunately, there are no complete cookbooks in existence, nor is one likely to be developed for quite some time. The number of possible code types and the variety of possible test populations relegates the complete cookbook to the future. Thus, the best one can hope for at this stage is an incomplete cookbook based upon one of the two existing efforts—Marks and Seeman or Gilberstadt and Duker—or perhaps upon a combination of the two.

Given the descriptive data included in a cookbook, the computer may be programmed to score the MMPI and to identify the code types for which actuarial data are included. When the computer identifies a case that fits the descriptive rules, it can print out a report that contains the relevant actuarial data. This may be presented in the form of a previously prepared report; or it may be presented in raw data form, that is, a print-out of the clinical data associated with the actuarial type. The principal advantage of using an actuarial base in developing a computerized interpretation is that the descriptive statements have, at least for the original population, a known frequency of attribution.

THE AUTOMATED CLINICIAN

The development of an automated interpretation system utilizing a clinical approach requires an experienced MMPI interpreter who is given the task of developing interpretative statements on the basis of MMPI profiles and is required to make explicit the test characteristics that evoke each statement. His interpretations become the statement library, and his explanation (e.g., F-K over 28, L over 70 T score) becomes the rule that elicits the interpretative statement. When the profile configurations to which the interpreter (or group of interpreters) can respond have been exhausted, and each statement has been keyed to a profile characteristic or configuration, the program is capable of simulating the clinician in the assignment of interpretative statements to MMPI test data.

The MMPI interpreter whose responses are utilized in the development of the interpretative system need not rely on clinical intuition to generate his statements. He may avail himself of all the existing literature relevant to MMPI interpretation including atlases, handbooks, research articles, and actuarial systems as well as his own accumulated clinical experience. The essential feature is that the choice of the statement and its wording are a function of human decision making as opposed to a statistical dictate.

This strategy of MMPI interpretation, an objective approach which remains close to the data but utilizes clinical experience and judgment when hard data are lacking, is the one traditionally associated with MMPI interpretation (in contrast to the more intuitive approach often associated with the projective tests). It is probably the optimum strategy in the present stage of MMPI research; in the opinion of many, including this author, it is a solution of expediency, a case of "what to do until the actuary comes."

The "automated clinician" approach falls short of the ideal of complete objectivity, and it must often rely on less than optimal data. Its advantages are that it can be done now without waiting for the ultimate cookbook, it can yield reports based on data at least as good as those used by human interpreters, and it can be made flexible enough to permit continuous modification as new interpretive information becomes available. For instance, a newly reported characteristic associated with a particular configuration (e.g., good prognosis for psychotherapy) can be added to the statement already prepared for that configuration.

Both the existing cookbooks and the existing computer systems are incomplete. The technology exists for the development of an automated system of psychological test interpretation based entirely upon actuarial data. Unfortunately, the actuarial data are, at this time, insufficient in quantity and quality to permit the attainment of this ideal. For the present, it appears that an automated clinician remaining as close to empirical data as possible is the best that can be attained. As additional actuarial data are accumulated, programs designed on the automated clinician model can integrate the new data and thus evolve into more sophisticated systems.

Interpreting by Computer

Computers have been used in the analysis of data derived from personality tests and in the development of some tests; but it is only recently that computers have been used to process test material with the object of deriving, on individual cases, machine-produced psychological reports. Most of the work in this area has been done so recently that much of it has not been published. Dreger (1966) presents a tabular listing of articles, books, and unpublished works in the general area of computer processing of test data. Only a small number of these refer to work in the area of automated psychological reports.

At the present time a complete description or even a bibliography of the programs that are operational or under development is not feasible. Instead, a brief reference will be made to some of the investigators in the area, followed by a more detailed presentation of the system developed by this author.

Non-MMPI Programs

Eber (1964) has developed a program that scores the Sixteen Personality Factor Questionnaire, computes a variety of scores that are difficult, if not impossible, to compute by hand, and attaches graded phrases to different factor scores and combinations of factor scores.

Piotrowski (1964) reports progress in the development of an automated report system for the Rorschach.

MMPI Programs

The first operational system for producing automated psychological test reports was developed at the Mayo Clinic by Swenson, Pearson, and Rome. Their work has been reported in a number of publications (Pearson & Swenson, 1967; Rome, Swenson, Mataya, McCarthy, Pearson, Keating, & Hathaway, 1962; Swenson, Rome, Pearson, & Brannick, 1965) and is now widely known. Faced with the familiar pattern of large intake and small psychology staff, the Mayo group developed a computer system by means of which the MMPI could be scored and analyzed and a series of descriptive phrases and sentences could be printed out for use by the medical staff as a part of a general medical evaluation. Since their aim was to provide the physician with a terse personality outline (Pearson & Swenson, 1967) rather than a detailed and exhaustive report, the Mayo print-out consists of a dozen or so statements selected from a library of approximately 60 descriptive statements. They derived their statements principally from single scale elevations, although some configurations (patterns) are included.

The Mayo program was highly successful in meeting the goals of its authors. It provided an efficient means of screening large numbers of medical patients who otherwise would have had no psychological or psychiatric screening. It was well accepted by the medical staff and by the patients (Rome et al., 1962). The technical achievements of the Mayo group also inspired other investigators to develop programs for a variety of other purposes. A scoring and report service utilizing the Mayo system is available through the Psychological Corporation.

The Mayo program, often in modified form, has been adapted for clinical use in several facilities where computers are available. Glueck and Reznikoff (1965) expanded the Mayo statements to produce a somewhat longer and more detailed report with more explicit attention to psychopathology for use in a private psychiatric hospital.

Marks (1966) utilized the Marks and Seeman *Atlas* (1963) to produce a print-out of the actuarial data associated with each of his code types. The print-out consists primarily of a list of most- and least-descriptive items from his *Q*-sort data. For cases that did not fit the specifications of any of his code types, the program printed out a report consisting of the Mayo statements. The Marks program, although necessarily incomplete, represents the only reported attempt to develop an interpretative system in the automated cookbook model. All the others are of the automated clinician variety, although some actuarial data are used in some of them.

Finney (1965) has reported progress in developing a system for use in psychiatric settings. His program is designed to produce an extensive report that will make use of new scales and new norms that he has developed. Finney's system has not yet been programmed for computer processing.

The MMPI interpretation system developed by Fowler (1964, 1965) was designed to be used by psychologists and psychiatrists as part of a diagnostic evaluation. The purpose was to program the computer to simulate, as nearly as possible, the interpretation and report-writing functions of the psychologist and to produce a report similar in style and content to a report written by a clinician. A more ambitious goal was to improve upon reports written by the usual method by taking advantage of the computer's capacity to store and recall relevant data.

The preceding review of existing interpretation systems is based on material from formal and informal sources. The purpose was to present a brief, nonevaluative summary of the systems that have been reported, using, whenever possible, the author's own description of his work.

A more detailed description of the system developed by this author will be presented to illustrate the procedures involved in preparing a program and to examine some of the professional, ethical, and theoretical issues raised by psychological automation.

THE DEVELOPMENT OF THE PROGRAM

Since the purpose of the program developed by Fowler was to simulate the human MMPI interpreter, the computer was programmed to follow the steps that might be followed by a clinician in analyzing an MMPI protocol. First, the various configurations of the validity scales to which an interpreter would attend were specified, and appropriate interpretative statements for each contingency were prepared. For instance the *F-K* ratio (Gough, 1950) is interpreted in the context of the elevation of *L* and *F* scales. When *F-K* is between -14 and $+3$, *L* is below 6, and *K* below 21, the applicable statement is, "In responding to the test items, it appears that the patient made an effort to answer truthfully without attempting to deny or exaggerate." However, if any one of six other statements relating to the validity of the patient's response has been printed, the above statement is suppressed. Similar operations are carried out with a number of other validity scale configurations. If any of the patterns that are indicative of questionable validity are found, the computer selects the appropriate paragraph from the statement library.

In responding to the clinical scales, most interpreters use a configural approach rather than an interpretation of single scale elevations. Because there is a great deal of published data on the two-point code, this configuration was selected as the approach to the interpretation of the clinical scales.

The computer is programmed to identify the two-point code and to locate the appropriate paragraph in the library. The development of the two-point code library was the most time-consuming part of the preparation of the program. First, a basic interpretative paragraph was prepared for each two-point code. Second, since the interpretation of the two-point code is influenced by the elevation of the two scales, variations were prepared to reflect various levels of elevation. Third, since the meaning of the two-point code is influenced by other profile characteristics, additional paragraphs were written to take other scale elevations and configurations into account. Fourth, such factors as sex, age, and marital status were considered, and alternative paragraphs were prepared. The result of this procedure was an elaborate set of interpretative rules and a number of alternative paragraphs for each two-point code.

Since other scale elevations may contribute to the clinical picture, additional statements were prepared for scales not accounted for in the two-point configuration. Also several of the special scales have been studied sufficiently to permit their use in profile interpretation. The choice of which scales to use is determined by the available data on the scales and the purpose for which the reports will be used. The computer is programmed to score for research purposes 100 special scales. It prints out scores for fourteen of these, but only four of them are utilized in the interpretation program: *Si* (Drake, 1946), *A* (Welsh, 1956), *Pr* (Gough, 1951), and *Es* (Barron, 1953).

Finally, some "decision rules" based on research were included in the program. The computer is programmed to score the Taulbee-Sisson rules (1957), the Peterson rules (1954), the Meehl-Dahlstrom rules (1960), and the Kleinmuntz rules (1963); but only the first two are used in the interpretation system at this time.

For each of the statements prepared, a set of rules specifying the conditions under which the statement is to be printed was required. These rules were arranged in the form of "decision trees," or flow charts. A schematic representation of one such chart is shown in Figure 6-1. Basically, it is a sequence of yes-no choices culminating in an instruction to print a particular statement or to proceed to the next chart.

The statement library and the interpretative rules were then converted

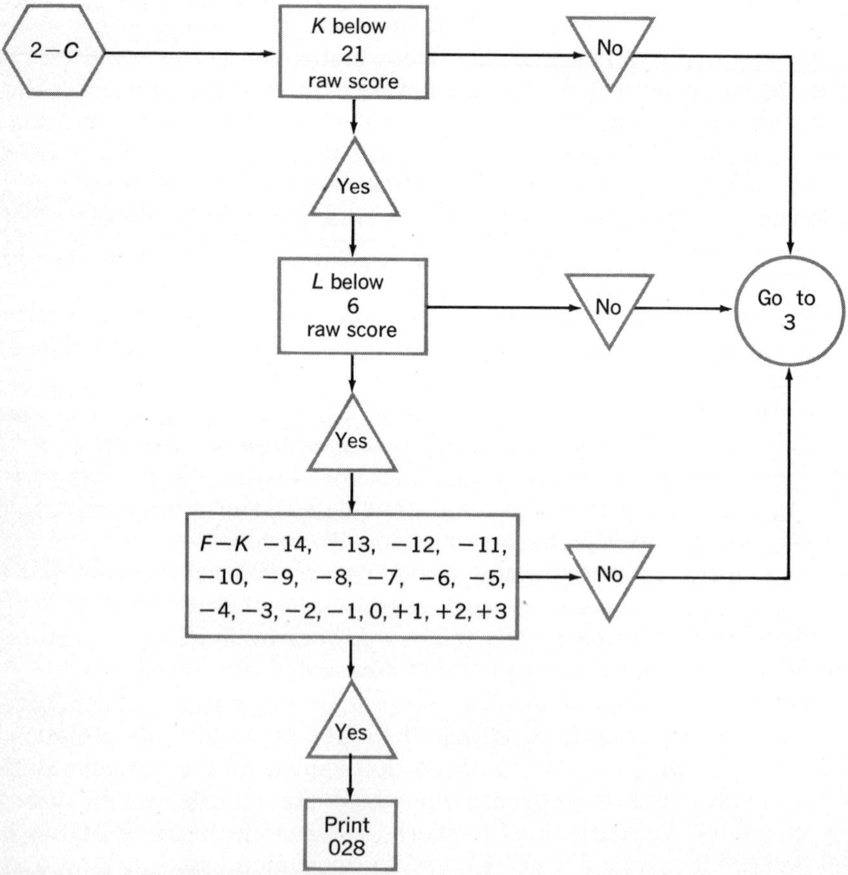

Fig. 6-1.

into a functional computer program by translating them into Fortran IV, a computer language.[1]

Computer Operations for MMPI Processing

The steps involved in processing an MMPI and the operations carried out by the computer are summarized below.

1 The MMPI is given in its standard booklet form to an individual or group. Special answer sheets are used.

2 The answer sheet is "read" by a 1232 optical scanner that punches the responses onto data cards.

3 The cards containing the true-false responses of the subject and identifying data are placed in the card reader by the computer operator.

4 The cards are read into a 1004 terminal that transmits the data by Dataphone to the remote computer center.

5 The following operations are performed by the computer:

- **a** The data are read in from the terminal.
- **b** The computer checks each test item sequentially, I through 566. For each item scored True there is a subroutine that instructs the computer to tabulate all the scales on which this item appears true. At this point, all scales that are affected because this item has been marked True are incremented by 1. This step is followed for each of the 566 items. The time differential between scoring 13 scales and scoring 110 scales or, for that matter, 1,000 is negligible.
- **c** After 566 iterations of the above-described sequence have been completed, the computer has stored internally the value for each MMPI scale. It compares these scales. The computer then checks a list of critical items that are identified in the program and prints out those which have been answered in the significant direction.
- **d** The computer, following the programmed decision rules, selects the appropriate descriptive statements.
- **e** The computer transmits the results of the analysis, which takes 2.5 seconds, to the original 1004 terminal.
- **f** The 1004 terminal prints the final report on 8½- by 11-inch paper.
- **g** The computer stores the material on tape for future use.

[1] The Fortran IV version of the program was prepared by Guy Marlowe. He was assisted by Joel Gilbert, and the scoring routine was prepared by Betty Whitten.

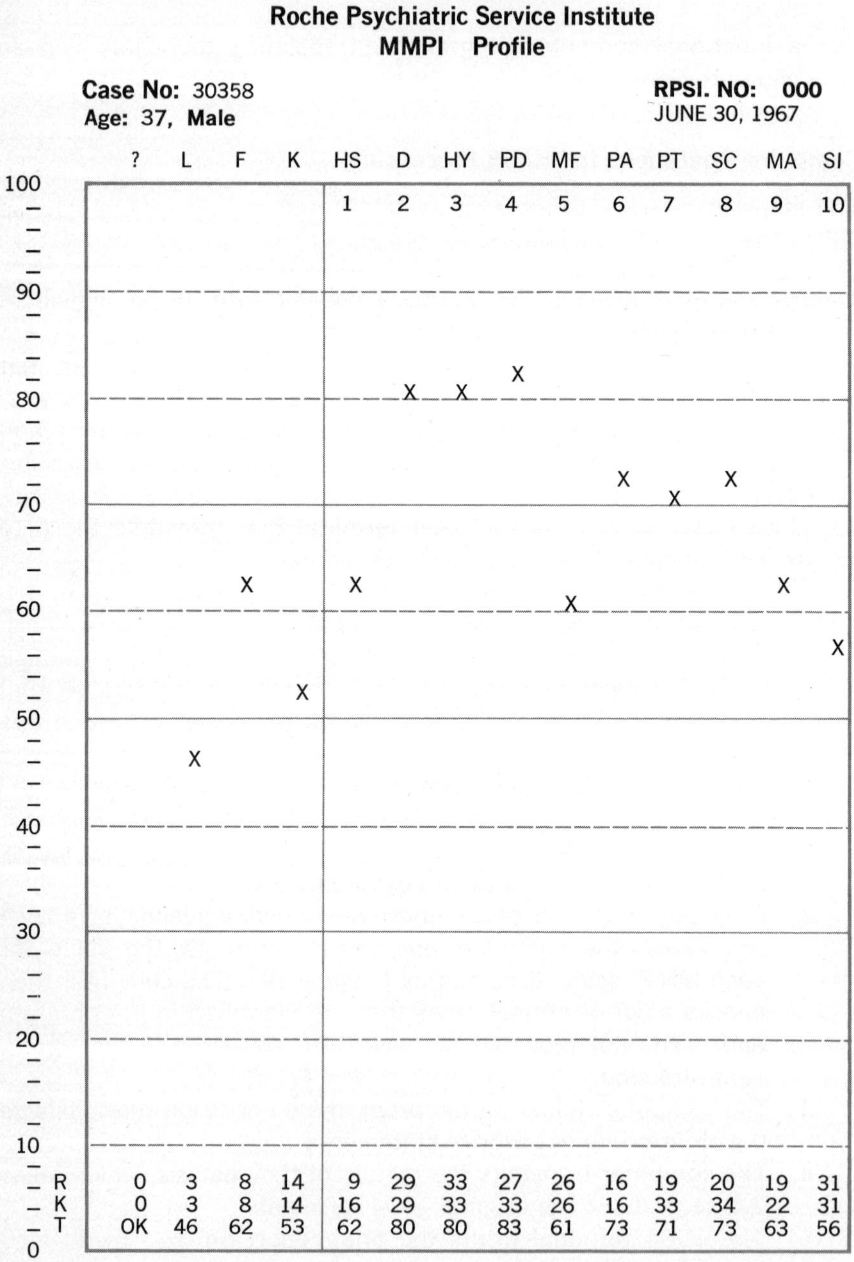
Roche Psychiatric Service Institute
MMPI Profile
Case No: 30358
Age: 37, Male
RPSI. NO: 000
JUNE 30, 1967
? L F K HS D HY PD MF PA PT SC MA SI
1 2 3 4 5 6 7 8 9 10
100
90
80
70
60
50
40
30
20
10
0
R 0 3 8 14 9 29 33 27 26 16 19 20 19 31
K 0 3 8 14 16 29 33 33 26 16 33 34 22 31
T OK 46 62 53 62 80 80 83 61 73 71 73 63 56

Fig. 6-2.

The output from the computer is a three-page print-out. The first page is a narrative report that is a compilation of the paragraphs which the computer has selected according to instructions. The second page is a technical sheet. The top half contains the raw scores and the *T* scores on 4 validity scales, 10 clinical scales, and 14 special scales. The bottom half of the page is a print-out of the critical items. These are selections of 38 MMPI items which relate to serious symptoms, impulses, or experiences (Grayson, 1951). Only the items answered in the deviant direction are printed. The items may alert the clinician to serious psychopathology or to areas that should be discussed in subsequent interviews.

The third page is a profile sheet that contains a print-out of the validity and clinical scales in graphic form.

An example of an automated report is given in Figure 6-2.

FIG. 6-2 BRIEF HISTORY

PATIENT NAME: 30358	RACE: Caucasian
BIRTHDATE: 8-05-29	SEX: Male
MARITAL STATUS: Married	AGE: 37
EDUCATION: B.S. degree in Mathematics	OCCUPATION: Engineer

REASON FOR TESTING: Diagnostic evaluation for purposes of outpatient treatment in an alcoholism clinic

PATIENT'S CHIEF COMPLAINT AND MEDICAL CONDITION

The patient reports his drinking has been out of his control for at least two years. He has had five admissions to a private hospital during the past two years. Drinking is interfering with his work and family life, and he has been arrested on drunkenness charges. He goes on a binge every week or oftener, has blackouts, morning drinks, and severe shakes during hangovers.

RELEVANT HISTORY

The patient was referred by his attorney after having wrecked his car while drinking. He was charged with attempt to leave the scene of an accident. He complains of marital discord whether he is drinking or sober. He and his wife are "sexually incompatible." He doesn't like being tied down, but stayed upon learning she was pregnant.

DIAGNOSTIC IMPRESSION

Extremely self-centered and immature; passive-aggressive personality pattern with strong sociopathic overtones.

ROCHE PSYCHIATRIC SERVICE INSTITUTE
MMPI REPORT

CASE NO.: 30358 RPSI. NO: 000
AGE: 37, MALE JUNE 30, 1967

IN RESPONDING TO THE TEST ITEMS, IT APPEARS THAT THE PATIENT MADE AN EFFORT TO ANSWER TRUTHFULLY WITHOUT ATTEMPTING TO DENY OR EXAGGERATE.

THIS PATIENT SEEMS TO BE DEPRESSED, AGITATED, AND RESTLESS. HE APPEARS TO BE A PERSON WHO HAS DIFFICULTY IN MAINTAINING CONTROL OVER HIS IMPULSES. WHEN HE DOES ACT OUT IN A SOCIALLY UNACCEPTABLE MANNER, HE FEELS GUILTY AND DISTURBED FOR A TIME, ALTHOUGH THE DISTRESS MAY REFLECT SITUATIONAL DIFFICULTIES RATHER THAN INTERNAL CONFLICTS. HE MAY EXHIBIT A CYCLIC PATTERN OF ACTING OUT, FOLLOWED BY GUILT, FOLLOWED BY FURTHER ACTING OUT. FREQUENTLY, HIS BEHAVIOR SHOWS A SELF-DEFEATING AND SELF-PUNITIVE TENDENCY. HE IS PESSIMISTIC ABOUT THE FUTURE AND DISTRESSED ABOUT HIS FAILURE TO ACHIEVE HIS GOALS. HIS INTENTIONS TO IMPROVE SEEM GENUINE, BUT THE PATTERN IS A PERSISTENT ONE, AND THE LONG-RANGE PROGNOSIS IS POOR. ASSISTING HIM TO A BETTER ADJUSTMENT WILL PROBABLY REQUIRE A COMBINATION OF FIRM LIMITS, WARM SUPPORT, AND ENVIRONMENTAL MANIPULATION.

HE APPEARS TO BE A PERSON WHO REPRESSES AND DENIES EMOTIONAL DISTRESS. ALTHOUGH HE MAY RESPOND READILY TO ADVICE AND REASSURANCE, HE IS HESITANT TO ACCEPT A PSYCHOLOGICAL EXPLANATION OF HIS DIFFICULTIES. IN TIMES OF PROLONGED EMOTIONAL STRESS, HE IS LIKELY TO DEVELOP PHYSICAL SYMPTOMS. HE IS PARTICULARLY VULNERABLE TO PSYCHOPHYSIOLOGICAL SYMPTOMS SUCH AS HEADACHES, TACHYCARDIA, AND GASTROINTESTINAL DISORDERS.

THERE ARE SOME UNUSUAL QUALITIES IN THIS PATIENT'S THINKING WHICH MAY REPRESENT AN ORIGINAL OR INVENTIVE ORIENTATION OR PERHAPS SOME SCHIZOID TENDENCIES. FURTHER INFORMATION WOULD BE REQUIRED TO MAKE THIS DETERMINATION.

HE APPEARS TO BE A RIGID PERSON WHO IS PRONE TO FEARS, COMPULSIVE BEHAVIOR, AND OBSESSIONS. DESPITE WORRY AND TENSION, HE IS LIKELY TO BE RESISTANT TO TREATMENT.

HE APPEARS TO BE AN IDEALISTIC, SOCIALLY PERCEPTIVE PERSON WHO IS AESTHETIC AND PERHAPS SOMEWHAT FEMININE IN HIS INTEREST PATTERNS. HE MAY PURSUE ARTISTIC AND CULTURAL INTERESTS AND REJECT COMPETITIVE ACTIVITIES.

THE PATIENT'S TEST PATTERN RESEMBLES THAT OF PSYCHIATRIC PATIENTS. PROFESSIONAL ATTENTION IS INDICATED.

NOTE: ALTHOUGH NOT A SUBSTITUTE FOR THE CLINICIAN'S PROFESSIONAL JUDGMENT AND SKILL, THE MMPI CAN BE A USEFUL ADJUNCT IN THE DIAGNOSIS AND MANAGEMENT OF EMOTIONAL DISORDERS. THE RE-

PORT IS FOR PROFESSIONAL USE ONLY AND SHOULD NOT BE SHOWN OR RELEASED TO THE PATIENT.

ROCHE PSYCHIATRIC SERVICE INSTITUTE

SCALE SCORES FOR MMPI

CASE NO: 30358 RPSI. NO: 000
AGE: 37, MALE JUNE 30, 1967

SCALE	?	L	F	K	HS	D	HY	PD	MF	PA	PT	SC	MA	SI
RAW	0	3	8	14	9	29	33	27	26	16	19	20	19	31
K-C	0	3	8	14	16	29	33	33	26	16	33	34	22	31
T-C	OK	46	62	53	62	80	80	83	61	73	71	73	63	56

SCALE	ES	MT	A	R	LB	CA	DY	DO	RE	PR	ST	CN	SO	SO-R
RAW	53	25	21	16	13	15	27	23	21	10	20	37	63	25
T-C	64	85	61	51	66	60	58	73	52	47	55	81	37	26

CRITICAL ITEMS

THESE TEST ITEMS, WHICH WERE ANSWERED IN THE DIRECTION INDICATED, MAY REQUIRE FURTHER INVESTIGATION BY THE CLINICIAN. THE CLINICIAN IS CAUTIONED, HOWEVER, AGAINST OVERINTERPRETATION OF ISOLATED RESPONSES.

20 MY SEX LIFE IS SATISFACTORY. (FALSE)
156 I HAVE HAD PERIODS IN WHICH I CARRIED ON ACTIVITIES WITHOUT KNOWING LATER WHAT I HAD BEEN DOING. (TRUE)
205 AT TIMES IT HAS BEEN IMPOSSIBLE FOR ME TO KEEP FROM STEALING OR SHOPLIFTING SOMETHING. (TRUE)
215 I HAVE USED ALCOHOL EXCESSIVELY. (TRUE)
251 I HAVE HAD BLANK SPELLS IN WHICH MY ACTIVITIES WERE INTERRUPTED AND I DID NOT KNOW WHAT WAS GOING ON AROUND ME. (TRUE)
337 I FEEL ANXIETY ABOUT SOMETHING OR SOMEONE ALMOST ALL THE TIME. (TRUE)

CLINICAL EVALUATION OF THE REPORTS

The interpretation program utilized the same data that are available to a clinician. The published literature, including articles, handbooks, and actuarial atlases, was the principal source for the interpretative statements. During a period of four years, the program was used to prepare reports on all the cases admitted to five outpatient clinics. On all these cases (approximately 2,000), background data, including social histories, medical examinations, and psychiatric evaluations, were available. The reports were compared with these data, and they were examined and evaluated by the professional staff members of the clinics in regular case conferences. The feedback thus obtained permitted the interpretation system to "gain clinical experience" in the same sense that a neophyte clinician might improve his reports by additional exposure to clinical cases.

In a formal sense, the computer-generated reports are neither more nor less "validated" than reports prepared by the usual methods. The evidence for individual interpretative statements can be cited, but the global accuracy of psychological reports, however derived, has not yet been established. One study that is currently in progress will compare *Q* sorts on case history data with independent *Q* sorts done on computer-derived reports and on reports prepared by clinicians of various levels of experience. Using the case history *Q* sorts as a criterion, the relative accuracy of the reports produced by various methods can be assessed.

THE PILOT TEST

To test the feasibility of offering a national service utilizing the system, a three-part pilot study was initiated.[2] The first phase of the study consisted of interviews with psychiatrists and psychologists in various parts of the country to obtain their reaction to the development of a computerized MMPI interpretation service. These interviews indicated that such a service would be accepted in concept and would be used by the professions.

The second phase consisted of a small-scale pilot test of the service (the prepilot). A letter and a brochure describing the proposed service were sent to each psychiatrist and psychologist in private practice in one New Jersey county with an invitation to participate in the service. Those elected to participate received, for a nominal fee, a kit containing an MMPI test booklet, 20 answer sheets, and a manual entitled *The MMPI Notebook: A Guide to the Clinical Use of the Automated MMPI* (Fowler, 1966).

The purposes of the prepilot were (1) to ascertain the response to the letter and educational material, (2) to establish a smooth work

[2] Roche Laboratories sponsored the pilot test to evaluate clinicians' response to computer-derived reports. As a first step, the Roche Psychiatric Service Institute (RPSI) was established, with Marvin L. Miller as director. An advisory committee was appointed to provide continuous counsel with respect to the scientific and professional aspects of the institute. The committee consists of Bernard C. Glueck, Jr., M.D., W. Grant Dahlstrom, Ph.D., and Raymond D. Fowler, Jr., Ph.D. On the basis of the pilot studies, RPSI now provides MMPI scoring and interpretation as a professional service to psychiatrists and clinical psychologists.

flow in the processing center, and (3) to test, in actual operation, the mechanics of the service.

The third phase was a large-scale pilot test designed to fulfill the following objectives:

1 To determine the need for and the usefulness and acceptability of the MMPI service and the educational material among users
2 To estimate the total use of the service on a national basis
3 To determine the reasons for failure to use the service by people to whom it was made available
4 To determine whether the control procedures assured an operation that was consistent with professional and ethical standards

Letters and educational material were sent to all practicing clinical psychiatrists and clinical psychologists in four metropolitan areas in the following sections:

1 Pacific Northwest
2 Middle West
3 Middle Atlantic
4 North Central

The initial contact by mail went to all the practicing psychiatrists and clinical psychologists in the four areas who met the qualifications recommended by the Professional Advisory Committee.

In order to assure appropriate use of the Roche Psychiatric Service Institute (RPSI) scoring and reporting service, the following controls were established:

1 The use is limited to psychiatrists and psychologists whose qualifications meet the standards of the respective professions. The qualifications established were as follows.

   Psychiatrists:

   a Member, American Psychiatric Association
   b Full-time psychiatric practice

   Psychologists:

   a Member, American Psychological Association
   b Ph.D. in psychology (or ABEPP, or state license, or state certification)

2 Each professional participant is assigned an identification number

and a control card. When a test protocol is sent in for processing, it must be accompanied by the control card with the signature of the clinician.

3 Reports are sent out only to the clinician's office address.

4 In order to assure the anonymity of the patient, the answer sheets are identified by code number, and only the clinician can identify the number with a specific patient.

The results of the pilot studies will be presented elsewhere. In general, they showed (1) that the service is readily accepted and will be be used when available, (2) that the participants feel that the reports serve a useful clinical function and that the service should be made available nationally, and (3) that the controls are sufficient to assure use consistent with the ethical standards of the professions.

ISSUES RAISED BY AUTOMATED PSYCHOLOGICAL REPORTS

> The advent of the computer is producing subtle changes throughout the entire fabric of society. Old ways of thinking, working and living are being transformed by the computer's impact on the ways man operates in relation to his daily environment.
>
> The changes are bound to require new sets of values concerned with human effort—its quality, quantity, motivation, reward and social utility [Kranzberg, 1967, p. 135].

The benefits of computer technology are not attained without profound impact upon the established order. Whether the impact is to be a positive or a negative one is a matter of critical importance to society.

The ethical questions raised by automated test interpretation have been given serious consideration by the American Psychological Association. An ad hoc Committee on Assessment studied the issue at length and proposed a detailed set of guidelines for automated test interpretation. These guidelines, with minor modifications, were adopted by the APA Council of Representatives to serve as an interim standard for the profession. Doubtless, the guidelines will be changed as practical experience accumulates. At the present time, they represent a carefully considered guide that, if adhered to, should assure appropriate professional use of these new techniques. The APA standards, as adopted in 1966, follow.

AUTOMATED TEST INTERPRETATION PRACTICES: AN INTERIM STANDARD FOR MEMBERS OF THE APA AND FOR ORGANIZATIONS BY WHOM MEMBERS ARE EMPLOYED

(Adopted by the Council of Representatives of the American Psychological Association, September, 1966)

The advent of sophisticated computer technology and recent psychological research has made it feasible and desirable for consulting and service organizations to offer computer-based interpretation services for diverse clinical psychological measurement instruments. Since these services will be rendered to clients with varying degrees of training in psychological measurement and since improper use of such interpretations could be detrimental to the well-being of individuals, it is considered proper for the American Psychological Association to establish various conditions which must be met before such services should be offered to clients.

1 Any organization offering the services described above must have on its staff or as an active consultant a member of the American Psychological Association who is a Diplomate of the American Board of Examiners in Professional Psychology or who has essentially equivalent qualification.

2 Such services will be offered only to individuals or organizations for use under the active supervision of qualified professional personnel with appropriate training. The qualified person must be either a staff member or a responsible, active consultant to the individual or organization receiving such services.

3 Organizations offering scoring services must maintain an active quality control program to assure the accuracy and correctness of all reported scores.

4 Organizations offering interpretation services must be able to demonstrate that the computer programs or algorithms on which the interpretations rest are based on appropriate research to establish the validity of the programs and procedures used in arriving at interpretations.

5 The public offering of an automated test interpretation service will be considered as a professional-to-professional consultation. In this the formal responsibility of the consultant is to the consultee but his ultimate and overriding responsibility is to the client.

6 The organization offering service is responsible that their reports adequately interpret the test materials. They should not misinterpret nor over-interpret the data nor omit important interpretations that the consultee would reasonably expect to be included.

7 The organization offering services is responsible that their report be interpretable by the consultee. The technical level of the report should be understandable and not misleading to the consultee. The professional consultee is responsible for integrating the report into his client relationship. Where technical interpretations could be misleading, the organization offering service would be responsible either not to accept the referral, to modify the form of their report, or to avoid otherwise its misinterpretation.

The guidelines adopted by the American Psychological Association propose, for the computerized psychological report, standards far higher than those which are usually required for reports prepared by traditional clinical methods. The contrast is made clear by imagining the effect of asking practicing clinicians to demonstrate (1) that their interpretations are based on research, (2) that valid procedures have been used in arriving at interpretations, (3) that an active quality control program is maintained to assure scoring accuracy, and (4) that they have not overinterpreted, underinterpreted, or misinterpreted the data. The fact that such demands are not only reasonable but minimal for a computer interpretation system is certainly significant in the assessment of the technique.

In the final analysis, computerized MMPI reporting systems have deeper significance than the practical considerations of speed, economy, and wide availability. They offer an alternative to the endless cycle of training new personnel, generation after generation, to do approximately the same thing with test data as their predecessors did. The prediction of human behavior and the description of personality are far too complex to be subject to half-remembered norms and subjective extrapolation. Even a simple actuarial formula can usually exceed clinicians' accuracy in the prediction of phenotypic and genotypic descriptors. The economics involved in training clinical psychology students to accomplish what computers can already do is questionable; to train them to do what computers can potentially do is impossible. The computer can be a powerful tool to free the psychologist from tasks that he does not do well, while releasing him for responsibilities for which he is uniquely qualified.

REFERENCES

Barron, F. An ego-strength scale which predicts response to psychotherapy. *Journal of Consulting Psychology*, 1953, **17**, 327–333.

Drake, L. E. A social I. E. scale for the MMPI. *Journal of Applied Psychology,* 1946, **30,** 51–54.

Drake, L. E., and Oetting, E. R. *An MMPI codebook for counselors.* Minneapolis: University of Minnesota Press, 1959.

Dreger, R. M. Objective personality tests. In I. A. Berg and L. A. Pennington (Eds.), *An introduction to clinical psychology.* (3rd ed.) New York: Ronald Press, 1966.

Eber, H. W. Computer reporting of 16 PF data. Paper presented at the meeting of the American Psychological Association, Los Angeles, 1964.

Finney, J. C. Purposes and usefulness of the Kentucky program for the automatic interpretation of the MMPI. Paper presented at the meeting of the American Psychological Association, Chicago, 1965.

Fowler, R. D. Computer processing and reporting of personality test data. Paper presented at the meeting of the American Psychological Association, Los Angeles, 1964.

Fowler, R. D. Purposes and usefulness of the Alabama program for the automatic interpretation of the MMPI. Paper presented at the meeting of the American Psychological Association, Chicago, 1965.

Fowler, R. D. *The MMPI notebook: A guide to the clinical use of the automated MMPI.* Nutley, N.J.: Roche Psychiatric Service Institute, 1966.

Gilberstadt, H., and Duker, J. *A handbook for clinical and actuarial MMPI interpretation.* Philadelphia: Saunders, 1965.

Glueck, B. C., Jr., and Reznikoff, M. Comparison of computer-derived personality profile and projective psychological test findings. *American Journal of Psychiatry,* 1965, **121,** (12), 1156-1161.

Gough, H. G. The F minus K dissimulation index for the MMPI. *Journal of Consulting Psychology,* 1950, **14,** 408–413.

Gough, H. G. Studies of social intolerance: II. A personality scale for anti-Semitism. *Journal of Social Psychology,* 1951, **33,** 247–255.

Grayson, H. M. *A psychological admissions testing program and manual.* Los Angeles: Veterans Administrative Center, Neuropsychiatric Hospital, 1951.

Kleinmuntz, B. MMPI decision rules for the identification of college maladjustment: A digital computer approach. *Psychological Monographs,* 1963, **77** (14 Whole No. 577).

Kranzberg, M. Computers: New values for society. *The New York Times,* January 9, 1967, 135–136.

Marks, P. A. Personal communication, 1966.

Marks, P. A., and Seeman, W. *The actuarial description of abnormal personality: An atlas for use with the MMPI.* Baltimore: Williams & Wilkins, 1963.

Meehl, P. E. Wanted—a good cookbook. *American Psychologist,* 1956, **11,** 263–272.

Meehl, P. E., and Dahlstrom, W. G. Objective configural rules for discriminating the psychotic from neurotic MMPI profiles. *Journal of Consulting Psychology,* 1960, **24,** 375–387.

Pearson, J. S., and Swenson, W. M. *A user's guide to the Mayo Clinic automated MMPI program.* New York: The Psychological Corporation, 1967.

Peterson, D. R. Predicting hospitalization of psychiatric outpatients. *Journal of Abnormal and Social Psychology,* 1954, **49,** 260–265.

Piotrowski, Z. A. Digital-computer interpretation of inkblot test data. *Psychiatric Quarterly,* 1964, **38,** 1–26.

Rome, H. P., Swenson, W. M., Mataya, P., McCarthy, C. E., Pearson, J. S., Keating, F. R., Jr., and Hathaway, S. R. Symposium on automation techniques in personality assessment. *Proceedings of the Mayo Clinic,* 1962, **37,** 61–82.

Sines, J. O. Actuarial methods and personality assessment. In B. A. Maher (Ed.), *Progress in experimental personality research.* New York: Academic Press, 1966. Pp. 133–193.

Swenson, W. M., Rome, H. P., Pearson, J. S., and Brannick, T. L. A totally automated psychological test: Experience in a medical center. *Journal of the American Medical Association,* 1965, **191** (11), 925–927.

Taulbee, E. S., and Sisson, B. D. Configurational analysis of MMPI profiles of psychiatric groups. *Journal of Consulting Psychology,* 1957, **21,** 413–417.

Welsh, G. S. Factor dimensions *A* and *R*. In G. S. Welsh and W. G. Dahlstrom (Eds.), *Basic readings on the MMPI in psychology and medicine.* Minneapolis: University of Minnesota Press, 1956. Pp. 264–281.

Chapter Seven
Content Dimensions in the MMPI

Jerry S. Wiggins
University of Illinois

The concept of item *content* has enjoyed neither precise specification nor active empirical exploration in the recent history of objective personality assessment. This situation may, in part, be attributed to the general disrepute into which "face validity" has fallen as a validity criterion (APA, 1954; Stagner, 1958) and to the tendency to regard responses to ambiguous items as reflecting "dynamic" aspects of personality. Meehl's (1945) now classic empirical manifesto raised the hope that dynamic aspects of personality might be assessed by means of true-false item pools superficially bearing little resemblance to the criterion at hand. A not infrequently encountered corollary of this belief is the superstition that knowledge of the content of an empirical scale may somehow vitiate the mysterious mediating process that links scale scores to empirical criteria.

Jackson and Messick's (1958) influential distinction between content and style in personality assessment was partly motivated by their desire to measure the former class of variables with more precision. Their methodological innovations enabled them to separate, within limits, components of content and style in the MMPI (Jackson & Messick, 1961). Several studies later, Jackson and Messick's (1962) view of content has a wistful tone: "Actually, we are very much concerned with measuring content, but content—like a tarpon being hunted by a spear fisherman at ten fathoms—usually appears somewhat closer, larger, and more easily captured than is actually the case." Without denying the rather poor showing that content made in their studies,

Portions of this chapter originally appeared in *Psychological Monographs* and are reprinted here with the permission of Gregory A. Kimble and the American Psychological Association. The early phases of this research were supported in part by a research grant, MH 07042-01, from the National Institute of Mental Health. The final phases of the project were supported by a grant from the University Research Board of the Graduate College, University of Illinois.

it should be noted that their criterion for content demanded interitem consistencies within the MMPI clinical scales that survived the partialing out of two potent sources of content-confounded stylistic variance—"acquiescence" and "social desirability." As will be indicated later, the assessment strategy of contrasted criterion groups (Wiggins, 1962) that was employed in the development of the MMPI clinical scales cannot be expected to ensure content homogeneity within empirical scales.

The most nihilistic position with respect to personality test item content has been taken by Irwin Berg (1955, 1959, 1961), the originator of the deviation hypothesis. The assessment *strategy* of statistical differentiation between deviant and normative groups has impressed Berg as being so fundamental to personality measurement as to render unimportant the item *content* whereby this differentiation is achieved (Berg, 1959). In many ways this position is a restatement of the pragmaticism of the empirical movement (Meehl, 1945) with a *non sequitur* corollary which makes the blindness of blind empiricism a virtue. Berg's main point with respect to content seems to be that any given content may be considered *in principle* to be as effective for a predictive task as any other content and that recourse should be made to empirical evidence as the final arbiter. Berg (1959) is careful to note that this does not mean that "any item is just as good as every other for discriminative purposes" [p. 89]. However, he tends to overstate his case:

> One should be able to construct the MMPI scales from the Strong interest blank and the strong occupational scales from the MMPI items by using the same technique. Or, for that matter, one should be able to develop the scales of both tests from almost any hodge-podge of a similar number of items. . . . Given enough deviant responses and clean criterion groups, one should be able to duplicate any existing personality, interest, occupational and similar scales without regard to particular item content [Berg, 1955, p. 70].

The basis of the above inference is not clear since Berg is unable to provide even a rudimentary rationale whereby one might be able to predict the suitability of a given content for a given assessment. Similarly, when Berg (1961) states, "The carefully described 26 categories of test item content employed by the MMPI are probably irrelevant for clinical measurement purposes" [p. 361], it is not clear how one might know this in advance of empirical test. One may argue that, *in principle,* alternative and equally effective item pools might be discovered for any given prediction situation, and such a principle cannot be disproved. To prejudge a given item pool requires a theory of content, however, and Berg's contribution to this enterprise has been mainly a negative one (Norman, 1963).

In light of the foregoing discussion it is not surprising that the 26 content categories involved in the original classification of the MMPI item pool have received little attention in the literature (Wiggins & Vollmar, 1959). The test authors themselves (Hathaway & McKinley, 1940) were reluctant to attribute much significance to either selection or classification of item content, although their aim "that more varied subject matter be included to obtain a wider sampling of behavior of significance to the psychiatrist" [p. 249] seems clearly to have been met. The content categories themselves have not excited the curiosity of many of the authors who have contributed to the nearly 1,000 articles (Dahlstrom & Welsh, 1960) on the MMPI that have since appeared.

Although the academic and professional community has seen fit to ignore or denigrate the content of the MMPI, other segments of our society ("subjects") have been less quiescent (Brayfield, 1965). Viewed from the other side of the desk, the 566 items of the MMPI appear to represent a massive invasion of privacy. Appeals to the principles of empiricism (Gordon, 1965) serve only to emphasize the insensitivity of the professionals involved, and such appeals hardly justify the use of any particular set of items for a given selection purpose. Attempts to placate the public by removing the more "offensive" items from the MMPI pool (Braaten, 1965; Butcher & Tellegen, 1966) cannot be justified on a scientific basis. In short, a legitimate issue has been raised concerning the content of personality inventory items, and the scientific and professional community has been stirred from an undeserved complacency. The viewpoint that a personality test protocol represents a communication between the subject and the tester (or the institution he represents) has much to commend it, not the least of which is the likelihood that this is the frame of reference adopted by the subject himself.

The present study represents a first step in the direction of clarifying the content of the MMPI item pool. Starting with the original content classifications of Hathaway and McKinley, both psychometric and intuitive procedures were employed in the development of a set of scales designed to be internally consistent, moderately independent, and representative of the major substantive clusters that appeared to exist in the total MMPI item pool.

There have been a number of previous attempts to provide bases for regrouping MMPI items in ways other than that provided by the standard empirical scales. For the most part, these studies have used existing empirical scales as the basis for further regrouping. Homogeneous subgroupings of items within each of the standard empirical scales have been identified on a rational basis by Harris and Lingoes (1955) and on a factor-analytic basis by Comrey (1957a, 1957b, 1957c, 1958a, 1958b, 1958c, 1958d) and Comrey and Marggraff (1958). Among other things, these studies have indicated that the standard MMPI empirical scales are far from homogeneous in item content and that the dimensionality of the MMPI item pool might be greater than that suggested by factorial studies of the individual scales (Lingoes, 1960). It is important to note, however, that the substantive dimensions which emerged in these studies are dimensions which are defined in relation to the original empirical scales. These clusterings are based on only a portion of the total MMPI and represent subclusters of content "filtered through" the strategy of contrasted groups employed in the construction of the original scales. Such clusterings, no doubt, contain meaningful dimensions of item content; but, in addition, they contain variance peculiar to all dimensions along which the originally contrasted normal and psychiatric groups differed (Wiggins, 1962).

Attempts at more efficient measurement through factorially derived scales have also been conducted within the limited context of the original empirical scales. Welsh (1956) cluster-analyzed nonoverlapping clinical scales to obtain markers for his item-analytic procedures that yielded the well-known *A* and *R* scales. Similarly, Eichman (1961, 1962) used the results of a factor analysis of clinical scales to derive his factor scales. Although working on the item level, Mees (1959) employed only 119 items selected from the standard clinical scales in developing his item factor scales. The fact that only subsets of items defined by the clinical scales were employed in these factorial studies probably does not seriously detract from their goal of more efficient measurement. Factor scales for the MMPI can be developed from almost any subsample of items (Wiggins & Lovell, 1965) and possibly from just a few direct statements (Peterson, 1965). Unfortunately, the factorial homogeneity of MMPI items has made the test particularly vulnerable to interpretations in which stylistic (Edwards & Diers, 1962; Jackson & Messick, 1961; Messick & Jackson, 1961) and method (Wiggins & Lovell, 1965) components are involved or contaminated with substantive components. The extent of this contamination cannot be fully assessed until a serious effort has been made to illuminate the substantive dimensions of the total item pool rather than simply that portion of it which is most responsive to the strategy of contrasted groups.

ORIGINAL CONTENT CATEGORIES

In selecting items for possible inclusion in the final version of the MMPI, the "universe of content" (Loevinger, 1957) was deemed to be "behaviors of significance to the psychiatrist" (Hathaway & McKinley, 1940). With this in mind, "the items were supplied from several psychiatric examination direction forms, from various textbooks of psychiatry, from certain of the directions for case taking in medicine and neurology, and from the earlier published scales of personal and social attitudes" (Hathaway & McKinley, 1940, p. 249). The names of the 26 categories suggested by the test authors as descriptive of item clusters in the MMPI pool are given in Table 7-1. To these 26

Table 7-1 Original content categories of the MMPI

Affect-Depressive (32 items): Sadness, despair, pessimism, futility; loneliness; guilt and expectation of punishment; worrying and brooding; sensitivity; anxiety; psychomotor retardation.

Social Attitudes (72 items): Introverted, seclusive; withdrawn; shy; non-outgoing; non-fun-loving; overly sensitive; irritable; feels misunderstood; lacking in self-confidence; social rigidity; uncommunicative; lacking in social aggressiveness; critical and resentful of others.

Morale (33 items): Lacks self-confidence; low self-esteem; works and lives under tension; difficulties in concentrating, planning, making decisions, completing tasks; expects failure and resents success of others; suggestible and immature; feels misunderstood and unappreciated; sensitive and pessimistic.

Political Attitudes—law and order (46 items): Sees world as jungle; identification with criminal code; distrust of motives of others; discipline problem in school; delinquent childhood; thrill seeking; resentment and distrust of authority; competitive and vindictive; independence from norms; lack of concern for family members' misbehaviors; opinionated.

Obsessive and Compulsive States (15 items): Obsessions, compulsions, rumination; destructive impulses; covert defiance; overt compliance.

General Neurologic (19 items): Headaches, nausea; seizures; lability; poor judgment; distractability; poor memory.

Vasomotor, Trophic, Speech, Secretory (10 items): Hot and cold sensations; sweating; blushing, dry mouth; poor reading comprehension.

Delusions, Hallucinations, Illusions, Ideas of Reference (31 items): Delusions of persecution and grandeur; ideas of influence; suspiciousness; hallucinations; bizarre experiences; malevolent forces in environment.

Phobias (29 items): Admission of general fearfulness and worry; specific irrational fears of animals, states of nature, disease, heights, crowds, etc.

Family and Marital (26 items): Lack of affection for parents; domination by parents; lack of parental support; desire to leave home; poverty; strife

Table 7-1 Original content categories of the MMPI *(Continued)*

within family; disapproval, resentment, ambivalence, and annoyance at family members; disappointment in love; never been in love.

Lie Items (15 items): Naïve and improbable claims to virtue with venial sins such as procrastination, vanity, gossip, citizenship, mild anger, bad thoughts, competitiveness, etc.

Masculinity-Femininity (55 items): Feminine interest pattern in literature, hobbies, and childhood games; preference for feminine as opposed to masculine vocations; confused sexual identity; admission of weakness, fears, worries, and distress.

General Health (9 items): Poor health; worry about health; high strung; weight fluctuation; easily tired.

Motility and Coordination (6 items): Muscular paralysis, contraction, tremor, weakness, and lack of coordination.

Gastrointestinal System (11 items): Excessive and poor appetites; stomach trouble; constipation and diarrhea; lump in throat.

Affect-Manic (24 items): Excitement, euphoria, high energy; restless and impulsive; irritability, quick temper, destructive impulses; optimism; flight of ideas; unpredictable; short memory; wide and short-term interests; unusual hearing.

Occupational (18 items): Rigid work habits; distractability; sensitivity to opinions and criticisms of others; obstinance; indecisiveness; timidity; lack of self-confidence and concern about work; resentment of boss.

Cardiorespiratory System (5 items): Chronic cough; asthma or hay fever; chest pains; vomiting or coughing blood; pounding heart and shortness of breath.

Habits (19 items): Sleep disturbance; sensitivity to dreams; absence of dreams; excessive drinking and use of alcohol; abstinence from alcohol; giving in to bad habits.

Cranial Nerves (11 items): Disturbances in vision, speech, audition, olfaction, and swallowing; facial paralysis.

Sensibility (5 items): Hypersensitivity to pain, touch, numbness; tingling skin sensations.

Educational (12 items): Dislike of reading—both fiction and nonfiction, likes funny papers and articles on crime; slow learner, disliked school.

Religious Attitudes (19 items): Fundamentalist beliefs; rejection of fundamentalist beliefs; unusual religious experiences; religiosity; magical beliefs; lack of praying and church attendance.

Sadistic, Masochistic Trends (7 items): Enjoys hurting and being hurt by loved ones; cruelty to animals; enjoys frightening people; fetishism.

Sexual Attitudes (16 items): Anxiety over sex; sexual preoccupation; sexual perversion; suppressive attitudes toward sex; permissive attitudes toward sex; disgust and embarrassment about sex.

Genitourinary System (5 items): Disturbance in urination; skin rash; something wrong with sex organs.

labels have been added phrases that are descriptive of the item content within each category.

Internal Consistency

As a first step in the investigation of the contribution of the original content categories to test variance, each category was considered to be a "scale" composed of *n* items that could be combined to yield a single total score for any individual. As a preliminary scoring method, each item was keyed in the direction of "deviance" as determined by the *infrequent* item option chosen in the Minnesota normal population (Hathaway & McKinley, 1951, pp. 26–29). It should be emphasized that this scoring procedure is not entirely consistent with the empirically determined keying direction of the MMPI clinical scales, since several of the clinical scales contain items that are keyed in the popular direction. More important, such a scoring procedure in no way ensures optimal scale homogeneity since both ends of an attitudinal continuum may be deviant with respect to population norms. In the case of sexual attitudes, for example, items admitting *both* antisexual attitudes and sexual acting out are deviant; hence both are keyed in the same direction although such keying is intuitively inconsistent. In the absence of detailed information concerning such things as interitem correlations, however, the preliminary scoring method was considered the one most compatible with the original purpose of the item pool.

The internal consistency of content categories thus formed was assessed from the full-scale MMPI protocols of 500 Stanford University students in introductory psychology. Total scores on odd and even items within each of the 26 content categories were obtained separately for 250 men and 250 women students. Correlations between odd- and even-item totals, corrected by the Spearman-Brown formula for double test length, are given in Table 7-2.

The internal consistencies of the original content categories can be seen to vary from near-zero coefficients to coefficients in the .80s. Directly comparable internal consistency appraisals of the standard MMPI clinical scales have not been reported for college students taking the group form (Dahlstrom & Welsh, 1960, p. 474). The most comparable data available, (Gilliland & Colgin, 1951) suggest, however, that the majority of content categories have internal consistency coefficients equal to or greater than those reported for the standard MMPI clinical scales. As indicated in Table 7-2, the internal consistencies of many of the content categories are hampered by containing small

Table 7-2 Corrected odd-even reliability coefficients for 26 original content categories of the MMPI

Category	n	r_{xx} ($N = 250$ men)	r_{xx} ($N = 250$ women)
Affect-Depressive	32	.865	.851
Social Attitudes	72	.850	.775
Morale	33	.802	.738
Political Attitudes	46	.727	.632
Obsessive-Compulsive	15	.668	.601
General Neurologic	19	.644	.693
Vasomotor	10	.632	.628
Delusions	31	.624	.470
Phobias	29	.622	.728
Family and Marital	26	.581	.471
Lie Items	15	.550	.652
Masculinity	55	.547	.505
General Health	9	.476	.307
Motility and Coordination	6	.475	.553
Gastrointestinal	11	.470	.353
Affect-Manic	24	.454	.510
Occupational	18	.436	.396
Cardiorespiratory	5	.422	.477
Habits	19	.418	.588
Cranial Nerves	11	.417	.538
Sensibility	5	.338	.397
Educational	12	.333	.261
Religious Attitudes	19	.258	.184
Sadistic-Masochistic	7	.244	.302
Sexual Attitudes	16	.216	.249
Genitourinary	5	.169	.176
Total	550		

numbers of items. Hathaway and McKinley (1940) were not explicit about the extent to which the number of items in a given category can be taken as representative of the relative significance of the category to a psychiatrist. Whether arising from implicit, explicit, or fortuitous circumstances, there are definite psychometric restrictions on the extent to which 5-item content categories may contribute to total test variance as contrasted with 55- or 72-item categories. When all content-category internal-consistency coefficients are corrected to the common base of the largest category (72 items), there is little to discourage an investigator from developing an expanded pool of items for any of the categories simply because some of them happen to be underrepresented in the MMPI. The obtained reliabilities are even more impressive in light of the previously mentioned fact that the scoring procedures which were employed did not ensure scale homogeneity.

It is of interest to note that the three content categories which have the highest internal consistencies for both men and women are Affect-Depressive, Social Attitudes, and Morale. As previously reported (Wiggins & Vollmar, 1959), these three categories account for some 70% of the item content of Welsh's *A* scale, the empirically derived marker of the potent first factor of the MMPI (Welsh, 1956). A decade ago such an observation would have lent encouragement to a substantive interpretation of the first factor of the MMPI. It is now generally recognized that an unfortunate confounding of item characteristics and content mitigates against any such straightforward interpretation (Block, 1965; Dicken, 1967; Wiggins, 1962; Wiggins & Goldberg, 1965).

Factorial Structure

Despite the fact that some of the original content categories are not reliably represented and that the present scoring method is less than optimal, it is of considerable interest to inquire into the number and kinds of substantive dimensions represented in the total MMPI item pool. Such an analysis would be the first to be based on a mutually exclusive and exhaustive classification of MMPI items.

Accordingly, product-moment intercorrelations among the 26 total scale scores were computed separately in the college samples of 250 men and 250 women. The matrices of content-category intercorrelations were factored by the method of principal components (Harman, 1960). Latent roots that exceeded unity were retained and rotated analytically to a varimax criterion (Kaiser, 1958).

The method of analysis employed yielded seven factors for men and six for women that accounted respectively for 60.9% and 55.1% of the total variance. The rotated factor matrices for men and women are presented in Tables 7-3 and 7-4. Factor loadings less than .33 have been omitted, and the matrices have been arranged in such a way as to facilitate comparison. Factor interpretation will be further facilitated by consulting the content-category descriptions provided in Table 7-1.

Factor I appears to be the familiar general maladjustment dimension of the MMPI clinical scales. The content categories that load this factor

Table 7-3 Rotated factor matrix of 26 original content categories ($N = 250$ men)

	I	II	III_a	III_b	IV	V	VI	h^2
Morale	.74							.81
Vasomotor	.74							.66
Social Attitudes	.70			−.34				.68
Affect-Depressive	.61	−.41		−.33				.82
Occupational	.45	−.53						.54
Phobias	.41		.39	−.39				.59
Affect-Manic	.40	−.54						.58
Obsessive	.40	−.52						.58
Masculinity	.33	−.35				.44	−.54	.62
Political Attitudes		−.63						.49
Sadistic		−.61						.53
Lie		.54						.61
Delusions		−.40	.39					.59
Sensibility		−.40	.53					.59
Cranial			.73					.61
Gastrointestinal			.55					.50
Genitourinary			.52		−.50			.56
General Neurologic			.50			.33		.63
Cardiorespiratory			.49	−.44				.51
Habits			.35			.45		.48
Motility				−.79				.69
General Health				−.68				.56
Sexual Attitudes					−.73			.64
Family and Marital					−.67			.62
Religious Attitudes						.74		.57
Educational							.85	.80
Variance, %	20.3	18.9	16.8	11.8	9.6	8.2	14.4	

most heavily reflect subjectively experienced distress on the part of the respondent. Low self-esteem, depressed mood, and feelings of inadequacy are coupled with social uneasiness and introversion. Anxiety is experienced directly with its usual physiological manifestations. This factor is loaded moderately by items reflecting irrational fears, restless irritability, and obsessional thinking. In men, this general maladjustment is also reflected in poor work habits and feminine interests. In women, maladjustment includes an unsatisfactory family background and a greater emphasis on poor physical health and undesirable habits.

Factor II is loaded by an intriguing combination of contents that have heretofore been observed to covary only in highly specialized

Table 7-4 Rotated factor matrix of 26 original content categories ($N = 250$ women)

	I	II	III	IV	V	VI	h^2
Morale	.75						.74
Vasomotor	.44						.52
Social Attitudes	.80						.70
Affect-Depressive	.78			.34			.81
Occupational				.55			.52
Phobias	.41			.52			.56
Affect-Manic	.41		−.41				.53
Obsessive	.47	.37	−.33				.59
Masculinity			−.33	.42		−.44	.57
Political Attitudes		.51	−.33		−.34		.58
Sadistic		.80					.66
Lie		−.35		−.56			.46
Delusions			−.57		−.34		.60
Sensibility			−.65				.52
Cranial			−.64				.43
Gastrointestinal			−.44				.44
Genitourinary			−.33			.44	.38
General Neurologic	.47		−.63				.63
Cardiorespiratory			−.56				.43
Habits	.37		−.38				.37
Motility			−.76				.71
General Health	.51		−.35				.50
Sexual Attitudes				.69			.50
Family and Marital	.54						.45
Religious Attitudes					−.84		.73
Educational						.63	.42
Variance, %	26.9	11.4	26.6	16.6	9.5	9.0	

instruments. The Political Attitudes category reflects authority conflict and authoritarian attitudes toward law and order. A sadomasochistic orientation is combined with obsessive-compulsive symptoms and overt compliance. Naïve and improbable claims to virtue may further suggest rigidity. Together these categories provide an almost classic description of the authoritarian personality syndrome that has been described in a variety of other contexts (Adorno, Frenkel-Brunswik, Levinson, & Sanford, 1950; Loevinger, 1962; Rokeach, 1960; Stern, Stein, & Bloom, 1956). Although this factor is most clearly defined for women, the additional categories that load it for men are compatible with the areas of maladjustment often associated with authoritarianism. In men, the mood disturbances, poor work habits, sensitivities, delusional thinking, and feminine interests may reflect a more deep-seated personality disturbance than is the case with authoritarianism in women.

Two dimensions of physical symptoms in men (factors IIIa and IIIb) appear to be combined in a single dimension of physical complaint for women (factor III). Factor IIIa in men is loaded by a variety of complaints presumably representative of disturbance in cranial nerve, gastrointestinal, sensibility, genitourinary, neurologic, and cardiorespiratory systems. Factor IIIb appears to center around general health concerns, symptoms of fatigue, and cardiorespiratory complaints. Both these factors are loaded slightly by categories of psychological symptoms as well. In women, fatigue and general health concern are combined with the aforementioned systemic symptoms into one general factor of somatic complaint. With the exception of the Manic category reflecting fast tempo and irritability, the psychological symptom categories appear quite secondary in their contribution to this factor.

Factor IV is highly and uniquely loaded by the category of Sexual Attitudes. Categories associated with deviant sexual attitudes vary remarkably for men and women. In men such attitudes are associated with family conflict and specific genitourinary complaints. In women, this factor is negatively loaded by improbable claims to virtue and positively loaded by feminine interests. Psychological symptoms in women take the form of irrational fears, poor work habits, and feelings of depression and guilt.

Factor V is strongly and uniquely loaded by deviant religious attitudes. In men, sleep disturbance, drinking habits, feminine interests, and, to a lesser extent, some somatic complaints tend to have loadings on this factor. In women, authoritarian attitudes and delusional thinking have very slight loadings on the deviant religious attitudes factor.

Factor VI is defined by deviant educational attitudes. In both men and women, antieducational attitudes are associated with masculine interests. In women, this factor is also loaded by the category of Genitourinary complaints.

In summary, a principal component analysis of the 26 mutually exclusive and exhaustive content categories of the MMPI yielded six interpretable factors in both men and women. The first three of these factors appear to represent general syndromes of complaint, while the last three appear to center around more specific substantive categories. The factors of general maladjustment and somatic complaint are familiar ones that might be anticipated on the basis both of clinical scale development and of the overrepresentation of such categories in the MMPI item pool. The factor of authoritarianism appears to represent a theoretically meaningful combination of substantive categories that has, until now, been obscured by the strategy employed in the development of the clinical scales. Deviant attitudes toward sex, religion, and education have likewise not been previously stressed as important substantive components of the MMPI item pool.

REVISION OF ORIGINAL CONTENT CATEGORIES

Given the encouraging internal consistencies and factorial structure of the original content categories, it seemed fruitful to attempt a more substantively consistent grouping of items within categories as a basis for subsequent development of actual content *scales*. Although many strategies of scale construction were possible at this point, the one chosen placed primary emphasis on the "rational" or substantive considerations involved in the classification of item content. Since this strategy is so antithetical to the traditional approach to MMPI scale construction, a brief justification seems required.

For better or (more likely) for worse, the MMPI represents a *fixed* item pool. Examination of the interrelationships among many characteristics of this item pool led Wiggins and Goldberg (1965) to conclude:

> Over- and under-representation of certain classes of desirability, endorsement, ambiguity, and grammatical characteristics tends to make the item pool unnecessarily homogeneous and may, in part, contribute to rather severe restrictions in criterion group discriminations. The fortuitous confounding of such item characteristics with substantive dimensions (Block, 1965; Wiggins, 1962) has created interpretative problems (Edwards, 1957; Jackson & Messick, 1961) which may never be satisfactorily resolved within any fixed item pool [pp. 394–395].

Although these authors stress the importance of basic research in item development, such research will not be of immediate value to the practical consumer of the MMPI. The present attempt to develop substantive scales for the MMPI was not initiated with the hope of overcoming the built-in shortcomings of the item pool. It was predicated, however, on the assumption that the interaction of item characteristics and stylistic tendencies with substantive dimensions might be better understood than the interaction of such sources of variance with the complex and poorly understood dimensions yielded by the strategy of contrasted groups (e.g., "hysteria").

The method whereby the original MMPI content categories were revised involved the collapsing of several categories into single categories, reassignment of items from one category to another, elimination of original categories, creation of new ones, and rekeying of item options within categories. Procedures were, with one minor exception, completely intuitive, and no claim is made for their replicability.[1]

The major item regroupings involved physical symptoms, interests, and items reflecting manifest hostility. Items from General Health, Cardiorespiratory, Gastrointestinal, and Genitourinary were combined in the single revised category of Poor Health. Items from General Neurologic, Cranial Nerves, Motility and Coordination, and Sensibility were combined into a single category of Organic Symptoms. Items reflecting hostility from the Sadistic-Masochistic category formed the nucleus of a new category of Manifest Hostility, to which 21 items from seven other original categories were added. A small group of items from the Habits category was considered separately as an Addiction category.

The Occupational Attitudes category was judged to be too heterogeneous, and items from this category were regrouped under Obsessive-Compulsive, Poor Morale, and four other revised categories. Original categories that were retained were purified around a central theme and items eliminated or borrowed from other categories in light of this theme. The category of Habits, for example, was redefined as Sleeping Habits, which eliminated seven of the original items and added three from other categories.

The categories of Educational Attitudes and Masculinity-Femininity were placed in a common pool, and from this pool preliminary attempts were made to differentiate feminine interest patterns from tendencies toward sexual inversion. When this differentiation was judged to be unsuccessful, a general category of Feminine Interests was developed which proved to be ambiguous with respect to keying direction. In the absence of a clear-cut rationale, the empirical norms of Drake (1953) were used as a basis for item keying. Items in the Feminine Interest category that significantly differentiated men and women in Drake's sample were retained and keyed in the female direction.

Internal Consistency of Revised Categories

A more consistent arrangement of items into content categories should be reflected in increased internal consistencies in the revised set.

[1] The assistance of Victor R. Lovell in performing these item regroupings is gratefully acknowledged.

Total scores on odd and even items were computed for each of the 18 revised categories in samples of 250 men and 250 women students from Stanford University. Since these samples had, in part, inspired the reclassification, odd and even totals were also computed in a mixed group of 203 men and women introductory psychology students from the University of Oregon.[2] Table 7-5 presents Spearman-Brown corrected internal consistency coefficients for the Stanford and Oregon samples. Since new content categories were created and old ones were considerably altered in the revision of the content categories, the success of the revision procedures cannot, in all cases, be directly assessed by comparison of each category with its revised counterpart. A slight decline in internal consistency occurred in depression, obsessive-compulsive, and vasomotor categories. This is more than offset by the increases in internal consistency which occurred in 14 categories which can be compared with their original counterparts. The most dramatic increase occurred in the category of Religious Attitudes, in which *deletion* of four items and rekeying of those remaining resulted in internal consistency increases from the low .20s to the high .80s. Regrouping sadistic-masochistic items into the more general category of Manifest Hostility resulted in increases from the low .30s to the middle .70s. Other increases may be noted by comparing Table 7-5 with Table 7-2.

CONSTRUCTION OF FINAL CONTENT SCALES

On the basis of the data presented in Table 7-5, it was decided that there were 15 substantive dimensions in the MMPI pool which possessed promising internal consistencies and sufficient numbers of items to warrant further exploration. These 15 dimensions appear as the first 15 categories in Table 7-5. The categories of Addiction, Lie, Vasomotor, and Sexual were dropped from further consideration at this point. The categories of Feminine Interests, Sleeping Habits, and Obsessive-Compulsive were carried along on a very tentative basis.

The Stanford sample was randomly divided into two groups of 300 and 200 subjects, with an equal number of men and women within each group. The group of 300 *S*s served as an item analysis group for scale purification, and the group of 200 *S*s was used for an independent assessment of the homogeneity of scales formed by item analysis.

[2] These data for 95 men and 108 women were made available by Lewis R. Goldberg.

Table 7-5 Corrected odd-even internal consistency coefficients of revised content categories in two college populations

Revised category	*n*	Stanford men ($N = 250$)	Stanford women ($N = 250$)	Oregon men and women ($N = 203$)
Religious	15	.87	.86	.81
Social	56	.84	.83	.80
Depression	33	.83	.82	.78
Morale	40	.84	.79	.74
Authority	43	.77	.71	.80
Phobias	27	.72	.80	.75
Hostility	27	.75	.73	.75
Organic	36	.71	.79	.72
Psychoticism	48	.75	.72	.71
Family	27	.74	.67	.73
Hypomania	25	.72	.71	.66
Health	28	.76	.70	.52
Feminine	56	.55	.60	.82
Sleep	15	.56	.58	.52
Obsessive	27	.52	.55	.50
Addiction	6	.67	.53	.42
Lie	15	.55	.65	.55
Vasomotor	10	.62	.60	.58
Sexual	16	.34	.51	.53

Point biserial correlations were computed between the 566 items of the MMPI[3] and each of the 15 total scale scores of the revised content categories. An item was retained in a given content scale if (1) its point-biserial correlation with the total scale of the category of which it was a member exceeded .30 and (2) its correlation with the total scale of the category of which it was a member exceeded its correlation with all 14 remaining revised content category scores.

Table 7-6 shows the number of items eliminated by each of the two criteria of item analysis. Among the Social Maladjustment items, for example, 26 items were eliminated because their correlation with the Social total scale score was less than .30. Three additional items were eliminated because their item-total correlations, although greater than .30, were equaled or exceeded by item-total correlations with one or more of the 14 additional content categories.

[3] Sixteen items are repeated in the group form of the MMPI. In all analyses reported here, only the first appearance of a repeated item was considered.

Table 7-6 Number of items eliminated by item analysis of revised content categories

Scale	Original	$r < .30$	Non-independent	Final *n*
Religious	15	3	0	12
Social	56	26	3	27
Depression	33	12	2	20*
Morale	40	15	3	23*
Authority	43	21	2	20
Phobias	27	7	1	19
Hostility	27	7	1	20*
Organic	36	13	0	23
Psychoticism	48	31	4	13
Family	27	11	0	16
Hypomanic	25	5	0	20
Health	28	15	0	13
Feminine	56	26	0	30
Sleep	15	3	1	11
Obsessive	27	14	3	10

* Includes one additional item from another content category.

It can be seen from Table 7-6 that item selection was made primarily on the basis of internal consistency. Only 20 items were eliminated on the basis of their being correlated with categories other than their own. Note, however, that the criterion of scale independence employed was quite minimal. Three items were judged to have been initially misclassified after examination of their correlations with other categories. Thus, one Obsessive item was transferred to the Depression category, one Social item to the Morale category, and one Psychoticism item to the Hostility category.

The 15 revised content categories and the 15 content scales formed by item analysis were then scored in the group of 200 *S*s originally set aside for this purpose. As a more general measure of scale homogeneity, Cronbach's (1951) coefficient alpha was computed for the 15 categories and 15 scales. Content scales were judged to be improved by item analysis if their alpha coefficient increased despite the elimination of substantial portions of items.

Table 7-7 presents alpha coefficients for the revised categories and the scales formed by item analysis. The contaminated correlation between the two sets of measures is presented in the final column. The Religion, Social, Morale, Authority, Family, and Feminine Interests scales were judged to be improved by item analysis. Scale purification

Table 7-7 Coefficient alpha internal consistency estimates for revised categories and item-analyzed content scales ($N = 200$ men and women)

Category	Revised	*n*	Final	*n*	Revised vs. final
Religious	81	(15)	83	(12)	98
Social	83	(56)	86	(27)	95
Depression	84	(33)	82	(20)	96
Morale	81	(40)	84	(23)	93
Authority	77	(43)	78	(20)	92
Phobias	70	(27)	67	(19)	96
Hostility	72	(27)	69	(20)	97
Organic	76	(36)	70	(23)	96
Psychoticism	76	(48)	61	(13)	85
Family	72	(27)	72	(16)	94
Hypomanic	69	(25)	67	(20)	97
Health	69	(28)	59	(13)	90
Feminine	77	(56)	84	(30)	96
Sleep	56	(15)	56	(11)	97
Obsessive	56	(27)	57	(10)	82

was extreme in several instances and resulted in improved alphas despite elimination of almost half the items in the scale.

Increased homogeneity was not achieved by item analysis for Depression, Phobias, Hostility, Organic, Psychoticism, Hypomania, or Health. Subsequent attempts to improve these scales by less stringent item-analytic criteria were not successful. It was decided, therefore, to retain these scales in their revised form. The Sleeping Habits and Obsessive scales were abandoned at this point on the grounds of unpromising homogeneity.

The foregoing procedures resulted in the adoption of 13 mutually exclusive scales that were considered internally consistent, moderately independent, and representative of the major substantive clusters of the MMPI. All these scales were based on rational regroupings of the original content categories proposed by Hathaway and McKinley. Six of these scales were further refined by item-analytic procedures. This final set of 13 scales will be referred to as the MMPI content scales.[4] The content of the items in the scales is described in Table 7-8.

[4] Item lists may be found in Wiggins (1966).

Table 7-8 Description of MMPI content scales

SOC *Social Maladjustment:* High SOC is socially bashful, shy, embarrassed, reticent, self-conscious, and extremely reserved. Low SOC is gregarious, confident, assertive and relates quickly and easily to others. He is fun-loving, the life of a party, a joiner who experiences no difficulty in speaking before a group. This scale would correspond roughly with the popular concept of "introversion-extraversion."

DEP *Depression:* High DEP experiences guilt, regret, worry, unhappiness, and a feeling that life has lost its zest. He experiences difficulty in concentrating and has little motivation to pursue things. His self-esteem is low, and he is anxious and apprehensive about the future. He is sensitive to slight, feels misunderstood, and is convinced that he is unworthy and deserves punishment. In short, he is classically depressed.

FEM *Feminine Interests:* High FEM admits to liking feminine games, hobbies, and vocations. He denies liking masculine games, hobbies, and vocations. Here there is almost complete contamination of content and form, which has been noted in other contexts by several writers. Individuals may score high on this scale by presenting themselves as *liking* many things, since this item stem is present in almost all items. They may also score high by endorsing interests that, although possibly feminine, are also *socially desirable,* such as an interest in poetry, dramatics, news of the theatre, and artistic pursuits. This has been noted in the case of Wiggins's *Sd* scale. Finally, of course, individuals with a genuine preference for activities that are conceived by our culture as "feminine" will achieve high scores on this scale.

MOR *Poor Morale:* High MOR is lacking in self-confidence, feels that he has failed in life, and is given to despair and a tendency to give up hope. He is extremely sensitive to the feelings and reactions of others and feels misunderstood by them, while at the same time being concerned about offending them. He feels useless and is socially suggestible. There is a substantive overlap here between the Depression and Social Maladjustment scales and the Poor Morale scale. The Social Maladjustment scale seems to emphasize a lack of social ascendance and poise, the Depression scale feelings of guilt and apprehension, while the present scale seems to emphasize a lack of self-confidence and hypersensitivity to the opinions of others.

REL *Religious Fundamentalism:* High scorers on this scale see themselves as religious, churchgoing people who accept as true a number of fundamentalist religious convictions. They also tend to view their faith as the true one.

AUT *Authority Conflict:* High AUT sees life as a jungle and is convinced that others are unscrupulous, dishonest, hypocritical, and motivated only by personal profit. He distrusts others, has little respect for experts, is competitive, and believes that everyone should get away with whatever he can.

Table 7-8 Description of MMPI content scales (*Continued*)

PSY *Psychoticism:* High PSY admits to a number of classic psychotic symptoms of a primarily paranoid nature. He admits to hallucinations, strange experiences, loss of control, and classic paranoid delusions of grandeur and persecution. He admits to feelings of unreality, daydreaming, and a sense that things are wrong, while feeling misunderstood by others.

ORG *Organic Symptoms:* High ORG admits to symptoms that are often indicative of organic involvement. These include headaches, nausea, dizziness, loss of motility and coordination, loss of consciousness, poor concentration and memory, speaking and reading difficulty, poor muscular control, tingling skin sensations, and disturbances in hearing and smelling.

FAM *Family Problems:* High FAM feels that he had an unpleasant home life characterized by a lack of love in the family and parents who were unnecessarily critical, nervous, quarrelsome, and quick tempered. Although some items are ambiguous, most are phrased with reference to the parental home rather than the individual's current home.

HOS *Manifest Hostility:* High HOS admits to sadistic impulses and a tendency to be cross, grouchy, competitive, argumentative, uncooperative, and retaliatory in his interpersonal relationships. He is often competitive and socially aggressive.

PHO *Phobias:* High PHO has admitted to a number of fears, many of them of the classically phobic variety such as heights, darkness, and closed spaces.

HYP *Hypomania:* High HYP is characterized by feelings of excitement, well-being, restlessness, and tension. He is enthusiastic, high-strung, cheerful, full of energy, and apt to be hotheaded. He has broad interests, seeks change, and is apt to take on more than he can handle.

HEA *Poor Health:* High HEA is concerned about his health and has admitted to a variety of gastrointestinal complaints centering around an upset stomach and difficulty in elimination.

Internal Consistency of Content Scales in Normal Populations

Since virtually all of the preliminary investigation and development of the MMPI content scales was based on a single college population, it was necessary to gather additional data from other populations to assess the psychometric characteristics of the final scales. Accordingly, complete MMPI protocols were obtained from the samples listed in Table 7-9. A group of Air Force enlisted men served as a noncollege normal population, while the remaining samples were college students of both sexes from several geographical regions.[5]

[5] The author is grateful to John D. Hundleby and to Leonard G. Rorer for making available the Air Force and Minnesota college data, respectively.

Table 7-9 Composition of normal sample ($N = 1{,}368$)

Group	Men	Women
Air Force enlisted men*	261	
Stanford University	250	250
University of Minnesota	96	125
University of Oregon	95	108
University of Illinois	100	83
Total	802	566

* Chanute Air Force Base, Rantoul, Ill.

The internal consistency of the MMPI content scales was assessed by computing alpha coefficients in samples not involved in scale derivation. These data are presented in Table 7-10. Reliability coefficients from the college samples are, with one notable exception, generally in accord with expectations gained from the derivation samples. The exception is Feminine Interests which, although among the most internally consistent scales in the derivation sample, is the least reliable scale in other college and Air Force samples. More in line with expectations are the generally high internal consistencies of Social Maladjust-

Table 7-10 Coefficient alpha internal consistency estimates for MMPI content scales in seven normal samples

	Air Force enlisted men	University of Minnesota		University of Oregon		University of Illinois	
		Men	Women	Men	Women	Men	Women
	($N = 261$)	($N = 96$)	($N = 125$)	($N = 95$)	($N = 108$)	($N = 100$)	($N = 83$)
SOC	.829	.856	.835	.830	.862	.856	.843
DEP	.872	.860	.831	.821	.756	.842	.854
FEM	.585	.523	.505	.594	.566	.650	.542
MOR	.857	.866	.825	.804	.753	.867	.804
REL	.674	.892	.861	.842	.756	.817	.793
AUT	.681	.794	.772	.743	.669	.766	.698
PSY	.877	.794	.687	.738	.662	.763	.806
ORG	.863	.772	.645	.652	.695	.749	.731
FAM	.707	.712	.789	.712	.694	.806	.643
HOS	.764	.819	.794	.788	.651	.776	.765
PHO	.765	.663	.721	.568	.701	.705	.770
HYP	.671	.701	.715	.682	.632	.679	.667
HEA	.743	.557	.713	.555	.537	.673	.651

ment, Religious Fundamentalism, Depression, and Poor Morale in the college groups. As before, Hypomania and Poor Health are among the lowest in internal consistency, but the obtained alpha coefficients are quite respectable in comparison with the majority of MMPI scales in use today.

With the exception of Feminine Interests, the alpha coefficients obtained in the Air Force sample are substantial, indicating a generality beyond college populations. Several differences in the relative internal consistencies of the content scales in an Air Force, as opposed to a college, population may be noted. Whereas Psychoticism and Organic Symptoms are only moderately reliable in college groups, they are among the most internally consistent scales in the Air Force sample. This may reflect, in part, the greater heterogeneity of the Air Force sample. It is also of interest to note that, whereas Religious Fundamentalism is consistently among the most reliable scales for college groups, it is one of the least reliable scales in the Air Force sample.

Group Differences in Content Scale Scores

Personality inventory scale scores that presumably reflect individual differences along dimensions of substantive interest should, at the very least, be expected to reflect such differences when diverse groups are compared. The standard MMPI clinical scales were *constructed* to reflect differences among certain groups, and initially substantive interpretations of clinical scales were rather narrowly restricted to such differences, whatever they may imply. By contrast, the MMPI content scales were designed to reflect reliable individual differences along interpretable substantive dimensions; and group differences, when found, will serve to enhance rather than define the meaning of the content scale involved.

The cooperation of two quite different psychiatric installations was obtained in securing complete MMPI protocols of patients on whom a final psychiatric diagnosis had been made.[6] One installation was a large state mental hospital whose inmates represent a wide spectrum of psychopathology, the most frequent diagnosis being that of chronic schizophrenia. The second installation was an outpatient clinic attached to an Air Force base whose clientele consists primarily of individuals with neurotic, sociopathic, and personality disorders. At each installation, an attempt was made to obtain the majority of recent

[6] The author is indebted to Paul Finkel, Clifford Broadway, and other staff of Kankakee State Hospital for their assistance in providing protocols and case folders.

and complete MMPI protocols on patients whose files were sufficiently complete to allow determination of the final psychiatric diagnosis. On the basis of information contained in the case folder, each patient was classified in terms of the first three digits of the diagnostic code given in the American Psychiatric Association's *Diagnostic and Statistical Manual: Mental Disorders* (1952). In the inpatient sample, several preliminary diagnostic impressions were available in addition to the final, official hospital diagnosis made by the diagnostic staff. When there was great discrepancy between preliminary and final diagnoses or when the final diagnosis was lacking in precision, the case was classified as "indeterminate." In the outpatient sample, only the final decision of the diagnostic staff was employed, and when this was imprecise, an "indeterminant" classification was assigned. The distribution of such classifications is given in Table 7-11 for both inpatient and outpatient samples. These distributions represent available records rather than any attempted sampling procedure. They are judged to be reasonably representative of the two kinds of installations involved.

Although the MMPI is given more or less routinely at both these installations, its contribution to final psychiatric diagnosis is probably less than at other installations that routinely give the MMPI. It should

Table 7-11 Composition of psychiatric sample ($N = 614$)

APA code	Diagnosis	Inpatients*		Outpatients†	
		Men	Women	Men	Women
000–199	Brain disorders	23	16	16	
200–213	Affective psychoses	20	27		
220–229	Schizophrenic psychoses	85	83	...	4
400–406	Psychoneurotic disorders	13	23	15	7
500–504	Personality pattern disturbance	15	5	17	2
510–513	Personality trait disturbance	17	8	36	6
520–524	Sociopathic personality disturbance	46	14	19	1
530–535	Special symptom reaction	...	...	6	
540–546	Transient situational disturbance	...	...	8	3
	Other‡	53	16	8	2
	Total	272	192	125	25

* Kankakee State Hospital, Kankakee, Ill.
† Chanute Air Force Base Outpatient Clinic, Rantoul, Ill.
‡ Rare category or indeterminant diagnosis.

be recognized, nevertheless, that an unknown degree of criterion contamination exists. In no instance, however, were MMPI content scale scores available to the institution prior to final diagnosis.

From the samples listed in Tables 7-9 and 7-11, it was possible to form seven fairly large groups that differed markedly among themselves in such characteristics as age, sex, education, and psychiatric status. These groups were (1) 261 Air Force men, (2) 272 inpatient men, (3) 192 inpatient women, (4) 125 outpatient men, (5) 25 outpatient women, (6) 96 University of Minnesota college men, and (7) 125 University of Minnesota college women. The 13 MMPI content scales were scored in each of these seven groups. For each content scale, a simple analysis of variance was performed to test the null hypothesis that mean scale scores are the same for the populations from which the seven groups were derived. This hypothesis was rejected for all 13 scales at $p < .01$ by the F ratio with 6 and 1089 degrees of freedom. Differences between certain group means across all content scales were further assessed by t tests for independent groups. Of 21 possible group comparisons across content scales, 11 were judged to be sensible, and only these were made. Even with this many comparisons, it is expected that at least several will not be replicable. The point of this analysis, however, was not to attach significance to any single comparison but rather to provide an overview of the content scales which differed most from sample to sample and of the sample comparisons which yielded the greatest differences.

The content scales which contributed most to differences among this particular sample of diverse groups were Poor Morale, Organic Symptoms, Phobias, and Depression. Lesser, but not insubstantial, differences occurred with Poor Health, Manifest Hostility, Feminine Interests, Authority Conflict, and Psychoticism. The means of content scales which did not differ greatly among the present samples were Social Maladjustment, Religious Fundamentalism, Family Problems, and Hypomania.

As might be expected, mean content scale scores differed most when college groups were compared with the same-sex patient groups—both inpatient and outpatient. What might not have been anticipated were the substantial differences between college and Air Force men. Large differences between outpatient men and women may have reflected the unrepresentative nature of a female sample at an Air Force installation. The Air Force "normal' sample differed very slightly from both inpatient and outpatient male samples. Differences between outpatient and inpatient men were also slight.

To provide a context of comparison for group differences obtained with the content scales, the same analysis was performed using the

13 standard MMPI clinical scales. The number of significant differences obtained with the clinical scales was similar to that obtained with the content scales. Again, the greatest mean scale score differences occurred when college groups were contrasted with patient groups. Relatively few differences were found between Air Force and patient samples or between inpatient and outpatient males. Although the number of significant differences was similar, the clinical scales, in general, tended to allow for rejection of the null hypothesis at a slightly higher level of significance than was possible with the content scales. Considering that the clinical scales were specifically constructed for the purpose of discriminating normal from abnormal samples, the slight edge they possessed over the content scales in the present analysis is not an impressive one. Whatever is represented in mean scale score comparisons across diverse groups is clearly present in the MMPI content scales as well.

Ordering of Group Means on Content Scales

In addition to assessing the overall contribution of content scale scores to group differences, it is of interest to examine the ordering of means for diverse groups within each of the separate content scales. Such a procedure is useful in suggesting underlying psychological continua that may be associated with scale scores (Gough, 1960). In the present instance, this approach should not be considered validational, since the content scales were not devised to serve specific group discriminative purposes. It is assumed that the dimensions underlying the content scales are substantive and, although primarily pathological in nature, not necessarily equivalent to the dimensions which contribute to the fact of membership in a socially or psychiatrically defined group. From the male samples described in Tables 7-9 and 7-11, sixteen subgroups were selected to represent a broad range of socioeconomic, educational, and psychiatric variables. Content scale means and standard deviations were computed for each subgroup. For each content scale, the groups were ordered by mean scale score.

Inspection of the group-ordered scale data revealed that the content scales do not provide measures of "pathology" that are consistent with the conventional psychiatric meaning of this term. Space limitations do not permit a detailed scale-by-scale analysis, but certain generalizations may be stated. When the rank order of each group within each scale is pooled across the 13 scales, four reasonably consistent groupings may be distinguished. In the first group are those with brain disorders, the outpatients with personality pattern and trait disturbances, and the Air Force normal subjects—all of whom tend to be among the highest scorers on the content scales. Next in order are the inpatients and outpatients with sociopathic disturbances, those with affective psychoses, and the special symptom outpatient group. Following this group are the inpatients and outpatients with neurotic disorders, those with schizophrenic psychoses, and the inpatients with personality trait disturbances. The lowest scoring group tends to consist of the inpatients with personality trait disturbances, the outpatients with brain disorders, college students, and outpatients with transient situational disturbances. It must be borne in mind that these generalizations tend to obscure large individual differences among the content scales.

DIFFERENTIAL DIAGNOSIS OF PSYCHIATRIC INPATIENTS

The preceding consideration of scale mean distributions across a variety of samples was designed to explicate the meaning of MMPI scales formed from substantive rather than group discriminative considerations. Should such scales be applied to problems of psychiatric classification, it is hoped that the approach would be multivariate rather than single scale. Further, the problem typically facing the practicing diagnostician is not that of distinguishing disparate groups such as Air Force personnel and college students but rather that of distinguishing putative subgroupings within a single population.

As an example of the use of MMPI content scales in a realistic diagnostic problem, multiple discriminant–analytic procedures were applied to the classification of psychiatric inpatients. From Table 7-11 it can be seen that by combining the diagnostic categories of personality disturbance (men = 32; women = 13) and by eliminating the rare and indeterminate categories (men = 53; women = 16), six major diagnostic groupings can be formed for men (N = 219) and women (N = 176), respectively. These groupings are (1) brain disorders, (2) affective psychoses, (3) schizophrenic psychoses, (4) psychoneurotic disorders, (5) personality disorders, and (6) sociopathic disorders.

Using the 13 MMPI content scales as predictors, multiple discriminant analyses were performed separately on these six groups of men and six groups of women inpatients. The main purpose of this analysis was to test the generalized, multivariate null hypothesis that these six diagnostic groups have similar content scale scores. Should rejection of this hypothesis seem tenable, the contribution of the separate content scales to the main discriminant functions would shed light on their relative diagnostic importance. Evaluation of the replicability of the functions derived and their efficiency in classifying other samples of psychiatric patients must await further data collection. The method of analysis employed is described by Cooley and Lohnes (1962).

When the number of groups is fewer than the number of predictors, the maximum number of discriminants is one fewer than the number of groups or, in the present instance, five. In both the male and female samples, five latent roots were examined along with their associated vectors (coefficients), which were adjusted to permit comparison of their relative contribution to each discriminant function. The generalized null hypothesis was evaluated by Wilks's lambda which expresses the ratio of pooled within-group cross-product deviation scores to total sample cross-product deviation scores. In testing the significance of lambda, the F approximation of Rao was employed (Cooley & Lohnes, 1962). In the male sample, $F = 1.56$, which for 65 and 954 df is significant at $p < .01$. For the women, $F = 1.53$, which for 65 and 750 df is also significant at $p < .01$. This makes tenable the rejection of the hypothesis of the equality of mean vectors for the six groups.

The coefficients associated with each of the five discriminant functions are of interest in assessing the relative contributions of the content scales to classification of an inpatient population. From a practical standpoint, it should be noted that three discriminant functions are probably sufficient for both men and women, since they account for approximately 88% of the discriminating power of the scales in each sample. It should also be noted that the three discriminant functions in each analysis were sufficiently different in pattern for men and women to discourage pooling data for sexes in hospital populations.

For men, the largest contributors to group discrimination along the first discriminant function were Hostility and Authority Conflict. Inspection of group means for these scales indicated that they were relatively effective in separating sociopathic and brain disorder groups from groups with schizophrenic, neurotic, and personality disturbances. Depression and Poor Morale contribute to group discrimination along the second discriminant. Mean Depression scale scores for brain disorder and neurotic groups were well above those for personality, affective, and schizophrenic groups. Mean scores for Poor Morale reflect a separation between the brain disorder group and the others just mentioned. Psychoticism and Hypomania were the largest contributors to the third discriminant function. Mean PSY scores suggest a clear psychotic-neurotic distinction with brain disorder, sociopathic, schizophrenic, and affective groups in the former category and neurotic and personality groups in the latter. Mean HYP scores suggest a similar dichotomy with the interesting exception of schizophrenic individuals, who are classified toward the neurotic pole of the implied continuum.

In the analysis based on women, the largest contributor to discrimination along the first discriminant function was Authority Conflict. Inspection of group means for this scale indicated, as with the men, a separation of sociopathic and brain disorder groups from schizophrenic, neurotic, and personality groups. The affective psychotic group attained the lowest mean score on this scale. The Psychoticism scale was the second largest contributor to the first discriminant function. In women, high mean PSY scores were obtained for schizophrenic and sociopathic subjects, while lower mean scores characterized neurotic, brain disorder, affective psychotic, and personality groups. Poor Morale contributed additionally to the first discriminant function and had the largest coefficient on the second. High MOR scores were obtained for personality pattern, neurotic, and affective psychotic groups. Lower scores were obtained by personality trait, sociopathic, and brain disorder groups.

Depression and Hostility (which were significant contributors to the first and second discriminants for men) contributed, along with Authority Conflict, to the third discriminant function for women. Mean DEP scale scores for women form a continuum on which personality pattern, neurotic, and schizophrenic groups are high, while affective and brain disorder groups are low. On the Hostility scale, schizophrenic and personality groups were high, and brain disorder and affective psychotic groups were relatively low.

Any attempt to summarize the relative importance of the content scales in contributing to classification of psychiatric patients by multiple discriminant analysis must be restricted in generalization to the present samples. In addition to possible problems of sample specificity, the present analysis was restricted to six diagnostic groupings that, although not arbitrary, may not be the groupings desired in other hospital settings. Nevertheless, it seems important to note that Authority Conflict, Poor Morale, Hostility, Psychoticism, and Depression were important contributors to group discrimination, as were, to a lesser extent, Family Problems, Organicity, and Hypomania. Scales that contributed relatively little to the present analysis were Religious Fundamentalism, Social Maladjustment, Phobias, Poor Health, and Feminine Interests.

Discriminant Analysis Based on MMPI Clinical Scales

Multiple discriminant analysis were also performed using the 13 standard MMPI clinical scales as predictors of the six diagnostic groupings. Although not the primary concern of the present study, it was hoped that such analyses would provide a context of comparison for the analyses of content scales as well as insight into the utility of a multivariate approach to this most familiar diagnostic problem.

As before, the significance of Wilks's lambda was evaluated by the F approximation of Rao. In the male sample, $F = 1.62$, which for 65 and 954 df is significant at $p < .01$. For the women, $F = 1.49$, which for 65 and 750 df allows rejection of the null hypothesis at $p < .01$. As with the content scales, the hypothesis of no difference between mean vectors for the six groups can be confidently rejected. Again, from a practical standpoint the dimensionality of the predictor space might be reduced to three, since the first three discriminant functions account for 86% and 88% of the discriminating power of the scales in male and female samples, respectively.

In the male sample, the predominant contribution of *Sc* and *Pt* to group discrimination was observed to be operative in all but the fourth discriminant function. *Hy* and *K* contributed additionally to the first discriminant, while *Si* and *Pd* were of importance to the second. The contribution of *F* to group discrimination was apparent in the third and fourth discriminant. *Pa* was involved in the last three discriminants, and *Hs* contributed to the fourth. Clinical scales *L*, *D*, *Mf*, and *Ma* contributed relatively little to classification of the male sample.

The first discriminant function in the female sample was even more clearly dominated by *Sc* and *Pt*, the latter scale in this instance being the more heavily weighted. *Hy* contributed additionally to the second discriminant and, with *Pd*, to the third as well. The scales that contributed most to classification of the female sample were clearly *Pt*, *Sc*, *Hy*, and *Pd*. Lesser contributions came from *F*, *Hs*, *D*, *Ma*, and *K*. Scales *L*, *Mf*, and *Si* were of only minor importance.

FACTORIAL STRUCTURE OF CONTENT SCALES

Unlike the standard MMPI clinical scales, the MMPI content scales do not share common items and were constructed in such a way as to maximize the homogeneity of each scale. Nevertheless, the criterion employed for scale independence (in the correlational sense) during item analysis was quite minimal, and the number of separate substantive dimensions involved in this set of scales is certainly fewer than 13. It is of interest, therefore, to examine the nature of the factor structure underlying the content scales and to do so with reference to the manner in which this structure is manifest in diverse populations. The samples selected for such analysis were (1) 261 Air Force enlisted men, (2) 258 male psychiatric inpatients, and (3) 100 University of Illinois male students. Although sex (male) and geographical locale (Illinois) are shared characteristics, the samples are assumed to vary on a large number of other demographic characteristics.

Matrices of intercorrelations among the 13 content scales were factored by the method of principal components. Factors were retained whose latent roots were greater than one. Three factors met this criterion in each of the samples. The retained factors accounted for 69%, 71%, and 62% of the total scale variance in the Air Force, psychiatric, and college samples, respectively. The factor matrices were rotated to a varimax criterion. The rotated factor matrices for each of the three samples are presented in Table 7-12.

Factor I. The first factor in the Air Force sample is a large (53% of common variance) and general dimension of self-reported maladjustment that is substantially loaded by all but three of the MMPI content scales. Organic Symptoms, Phobias, Poor Health, and Depression are

Table 7-12 Rotated factor matrices of content scales in three male samples

	Chanute Air Force Base normal subjects ($N = 261$)				Kankakee psychiatric inpatients ($N = 258$)				Illinois college men ($N = 100$)			
	I	II	III	h^2	I	II	III	h^2	I	II	III	h^2
ORG	86	19	−05	79	87	19	12	80	28	35	62	59
PHO	83	16	10	73	68	27	36	67	63	09	39	56
HEA	78	19	06	64	80	14	08	66	22	45	56	57
DEP	76	47	22	85	66	63	08	84	75	38	26	78
PSY	74	48	00	77	46	68	33	78	43	59	44	72
MOR	67	46	32	77	57	67	13	79	78	36	11	76
FEM	58	−17	−22	41	20	05	75	61	−09	−17	71	54
SOC	57	03	50	57	59	16	−08	38	83	−06	−11	71
FAM	53	46	−12	50	26	73	−12	61	44	40	11	36
AUT	01	85	−05	73	03	83	05	69	30	78	06	69
HYP	11	82	13	71	19	84	23	80	27	67	20	56
HOS	41	77	−02	76	27	86	19	85	47	69	04	71
REL	−07	−01	85	73	−05	15	82	69	21	−66	04	48
Variance, %	53	33	14		37	45	18		40	39	21	

especially highly loaded on this factor in the psychiatric sample, as they are in the Air Force sample.

The maladjustment factor in the Air Force sample is highly loaded by categories of physical complaint but is clearly a general factor of psychological complaint as well. In the psychiatric sample, the factor is less general, hence the emphasis on physical complaint is more prominent. In the college sample this trend is reversed. Here the first factor is one that predominately emphasizes Social Maladjustment, Poor Morale, and Depression. The Phobias category is highly loaded on factor I, but those of Organic Symptoms and Poor Health are loaded on another factor (factor III). One of the factors underlying the relations among the content scales would thus appear to be a maladjustment or complaint factor. Its generality and relative emphasis on psychological, social, and somatic symptoms would seem to vary with the population studied, however.

Factor II. The second factor in the Air Force sample is primarily loaded by Authority Conflict, Hypomania, and Manifest Hostility. More moderate loadings are contributed by Psychoticism, Depression, Family Problems, and Poor Morale. In the psychiatric sample this factor is more prominent, emerging as the first factor in the analysis and accounting for 45% of the common variance. Again, the primary loadings are on Manifest Hostility, Hypomania, and Authority Conflict. Somewhat more substantial loadings occur on Family Conflict, Psychoticism, Poor Morale, and Depression than was the case in the Air Force sample. In the college sample this factor appears to be a slightly more general one which is distinguished by a substantial negative loading on Religious Fundamentalism. In all samples, the second factor underlying the relations among content scales is one emphasizing a cynical, distrustful, exploitive attitude toward life, hostility toward others, and restless, high-strung energy (Table 7-8). This aggressive orientation is accompanied by generally low morale and self-esteem and by indications of coming from a home with a similar orientation (FAM). In college students this orientation seems to include an element of atheism or, at least, deviation from fundamentalist religious convictions.

Factor III. In the Air Force sample the third factor is defined uniquely by Religious Fundamentalism with a secondary loading on Social Maladjustment. In the psychiatric sample, Religious Fundamentalism and

Feminine Interests define the factor. Feminine Interests defines the third factor in college males, but Religious Fundamentalism is noticeably *not* involved. Organic Symptoms and Health Concern emerge as scales not involved in the third factor for the Air Force or psychiatric samples. The three samples rather clearly differ with respect to the manner in which Religious Fundamentalism and Feminine Interests enter into the underlying factor structure. In the Air Force and college samples, Feminine Interests loads a factor characterized by both somatic and psychological complaint. In the psychiatric sample, however, Feminine Interests loads a factor primarily characterized by Religious Fundamentalism. Whereas Religious Fundamentalism defines a relatively distinct factor in the Air Force and psychiatric samples (i.e., factor III), this category is associated with the Hostility factor (factor II) in the college sample.

Interpretation of Factorial Dimensions underlying Content Scales

The preceding analyses suggested that the number of dimensions underlying the MMPI content scales is the same for quite different populations but that the specific structuring of these dimensions varies with the population studied. Although the meaning of the content scales is, to some extent, self-explanatory, there was little attempt to make substantive interpretations of the three factors in the different populations. Such interpretations will require, as a minimum, the employment of marker scales that will coordinate the present findings with the extensive empirical literature of the factorial structure of the MMPI. In addition to the statistical identification of factors, it will also be necessary to relate the apparent substantive nature of the factors identified to what is known about their *extratest* correlates. Such an analysis will first require a brief consideration of the considerable literature that exists on the factorial structure of the MMPI.

With the exception of certain factorially derived inventories such as Cattell's Sixteen Personality Factor Questionnaire (Cattell & Stice, 1962), the MMPI has been subjected to more factor-analytic investigations than any other test in widespread use. Although the MMPI is subject to considerable interpretative controversy, a rather remarkable agreement exists on the dimensionality of this instrument. When the intercorrelations of MMPI clinical scales are factored, two substantial factors emerge which account for the vast majority of common variance. These factors are consistently marked by Welsh's (1956) *A* and *R* respectively, which were developed for this purpose. Depending on the investigator's tolerance for percent of variance extracted, several additional smaller factors have been identified which appear more subject to variation, as a function of scales included and populations studied, than do the first two factors.

Early factorial studies of the MMPI tended to label the first factor "personality maladjustment" (Cook & Wherry, 1950), "psychotic maladjustment" (Cottle, 1950; Wheeler, Little, & Lehner, 1951), and "anxiety" (Eichman, 1962; Welsh, 1956). More recent studies tend to interpret both poles of the first factor and to relate it to a broader theoretical context such as "anxiety versus dynamic integration" (Karson & Pool, 1957, 1958), "ego weakness versus ego strength" (Kassebaum, Couch, & Slater, 1959), and "general complaint versus dynamic integration" (Gocka & Marks, 1961). In a similar fashion, interpretations of the second factor of the MMPI have changed from "overactivity and recklessness" (Cook & Wherry, 1950), "neurotic adjustment" (Cottle, 1950; Wheeler et al., 1951), and "repression" (Eichman, 1962; Welsh, 1956) to the broader category of "extraversion versus introversion" (Gocka & Marks, 1961; Karson & Pool, 1957, 1958; Kassebaum et al., 1959). Additional factors, beyond the first two, have been variously labeled "paranoia" (Cook & Wherry, 1950; Wheeler et al., 1951), "feminine interests" (Cook & Wherry, 1950; Cottle, 1950), "somatization" and "unconventionality" (Eichman, 1962), and "tender-minded sensitivity" (Gocka & Marks, 1961; Kassebaum et al., 1959).

During the last decade, the foregoing substantive interpretations of MMPI factors have been seriously challenged by an argumentative and prolific group of writers devoted to the demonstration of response styles and sets in the MMPI that are alleged to vitiate or, at best, severely limit the credibility of such substantive interpretations (Rorer, 1965). Edwards and his colleagues have steadfastly maintained that the first factor of the MMPI is best thought of as reflecting "social desirability" (Edwards, 1957, 1961, 1962; Edwards & Diers, 1962; Edwards, Diers, & Walker, 1962; Edwards & Heathers, 1962; Edwards & Walker, 1961; Edwards & Walsh, 1963). Others have maintained that such stylistic tendencies as "acquiescence" (Messick & Jackson, 1961) or the tendency to answer "deviantly true" (Barnes, 1956a, 1956b; Wiggins, 1962) are involved in the first factor as well. The second factor of the MMPI has been interpreted as reflecting acquiescence, most notably by Jackson and Messick (1958, 1961, 1962). A third stylistic factor was first identified by Edwards et al. (1962) and subsequently replicated by others (Edwards & Walsh, 1964; Liberty, Lunneborg, & Atkinson, 1964; Wiggins, 1964; Wiggins & Lovell, 1965). This factor has been referred to as a "lying" factor (Edwards et al., 1962; Liberty et al., 1964) and as a "social desirability role-playing" factor (Wiggins, 1964). Although this third factor appears to be somewhat of a "pure" response style factor which is not highly related to other sources of variance in the test, it is highly loaded by special scales which are themselves correlated with the tendency to modify answers to the test in a socially desirable direction under instructions to do so (Boe & Kogan, 1964; Cofer, Chance, & Judson, 1949; Hunt, 1962; Skrzypek & Wiggins, 1966; Walker, 1962; Wiggins, 1959).

The practical relevance or even existence of response styles in the MMPI has recently been called into question (Block, 1965; McGee, 1962; Rorer & Goldberg, 1965). The most effective defense of substantive interpretations of MMPI factors has been made by Block (1965), who not only challenged stylistic interpretations on logical and statistical grounds but provided empirical data that were, to him, demanding of substantive interpretation. To demonstrate that stylistic interpretations of the first two factors of the MMPI are not *sufficient*, Block developed what he considered a desirability-free measure of the first factor and an acquiescence-free measure of the second factor. To the extent that these two scales mark the factors involved, one must concede that something other than response styles is involved. More decisive, however, was Block's appeal to the long-overdue criterion of *external* evidence of substantive dimensions being measured by the first two factors. By the method of contrasted groups, Block obtained *Q*-sort descriptions by professional psychologists of high- and low-scoring subjects on the first two factors of the MMPI. These descriptions were obtained independently of the MMPI in five diverse samples of subjects under a variety of assessment circumstances. The constellation of *Q*-sort adjectives characterizing high- and low-scoring subjects on these factors led Block to conclude that the first factor of the MMPI measures "ego resiliency," while the second factor measures "ego control." Space limitations prohibit documentation of the full range of closely reasoned arguments that led Block to the foregoing conclusion. For present purposes, it will simply be noted that Block has convincingly demonstrated the *necessity* for substantive interpretations of these factors regardless of their degree of contamination with other sources of variance.

For reasons dictated by the availability of original protocols, a substantive interpretation of the factors underlying the MMPI content scales will here be attempted only in college populations. An attempt was made to align the three factors found in the small sample of Illinois college men (Table 7-12) with reference to the principal stylistic and substantive dimensions suggested by the recent factor-analytic literature of MMPI clinical scales. This alignment was accomplished in the considerably larger samples of Stanford men and women undergraduates.

Factor analysis of the intercorrelations of MMPI content scales in the sample of Illinois undergraduate men revealed three factors (Table 7-12). The first factor was loaded principally by Social Maladjustment, Poor Morale, and Depression. The second factor was loaded positively by Authority Conflict, Manifest Hostility, and Hypomania and negatively by Religious Fundamentalism. The third factor was loaded by Feminine Interests and by the Organic Symptoms and Poor Health scales.

Additional factor analyses were performed on samples of 250 men and 250 women from Stanford University. In addition to the 13 MMPI content scales, six marker variables were included to define the tradi-

Table 7-13 Rotated factor matrices of content scales plus six marker variables

	Stanford women ($N = 250$)						Stanford men ($N = 250$)					
	I	II	III	IV	V	h^2	I	II	III	IV	V	h^2
MOR	81	...	...	...	...	80	79	...	36	...	...	77
A	80	...	37	...	...	88	85	...	40	...	...	91
SOC	79	−36	...	...	...	81	62	−56	...	...	...	81
DEP	78	...	38	...	...	81	78	...	42	...	...	82
ER-S	−57	−42	−37	...	...	67	−69	...	−34	...	...	63
PHO	53	...	...	...	34	49	47	...	58	...	...	57
HOS	40	72	...	...	...	69	68	37	...	...	...	69
Cof	−40	...	...	75	...	79	−44	...	...	71	...	78
FAM	37	34	...	...	...	33	...	40	40	...	...	47
PSY	33	37	56	...	...	59	53	...	61	...	...	69
R	...	−83	...	...	...	74	−38	−72	...	...	...	78
HYP	...	70	...	...	...	66	52	58	...	...	...	71
EC-5	...	−70	...	40	...	80	...	−80	...	...	...	83
AUT	...	55	...	...	...	49	−8	33	34	...	−35	59
ORG	...	...	82	...	...	75	34	...	77	...	...	71
HEA	...	...	78	...	...	74	...	...	76	...	...	69
Sd	...	...	...	88	...	78	...	...	...	83	...	77
REL	...	...	...	72	...	58	...	...	...	75	...	62
FEM	...	...	...	...	85	74	...	...	...	...	87	80
Variance, %	50	18	15	9	8		36	17	22	16	9	

tional MMPI clinical scale space. Four of these markers are subject to stylistic interpretation, while the remaining two are not. Welsh's (1956) factor scales *A* and *R* were included as markers of the first two factors of conventional MMPI space. Wiggins's *Sd* (Wiggins, 1959) and the *Cof* of Cofer et al. (1949) were included to permit investigation of the possible convergence of the third content factor with the third stylistic dimension previously mentioned (Edwards et al., 1962). Block's (1965) *ER-S* and *EC-5* were included as desirability-free and acquiescence-free measures of the factors he describes as "ego resiliency" and "ego control," respectively. As before, the intercorrelation matrices were factored by the method of principal components, and factors with latent roots greater than unity were rotated analytically to a varimax criterion. The rotated factor matrices for samples of Stanford men and women are presented in Table 7-13. Factor loadings less than 0.33 have been omitted and the matrices have been arranged to facilitate comparison.

Whereas three factors were obtained from the analysis of content scales in the sample of Illinois men, five factors emerge when six marker scales are included. These five factors account for 69% and 72% of the total variance in the female and male samples, respectively. The first three factors are recognizable as the same obtained in the earlier analysis. The fourth factor is a "stylistic" factor determined by the inclusion of *Sd* and *Cof*. These stylistic scales have little in common with content scales other than Religious Fundamentalism, although this, in itself, is an intriguing finding. The present space is such that Feminine Interests emerges as a fifth quite specific factor distinct from factor II.

Factor I. Anxiety Proneness versus Ego Resiliency. The first factor in both samples is clearly and unambiguously marked by Welsh's *A*, which coordinates the first factor of content scales with the first factor obtained in all studies of clinical scales to date. Although scale *A* provides a statistical identification of the factor, it does not allow a choice between stylistic and substantive interpretations. Block's *ER-S*, which does not admit of stylistic interpretation, has a substantial, but not unique, loading on this factor in the present analyses. It will not be argued that the present factor is free of the contaminating influence of social desirability. However, the nature of the content scales that load this particular factor is of more than passing interest. Poor Morale, Social Maladjustment, and Depression have high loadings on the first factor in both groups. The item content of these scales (Table 7-8) suggests an individual lacking in self-confidence who is socially inhibited and given to feelings of guilt and apprehensiveness. An individual at the other end of the implied continuum would be characterized by self-confidence and optimism, social ascendance and poise, and a confident, resilient approach to the future. The item content of the scales that mark this factor is so close to the independent behavior descriptions obtained by Block (1965) for individuals with high and low scores on the same psychometric dimension that Block's suggested label of "ego resiliency" is here applied to the first factorial dimension of MMPI content scales.

Factor II. Impulsivity versus Control. The second factor is marked by Welsh's *R* and Block's *EC*-5, with *R* predominating in the sample of women and *EC*-5 marking the factor in the sample of men. Although *R* is highly subject to stylistic interpretation, *EC*-5 is not. In light of the recent criticisms directed at the interpretation of this dimension as "acquiescence" (Block, 1965; McGee, 1962; Rorer, 1965; Rorer & Goldberg, 1965), the burden of proof of the *utility* of such an interpretation is shifted to its proponents. More germane to the present analyses is the nature of the content scales that load this factor. Hypomania has high loadings on the second factor in both samples. The items that constitute this scale emphasize excitement, restlessness, hotheadedness and overcommitment. Such items are suggestive of impulsivity or lack of control at one pole of the dimension and control, or possibly, overcontrol at the other. Manifest Hostility and Authority Conflict have high loadings on this factor in the female sample. The items in these scales reflect the free expression of aggressiveness and the cynical, distrustful attitude that everyone should get away with what he can. Such items are seen as consistent with the lack of impulse control suggested by the Hypomania scale. In the male sample, Manifest Hostility and Authority Conflict have smaller loadings, while Social Maladjustment and Family Problems contribute more. Again, the constellation of content scales marking the second factor is highly similar to the independent behavior descriptions obtained by Block (1965) for this dimension which caused him to label the factor a "control" dimension. It is also of interest to note that Block (1965) has argued that the control dimension is expressed differently in men and women, which also appears to be the case in the present analyses.

Factor III. Health Concern. In both samples, the third factor is characterized by high loadings on Organic Symptoms and Poor Health. The relationship between these two scales is rather obvious and would seem to warrant the general label of "health concern" for the factor. In college populations, at least, there appears to be an underlying factor of concern with health that includes both the headaches, dizziness, etc., from the Organic Symptoms content scale and the gastrointestinal complaints from the Poor Health content scale. Lacking the independent behavior descriptions that were available for the first two factors and lacking a factor marker that would relate the present dimension to previous ones, it seems best to view this factor as one involving "reported poor health." Considering the large number of items in the MMPI pool that relate to health, it is not surprising that such a factor should emerge. A "poor physical health" factor has emerged from factor analysis of items from several of the standard MMPI clinical scales (Comrey, 1957a, 1957b, 1957c, 1958c; Comrey & Marggraff, 1958). Factor analysis of groups of MMPI scales has also yielded a "somatization" factor (Eichman, 1961; Fisher, 1964).

Factor IV. Social Desirability Role Playing. This factor was rather clearly determined by the inclusion of the stylistic role-playing scales which define it: Wiggins's (1959) *Sd* and the *Cof* of Cofer et al. (1949). As previously indicated, a considerable number of studies attest to the behavioral correlates of these scales, namely, the tendency to modify answers to the MMPI in a socially desirable direction when instructed to do so. The content scale of Religious Fundamentalism has a high and unique loading on this factor in both samples. The most conservative interpretation of this finding would be that the items in the Religious Fundamentalism scale are those which are most subject to change under conditions which encourage faking. However, in view of the fact that the Marlowe-Crowne Social Desirability Scale (Crowne & Marlowe, 1960) is known to load this factor (Edwards et al., 1962; Edwards & Walsh, 1964; Liberty et al., 1964), a further inference seems justified. On the basis of the extensive documentation of the correlates of the Marlowe-Crowne scale (Crowne & Marlowe, 1964) that is known to load this factor, it seems likely that, in these college samples, individuals who describe themselves as religious, churchgoing people may be operating under a strong motive to gain social approval (Crowne & Marlowe, 1964). Such a phenomenon may be quite specific to these particular samples, however.

Factor V. Feminine Interests. When the present set of marker scales are included in the factor analysis of MMPI content scales, Feminine Interests emerges as a specific factor. In the earlier factor analyses of content scales in several male samples (Table 7-12), the Feminine Interests scale was seen to vary from sample to sample in its factorial contribution. Such a factor is reminiscent of the "feminine interests" factor which has been reported from time to time in the literature (Cook & Wherry, 1950; Cottle, 1950; Kassebaum et al., 1959; Wheeler et al., 1951) and which has exhibited considerable fluctuation from sample to sample. Interpretation of this factor must be restricted to the content of the items in the Feminine Interests scale (Table 7-8) since its non-MMPI correlates have not been investigated.

In summary, when the factorial dimensions of the MMPI content scales were aligned with previously reported dimensions of MMPI clinical scales, considerable convergence was evident. In a college population, the first two factors were clearly marked by Welsh's (1956) A and R which permitted their identification as the first two factors of previously reported studies. Although the possible contaminating effect of "social desirability" could not be ruled out, the first factor was interpreted as reflecting "anxiety-proneness versus ego resiliency." The second factor was interpreted as "impulsivity versus control" with less concern for the possible alternative interpretation of "acquiescence." The third factor appeared to reflect "health concern" as judged from the item content of the scales that loaded it. A relatively specific factor of "feminine interests" was identified, although its generality across populations was questioned. The possibility that high scores on the Religious Fundamentalism content scale may be associated with high approval motivation (Crowne & Marlowe, 1964) was also raised.

Implications for Clinical Interpretation of the MMPI

In several of the analyses previously presented, the MMPI clinical scales were used as a base line or frame of reference for comparison with the content scales. These comparisons involved such issues as internal consistency, group differences, and differential diagnosis. Although the clinical and content scales were found to be similar in many respects, they should not be viewed as equivalent from the standpoint of clinical application. This point is best illustrated by use of an artificially constructed profile of MMPI clinical scale scores. Such a profile is presented in Figure 7-1.

The profile in Figure 7-1 bears a resemblance to that of "John Doe" presented by Shneidman (1951). Shneidman's patient was a twenty-five-year-old single male whose primary diagnosis was that of anxiety reaction but for whom there were indications (especially in the MMPI) of an incipient schizophrenic reaction. The hypothetical profile

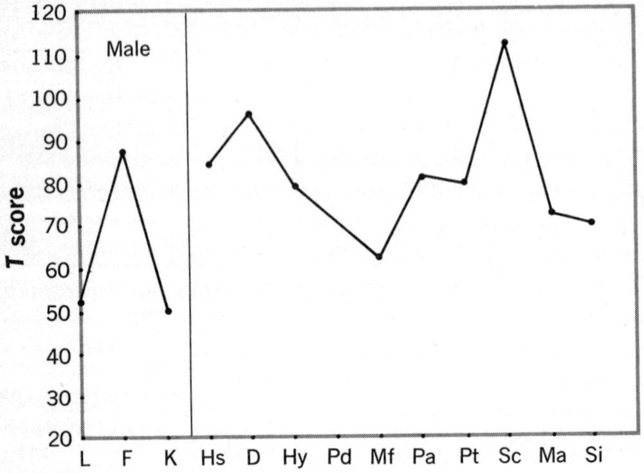

Figure 7–1 Profile of hypothetical patient on standard MMPI scales.

in Figure 7-1 differs from John Doe's principally in *Pt*, which is lower, and in *Mf* and *Sc* (also lower) plus a slightly higher *F*. Configurally, the hypothetical profile resembles that of a twenty-one-year-old single male reported in the *MMPI Atlas* (Hathaway & Meehl, 1951). The diagnosis for this patient was reactive depression with a lingering doubt concerning organic pathology. The overall elevation of the profile reported in the *Atlas* was much less than that of the hypothetical profile. The hypothetical profile is not easily classified within Marks and Seeman's (1963) system, although this is, by itself, no indictment of its typicalness (Huff, 1965). All the promising diagnostic signs employed by Goldberg (1965) classify this profile as "psychotic." Perhaps the best appeal is to "clinical experience" which for many will verify the plausibility of encountering in a hospital setting a profile such as that represented in Figure 7-1.

The profile in Figure 7-1 may be used to illustrate the manner in which content scales may supplement interpretation of standard MMPI profiles. Starting with two identical 566-item protocols, each of which yielded the clinical scale profile in Figure 7-1, content scale scores were varied under the restriction that clinical scale scores remain the same. This was done to illustrate the point that the same profile of clinical scale scores can be obtained in two protocols that differ markedly from each other in their content scale scores. Table 7-14 presents the raw content scale scores for two hypothetical patients (patient A and patient B), each of whom produces the identical MMPI clinical profile illustrated in Figure 7-1.

Table 7-14 Raw scores on content scales for two hypothetical patients with identical clinical scale profiles

Content scale	Patient A	Patient B	Difference
ORG	28	5	+23
PSY	8	21	−13
HEA	7	20	−13
FEM	6	17	−11
FAM	11	6	+5
DEP	15	19	−4
HYP	8	12	−4
PHO	13	9	+4
SOC	10	13	−3
HOS	9	12	−3
AUT	13	11	+2
REL	7	9	−2
MOR	12	11	+1

Patient A has admitted to a large number of symptoms thought to be indicative of organic pathology. Additionally, he admits having family problems and a number of fears. In contrast, patient B admits to a large number of psychotic symptoms of a primarily paranoid nature. He is greatly concerned about his health and admits to liking an unusual number of feminine pursuits. By comparison with patient A, patient B is generally more deviant with respect to content categories reflecting poor morale, mood instability, social maladjustment, and hostility.

The configuration of content scale scores of patient B readily confirms the impression of psychopathology gained from an inspection of the clinical profile in Figure 7-1. This could be the profile of a paranoid schizophrenic with an underlying homosexual component and a body concern that is delusional in nature. Poor morale, social maladjustment, and hostility are, of course, compatible with this picture.

Although patient A's raw content scale scores are sufficiently deviant to be considered those of a hospitalized patient, they are in sharp contrast to those of patient B. By comparison, patient A is almost exclusively concerned with organic symptoms and, to a lesser extent, family problems. Evidence of delusional thinking, health concern, feminine interests, and general maladjustment is comparatively weak for patient A. The clinical scale profile in Figure 7-1 may now be viewed in a quite different light.

The present example does *not* imply that the long-awaited method of differentiating schizophrenic from brain disorder patients has been discovered within the MMPI. It is meant to imply that a given clinical scale profile may be viewed in quite different perspective as a function of variation in the underlying content components which determine profile elevation. The interpretative significance of content scale configurations cannot be taken at face value, and a great deal more research and experience with these scales must precede any recommendations for clinical application. Curiosity concerning the nature of patients' communications to us would seem to be a healthy interest, however, and some may prefer to adopt the MMPI content scales as the most promising procedure for satisfying this interest. It is hoped that such interim applications will be strictly supplemental to the tried and, occasionally, true procedure for clinical scale interpretation.

SUBSTANTIVE HOMOGENEITY OF CLINICAL SCALE PROFILES

The preceding example provided a dramatic demonstration of the extent of discrepancy that might exist between the implications of a given clinical scale profile and the actual content of a patient's communication to an institution. This particular example should not be accepted uncritically, however, as has been noted by Tellegen (1966).[7] Tellegen contends that configural interpretations of MMPI clinical profiles often represent an attempt to describe the substantive nature of patients' communications. For example, a high *Hy* combined with a relatively low *Hs* would suggest that the *Hy* score was not primarily determined by response to somatic content. The issue, as Tellegen (1966) sees it, is not whether a given clinical profile *could* reflect different content patterns but whether configurally classified clinical profile types *do* show wide variability in their underlying content. The implication here is that, given the factorial constraints of the MMPI item pool, profiles belonging to the same narrowly defined configural type would not vary widely on additional scales not employed in this type classification. Hence, two profiles classified as similar by the practicing clinician would tend to reflect similar patient communications.

Tellegen's question has the merit of being an empirical one, and a first step toward providing a definitive answer has been taken by Payne (1968). The principal hypothesis of Payne's study was that increases in the substantive homogeneity of clinical profile types would

[7] Auke Tellegen read an earlier version of the present chapter and provided critical comments that inspired the research reported in this section.

occur with increases in the configurality (specificity) of the rules for forming profile groupings. Recent admissions were added to the inpatient psychiatric sample employed in the present study (Table 7-11) to make a grand total of 566 patients. Raw clinical scale scores were obtained and transformed to K-corrected T scores for purposes of profile analysis. These 566 patients were then classified under eight different systems of profile classification which ranged from very simple to highly complex in terms of the number and type of rules employed for assignment. This continuum of complexity of profile classification is represented in the first column of Table 7-15.

From Table 7-15 it can be seen that the lowest order of complexity of profile classification involved the assignment of patients to one of eight groups on the basis of their single highest clinical scale score (*Mf* and *Si* were not included). The second level of complexity of classification involved the assignment of patients to one of eight groups on the basis of their single highest clinical scale score that exceeded a T score of 70. Only 68% of the sample could be classified under this system, since there were a number of profiles that did not have a clinical scale above 70. Next, the patients were classified in terms of their two highest clinical scale scores, their two highest scales above 70, their three highest scale scores, and their three highest scale scores above 70. The latter classification system allowed for classification of only 29% of the sample. Finally, the highly configural cookbook (see Chapter 3) classification systems of Gilberstadt and Duker (1965)

Table 7-15 Multivariate analyses of variance of 13 content scales under clinical profile classification systems varying in complexity

Classification system	(1) Total *Ss*	(2) % classified	(3) Number employed	(4) Number of groups	(5) Wilks's lambda	(6) $\frac{\lambda}{1+\lambda}$	(7) variance, %
Singles	556	100	556	8	.279	.39	41
Singles>70	556	68	381	8	.204	.47	44
Doubles	556	100	517	19	.115	.51	37
Doubles>70	556	44	197	11	.083	.62	46
Triples	556	100	462	23	.078	.58	41
Triples>70	556	32	113	9	.060	.64	45
Gilberstadt-Duker	541	29	137	6	.050	.84	76
Marks-Seeman	541	27	122	4	.072	.85	86

and Marks and Seeman (1963) were employed in the classification of clinical profiles. The cookbook systems resulted in the classification of only slightly more than one-quarter of the present sample.[8] Nevertheless, these systems are probably the best representatives of the manner in which profiles are actually interpreted in clinical practice.

The next step in Payne's (1968) analysis involved discarding profile groupings that contained too few members to permit a reliable estimate of within-group variance. Columns 3 and 4 of Table 7-15 indicate the total number of patients retained in each classification system and the number of groups that were formed within each system. Only four groups met this criterion within the Marks-Seeman system, and the vast majority of these patients fell within the heterogeneous K^{+} categorization. Although this was a somewhat unfortunate distribution within a classification system, it should be noted that it tended to operate against the principal hypothesis.

It is now possible to state Tellegen's (1966) hypothesis more precisely in relation to the design of Payne's (1968) study. Given a number of clinical scale classification systems that vary in complexity, the between-group–within-group variance ratio of *content scale scores* should increase as the complexity of classification increases. Considering the extreme case, there should be much greater within-group homogeneity of content scale scores in the four Marks-Seeman groups than is found in the single scale groups. This would mean that patients classified as falling within one of the highly configural Marks-Seeman categories are saying more similar things about themselves on the content scales than patients classified as falling within one of the less specific single scale categories.

For each of the eight classification systems employed by Payne (1968), there were 13 dependent variables (content scales) and several treatments (clinical profile groups). As such, it was possible to perform a one-way, or simple, multivariate analysis of variance for each of the separate classification systems. In the one-way case, a multivariate analysis of variance is equivalent to a multiple discriminant analysis. Thus, for each classification system it was possible to test the generalized, multivariate null hypothesis that the mean vectors for the 13 content scales were the same in all the profile groups within that classification system. As in the earlier discriminant

[8] Payne (1967) also found that relaxing any one rule (other than the important first rule) allowed for classification of 57% and 47% of cases in the two systems. Relaxing two rules (other than the first one) allowed for 59% classification in both systems. Further relaxation of rules did not appear to be profitable.

analysis, this hypothesis was evaluated by Wilks's lambda which is given in column 5 of Table 7-15. Since lambda expresses the ratio of within-group to total group cross-product deviation scores, values become smaller as between-group variance increases. In testing the significance of lambda by Rao's F approximation, the multivariate null hypothesis was confidently rejected ($p < .001$) for *all* eight classification systems. Since the degrees of freedom for groups and subjects varied widely between classification systems, it was difficult to perform a direct comparison of these eight significance tests. Consequently, other criteria were considered.

Several criteria have been proposed for evaluating the significance of the results of a multivariate analysis of variance (Jones, 1966), one of which emphasizes the properties of the largest root (Roy, 1953). The last two columns of Table 7-15 present the largest root [expressed as $\lambda/(1 + \lambda)$] and the percentage of variance accounted for by this root for each of the eight multivariate analyses. No attempt was made to correct for the varying degrees of freedom in the different analyses, and these statistics must be considered descriptive rather than inferential. Nevertheless, it seems clear from inspection of Table 7-15 that, regardless of the statistical criterion employed, there was a clear-cut tendency for an increase in substantive homogeneity to be associated with an increase in the specificity of rules for profile groupings. At the very least, it may be concluded that the highly configural cookbook systems generate profile groupings which possess greater homogeneity of self-report than groups classified by simple high-point scale rules. Application of more analytic techniques of statistical inference is unlikely to contradict such an assertion.

The results of Payne's study suggest that certain classifications of clinical profiles into narrowly defined groups tend to ensure homogeneity of self-report within these groups. Such a result is, to some extent, psychometrically determined, although empirical exceptions are quite possible. It would be premature to view this finding as evidence for a rapprochement between conventional and substantive interpretations of the MMPI. First, it would have to be established that clinicians actually classify profiles in a manner similar to that used in the more configural systems of Payne's study. Since there is reason to be skeptical about the manner in which clinicians *actually* utilize profile information (Hoffman, 1960), it would be more realistic to restrict the range of inquiry to those clinicians who employ cookbook systems of the Gilberstadt-Duker and Marks-Seeman variety. Here we might compare the nature of interpretations generated from empirical (cookbook) and substantive (content) bases. Careful scrutiny of both convergent and discrepant interpretations would enhance our knowledge of the dynamics of verbal behavior that are operative in assessment by personality inventories.

DISCUSSION

To encourage further investigation of the empirical properties of the content scales is to imply that they possess advantages over the currently employed clinical scales. Since such a position is taken by the present investigator, it seems appropriate to review these claimed advantages and to discuss their relevance for both clinical and research applications of the MMPI.

Viewed from the convenient hindsight of 25 years, the MMPI appears to have been poorly conceived for the purposes it was eventually to serve. The Kraepelinian categories to which it was committed were soon to pass into disfavor. Moreover, the predictive success of the individual scales in making such psychiatric categorizations was considerably less than had been anticipated. Under the impetus of an unprecedented amount of research, there was a shift of emphasis from the psychiatric to the personological implications of the clinical scales, and the application of the scales was extended far beyond the original context of personnel decisions.

The MMPI clinical scales are poorly equipped to serve as personality trait scales for several reasons. Several of the scales lack the internal consistency that is usually taken as evidence of an organized pattern of behavior. Also, an interpretative ambiguity exists with respect to the meaning and significance of low scores on the scales, since "normal" subjects rarely achieve a score of zero (Wiggins, 1962). Indeed, the hodgepodge of content that contributes to a high score on a given clinical scale is not suggestive of any consistent personality trait or structure. The fact that this makes the inventory difficult to fake would seem, at best, a mixed blessing. Given the substantive heterogeneity of the clinical scales, a configural "pattern" may be achieved in a wide variety of ways, and it seems cavalier to apply standard "blind" interpretations to such patterns, as is done in clinical practice. Finally, a minor but irritating characteristic of the scales is the extensive degree of item overlap that exists among them (Adams & Horn, 1965; Shure & Rogers, 1965).

It seems likely that the MMPI item pool, which was once considered so rich and untapped, may be too limited as a source of items for building general purpose personality scales (Wiggins & Goldberg, 1965). This may be true with respect to both content and item characteristics and is certainly true of the extent to which the two are confounded. Nevertheless, in the absence of any immediate replacement, it would seem unwise to abandon an inventory that has the empirical virtues, however limited, of the MMPI. Rather, it would seem appropriate to explore the utility of supplemental measures that are not encumbered by all the substantive and psychometric shortcomings of the clinical scales.

The MMPI content scales possess a respectable degree of internal consistency. This internal consistency must, in part, be attributed to homogeneous organization of psychological, physical, and social complaints that seem appropriately combined by a cumulative scoring model (Loevinger, 1957). Although no claim is made for scale unidimensionality or Guttman-type item properties, each scale has a compelling, though prosaic, feature. Subjects who achieve high scores on the scales do so by admitting to, or claiming, an unusual amount of the substantive dimension involved. Subjects who achieve low scores claim a small amount and, by so doing, may or may not be similar to certain abnormal groups. But subjects who say they are hostile are saying just that and not that they have organic symptoms or strong religious convictions. A return to this type of Woodworthian simplicity has been long overdue.

The present study was able to provide only very limited evidence bearing on the effectiveness of the content scales in discriminating among traditional psychiatric groups. However, the preliminary evidence obtained was not discouraging in this respect. Although the burden of proof is clearly on the content scales, the superiority of scales derived by a contrasted groups strategy need not be conceded a priori when populations other than the derivation samples are involved (Hase & Goldberg, 1967).

Although apparently heterogeneous in content, covariation among content scales may be reduced to three underlying factors. The first two of these factors were found to be colinear with the first two factors consistently found in analyses of the MMPI clinical scales. This result is not surprising within the domain of MMPI items and may even reflect an upper limit on the number of parsimoniously interpretable factors within the conventionally defined questionnaire realm (Peterson, 1965). However, the content scales tend to clarify the specific manner in which the ubiquitous two factors of personality questionnaires manifest themselves within the MMPI item pool. The item content of the scales that mark these two factors lends itself readily to the substantive interpretations placed upon these dimensions by Block (1965). This is especially important when it is recognized that Block's interpretations were buttressed by independently obtained empirical evidence.

Coming from the same item pool, the content scales are no less free than the clinical scales of confounding item characteristics that lend themselves to stylistic interpretations. The tenor of recent critical thinking on this issue suggests, however, that the burden of proof of the utility of stylistic interpretations has been shifted to the proponents of such styles. In any event, *what* is being confounded by item characteristics in the case of the content scales seems clearer. Future studies of item characteristics would do well to examine their effects on substantive dimensions rather than on the poorly understood dimensions yielded by the scale construction strategy of contrasted groups. Such research would naturally be facilitated by scales composed of nonoverlapping items.

The case for further investigation of substantive aspects of the MMPI may best be presented by calling attention to a basic feature of assessment situations that has tended to be ignored or belittled by sophistic arguments. Regardless of psychologists' views of a test response, the respondent tends to view the testing situation as an opportunity for *communication* between himself and the tester or institution he represents (Carson, 1969; Leary, 1957). Obviously, the respondent has some control over what he chooses to communicate, and there are a variety of other factors which may enter to distort the message, many of them attributable to the testing media themselves (Cattell, 1961; LaForge, 1963). Nevertheless, recognition of such sources of "noise" in the system should not lead us to overlook the fact that a message is still involved. The MMPI content scales may be closely attuned to this message and, as such, may provide a useful supplement to the standard clinical scales.

REFERENCES

Adams, D. K., and Horn, J. L. Nonoverlapping keys for the MMPI scales. *Journal of Consulting Psychology*, 1965, **29**, 284.

Adorno, T. W., Frenkel-Brunswik, E., Levinson, D. J., and Sanford, R. N. *The authoritarian personality*. New York: Harper, 1950.

American Psychiatric Association. *Diagnostic and statistical manual: Mental disorders*. Washington, D.C.: APA Mental Hospital Service, 1952.

American Psychological Association. Technical recommendations for psychological tests and diagnostic techniques. *Psychological Bulletin Supplement*, 1954, No. 2, Pt. 2.

Barnes, E. H. Factors, response bias and the MMPI. *Journal of Consulting Psychology,* 1956, **20,** 419–421. (a)

Barnes, E. H. Response bias and the MMPI. *Journal of Consulting Psychology,* 1956, **20**, 371–374. (b)

Berg, I. A. Response bias and personality: The deviation hypotheses. *Journal of Psychology,* 1955, **40,** 61–72.

Berg, I. A. The unimportance of test item content. In B. M. Bass and I. A. Berg (Eds.), *Objective approaches to personality assessment.* Princeton: Van Nostrand, 1959.

Berg, I. A. Measuring deviant behavior by means of deviant response sets. In I. A. Berg and B. M. Bass (Eds.), *Conformity and deviation.* New York: Harper, 1961.

Block, J. *The challenge of response sets.* New York: Appleton-Century-Crofts, 1965.

Boe, E. E., and Kogan, W. S. Effect of social desirability instructions on several MMPI measures of social desirability. *Journal of Consulting Psychology,* 1964, **28,** 248–251.

Braaten, D. Kooky personality test. *The Washington Star,* June 8, 1965.

Brayfield, A. H. (Ed.), Special issue: Testing and public policy. *American Psychologist,* 1965, **20,** 857–1002.

Butcher, J. N., and Tellegen, A. Objections to MMPI items. *Journal of Consulting Psychology,* 1966, **30,** 527–534.

Carson, R. C. Issues in the teaching of clinical MMPI interpretation. In J. N. Butcher (Ed.), *MMPI: Research developments and clinical applications.* New York: McGraw-Hill, 1969.

Cattell, R. B. Theory of situational, instrument, second order, and refraction factors in personality structure research. *Psychological Bulletin,* 1961, **58,** 160–174.

Cattell, R. B., and Stice, G. F. *The sixteen personality factor questionnaire.* (3rd ed.) Champaign, Ill.: Institute for Personality and Ability Testing, 1962.

Cofer, C. N., Chance, J., and Judson, A. J. A study of malingering on the MMPI. *Journal of Psychology,* 1949, **27,** 491–499.

Comrey, A. L. A factor analysis of items on the MMPI depression scale. *Educational and Psychological Measurement,* 1957, **17,** 578–585. (a)

Comrey, A. L. A factor analysis of items on the MMPI hypochondriasis scale. *Educational and Psychological Measurement,* 1957, **17,** 568–577. (b)

Comrey, A. L. A factor analysis of items on the MMPI hysteria scale. *Educational and Psychological Measurement,* 1957, **17,** 586–592. (c)

Comrey, A. L. A factor analysis of items on the MMPI hypomania scale. *Educational and Psychological Measurement,* 1958, **18,** 313–323. (a)

Comrey, A. L. A factor analysis of items on the MMPI paranoia scale. *Educational and Psychological Measurement,* 1958, **18,** 99–107. (b)

Comrey, A. L. A factor analysis of items on the MMPI psychasthenia scale. *Educational and Psychological Measurement,* 1958, **18,** 293–300. (c)

Comrey, A. L. A factor analysis of items on the MMPI psychopathic deviate scale. *Educational and Psychological Measurement,* 1958, **18,** 91–98. (d)

Comrey, A. L., and Marggraff, W. M. A factor analysis of items on the MMPI schizophrenia scale. *Educational and Psychological Measurement,* 1958, **18,** 301–311.

Cook, E. B., and Wherry, R. J. A factor analysis of MMPI and aptitude test data. *Journal of Applied Psychology,* 1950, **34,** 260–266.

Cooley, W. W., and Lohnes, P. R. *Multivariate procedures for the behavioral sciences.* New York: Wiley, 1962.

Cottle, W. C. A factorial study of the Multiphasic, Kuder, and Bell inventories using a population of adult males. *Psychometrika,* 1950, **15,** 25–47.

Cronbach, L. J. Coefficient alpha and the internal structure of tests. *Psychometrika,* 1951, **16,** 297–334.

Crowne, D. P., and Marlowe, D. A new scale of social desirability independent of psychopathology. *Journal of Consulting Psychology,* 1960, **24,** 349–354.

Crowne, D. P., and Marlowe, D. *The approval motive.* New York: Wiley, 1964.

Dahlstrom, W. G., and Welsh, G. S. *An MMPI handbook: A guide to use in clinical practice and research.* Minneapolis: University of Minnesota Press, 1960.

Dicken, C. Content and acquiescence in the MMPI. Unpublished manuscript, San Diego State College, 1967.

Drake, L. E. Differential sex responses to items of the MMPI. *Journal of Applied Psychology,* 1953, **37,** 46.

Edwards, A. L. *The social desirability variable in personality assessment and research.* New York: Dryden Press, 1957.

Edwards, A. L. Social desirability or acquiescence in the MMPI? A case study with the *SD* scale. *Journal of Abnormal and Social Psychology,* 1961, **63,** 351–359.

Edwards, A. L. Social desirability and expected means of MMPI scales. *Educational and Psychological Measurement,* 1962, **22,** 71–76.

Edwards, A. L., and Diers, C. J. Social desirability and the factorial interpretation of the MMPI. *Educational and Psychological Measurement,* 1962, **22,** 501–509.

Edwards, A. L., Diers, C. J., and Walker, J. N. Response sets and factor loadings on sixty-one personality scales. *Journal of Applied Psychology,* 1962, **46,** 220–225.

Edwards, A. L., and Heathers, L. B. The first factor of the MMPI: Social desirability or ego strength? *Journal of Consulting Psychology,* 1962, **26,** 99–100.

Edwards, A. L., and Walker, J. N. Social desirability and agreement response set. *Journal of Abnormal and Social Psychology,* 1961, **62,** 180–183.

Edwards, A. L., and Walsh, J. A. The relationship between the intensity of the social desirability keying of a scale and the correlation of the scale with Edwards' *SD* scale and the first factor loading of the scale. *Journal of Clinical Psychology,* 1963, **19,** 200–203.

Edwards, A. L., and Walsh, J. A. Response sets in standard and experimental personality scales. *American Educational Research Journal,* 1964, **1,** 52–61.

Eichman, W. J. Replicated factors on the MMPI with female NP patients. *Journal of Consulting Psychology,* 1961, **25,** 55–60.

Eichman, W. J. Factored scales for the MMPI. *Journal of Clinical Psychology,* 1962, **15** (Monogr. Suppl.), 363–395.

Fisher, J. Some MMPI dimensions of physical and psychological illness. *Journal of Clinical Psychology,* 1964, **20,** 369–375.

Gilberstadt, H., and Duker, J. *A handbook for clinical and actuarial MMPI interpretation.* Philadelphia: Saunders, 1965.

Gilliland, A. R., and Colgin, R. Norms, reliability, and forms of the MMPI. *Journal of Consulting Psychology,* 1951, **15,** 435–438.

Gocka, E. F., and Marks, J. B. Second-order factors in the 16 PF and MMPI inventory. *Journal of Clinical Psychology,* 1961, **17,** 32–35.

Goldberg, L. R. Diagnosticians vs. diagnostic signs: The diagnosis of psychosis vs. neurosis from the MMPI. *Psychological Monographs,* 1965, **79** (12, Whole No. 602).

Gordon, J. E. A communication: Snooping and testing. *The New Republic,* Jan. 9, 1965, 28–30.

Gough, H. G. Theory and measurement of socialization. *Journal of Consulting Psychology,* 1960, **24,** 23–30.

Harman, H. *Modern factor analysis.* Chicago: University of Chicago Press, 1960.

Harris, R. E., and Lingoes, J. C. Subscales for the MMPI: An aid to profile interpretation. Unpublished manuscript, The Langley Porter Neuropsychiatric Institute, San Francisco, 1955.

Hase, H. D., and Goldberg, L. R. The comparative validity of different strategies of deriving personality inventory scales. Unpublished paper, Oregon Research Institute, Eugene, 1967.

Hathaway, S. R., and McKinley, J. C. A multiphasic personality schedule (Minnesota): I. Construction of the schedule. *Journal of Psychology,* 1940, **10,** 249–254.

Hathaway, S. R., and McKinley, J. C. *The Minnesota Multiphasic Personality Inventory manual.* (Rev. ed.) New York: The Psychological Corporation, 1951.

Hathaway, S. R., and Meehl, P. E. *An atlas for the clinical use of the MMPI.* Minneapolis: University of Minnesota Press, 1951.

Hoffman, P. J. The paramorphic representation of clinical judgment. *Psychological Bulletin,* 1960, **57,** 116–131.

Huff, F. W. Use of actuarial description of abnormal personality in a mental hospital. *Psychological Reports,* 1965, **17,** 224.

Hunt, D. E. Personality patterns in adolescent boys. Progress Report No. 7, 1962, Syracuse University, PHS Grant M-3517.

Jackson, D. N., and Messick, S. Content and style in personality assessment. *Psychological Bulletin,* 1958, **55,** 243–252.

Jackson, D. N., and Messick, S. Acquiescence and desirability as response determinants on the MMPI. *Educational and Psychological Measurement,* 1961, **21,** 771–790.

Jackson, D. N., and Messick, S. Response styles and the assessment of psychopathology. In S. Messick and J. Ross (Eds.), *Measurement in personality and cognition.* New York: Wiley, 1962, pp. 129–155.

Jones, L. V. Analysis of variance in its multivariate development. In R. B. Cattell (Ed.), *Handbook of multivariate experimental psychology.* Chicago: Rand McNally, 1966, pp. 244–266.

Kaiser, H. F. The varimax criterion for analytic rotation in factor analysis. *Psychometrika,* 1958, **23,** 187–200.

Karson, S., and Pool, K. B. The construct validity of the Sixteen Personality Factors Test. *Journal of Clinical Psychology,* 1957, **13,** 245–252.

Karson, S., and Pool, K. B. Second-order factors in personality measurement. *Journal of Consulting Psychology,* 1958, **22,** 299–303.

Kassebaum, G. G., Couch, A. S., and Slater, P. E. The factorial dimensions of the MMPI. *Journal of Consulting Psychology,* 1959, **23,** 226–236.

LaForge, R. Interpersonal domains or interpersonal levels? A validation of Leary's "MMPI Level 1 indices." Paper presented at the meetings of the Western Psychological Association, Santa Monica, Calif., April, 1963.

Leary, T. *Interpersonal diagnosis of personality.* New York: Ronald Press, 1957.

Liberty, P. G., Jr., Lunneborg, C. E., and Atkinson, G. C. Perceptual defense, dissimulation and response styles. *Journal of Consulting Psychology,* 1964, **28,** 529–537.

Lingoes, J. C. MMPI factors of the Harris and the Wiener subscales. *Journal of Consulting Psychology,* 1960, **24,** 74–83.

Loevinger, J. Objective tests as instruments of psychological theory. *Psychological Reports Monograph,* 1957, **3,** 635–694.

Loevinger, J. Measuring personality patterns of women. *Genetic Psychology Monographs,* 1962, **65,** 35–136.

Marks, P. A., and Seeman, W. *The actuarial description of abnormal personality: An atlas for use with the MMPI.* Baltimore: Williams & Wilkins, 1963.

McGee, R. K. Response style as a personality variable: By what criterion? *Psychological Bulletin,* 1962, **59,** 284–295.

Meehl, P. E. The dynamics of "structured" personality tests. *Journal of Clinical Psychology,* 1945, **1,** 296–303.
Mees, H. L. Preliminary steps in the construction of factor scales for the MMPI. Unpublished manuscript, University of Washington, 1959.
Messick, S., and Jackson, D. N. Acquiescence and the factorial interpretation of the MMPI. *Psychological Bulletin,* 1961, **58,** 299–304.
Norman, W. T. Relative importance of test item content. *Journal of Consulting Psychology,* 1963, **27,** 166–174.
Payne, F. The substantive homogeneity of MMPI clinical profile classification systems. Unpublished master's dissertation, University of Illinois, 1968.
Peterson, D. R. The scope, generality and meaning of verbally defined "personality" factors. *Psychological Review,* 1965, **72,** 48–59.
Rokeach, M. *The open and closed mind.* New York: Basic Books, 1960.
Rorer, L. G. The great response-style myth. *Psychological Bulletin,* 1965, **63,** 129–156.
Rorer, L. G., and Goldberg, L. R. Acquiescence in the MMPI? *Educational and Psychological Measurement,* 1965, **25,** 801–817.
Roy, S. N. On a heuristic method of test construction and its use in multivariate analysis. *Annals of Mathematical Statistics,* 1953, **24,** 220–238.
Shneidman, E. S. *Thematic test analysis.* New York: Grune & Stratton, 1951.
Shure, G. H., and Rogers, M. S. Note of caution on the factor analysis of the MMPI. *Psychological Bulletin,* 1965, **63,** 14–18.
Skrzypek, G. J., and Wiggins, J. S. Contrasted groups vs. repeated measurement designs in the evaluation of social desirability scales. *Educational and Psychological Measurement,* 1966, **26,** 131–138.
Stagner, R. The gullibility of personnel managers. *Personnel Psychology,* 1958, **11,** 347–352.
Stern, G. G., Stein, M. I., and Bloom, B. S. *Methods in personality assessment.* Glencoe: Free Press, 1956.
Tellegen, A. Personal communication, Oct. 3, 1966.
Walker, J. S. An examination of the role of the experimentally determined response set in evaluating Edwards' Social Desirability Scale. *Journal of Consulting Psychology,* 1962, **26,** 162–166.
Welsh, G. S. Factor dimensions *A* and *R*. In G. S. Welsh and W. G. Dahlstrom (Eds.), *Basic readings on the MMPI in psychology and medicine.* Minneapolis: University of Minnesota Press, 1956, pp. 264–281.
Wheeler, W. M., Little, K. B., and Lehner, F. J. The internal structure of the MMPI. *Journal of Consulting Psychology,* 1951, **15,** 134–142.
Wiggins, J. S. Interrelationships among MMPI measures of dissimulation under standard and social desirability instructions. *Journal of Consulting Psychology,* 1959, **23,** 419–427.
Wiggins, J. S. Strategic, method, and stylistic variance in the MMPI. *Psychological Bulletin,* 1962, **59,** 224–242.

Wiggins, J. S. Convergences among stylistic response measures from objective personality tests. *Educational and Psychological Measurement,* 1964, **24,** 551–562.

Wiggins, J. S. Substantive dimensions of self-report in the MMPI item pool. *Psychological Monographs,* 1966, **80** (22, Whole No. 630).

Wiggins, J. S., and Goldberg, L. R. Interrelationships among MMPI item characteristics. *Educational and Psychological Measurement,* 1965, **25,** 381–397.

Wiggins, J. S., and Lovell, V. R. Communality and favorability as sources of method variance in the MMPI. *Educational and Psychological Measurement,* 1965, **25,** 399–412.

Wiggins, J. S., and Vollmar, J. The content of the MMPI. *Journal of Clinical Psychology,* 1959, **15,** 45–47.

Chapter Eight
Parent Personality and Childhood Disorders: A Review of MMPI Findings

A. Jack Hafner, James Neal Butcher, Marian D. Hall, and Wentworth Quast
University of Minnesota

Parent personality as it influences or is related to the development of behavioral disturbance in the child has been intensively investigated in recent years. These studies have been an outgrowth of the desire to understand more adequately origins of the child's behavior problem by examining events within the family situation. Many of these studies have also developed out of an attempt to understand the family dynamics and the quality of parent-child interactions in order to provide information for making treatment dispositions, since parents are becoming increasingly involved in the treatment of the child.

Two recent articles have reviewed some of the literature in the general area of parent or family characteristics related to childhood disorders. Handel (1965) pointed out that a wide variety of psychological phenomena can be better understood by the psychological study of whole families. He reviewed research related to the study of families and family interaction patterns in order to obtain a view of how a family functions. The methods he reviewed for studying families included therapy, field methods, projective methods, and controlled experiments; he did not include any of the MMPI research on parents in his review. He pointed out that there are no established methods for studying families at this time.

Frank (1965) reviewed a number of studies on the role of the family in the development of personality in the child. He concluded that there are no consistent relationships between specific emotional experiences in the home and the development of personality or personality disturbance in the child.

The literature review of Frank, like that of Handel, did not deal with the studies that used the MMPI to examine parent personality associated with behavior disorders in children. There has been a considerable amount of clinical use of parent MMPIs in relation to the child groups as well as a growing body of literature pertaining to parent MMPIs and child behavior. The purpose of the present review is to summarize and evaluate the MMPI research studies concerned with parent personality and childhood psychopathology and to make some suggestions for future research on this problem. The studies that have used the MMPI to examine parent personality associated with childhood disorders are presented in Appendix B.

A number of investigations have been directed toward determining if parents of disturbed children are themselves more disturbed than adults in general as measured by the MMPI: Adrian (1957), Adrian, Vacchiano, and Gilbart (1966), Burien (1957), Goodstein and Rowley (1961), Hanvik and Byrum (1959), Kalhorn (1947), L'Abate (1960), Lauterbach, London, and Bryan (1961), Liverant (1959), Marks (1961), Stennett (1966), Toms (1955), and Wolking, Quast, and Lawton (1966).

These studies generally have used significance tests to examine group mean differences between parents of clinically disturbed children and parents of "normal" children. The most consistent finding has been that parents of disturbed children produce more deviant MMPI profiles than nonclinic parents. Another frequent finding has been that, although mean profile elevations for the clinic parents were above that of normal adults, they were below that of a psychiatrically disturbed adult population. There is a tendency for the *Hy* and the *Pd* scales to be elevated with fairly high frequency for the parents of the disturbed children.

However, no consistent scale elevations have appeared in all the studies mentioned. This may, to some extent, be the result of the use of quite different psychiatric samples in the various studies. A second possible reason for the lack of consistent parent patterns may be the failure of investigators to examine homogeneous subject groups. The study of a complicated variable such as parent personality associated with the psychopathology of children requires the utmost care in providing "pure" samples. Some studies have not assured homogeneity of the behavioral problem in question. Zigler and Phillips (1961) have pointed out the lack of homogeneity within diagnostic categories. Patients who are grouped under a general diagnostic rubric may actively exhibit widely different types of behavior. This is particularly a problem with diagnostic categorization for children. Consequently, selecting a group of "neurotics" and "behavioral problems" does not guarantee that children within a group are similar or that the characteristics between contrast groups are different. When behavioral characteristics in the children are not closely matched, it is not surprising that the parent personality characteristics are confounded. Other control problems resulted because many of these studies did not control for age and sex of the child and socioeconomic level of the family. These variables seem to be important in studying psychological attributes of the child and are probably even more important in studying the associated parental personality.

In an attempt to understand more precisely what relationships exist between specific parent personality configurations and particular forms of childhood pathology, a number of studies have utilized relatively more homogeneous groupings of childhood disorders. Liverant (1959), studying parent MMPI differences of a number of clinical groups, found differences primarily between mean father profiles but not between profiles of the mothers. Goodstein and Rowley (1961), in a replication, found significant MMPI scale differences between mothers of four groupings of psychiatrically disturbed children (schizophrenic, acting-out, personality trait, and neurotic). No significant differences were found, however (unlike Liverant's findings), in the comparisons made between the fathers for the same child groupings. Wolking, Quast, and Lawton (1966) compared mothers' and fathers' MMPI profiles with eight diagnostic groupings of children (organic brain syndrome, psychosis, psychosomatic reaction, conversion reaction, obsessive-compulsive, anxiety reaction, behavior disorder, mental deficiency). They found that the mothers' profiles did not vary according to the diagnostic groups but that the fathers' profiles tended to vary with the diagnostic groups. In a different study, Wolking, Dunteman, and Bailey (1966) compared parent profiles for four diagnostic groups according to the sex of the child. They found no differences between mothers of female children according to diagnostic groups, between fathers of female children and the diagnostic groups, and between fathers of male children and the diagnostic groups. They did find significant differences between mothers of male children grouped according to the diagnostic groups.

Erickson (1966) compared mother MMPI profiles for a group of young retarded, emotionally disturbed children with mother profiles for a group of young organically retarded children. She found no significant differences in profiles between these mothers, but found both groups of mothers to differ significantly from the female MMPI norm group.

Some investigators have made comparisons of parents of children with other types of disorders. Goodstein (1956, 1960) made MMPI comparisons of parents of children with cleft palates and children with stuttering problems in contrast to parents of children without these difficulties. He found that the MMPI profiles were not helpful in making discriminations between these groups of parents. Grossman (1952) compared parents of stutterers with a group of parents of nonstutterers and also found no significant differences in MMPI scales for the parents; but he did find that parents of stutterers interpreted the MMPI items "more atypically" than nonstutterers' parents.

There have been several other studies which have utilized the approach of examining parent MMPIs in relation to specific problems in homogeneous groups of children. Butcher and Messick (1966) used a measure of profile similarity to compare adolescents' MMPIs with those of their parents. Adolescent boys rated as "normally assertive" by teachers and peers were found to be more like both parents than passive boys who were less like their fathers and more like their mothers. MMPI profiles of highly aggressive boys were less like their mothers' and more like their fathers'.

Sopchak (1958) also made a comparison between parent MMPIs and those of their offspring. Male and female college students' MMPIs were compared with those of their mothers and fathers. Sopchak found males were more similar to their fathers than their mothers, and females were more similar to their mothers than their fathers in regard to the MMPI. The greatest degree of similarity was between the females and their mothers.

Butcher (1966) compared parent MMPI profiles of adolescent boys who were brought to a child guidance clinic for treatment. The groups of externalizing and internalizing adolescents were selected using Achenbach's (1966) factor-analyzed symptom clusters. Both groups of boys were found to be homogeneous (in terms of behavioral symptoms) and different in a number of personality attributes. He found that fathers of externalizing boys had greater and more frequent elevations on the *Pd* scale of the MMPI than fathers of internalizing boys.

In a similar study, using preadolescent boys, Anderson (1968) examined personality differences among parents of "aggressive" and "neurotic" boys (grouped according to Achenbach's factor ratings) and "normal" control parents. Experimental parents were more deviant (as measured by the MMPI) than control parents, and parents of aggressive boys were more deviant than parents of neurotic boys. There was a high degree of similarity in scale elevation and configuration in the three groups of mothers. However, marked differences appeared in the fathers—with fathers of aggressive boys having greater elevation on the *Pd* scale.

Boveng (1963) demonstrated that parents of boys with a learning inhibition had twice as many MMPI scales equal to or greater than 70 than did parents of normal boys. Hall (1963) also investigated parents of a group of boys with learning inhibitions and found a number of MMPI scale differences between these parents and the MMPI standardization sample. MMPI profiles for mothers and fathers of learning-inhibition sons indicate the presence of personality traits consonant with interview-based descriptions. More information was gained by looking at MMPI profiles of parents conjointly than by looking at mother and father profiles separately.

Several studies have directed their attention to the mother-father relationships and the MMPI. Adrian (1957) found that moderate or marked dissimilarity in the MMPI profiles for husbands and wives appeared to be associated with poor child adjustment. Lauterbach, Vogel, and Hart (1962) showed that parents of disturbed boys were less similar to each other than are parents of normal boys as measured by the MMPI. In contrast, Stennett (1966), comparing parent pairs on the MMPI for "troubled families," found that these parents did not have either complementary or conflicting personality characteristics to a greater or lesser degree than expected by chance.

Two other studies have been reported that deal with parent MMPI characteristics. L'Abate (1960) found that mothers who brought their sons to a clinic alone were more disturbed, as measured by the MMPI, than mothers who came with their husbands. Loeb and Price (1966) compared parent MMPIs of continuously married parents, of divorced or separated parents, and of remarried parents. In general they found more disturbance was evident in the MMPIs of the divorced, separated, or remarried parents in comparison with the group of continuously married parents.

SUMMARY AND CONCLUSIONS

The results of a number of studies on the relationship between parent personality and childhood disorders strongly suggest that parents of children who are psychiatrically disturbed are themselves more disturbed than parents in general. However, there is some indication that they are not as disturbed as adult psychiatric patients.

Although the *Hy-Pd* code type has frequently been found among groups of parents of disturbed children, no reliable parent code types have been established. The reasons for this are the use of different types of problem cases (and the lack of replication) and possibly the failure to assure homogeneity in the problems studied—including manifest behavior, child's age, child's sex, parents' sex, and socioeconomic level.

The findings concerning parent personality and child behavior problems that have appeared in the literature and the rapidly expanding clinical use of the MMPI with parents in child guidance settings provide a great deal of stimulus for continued research in the area.

The future study of such a complex variable as parent personality (as measured by the MMPI) in relation to childhood disorders should take into consideration a number of points:

1. There is an absence of a suitably large reference group of parents of normal children to provide an adequate comparative group for clinical samples.
2. Future studies should make every effort to provide adequate controls—assuring similarity of behavioral problems and subject characteristics under investigation. There is also an apparent need for more replication in areas that have been studied.
3. Rather than using the MMPI as the sole parent measure, as these studies have done, it may prove more valuable to supplement this with other types of information and procedures.
4. It may be fruitful to think in terms of developing a "cookbook" typology for parent personality. No study, to date, has approached the problem with this goal. An approach such as this might well include a consideration of high- and low-point codes and combinations of them. Parent code types of normal as well as abnormal children could be determined.
5. Another possibly fruitful approach to parent personality and child behavior might involve the study of children of psychiatrically disturbed parents. No studies, to date, have approached the problem in this way. However, it would seem that, if a parent responds to a child in a consistently suspicious, hostile, and paranoid fashion, this would produce a different sort of behavior in the child than a more stable or balanced parental response.
6. The method of comparing MMPI scores for parents is another area that needs clarification. Mean profiles of parent groups have often been used in making comparisons. The averaging of scores, however, may mask important differences both within and between the groups. Comparisons are also made frequently by comparing single scales between parent groups. However, a multiple code-type analysis may be needed since the differences between the parent groups may be reflected in more complex relationships.
7. The use of parent profiles as data for the study of personality

patterns in children poses different problems than the customary practice of relating the MMPI profile to the behavior of the individual or a diagnostic group. In the parent-child case, inferences are a further step removed. Parents' MMPIs may be hypothesized to reflect, more or less adequately, a map of the child's psychological environment insofar as it is determined by parental personalities. It is, then, not merely the degree of elevation of high-point scales that provides the most relevant information but the patterning of the two parent profiles in conjunction with specific observations of the child's behavior. Interprofile analysis may provide essential information about significant interpersonal dimensions of the child's life situation, such as the prevailing emotional climate, the potential for communication within the family, and the type of models provided. Useful clinical interpretation of parent MMPIs may involve interprofile analysis.

REFERENCES

Achenbach, T. M. The classification of children's psychiatric symptoms: A factor analytic study. *Psychological Monographs,* 1966, **80** (7, Whole issue).

Adrian, R. J. The relationships of parental personality structures to child adjustment and adoption selection. *Dissertation Abstracts,* 1957, **17,** 138.

Adrian, R. J., Vacchiano, R. B., and Gilbart, T. E. Linear discriminant function classification of accepted and rejected adoptive applicants. *Journal of Clinical Psychology,* 1966, **22,** 251–254.

Anderson, L. Personality characteristics of parents of neurotic, aggressive and normal pre-adolescent boys. Unpublished doctoral dissertation, University of Minnesota, 1968.

Boveng, T. An MMPI study of the parents of learning-inhibition boys. Unpublished master's dissertation, University of Minnesota, 1963.

Burien, G. J. MMPI characteristics of parents of child psychiatry inpatients. Unpublished master's dissertation, University of Minnesota, 1957.

Butcher, J. N. MMPI characteristics of externalizing and internalizing boys and their parents. Paper presented at the First Conference on Recent Developments in the Use of the MMPI, Minneapolis, March, 1966.

Butcher, J. N., and Messick, D. N. Parent-child profile similarity and aggression: A preliminary study. *Psychological Reports,* 1966, **18,** 440–442.

Erickson, M. T. MMPI comparisons between parents of young emotionally disturbed and organically retarded children. Paper presented to the Southeastern Psychological Association, New Orleans, March, 1966.

Frank, G. H. The role of the family in the development of psychopathology. *Psychological Bulletin,* 1965, **64,** 199–205.

Goodstein, L. D. MMPI profiles of stutterers' parents. *Journal of Speech and Hearing Disabilities*, 1956, **21**, 430–435.

Goodstein, L. D. MMPI differences between parents of children with cleft palates and parents of physically normal children. *Journal of Speech and Hearing Research*, 1960, **3**, 31–38.

Goodstein, L. D. Personality test differences in parents of children with cleft palates. *Journal of Speech and Hearing Research*, 1960, **3**, 39–43.

Goodstein, L. D., and Dahlstrom, W. G. MMPI differences between parents of stuttering and non-stuttering children. *Journal of Consulting Psychology*, 1956, **20**, 365–371.

Goodstein, L. D., and Rowley, V. N. A further study of MMPI differences between parents of disturbed and non-disturbed children. *Journal of Consulting Psychology*, 1961, **25**, 460.

Grossman, D. J. A study of parents of stuttering and nonstuttering children using the MMPI and the Minnesota Scale of Parent's Opinions. Master's dissertation, University of Wisconsin, 1951. (Also abstracted in *Speech Monographs*, 1952, **19**, 193–194.)

Hall, M. D. Personality characteristics of parents of children with learning problems, 1963. Paper presented at the First Conference on Recent Developments in the Use of the MMPI, Minneapolis, March, 1966.

Handel, G. A psychological study of whole families. *Psychological Bulletin*, 1965, **63**, 19–41.

Hanvik, L. J., and Byrum, M. MMPI profiles of child psychiatry patients. *Journal of Clinical Psychology*, 1959, **15**, 427–431.

Kalhorn, J. Personality and parent behavior. *American Psychologist*, 1947, **2**, 425.

L'Abate, L. Personality correlates of manifest anxiety in children. *Journal of Consulting Psychology*, 1960, **24**, 342–348.

Lauterbach, C., London, P., and Bryan, J. MMPI's of parents of child guidance cases. *Journal of Clinical Psychology*, 1961, **17**, 151–154.

Lauterbach, C., Vogel, W., and Hart, J. Comparison of the MMPI's of male problem adolescents and their parents. *Journal of Clinical Psychology*, 1962, **18**, 485–487.

Liverant, S. MMPI differences between parents of disturbed and non-disturbed children. *Journal of Consulting Psychology*, 1959, **23**, 256–260.

Loeb, J., and Price, J. R. Mother and child personality characteristics related to parental marital status in child guidance cases. *Journal of Consulting Psychology*, 1966, **30**, 112–117.

Marks, P. A. An assessment of the diagnostic process in a child guidance setting. *Psychological Monographs*, 1961, **75**, No. 3.

Sopchak, A. L. Spearman correlations between MMPI scores of college students and their parents. *Journal of Consulting Psychology*, 1958, **22**, 207–209.

Stennett, R. G. Family diagnosis: MMPI and CTP results. *Journal of Clinical Psychology,* 1966, **22**, 165–167.

Toms, E. C. Personality characteristics of mothers of schizophrenic veterans. Doctoral dissertation, University of Minnesota, 1955. (*Dissertation Abstracts,* 1955, **15**, 2580.)

Vogel, W., and Lauterbach, C. G. Relationships between normal and disturbed sons' percepts of their parents' behavior and personality attributes of the parents and sons. *Journal of Clinical Psychology,* 1963, **19,** 52–56.

Williams, J. F. A study of the parents of cerebral palsied and non-cerebral palsied children using the MMPI. Master's dissertation, University of Wisconsin, 1951. (Also abstracted in *Speech Monographs,* 1952, **19,** 199.)

Wolking, W. D., Dunteman, G. H., and Bailey, J. P. Multivariate analyses of parents' MMPI's based on the psychiatric diagnoses of their children. Revision of paper presented to the Southeastern Psychological Association, New Orleans, March, 1966.

Wolking, W. D., Quast, W., and Lawton, J. J. MMPI profiles of the parents of behaviorally disturbed children and parents from the general population. *Journal of Clinical Psychology,* 1966, **22,** 39–48.

Zigler, E., and Phillips, L. Psychiatric diagnosis: A critique. *Journal of Abnormal and Social Psychology,* 1961, **63,** 607–618.

Chapter Nine
MMPI Profiles Associated with Outcomes of Group Psychotherapy with Prisoners

James L. Jacobson
Robert D. Wirt
Minnesota State Department of Corrections
and the
University of Minnesota

J. L. Moreno (1932), the founder of group therapy and the most prolific writer and innovator in the field, first suggested the term "group therapy" in relation to its use with prisoners. It is remarkable that in the 35 years since, although methods of group work in many settings with many kinds of participants have spread widely, relatively little systematic work has been done in prisons.

The research, training, and service described in the following account was begun over 10 years ago in the fall of 1956. In that same year, Slavson had written that only two per cent of published papers in group psychotherapy can be regarded as experimental research. We hoped to increase that small percentage a bit by designing a program of study that might relate characteristics of group members, group process, and outcome in a systematic fashion. Over a period of 11 years, with the help of a great many people and with the cooperation of some hundreds of prison inmates, we believe that some progress was made in objectifying processes of group psychotherapy.

In their exciting book on group therapy, Whitaker and Lieberman (1964) made, as others have, a special point of distinguishing between group psychotherapy as construed to mean treatment of the group and group psychotherapy as a process for treatment of individuals

The research reported in part here was made possible through a series of grants awarded by the Minnesota State Department of Public Welfare, by the cooperation of many individuals at the Minnesota State Prison and in the Minnesota Department of Corrections, by the cooperation of the University of Minnesota's Numerical Analysis Center, and by the generous support of the Graduate School of the University of Minnesota. To all these individuals and institutions, the authors wish to express their gratitude.

in a group setting. Research in group therapy can also be directed at these two levels of abstraction: the analysis of group processes or the interpretation of change among individuals. Whitaker and Lieberman's analysis of group processes in therapeutic interactions is a brilliant model for study of the group. We did not choose to emphasize that level of observation of our groups, however. Much of our research was, rather, directed at understanding intrapersonal and interpersonal relationships within and between individual group members and among subgroups having similar characteristics.

We wished first to provide an opportunity for imprisoned men to come to a better understanding of themselves and their relationships with other people. It was, and is, our belief that faulty relationships in these areas of human behavior are basically causal in the chain of tragic events which leads citizens to become criminals. The moral, economic, political, sociological, and physical blight and neglect that characterize the early histories of the vast majority of prisoners certainly contribute massively to the distortion of behavior that results in crime. It is the effect of these and of the individual's interpersonal experiences which warps development and produces criminal pathology. Our approach to group therapy, therefore, borrowed heavily from the psychiatric and psychological literature. Insofar as our data demonstrate that members of therapy groups have been able to provide themselves with more comfortable personal adjustments and better tolerated social adjustments, we may conclude that the program of group psychotherapy at the Minnesota State Prison was indeed of service. Insofar as our data show, as we shall describe shortly, that most were not helped, we may indeed have done some individuals a disservice in the interest of a science and an art which may, we believe, be of value to another generation of caged human beings.

At the beginning of the group therapy program at the Minnesota State Prison, no one on the prison staff had had much experience or training in group psychotherapy. One of us (Wirt), therefore, acted as a consultant on treatment. He met weekly with the groups for the first 20 sessions of therapy, acting as leader therapist, with one person from the prison staff acting as co-therapist. It was felt that if the psychologist, social worker, or chaplain could have an apprenticeship experience of this kind with two successive groups, he should then have sufficient psychotherapeutic skill to take on the role of leader therapist for subsequent groups. Each week, after seeing three or more therapy groups, the consultant and the co-therapists met for training sessions to exchange ideas, discuss problems as they came up in the treatment groups, and plan future therapeutic tactics. In all, 25 members of the prison staff engaged in these functions, each receiving about a year of supervised experience. The group therapy program is now continuing at the prison as a regular function of the personnel in the treatment and classification department.

We had two research goals in addition to the service and training goals described above. First, we wanted to develop psychological methods for prediction of behavior; and, second, we wanted to develop psychological treatment methods. The overall research strategy for the development of these methods was based upon empirical observation and relationships rather than on theoretical structure. The result is that our predictions and treatment instruments will be item scales and sign indicators.

As we indicated, in the beginning there was little to go on in terms of methods of treating prisoners in group therapy. We had to rely on our experience in other settings with other groups and on some general principles of group work which we found in the literature. At first there were structural and logistic problems to overcome ranging from group size, frequency and place of meetings, etc., to more important considerations of making the program acceptable to inmates, the possible compromise of therapeutic goals in order to meet research and training needs, etc.

The answers we gave to these and similar questions were based on certain assumptions we made and certain practical limitations. All of our experience, and most of the literature, involved voluntary groups. We felt that this consideration might be especially important in a prison setting, where so little that a man does is through his own volition. It is ironical that our social institutions have so evolved that we make nearly impossible any opportunity to learn self-discipline and the assumption of social responsibility for the very people we find most lacking in these skills. Making participation voluntary produced a number of problems. It meant that group members must have an opportunity to understand something about the nature of group therapy, that they could quit, and that this voluntary activity had to seem rational to the custody staff and the shop foremen.

Most therapists insist that trust cannot be developed in a therapeutic relationship unless there is a feeling of assurance that the proceedings are private and the content of the discussions is confidential. These are not easily provided in prison.

We arranged to meet in the dressing room behind the stage in the prison auditorium. This room accommodated up to 20 people comfortably, was well lighted and quite some distance from any prison activity. Most groups sat around a table brought in for the purpose, although a few groups sat in chairs arranged, roughly, in a circle, without using a table.

Before the first groups began, the editor of the prison newspaper, *The Mirror,* interviewed us and published an article describing the service and research purposes of the group therapy program. At about the same time, we met with the entire prison staff and explained our plans to them and answered their questions. The staff was chiefly concerned about custody problems and the difficulties which an hour's absence from work would create. Through the eight years of the research program (and continuing at the present time) the prison administration has consistently supported the group therapy program, despite some inconveniences to the staff. We were able to work out a system for ensuring passes, and with few exceptions the men who chose to come showed up on time; a few were discouraged from attending by negative reactions from officers and work supervisors and especially by fellow prisoners. Over the years these reactions moderated considerably.

After the files had been searched for inmates fitting varying selection criteria for each project, those who fitted the characteristics were interviewed individually. They were told that we wanted to establish a program of group therapy at the prison if it proved to be a helpful service to inmates. They were also told that we did not have enough trained staff members to provide therapy for everyone, that of those who volunteered not all could be selected, but that selection among those interviewed would be on a random basis. We asked that all who volunteered pledge themselves to take a number of psychological tests before and after the series of meetings whether or not they were chosen to participate in the sessions. We assured them that the results of these tests and what they said in the treatment sessions would not be disclosed to anyone except the leader therapist, the co-therapists, and the research analyst. They were informed that these data would be kept separate from the prison files, that they would not be available to the warden, his staff, or the parole board, and that the fact that they had participated in group therapy at all would not be known to the parole board unless the inmate himself mentioned it to the board. We said that any report of findings would be in terms of group statistics. They were told that participation was voluntary, that they could quit at any time, and that they could continue after the 20 weeks with the co-therapist if they wished, but would not be dropped by us. This last condition caused us concern in some groups when we found that some individuals appeared to be destructive of the group process. However, we concluded that it would be better to depend upon research findings to reveal which individuals were really benefiting and which were really an asset in the group than to trust our own clinical judgment at that time. We also said that we hoped it would be a useful experience for them and that we were conducting the research aspects of the program in order to improve our skills in finding men for whom it would be helpful and to determine the most effective methods of conducting treatment. All these assertions were true, and all these conditions were kept faithfully, though most inmates, of course, were highly suspicious and could not believe that we had motivations which were in their interest.

We elected to begin with 12 men in each therapy group, when possible, which generally required finding 24 inmates (to provide both experimental and control groups) who fitted selection criteria and could be matched on various characteristics. This rather arbitrary figure was chosen with the hope that about eight men would stay with the group throughout the experimental period. There was some clinical evidence in the literature and in our own experience which suggested that a group of that size would be optimal. This guess turned out to be quite good, and we were able to treat groups of what seemed to be an appropriate size. Eight or ten people can get to know each other fairly well in 20 weeks' time, and each has an opportunity to be heard.

We decided to meet once a week for a period of 50 minutes for 20 weeks. To some degree, most of the group members suffered from character defects and their chief mechanism was projection. Most of them were egocentric and immature. Clearly, 20 weeks would not be sufficient time to permit great advances in maturing. However, we believed that five months should provide sufficient time to observe change, if any were to occur. It did appear to provide sufficient help for some and to be a foundation for more extended treatment for others. Following the experimental period, most of the group members continued in therapy with the co-therapist. The 50-minute-hour once a week was used because our time was limited and we wanted to see as many groups as possible.

Having made these initial decisions on rational and practical grounds before we had obtained any research data, we thought it necessary to maintain the same structure throughout successive projects in order not to complicate the research design. In retrospect, we would guess that two meetings a week of 90 minutes would be more effective.

After the group sessions each week, the leader therapist met with the co-therapists for a training meeting. In these meetings general problems of theory and technique in group psychotherapy were discussed, and detailed analysis of each group was conducted. Some effort was made to evaluate the current progress of each group and its members; methods for dealing with current situations were developed. Each of the co-therapists was given an opportunity to discuss his group including his concerns in handling his own feelings and the interactions that developed among the group members. All the therapists contributed ideas and solutions to problems, with the consultant taking the leading role. Perhaps at times it had the quality of group therapy for group therapists.

At the first meeting of each group, the leader therapist usually began the session with a restatement of the goals and conditions of the group, which had been discussed with the individual when he was interviewed and asked to volunteer. He went on to suggest that the purpose of the meetings was to help the men better understand themselves and their interactions with other people and that group therapy provided a means for examining these patterns that was not provided by an ordinary bull session.

The orientation toward treatment was rather eclectic, having greatest similarity to contemporary ego psychology, and undoubtedly reflected the consultant's own interests in the theories of Sullivan (1953) and Erikson (1950) (neither of whom actually had much to say about group therapy, however).

The members were invited to bring up any subject they wished for discussion. In beginning weeks this tended to result in lengthy gripe sessions about the prison, its rules, and its staff, and complaints about society, the law, and parole officers. As the men got to know each other better and to trust the therapists, there was more discussion of personal problems, family conflict, and historical material. The therapists permitted discussion of any material. Some sessions were quite emotional, but it was never necessary to restrain anyone from physical attack. The therapists did fail in a few instances to maintain a tolerable level of anxiety, which resulted in one member's leaving a group. Generally, the problems raised by these periods could be worked through profitably, or so it seemed at the time. Most sessions were frustrating to the therapists because they seemed too superficial.

The group therapy program consisted of a series of eight projects. In nearly every project the consultant (Wirt) acted as leader therapist and one of the prison staff acted as co-therapist. Approximately 12 inmates who had volunteered to participate were group members. The meeting lasted 50 minutes, once a week, for 20 weeks. Most groups were matched with a control group. In general, the members of both experimental and control groups took a number of psychological tests both before and after the series of sessions, and both therapists rated each member on a number of behavior items after each therapy session. Group members who chose to continue in therapy after the 20 weeks—as most did—were seen in weekly meetings indefinitely by the co-therapist.

The first project consisted of three experimental and three matched control groups. These groups were chosen largely on the basis of clinical judgment: One was a group of new admissions, one a group of sexual offenders, and one a group which we considered to have emotional problems as distinct from fundamental character defects.

The second project consisted of eight therapy groups matched person for person on a set of variables with eight control groups. These groups were chosen to be representative of the prison population in terms of crimes committed, personality as measured by the MMPI, age, and intelligence.

The third group psychotherapy project included six groups of inmates selected for therapy and three matched control groups. Data from the previous projects were used to develop a prediction of response to group psychotherapy. Group members were selected so that each group consisted of five poor candidates, four median-response candidates, and three good-response candidates.

The fourth group therapy project included eight experimental and eight control groups. A five-variable profile had by now been constructed, configurations on which were used to select good and poor responders to group therapy. By using these methods, we were able to improve accuracy of prediction and selection.

The fifth group therapy project was devoted to obtaining data from behavior exhibited in the group meetings that would be predictive of postprison adjustment. Therefore, candidates were selected randomly from among men who were likely to be paroled shortly after the 20 weeks of therapy. There were three experimental groups; control groups were not used. The behavior-rating items were refined into an instrument we called the Stillwater Group Psychotherapy Rating Scale.

In the sixth group therapy project, further analyses of the sorts attempted in the first four projects and that of the fifth project were combined.

The seventh project was essentially a replication of the sixth. Six control and six experimental groups were selected and studied in the same manner as we employed in the previous project.

The eighth project was a follow-up study. All the inmates who were seen in group therapy, those in control groups, and those who refused

Table 9-1 An overview of the group psychotherapy research program

Project	Time period	Experimental groups: Group number	Experimental groups: N	Control groups: Number of groups	Control groups: N	Number refused to volunteer	Research purpose
One	1/57–6/57	1	11	3	35	35	Clinical
		2	12				
		3	12				
Two	10/57–8/58	4	9	8	87	50	Representative groups
		5	12				
		6	12				
		7	12				
		8	10				
		9	10				
		10	11				
		11	11				
Three	1/59–5/59	12	12	3	37	76	Structured groups
		13	12				
		14	12				
		15	12				
		16	12				
		17	12				
Four	5/60–10/60	18	12	8	72	15	Behavior pathology
		19	12				
		20	12				
		21	12				
		22	12				
		23	12				
		24	12				
		25	12				
Five	6/61–10/61	26	12	0	0	18	Behavior pathology
		27	12				
		28	12				
Six	1/62–6/62	29	12	6	36	77	Behavior pathology
		30	12				
		31	12				
		32	9				
		33	8				
		34	10				
Seven	7/63–6/64	35	10	6	53	61	Behavior pathology
		36	10				
		37	10				

Table 9-1 An overview of the group psychotherapy research program *(Continued)*

Project	Time period	Experimental groups: Group number	Experimental groups: N		Control groups: Number of groups	Control groups: N	Number refused to volunteer	Research purpose
		38	10					
		39	10					
		40	7					
Eight	7/64–1/65		None			None	None	Follow-up
Totals	8 years	40 groups	446 individuals	26 therapists	34 groups	300 individuals	332 individuals	Selection, treatment prediction

to volunteer were followed, using methods adapted from Mandel's study (1963) of recidivism among state reformatory inmates. (For an overview of the projects, see Table 9–1.)

Overall, 446 inmates were seen in group therapy. Over a period of eight years, 40 groups were seen by 26 therapists. There were 34 control groups which included 300 men. Among prisoners meeting selection criteria, 332 of them refused to volunteer for group therapy. In total, then, the studies were concerned with something over 1,000 men.

On any given day there are about 1,000 men in the cells of the Minnesota State Prison. They stay there for an average of three years on a given sentence. But the recidivism rate is about 60%, which means that most of them stay longer. The cost of maintaining these people in that fashion, plus the cost of their failure to contribute to the tax rolls, plus the cost of their destructiveness in terms of personal and property damage is uncalculated, but is, doubtless, enormous. If methods can be found to reduce that cost by even a small percentage, the number of dollars saved and, more importantly, the number of persons benefited would be considerable.

The follow-up of our groups included an effort to obtain an estimate of each inmate's adjustment at home and in the community following his parole or discharge from the prison. At the time of the follow-up, January, 1965, some of the men were still in prison, of course, and others had been returned to prison either because of a technical viola-

Table 9-2 Follow-up results

Follow-up	Research group			
	Experi-mental	Control	Dropout	Totals
Group 1: Acceptable Behavior: excellent, marginal, or poor adjustment ($N = 149$)	60	62	27	149
Group 2: Unacceptable behavior: commit new offences, parole violation, legal problem ($N = 149$)	67	50	32	149
Total	127	112	59	298

tion of their parole agreement or because of having been convicted of a new crime. Overall the control groups appeared to be making a somewhat better adjustment than the experimental groups, as shown in Table 9-2. The best predictors of success were our behavior-rating measures and the Kuder Preference Record, not the MMPI.

We obtained the follow-up data by contacting the local police departments in each of the 50 states. A more effective way to determine whether a person has been arrested is through the files of the Federal Bureau of Investigation, since each of our men has an FBI number; but the FBI will not cooperate in research of the sort we conducted. Most of the former inmates were still in Minnesota, of course; it takes special arrangements to be paroled to another state—no one is very eager to get someone else's felons. For those within the state, it was possible to obtain a fairly detailed description of their adjustment from the parole agents and to find out which men had been arrested and what the nature of the crime was. The men were categorized into nine classes, as follows:

1 Still in Minnesota State Prison
2 Discharged directly to another institution on detainer
3 Satisfactory adjustment on parole
4 No follow-up data available
5 Released and making excellent adjustment

6 Released and making marginal or poor adjustment
7 Released and committed new crime
8 Released, has not committed new crime, but in trouble with the law, and returned as parole violator
9 Released, has not committed new crime, in trouble with the law, but not returned as parole violator

These were combined into two groups, labeled *acceptable* behavior and *unacceptable* behavior. The ratings were made by our two research assistants, Mr. Kenneth Hampton and Mrs. Mary Tosick, after a careful reading of the follow-up data. Mr. Jacobson (the research analyst) then matched the two groups for date of discharge. That is, he would pick a man in the unacceptable group, for example, and look for a man in the acceptable group who had been released at about the same time. Our best matches are for those released on the same day; all are matched within a three-month span. Thus, the people in each group had about the same amount of time to make a good adjustment in the community or to commit new crimes and be apprehended. There are 149 men in each group, and it is these two groups on which most subsequent data analysis has been done.

We have a special interest in group therapy and have tried to develop methods which would be useful in selecting members who would benefit, in assessing those who had benefited, and in suggesting behavior on the part of therapists which is constructive. We have made progress on all these counts using a variety of psychometric instruments and ratings as well as demographic variables.

One such method was to assess "positive" and "negative" movement in therapy. For this the acceptable and unacceptable groups were used as criterion groups. Each was split so that cross-validation groups were available. For each, empirically derived scales were developed and cross-validated for both the California Personality Inventory and the Edwards Personal Preference Schedule. A group member was considered to have made positive movement in group therapy if his scores on these scales moved in the direction of the acceptable group and if his scores on the MMPI became less like prison T scores and more like the T scores of the original normative samples. For the statistical analysis, we categorized persons showing improvement on two of these three measures in the positive movement group. There is not space here to describe the many characteristics which differentiate those who showed positive change from those who did not, but generally the demographic differences show a more pathological early history for those who did not improve.

Regarding the MMPI, our study was wholly empirical. Since the data were computerized, it was possible to score any group on any scale for which we had the key. We used all the scales reported in Dahlstrom and Welsh (1960), the acceptable and unacceptable groups being compared on some 240 MMPI scales. However, the point is that we did compare these groups on a number of scales for which there was no a priori—nor indeed any a posteriori—rationale for running such a contrast. A good many of these scales were derived from quite different populations—e.g., psychiatric groups, college students, or neurology patients, and from special occupational, educational, and social groups—so that we had no reason to suppose that our prison groups should differ from each other or from the norm groups on many of these scales. It is not surprising, therefore, that many of the scales failed to differentiate the two groups. What is more impressive, however, is the number of scales that did differentiate the groups. Of the 240 we tested, a little fewer than one-fourth significantly differentiated between acceptable and unacceptable postprison adjustment. Nearly all these differences are statistically quite significant. We are dealing here with fairly large numbers, of course, so that, in many cases, though the statistical differences appear quite reliable, the raw score differences are as small as one item. What is important, we believe, is not the statistical differences on any given measure—which as Lykken (1966) points out is the least important datum in the results of most psychological research—but the large number of such differences and the clustering. These show, we think, quite clear and logically congruent patterns which explain the therapists' reactions to these group members, indicate why the approach to treatment was probably wrong, and explain the recidivism rates.

The demographic and psychological variables involved in this study are too numerous to be reported here. There are, in addition, too many multiphasic scales showing potentially interesting differences to be discussed in detail here. All the scales we used are shown in Appendix C. The data there give means and standard deviations for each scale for the acceptable, unacceptable, and Hathaway and McKinley's (1951) normal males. Appendix C also shows the magnitude of t for the difference between the means of the acceptable and unacceptable groups.

We begin with the familiar profile used in daily clinical practice. Both groups look very much alike and much like "prisoners in general." That profile is essentially a 4′ pattern, hardly a surprising finding. Though slight in absolute magnitude, the scales that differentiate the groups at a statistically acceptable level are as follows: The unacceptable group is higher on *Pd* and *Ma*, and the acceptable group is higher on *Hs* and *Si*. The associations of these syndromes run throughout the results. As a group, the inmates making acceptable adjustments in the community are, relative to those making unacceptable adjustments, more neurotic and inhibited, while the poorly adjusting individuals are deviant, more psychopathic, and more impulsive.

In terms of code types, those including a high *Pd* element uniformly fall into the recidivism class, while those having a heavy neurotic factor are in the acceptable group. Thus the following code types occur significantly more often in the acceptable group: 137, 213, 1238, 13, 21, 31, and 12; the following character-disordered and psychotic code types are heavily represented among the unacceptable group: 4, 49, 274, 248, 98, and 9.

Similarly, scales designed to measure such syndromes as single measures yield predictable results: Acceptable subjects are higher on the following scales: Admission of Symptoms, Religiosity, Judged Anxiety, Pharisaic Virtue, Rigidity, Somatic Complaint, Neuroticism, Ulcer Personality, Somatization Reaction, and Ego Overcontrol; the unacceptable group scores higher on scales labeled Familial Discord, Impulsivity, Authority Problems, Delinquency, Escapism, Amorality, Recidivism, Alcoholism, and Underachievement.

As we pointed out, these absolute differences are small—and some of the statistical differences are not great—so that prediction probably requires a sign approach for many scales. The biggest differences are on some scales not used in typical clinical practice.

The greater anxiety and depression among the better-adjusted group is further confirmed by their higher scores on scales derived from neuropsychological research, such as the Parietal-Frontal and Caudality scales. Psychological distress is more commonly observed in patients with lesions in the back rather than the front of their heads.

There is a very long history of attempts at psychological intervention into untoward social behavior, and it seems not an unfair summary of those efforts to suggest that, whatever the form of so-called therapeutic efforts, they have rather uniformly been more successful with people whom one might grossly characterize as neurotic than they have with individuals more properly diagnosed as character-disordered or psychotic. Our groups were, nearly always, selected to be representative of the prison population or to include a heavy proportion of those predicted to do poorly. Since the results show the acceptable group to have a highly neurotic quality in comparison to the unacceptable group, it may well be that group therapy was helpful for these inmates. Further inspection of the data will reveal if that is the case.

We typically misjudged who would improve and who would not. We had some intermediate criteria of improvement such as disciplinary problems in prison, and, even with this feedback, the therapists continued to be misled. One of the scales on which the unacceptable group scored higher than the acceptable group is the Adjustment to Prison scale. We responded favorably to inmates who began by complaining about the travail of prison life, who told us how much they appreciated the opportunity to get help, who said they knew they were mixed-up and were motivated to find new patterns of living. Note some scales on which the unacceptable subjects scored high: Social Participation, Social Presence, Social Imperturbability, Social Status, Intellectual Efficiency, and Ego Strength. In contrast, those who in fact turned out well scored high on Ego Overcontrol, Pedophile, Health Concern factor, Aging, Rigidity, Somatic Complaints, and Introversion. It is clear which group was more interesting to talk with. Of course, the glib fellows sounded just the same after 20 weeks, and the silent, doubtful ones were making progress. But that is a hard lesson to learn. Ten years later, we are still trying to learn it.

What does this mean in terms of our treatment approach? We rather wonder if our traditional, passive, analytic, supportive, accepting approach might not be construed by the prisoners as implicit approval of their ideas and behavior, thus inadvertently reinforcing the very actions and orientation we might have hoped to modify. If so, the more sociopathic individual might have become more confirmed in his ways, while the borderline neurotic might have been helped to give up his inhibitions and act out. We rather see some value in the ventilation of the early gripe sessions—we have quite clear evidence which is not presented here that imprisonment itself is damaging for most inmates. However, having shown that ventilation is permitted, even necessary and desirable, the leader should then move into a more assertive, reality-orienting role. Again, we believe our behavior-rating data (to be published at a later date) will show that when the therapist behaved that way it was fruitful.

In summary, we think these data will now make it possible to make a better selection of inmates who can benefit from one or another approach to group treatment, will suggest constructive behavior for the therapists, and will make possible more reliable predictions of parole success. If these statements are correct and these findings can be incorporated into prison treatment programs, then the result should be more effective treatment.

REFERENCES

Dahlstrom, W. G., and Welsh, G. S. *An MMPI handbook: A guide to use in clinical practice and research.* Minneapolis: University of Minnesota Press, 1960.

Erikson, E. H. *Childhood and society.* New York: Norton, 1950.

Hathaway, S. R., and McKinley, J. C. *The Minnesota Multiphasic Personality Inventory manual.* (Rev. ed.) New York: The Psychological Corporation, 1951.

Lykken, D. T. Statistical significance in psychiatric research. Report No. PR-66-9 from the Research Laboratories of the Department of Psychiatry, University of Minnesota. Minneapolis: Author, 1966.

Mandel, N. *Crime revisited: A study of recidivism.* St. Paul: Minnesota State Printing Office, 1963.

Moreno, J. L. *Application of the group method to classification.* New York: National Committee on Prisons and Prison Labor, 1932.

Slavson, S. R. *Fields of group psychotherapy.* New York: International Universities Press, 1956.

Sullivan, H. S. *The interpersonal theory of psychiatry.* New York: Norton, 1953.

Whitaker, D. S., and Lieberman, M. A. *Psychotherapy through the group process.* New York: Atherton Press, 1964.

Chapter Ten
The Personality of Delinquents

Elio D. Monachesi and Starke R. Hathaway
University of Minnesota

In recent years much has been said and written about juvenile delinquency. Many persons have expressed concern about the increasing volume of cases of youngsters seen in our juvenile courts and other public agencies. Some authors have insisted that delinquency cannot really be measured accurately; even if it could be, any comparison of the ascertained rate of delinquency at any two points in time would be misleading unless it were possible to determine and control a complex of social variables that are assumed to be related to delinquency. For example, some authors argue that the volume of delinquency in any specific community is concomitant with the attitudes and activities of the dominant and articulate groups of the community. Since delinquency is socially defined, what is or what is not regarded as deviant behavior is socially determined, and any changes in such definitions, any shifts in the degree to which a community is willing to tolerate deviant behavior, will be reflected in the volume of delinquency.

Although it is virtually impossible to state with any comfortable degree of accuracy whether delinquency is increasing—whether the present generation of adolescents is more deviant than past generations—the problem of delinquency not only has increasingly received public attention but has also become the object of numerous large-scale studies designed to determine its causes and its prevention at considerable cost to governmental and private funding agencies.

Thus, Congress in 1961 passed the Juvenile Delinquency and Youth Offenses Control Act, which provided funds for the President's Committee on Juvenile Delinquency and Youth Crime to mount large-scale demonstration preventive programs in many of the country's urban

The results to be reported are derived from a study supported by grants from the Graduate School of the University of Minnesota, and from the National Institute of Mental Health, Public Health Service, United States Department of Health, Education, and Welfare. The authors gratefully acknowledge this support.

centers. In general these programs have focused upon providing opportunities for underprivileged youth to develop skills that would enable them to participate successfully in our dominant middle-class society. In order to attain this objective, a variety of programs has been launched. Employment-focused, school-focused, and recreation-focused programs have been established in many metropolitan centers to prevent and to control delinquency. This is the reason for the establishment (to list only a few such projects) of the Harlem Youth Opportunities Unlimited, the Mobilization for Youth in New York City, the Chicago Joint Youth Development Program, the New Haven Manpower Program, the St. Louis Gateways for Youth Program, the Minneapolis Youth Development Project, and the Girls at Vocational High experiment in New York City (Meyer, Borgatta, & Jones, 1965). As of the moment, however, the success of these and other such projects in the prevention and control of delinquency remains to be determined.

The empirical study of crime and delinquency has been the focus of attention of many scholars for over a century. We still, however, find it impossible to formulate a comprehensive explanation of delinquent behavior that is sound and capable of fitting the empirical world. Studies in this field have resulted in the discovery of a plethora of factors, personal and social, that are related in one way or another to delinquent behavior. It is currently possible to point to a variety of ways in which delinquents and nondelinquents differ from one another, but efforts that have been made to control and to prevent delinquent behavior based upon these differences have produced indifferent and unencouraging results.

In general most of the available studies of delinquents have attempted to correlate the social and personal characteristics in the delinquent's developmental history with his behavior at some point in time. These characteristics, which presumably explain behavior, are actually determined after the behavior in question has occurred. The soundness of such explanations of behavior is completely dependent upon the accuracy of the reconstruction of the developmental history of individuals. It is impossible, however, to reconstruct many phases of an individual's past history reliably because of circumstances beyond the control of the investigator. The emotional and mental history of a person is especially susceptible to distortion. Still another difficulty encountered in the study of delinquency involves postdiction in contrast to prediction. Once a child has been adjudicated delinquent, he, as well as his parents and others who know him, cannot be wholly free from the changes in attitudes and the biases that result from his being labeled a delinquent. Studies that compare known delinquents with nondelinquents to determine "causes" of delinquency in those characteristics differentiating delinquents and nondelinquents can lead to false conclusions based on contaminated data. It is impossible to know reliably how many of the differentiating characteristics found are the result of delinquent behavior itself. Thus, delinquency, the variable under study, may be responsible for many of the variables differentiating delinquents and nondelinquents.

One way to circumvent some of the hazards of research in delinquency is to take a longitudinal approach to the problem. Such an approach involves the collection of data on the social and personality characteristics of a large group of children, the majority of whom have not engaged in serious deviant behavior. Essentially, the objective of research of this kind is the collection of a large body of data considered pertinent to the problem under study in order to determine how persons differed in characteristics before the behavior in question occurred. A summary of the results of one phase of a longitudinal study of social adjustment will be presented in this paper. This phase deals with the personality characteristics of delinquents and nondelinquents.

DESCRIPTION OF THE PROJECT

Early in 1947, data collection on the personality and social characteristics of some 4,000 schoolchildren was begun. In order to minimize problems of interpretation and classification of data, it was decided to use a personality inventory whose reliability and validity were known. The Minnesota Multiphasic Personality Inventory seemed best to fit the requirements of the study (Hathaway & McKinley, 1951). The results of published research (Capwell, 1945; Monachesi, 1948, 1950) that utilized the MMPI demonstrated that several of the scales had repeatedly discriminated significantly between groups of male and female delinquents and nondelinquents.

Several considerations determined the choice of the population for study. Although it was desirable to study a single age group, the difficulties of collecting data on such a group were judged to outweigh the advantages to be gained. The inappropriateness of some of the items of the MMPI, considered such by school authorities, for very young children seemed to dictate the choice of a senior high school population. However, the abrupt rise in the number of reported delinquency cases at about the age of 14 years made such a choice undesirable. As a compromise, it was finally decided to study the ninth-grade school children of Minnesota.

The first ninth-grade MMPI study was made in the Minneapolis public school system in the school year 1947–1948. The official enrollment in the ninth grade at the beginning of the school year was 4,572 children, and of this number 3,971 were tested. One school refused to cooperate because of objections raised about several of the MMPI items, and thus 241 pupils were eliminated. Other losses were due to absences and dropouts during the school year. Despite all efforts, only 87% of the official ninth-grade registration became available.

Approximately two years after the MMPI data were collected the first follow-up study of the sample of youngsters was made. This investigation was designed to determine what children in the sample were known to law-enforcing agencies in Minneapolis and Hennepin County. The records examined revealed that 591 of the ninth graders were known to the police and/or courts—22% of all the boys and 8% of all the girls.

Another follow-up study of the original 1947–1948 Minneapolis sample designed to determine the association of MMPI variables and delinquent behavior was completed four years after the MMPI had been administered. This study, more extensive and intensive than the first, involved again a careful search of the records of law-enforcing agencies as well as the records of private and public social agencies. In addition, a staff of field workers were employed to collect, through interviews with each child, his parents, and others, data about the child's adjustment to his family, school, neighborhood, work situations, etc. The data contained in the records of law-enforcing agencies were employed to rank the severity of the deviant behavior of the children involved. The following ranking categories were formulated:

Delinquency 0: No definite evidence of significantly deviant behavior. These were the children with no police or court contact.

Delinquency 1: Appearance of names in police records for at least one minor difficulty such as traffic contact (for example, overtime parking) or being picked up; but involvement was poorly established, or the individual was contributing in such a minor way that it would not justify classification into one of the following groups.

Delinquency 2: The youngsters placed in this class had committed minor offenses such as destruction of property (especially when this was connected with play activities), drinking, one or more traffic offenses (escapades involving speeding, driving without a license, and/or going at high speed through a stoplight or sign), curfew violation, and immoral conduct. The misbehavior was relatively nondelinquent in comparison to that of the other two categories. Nevertheless, these children as a group were considered to have demonstrated evidence of undesirable conduct.

Delinquency 3: This classification involves the commission of one serious offense such as auto theft, grand larceny, or gross immorality or more than one less-serious offense such as petty larceny, immoral conduct, assault, disorderly conduct, malicious destruction of property, shoplifting, flagrant curfew violations, truancy, and incorrigibility. The youngsters placed in this class were, therefore, not clearly established delinquents; but nevertheless they were showing behavior that needed more than casual explanation.

Delinquency 4: This level of misconduct is used to denote those who committed repeated offenses such as auto theft, burglary, grand larceny, holdup with a gun, and gross immoral conduct (girls), accompanied by less-serious offenses. In this category were placed all youngsters who were considered to have demonstrated a well-established delinquent pattern.

Each follow-up study made it possible to give each child a delinquency rating, and these two ratings when added together result in eight behavior categories (0 to 8) suggesting the duration and severity of the misconduct of each child in the group. For example, a ranking of four indicates that the child has been found to be either severely delinquent in one follow-up study or mildly deviant in both studies.

The number and percentage of boys within each of the rating categories are presented in Table 10-1. (Only the data for boys are presented because a small number of girls, 156, had encountered difficulties with law-enforcing agencies.) As will be noted, 7.5% of the boys had a delinquency rating of four or more while 59.1% had no record.

The next step in the analysis of the collected data was taken in order to determine whether boys with a delinquency record differed from boys without such records on the several MMPI scales. Only boys who became delinquent after the MMPI was administered were used in this analysis. These boys were, therefore, true prediction cases in the sense that their personality characteristics were assessed before

Table 10-1 Number and percentages, and cumulative frequencies and percentages of boys assigned to various behavior categories

Delinquency rating	Frequency	Percentage	Cumulative frequency	Cumulative percentage	Cumulative frequency	Cumulative percentage
0	1,158	59.1	1,158	59.1	1,958	100.1
1	193	9.9	1,351	69.0	800	41.0
2	203	10.4	1,554	79.4	607	31.1
3	259	13.2	1,813	92.6	404	20.7
4	54	2.8	1,867	95.4	145	7.5
5	42	2.1	1,909	97.5	91	4.7
6	25	1.3	1,934	98.8	49	2.6
7	15	.8	1,949	99.6	24	1.3
8	9	.5	1,958	100.1	9	.5
Total	1,958	100.0				

Source: S. R. Hathaway and E. D. Monachesi, The personalities of pre-delinquent boys. *Journal of Criminal Law, Criminology and Police Science,* (1957), **48,** 154.

the fact of delinquency. Furthermore, all boys with a delinquency rating of 1 were also excluded since they could not be considered delinquents in the usual sense. It would have been desirable, had it been possible, to exclude boys with ratings of 2 and 3; however, sample size made this impossible. The number of severely delinquent children was too small to produce statistically reliable results if the data were subjected to extensive cross-tabulation analysis. The inclusion of mildly delinquent boys in the group attenuates the findings since these boys had personalities very similar to those of nondelinquent boys.

Before presenting data indicative of the relations between personality characteristics of boys and delinquency, it is necessary to keep in mind some important methodological problems. The scales of the MMPI have been found to be related to various known forms of adult mental illness such as hypomania, schizophrenia, hysteria, psychopathic deviance, and the like. The scores made on these scales are not, however, perfect measures of adult maladjustment; and, when these scales are employed in the study of adolescents, further validity is undoubtedly lost. This cannot be avoided; but it seems reasonable to assume tentatively that if the MMPI scales are found to be related to delinquent behavior in an orderly and clinically meaningful way, the variables being measured are related to the adult maladjustment patterns the MMPI scales have been shown to measure. If it is found that the occurrence of delinquent behavior varies with patterns of adult maladjustment, as measured by the MMPI scales, it may be that delinquent behavior in adolescents is a symptomatic manifestation of the same variables related to adult mental maladjustment.

The data on the relationship between delinquency and the MMPI scales are presented in Table 10-2. The sample consists of 1,467 boys of whom 21.1% had a delinquency rating of 2 through 8 inclusive. The data presented were obtained by coding (Hathaway, 1947; Hathaway & McKinley, 1951) the MMPI profiles of every boy and by

Table 10-2 Delinquency rates among groupings of the profiles by most deviant single scale

Scales	All profiles			Primed profiles (70 *T* score and above at highest)		
	Total *N*	After-test delin-quents	Rates for the class, %	Total *N*	After-test delin-quents	Rates for the class, %
Inhibitory scales:						
0 (*Si*)	91	10	11.0	10	1	10.0
2 (*D*)	67	9	13.4	24	3	12.5
5 (*Mf*)	87	10	11.5	22	1	4.5
No high points	35	4	11.4			
Total	280	33	11.8	56	5	8.9
Variable scales:						
1 (*Hs*)	48	10	20.8	24	4	16.7
3 (*Hy*)	39	7	17.9	5	1	20.0
6 (*Pa*)	38	7	18.4	14	3	21.4
7 (*Pt*)	89	17	19.1	49	6	12.2
Total	214	41	19.2	92	14	15.2
Excitatory scales:						
4 (*Pd*)	276	65	23.6	116	37	31.9
8 (*Sc*)	202	48	23.8	119	31	26.1
9 (*Ma*)	317	68	21.5	166	48	28.9
Invalid	97	35	36.1			
Indeterminate	81	19	23.5	11	3	27.3
Total	973	235	24.2	412	119	28.9
Total valid profiles	1,370	274	20.0			
Overall totals	1,467	309	21.1	560	138	24.6

Source: S. R. Hathaway and E. D. Monachesi, The personalities of pre-delinquent boys. *Journal of Criminal Law, Criminology and Police Science,* (1957), **48,** 158.

grouping them according to which of the 10 scales was the most deviant point in the profile. Thus, the profile of 91 boys had the 0 (*Si*) scale as its most deviant point, and 10 of these boys were delinquent. Further, in 10 of these profiles the 0 scale score was a standard score of 70 or above, which means that the score was at least two standard deviations above the average for adult norms. Only one of the ten boys with primed (T score $=$ 70) score on the deviant 0 scale was delinquent. When scale 0 is elevated, it generally suggests social introversion and nonparticipation in social groups. The remainder of the data in Table 10-2 indicate how the MMPI scales are variously related to delinquency. Scales 0, 2, and 5 are designated as inhibitory scales, since they are associated with low rates of delinquency. Scales 4, 8, and 9 are called excitatory scales. These are the scales related to high delinquency rates. The data suggest that boys who tend to be socially introverted, unhappy, sensitive, and feminine are less apt to engage in delinquent behavior than boys who are rebellious, unconventional, aggressive, negative, difficult, expansive, and decisive. The remaining four scales, 1, 3, 6, and 7, are called variable scales since they seemed to have a variable effect or no effect on delinquency rates. The delinquency rate associated with this group of scales is roughly the same as the overall rate of 21.1%.

Again, it should be stated that in evaluating the delinquency rates related to groups of scales, it is important to remember that, in order to arrive at a sufficiently large sample of cases, it was necessary to use data on boys that were relatively nondelinquent whose contact with law-enforcing agencies involved minor incidences of misconduct. In effect this means that all the differences in rates were somewhat attenuated. Evidence that attenuation occurs is supplied by data at hand. It was found that when scales 4, 8, and 9 were highly elevated, a large number of these boys were seriously delinquent (delinquency rating of 4 or above).

Other data in Table 10-2 indicate that boys who score high on the F and/or the L scales, thus rendering their MMPI protocols invalid, had the highest delinquency rate. Of these 36% were delinquent and 20.2% were severely delinquent. In contrast, only four of the boys whose profiles had no abnormal deviation on any scale, that is to say, none of the scales had a standard T score above 54, were delinquent. Boys whose profiles were classed as indeterminate, meaning that the scores on three or more of the scales were equal or within one point of one another, had a delinquency rate roughly similar to the overall rate.

The analysis of the 1947–1948 Minneapolis data demonstrated

that it requires a very large initial sample to provide adequate data for longitudinal studies. It was impossible to do the many necessary cross tabulations since many of the cells contained frequencies too small to be statistically reliable. A much larger sample was needed, and it seemed desirable to obtain data on rural ninth graders as well as more data on urban children. In the spring of 1954, MMPI data as well as other data relating to the social, economic, and scholastic characteristics were collected on 11,329 additional ninth graders. These children attended 92 schools situated in 86 communities located in 47 of Minnesota's 87 counties. The schools were chosen to be representative of Minnesota's diverse geographic and economic areas. Of the total ninth-grade population of Minnesota for 1954, 28% is included in the sample, and it contains 36% of all ninth graders outside the Twin Cities. The sample also includes 101 boys and girls attending two Roman Catholic parochial schools.

Three years after the initial data were collected a follow-up study was made of the statewide sample. In addition to various other social and psychological data, an intensive search of the files of law-enforcing agencies was made to determine which of the children were known to the police and the courts. Again, children who had contacts with the law were given a delinquency rating similar to that given the Minneapolis group in previous studies.

The data on delinquency rating for the Minnesota statewide sample are in Table 10-3. The table shows the frequency and proportion of

Table 10-3 Cumulative delinquency ratings for 11,329 Minnesota 17-year-olds

Delinquency rating	Male		Female	
	f	%	*f*	%
0	3,665	64.3	4,945	87.9
1	591	10.4	232	4.1
2	857	15.0	232	4.1
3	352	6.2	74	1.3
4	136	2.4	37	0.7
No information	100	1.8	108	1.9
Total	5,701	100.1	5,628	100.0

Overall delinquency rate:
Boys: 1,936/5,601 = 34.6
Girls: 575/5,520 = 10.4

Source: S. R. Hathaway, E. D. Monachesi, and L. A. Young, Delinquency rates and personality. *Journal of Criminal Law, Criminology and Police Science*, 1960, **50**, 434.

the total group placed in each of five delinquency classifications. The ratings are based on the information gathered during the follow-up survey. Most of the children were attending the twelfth grade when the survey was conducted. Their average age was then 17.5 years. Each individual was rated on the basis of his total delinquency record at the time of the survey.

Some comparisons can be made between the data in Table 10-3 and the information obtained earlier for Minneapolis adolescents. There were two surveys of the total Minneapolis sample; the first occurred when most of the members of the group were in the eleventh grade (average age 16.5 years); the second survey was made the year following high school graduation (average age 18.5 years). The data in Table 10-3 were collected while the statewide children were in the twelfth grade (average age 17.5 years), a point approximately between the average ages of the Minneapolis group when the two follow-up studies were made. By interpolation, estimation of the delinquency rate for Minneapolis adolescents, equated to the age of the statewide group, may be derived for comparison. Table 10-4 presents the data.

The rates for the two samples are remarkably similar. By the time they had reached 17.5 years of age, approximately 35% of the 1958 Minneapolis boys had been in sufficient trouble to have had their names recorded by either the police or the courts, while 34% of the 5,701 boys in the statewide sample were similarly identified. The corresponding delinquency rates for girls at 17.5 years of age were 10.5% for the 2,013 Minneapolis girls and 10.2% for the 5,628

Table 10-4 Comparative cumulative delinquency rates for Minneapolis and Minnesota statewide adolescents

Average age	Boys		Girls	
	Minneapolis	Statewide	Minneapolis	Statewide
16.5	29.9		9.1	
17.5	35.4*	34.6	10.5*	10.2
18.5	40.9		11.9	
N =	1,958	5,701	2,013	5,628

* Delinquency rate for Minneapolis boys and girls at age 17.5 years is an estimate that assumes a constant delinquency rate during the two-year interval between the first and second follow-up surveys.

Source: S. R. Hathaway, E. D. Monachesi, and L. A. Young, Delinquency rates and personality. *Journal of Criminal Law, Criminology and Police Science*, 1960, **50**, 435.

statewide girls. The similarity of these rates is somewhat surprising, for the Minneapolis sample represents a purely urban population and the Minnesota statewide sample has a heavy rural population, with 28% living on farms and 45% living in small towns and villages throughout the state. There is also a seven-year difference in time between the two investigations.

Associational analyses (Hathaway & Monachesi, 1963) of MMPI variables and delinquency rates for the statewide sample yield essentially the same findings as did the 1947–1948 Minneapolis sample data. Scales 4, 8, and 9, the excitatory scales, were found to be associated with high delinquency rates. Boys whose profiles were deviant on these scales, singly or in combination, have delinquency rates that are considerably larger than the overall rate. Thus, it was found that boys with the excitatory MMPI scale codes (when scales 4, 8, and 9 in combination are the most deviant scales in the profile) had a delinquency rate of 41.9% in contrast to an overall rate of 34.6%. Again, scales 0, 2, and 5, or the suppressor scales, were the dominant scales in the profiles of boys with low delinquency rates—27.1% as against 34.6%. The variable scales 1, 3, 6, and 7 were again found to have little relation to delinquency. Boys with "no high" point profiles again had a low delinquency rate. These data, as well as the 1947–1948 Minneapolis sample data, would seem to suggest that delinquents are more frequently psychopathic, schizoid, or hypomanic than are nondelinquents. Further, boys who tend to be more feminine, depressed, and introverted are less apt to become delinquent.

Of great interest is the fact that some of these relationships are even more marked for girls. In this case, the MMPI data are so closely related to delinquency that it was found that girls with excitatory code profiles had a delinquency rate twice as large as the overall rate. Again, the more deviant scores are on scales 4, 8, and 9, the higher the delinquency rate. Girls with inhibitory or suppressor scale codes had lower delinquency rates than the overall rate.

The data indicate that the personality patterns related to higher delinquency rates of boys are the same as those associated with higher delinquency rates of girls. It was found that, by selecting all code types in the statewide sample that contained at least 30 cases, the correlation between the delinquency rates of girls paired with those of boys of the same code type produced a correlation coefficient of .71. A similar analysis of the Minneapolis data yielded a coefficient of .53; however, the Minneapolis data, because of the small sample size, are less reliable.

CONCLUSION

Personality patterns identified by the MMPI are widely known in professional work with adult maladjustment. It seems reasonable to assume that the procedures considered appropriate for the treatment of adult problems can, with modification, be applied to give direction to the therapeutic efforts with adolescents who display similar patterns.

The data presented do indicate the existence of an association between certain MMPI scale patterns and future deviant behavior. These data can be used to identify possible problem children before deviant behavior actually occurs. Any device that can be used to detect such children makes it possible to focus preventive and therapeutic efforts upon predictable deviants before the onset of serious problems.

Although the frequency of moderately abnormal personality patterns among adolescents is observed to be high, it is obvious that as they grow older the trend is toward normal adjustment for the majority of these offenders (Hathaway & Monachesi, 1953). We cannot suggest, therefore, that all children need special help to become acceptable adults; on the contrary, most of them, even though they are temporarily delinquent, seem to work their way through to normal adult adjustment. It is hoped, however, that we may discover methods that will decrease the number of those who do carry into adulthood their delinquent behavior tendencies. Possibly even more significantly, we hope to identify and help whose who could achieve adjustment in time to do so more quickly and with less stress on themselves and others through effective programs of treatment.

It is probable that the delinquency rate of any community will never be reduced to zero. Some boys and girls will become delinquent no matter how effective or efficient our preventive measures are or will be because of the small proportion of children who possess certain personality characteristics that can be modified only slightly or not at all. It is to be hoped that the approach to understanding delinquency suggested by our findings will make possible an earlier identification of these problem children. Once the extremely resistant type of delinquency-prone child is isolated, new and more adequate treatment approaches or more effective management techniques may be instituted.

The findings reported here, if properly used, can be of value to community agencies, public or private, whose goal is to assess personality disorders in children in order to help them live more useful and happy lives and prevent them from creating serious social problems. The results of the studies reported here suggest that the MMPI may be effectively employed in the early identification of delinquency-prone children.

REFERENCES

Capwell, D. F. Personality patterns of adolescent girls: II. Delinquents and non-delinquents. *Journal of Applied Psychology,* 1954, **29,** 284–297.

Hathaway, S. R., A coding system for MMPI profile classification. *Journal of Consulting Psychology,* 1947, **11,** 334–337.

Hathaway, S. R., and McKinley, J. C. *The Minnesota Multiphasic Personality Inventory manual.* (Rev. ed.) New York: The Psychological Corporation, 1951.

Hathaway, S. R., and Monachesi, E. D. *Analyzing and predicting juvenile delinquency with the MMPI.* Minneapolis: University of Minnesota Press, 1953.

Hathaway, S. R., and Monachesi, E. D. The personalities of pre-delinquent boys. *Journal of Criminal Law, Criminology and Police Science,* 1957, **48,** 149–163.

Hathaway, S. R., Monachesi, E. D., and Young, L. A. Delinquency rates and personality. *Journal of Criminal Law, Criminology and Police Science,* 1960, **50,** 433–440.

Hathaway, S. R., and Monachesi, E. D. *Adolescent personality and behavior.* Minneapolis: University of Minnesota Press, 1963.

Meyer, H. J., Borgatta, E. F., and Jones, W. C. *Girls at Vocational High.* New York: Russell Sage Foundation, 1965.

Monachesi, E. D. Some personality characteristics of delinquents and non-delinquents. *Journal of Criminal Law and Criminology,* 1948, **38,** 487–500.

Monachesi, E. D. Personality characteristics and socioeconomic status of delinquents and non-delinquents. *Journal of Criminal Law and Criminology,* 1950, **40,** 570–583.

Chapter Eleven
Personality Characteristics of Members of a Serpent-handling Religious Cult

Auke Tellegen
University of Minnesota
Nathan L. Gerrard
Morris Harvey College
Louise B. Gerrard
West Virginia
Department of Mental Health
James Neal Butcher
University of Minnesota

Religious beliefs and practices take many forms. Even within the Protestant religion one can find a wide variety of religious beliefs and rites; in somewhat isolated religious groups, not under the influence of a centralized church structure, highly individualized religious practices occur. One extreme and seemingly bizarre religious practice, the handling of poisonous snakes and drinking deadly poison as tests of faith, has developed in this country in a relatively short time over the last 60 years. The cultural factors that enter into the development and perpetuation of these unusual and rather dangerous practices, which have grown even in the face of broader community disapproval and legislation against them, are intriguing.

Among these factors are no doubt social and economic conditions, cultural isolation, and level of education as well as individual personal-

Acknowledgment is made of support in part by Public Health Service Grants to the Gerrards, MH 07472-01 and MH 10048-01, from the National Institute of Mental Health, Public Health Service; by the Wenner-Gren Foundation for Anthropological Research, Inc., New York, Project #1453; and to Dr. Tellegen by the Vocational Rehabilitation Administration Research and Training Grant No. 2 University of Minnesota Hospital.

We express our gratitude to Drs. John Brantner, Jan Duker, Jack Hafner, Marion Hall, Leo Hanvik, Jerome Pauker, William Schofield, Lloyd Sines, Zigfrid Stelmachers, and Anne Wirt for their participation as clinical judges in one of the phases of this study.

ity attributes. The study of these religious cults and their members can lead to a better understanding not only of sociological and social-psychological factors but also of personality factors involved in the development of deviant subcultural groups.

Serpent-handling cults in the Southern Appalachian region have attracted the attention of anthropologists. La Barre (1962) gives a historical account of the origin and spread of this cult through several states and provides a detailed discussion of symbolic meanings of serpent handling and other practices of the cult. In addition, La Barre presents a detailed case history analysis of one cult leader and attempts to formulate certain conclusions concerning the sociology and psychology of serpent-handling cults. La Barre's formulation relies heavily on psychoanalytic concepts of intrapsychic conflict. The serpent handler is portrayed as the victim of a repressive, subservient, and deprived "poor white" culture, who in the practices of his sect, particularly in the snake-handling ritual, symbolically enacts his unconscious sexual impulses and conflicts. The serpent handler is said to achieve in this fashion temporary release and some indirect impulse gratification without, however, resolving his underlying conflicts and frustrations. La Barre's monograph draws on an impressive array of sociological and anthropological information and offers a thorough and sometimes convincing psychological analysis. A difficulty, however, in evaluating the merits of his formulations is the highly inferential nature of his interpretations embedded in a complex Freudian framework. Although a psychodynamic interpretation of this kind may prove to have merits, its proper evaluation would require an extremely rich network of observations. In this respect La Barre's study falls short. As a matter of fact, his psychological assessment is, strictly speaking, limited to clinical observations of one atypical individual, the leader of a sect. It would not be surprising if studies of different subjects were to result in different findings. Add to this the problem of selective data recording, coupled with the probability that selectivity will take different directions depending on one's theoretical orientation, and one would have to expect discrepancies between the reports of different investigators even on a descriptive level.

Two of the present investigators, after several years of observation and intimate contact with a serpent-handling group, became dissatisfied with some of La Barre's views. They began to question in particular the important explanatory role that La Barre appears to assign to the psychopathology of the individual sect members, psychoanalytically conceived in terms of repression, conflict, and symptoms representing symbolic impulse expression. The emerging difference in views suggested the need for more descriptive data concerning the personality characteristics of individual sect members. At this point it was decided to introduce the MMPI into the study, in the hope of obtaining a useful supplement to the behavioral observations. The selection of the MMPI was based, first of all, on the comparative soundness of the instrument particularly for the assessment of psychopathology. Other pertinent advantages were the simple true-false format of the test, its relatively undemanding language level, and the objectivity of the scoring.

It cannot be denied that the use of psychological tests in a subcultural study creates certain problems not unlike those encountered in cross-cultural research (Lindzey, 1961). A primary difficulty in subcultural studies is that the test typically is being used in a population which almost by definition differs in several critical respects from the one in which the test was developed and validated. These differences (including, for example, differences in language usage) are likely to affect the meaning of the test results that are obtained and make it necessary to observe more than the usual amount of interpretative caution. More importantly, the test results would have to be compared with other data obtained in the same study. Independent confirmation of any conclusion based on the test would not only strengthen that particular conclusion but also indirectly increase the credibility of other interpretations based on the same instrument. This opportunity for confirmation did exist in the present study and yielded encouraging results.

Although the main objective of this investigation was to examine MMPI characteristics of a serpent-handling group, it was clear that the results would be more illuminating if a comparison group were included. Such a group could consist of individuals who were not serpent handlers but who nevertheless possessed some of the same background characteristics. Comparison of this group with the snake handlers would aid in deciding which MMPI characteristics are indeed unique to snake handlers and which are also found among other individuals with a similar cultural background. Accordingly, a second sample of MMPIs was obtained from a group of persons living in the same region as the snake handlers who belonged to a conventional denomination.[1] The analysis to be presented later is based on a comparison between members of the two church groups.

The present paper, then, will focus on the psychometric findings obtained with the MMPI; it is not an exhaustive report on the entire field study.

[1] The identity of this "control group" must remain confidential. However, the two denominations with largest memberships in West Virginia are the Methodist and the Baptist.

METHOD

Subjects

Both church groups reside in southern West Virginia in a region that is rural nonfarm with only about one-tenth of the population living in settlements of more than 2,500. The dominant industry in the area was coal mining, which has, in the last 15 years, been drastically curtailed. Unemployment is now widespread. The members of both churches are of predominantly Scotch-Irish or Pennsylvania Dutch descent. One or two generations ago many families from both churches lived in the same mining community, and their backgrounds were highly similar. The central difference between the groups at the time of this study is that the serpent handlers have remained members of the lower working class and the members of the conventional denomination are upwardly mobile and have managed to become members of the upper working class or middle class.

Serpent handlers are employed in a variety of unskilled or semiskilled occupations, such as truck driver, janitor, mechanic, or small business operator. Some have been on welfare for varying lengths of time. The average income is seldom over $3,000 a year. About one-third own their own homes, valued at about $3,000, and the rest rent houses for about $30 a month. None of the adults over 40 attended high school, and few under 40 have completed high school. Except for their church, which they attend about three times a week for three to six hours, they do not participate in community activities. Except for serpent handling, their religion is typically Holiness. They believe in a literal interpretation of the Bible. They are puritanical in their morality, although their attitude toward "sinners" is quite tolerant. They believe that a state of holiness can be achieved instantaneously through the direct operation of the Holy Spirit; during this state they speak in tongues, dance ecstatically, and sometimes become unconscious. The services do not adhere to a fixed schedule; on the contrary, they are quite unstructured and allow for free emotional expression. Enactment of the various roles (dancer, singer, testifier) is spontaneous and depends on the mood of the moment of the individual member. The serpent handlers are maintaining their beliefs and values despite their increased contact with the dominant culture.

The members of the conventional denomination are employed in a variety of skilled occupations: carpenter, barber, electrician, etc. Employment is regular, and the income averages about $5,000. Wives often work as clerks or stenographers. Most own their own homes valued at about $8,000. Most of the *S*s under 30 finished high school, but few over 50 attended high school. Several are active in PTA and other organizations, but church is the center of social activity (once or twice weekly). Literal interpretation of the Bible is not characteristic of this group. Services and activities in the church are tightly scheduled, and role playing is stable.

ADMINISTRATION OF THE MMPI

The MMPI was group-administered to most of the serpent handlers during a special evening session at the church. Although the administration was somewhat unusual involving elaborate instructions, false starts, and interruptions—popcorn and Coke breaks and occasional uninvited bystanders—the motivation and cooperation of the subjects remained high. A few core members of the sect, who were absent at this session, were later followed up individually. An audio form of the MMPI was used to solve the problem posed by low reading level. A total number of 46 serpent handlers completed the MMPI. The MMPI was administered to 90 members of the conventional congregation in two sessions. These *S*s volunteered at the minister's request. The MMPI profiles used in the analysis were matched as closely as possible for socioeconomic status and age.

ANALYSIS OF THE DATA

The analysis will be presented in four main sections. The content of the first section deviates somewhat from the main descriptive purpose of this investigation but concerns an important related issue. The issue involves the possible influence of bias in the evaluation of an unusual social phenomenon like snake handling. Specifically, using our data we wanted to determine how the knowledge that a person belongs to a snake-handling sect might affect an experienced diagnostician's impression of that person. We believed that perspective could be gained from data showing the influence, direction, and accuracy of existing preconceptions as they affect clinical impressions. If it were found that clinical psychologists do have certain preconceptions in this area which affect their evaluation of the individual's adjustment, we would, of course, wonder about the possible operation of similar biases in other subcultural studies. Such preconceptions might appear reasonable, even have some validity, and still carry undue weight in the final judgment of those investigators who place little emphasis upon objective methods of data collection and interpretation.

The second section contains a descriptive analysis of the actual test findings, and will consist of statistical comparisons of the two church groups on a series of MMPI scales. The third section will describe our efforts to move beyond a purely descriptive-statistical analysis by means of an interpretative analysis conducted with the help of experienced clinicians. A fourth section presents the results of an analysis in which the qualitative statements made in the interpretative analysis are subjected to a quantitative evaluation. We hope that the last two sections will aid substantially in communicating the psychological significance of our findings.

A Priori Notions Concerning the Psychological Significance of Church Group Membership

As stated earlier, the focus of interest in this section concerns the following question: What relationships do experienced psychologists, well-trained in personality assessment but with no special expertise in the area under study, tend to see on an a priori basis between personality characteristics—as revealed by the MMPI—and church membership? An attempt was made to answer this question using our MMPI data. Four judges, all experienced clinicians, were given an expanded version of the group descriptions presented in the "Method" section, which described common as well as distinguishing characteristics of the two church groups and contained information concerning local socioeconomic conditions, employment status, occupational characteristics, and religious practices of the two groups.[2] The judges were also given 96 individual MMPI profiles which contained scores on the validity scales and all clinical scales with the exception of the *Mf* scale; sex and age were not indicated.

The four clinicians were asked, after studying the descriptions of the two church groups, to sort the 96 profiles into two groups: (1) those which they thought belonged to members of the *conventional* denomination and (2) those they thought belonged to the *serpent-handling* denomination. After this was completed, the judges were asked to rate the adjustment of each individual by classifying the

[2] A copy of the instructions referred to here, or of the instructions of clinicians' reports to be discussed later, may be obtained on request from the authors, Department of Psychology, University of Minnesota, Minneapolis.

profiles in one of the following diagnostic categories: normal, neurotic, behavior disorder, and psychotic.

First the agreement among the judges was examined. It was found that the percentages of agreement of the six possible pairs of judges in sorting the individual profiles into church groups ranged from .55 to .75. For the classification of profiles according to diagnostic category (normal, neurotic, behavior disorder, and psychotic), the percentages of agreement ranged from .60 to .83.

At this point our primary interest was, of course, in examining the relationships between assigned church membership and diagnostic impression. For our analysis, we singled out those 58 MMPI profiles out of the total (96) on which there was agreement of at least three out of four judges with respect to both classifications—church membership and diagnostic impression. Each of these profiles was classified according to the judgment of the majority. The results are summarized in Table 11-1.

Table 11-1 shows clearly that the experienced judges tended to assign "normal" profiles to the conventional denomination (31 out of 35) and "abnormal" profiles to the serpent-handling groups (15 out of 23, including all 8 "psychotic" profiles and 3 out of the 4 profiles labeled "behavior disorder").

The same trend is revealed by the results shown in Table 11-2, which lists averages of those profiles that had been assigned unanimously to one of the two church groups. The results shown in Table 11-2 indicate that the average of the profiles assigned to the conventional denomination is essentially normal, while the average of the profiles assigned to the serpent-handling cult presents a clearly "abnormal" picture with elevations on *F*, *Pd*, *Pa*, *Pt*, *Sc*, and *Ma*.

These data clearly indicate that the judges considered membership

Table 11-1 Relationship between judged church membership and diagnostic MMPI classification. Only for cases on which 3 out of 4 judges agreed on church membership and category ($N = 58$)

Judged church membership	MMPI classification				
	Normal	Neurotic	Behavior disorder	Psychotic	Total
Conventional church	31	7	1	0	39
Serpent-handling sect	4	4	3	8	19
Total	35	11	4	8	58

Table 11-2 *T*-score averages of MMPI profiles assigned by 4 out of 4 judges to conventional denomination ($N = 25$), and to serpent-handling sect ($N = 18$), respectively.

Scale	Assigned to conventional denomination	Assigned to serpent-handling sect
L	52	47
F	53	71
K	50	45
Hs	55	56
D	57	56
Hy	55	57
Pd	55	67
Pa	50	71
Pt	53	68
Sc	50	74
Ma	49	69
Si	60	59

in the serpent-handling sect as more indicative of psychopathology than membership in the conventional denomination.

How accurate were the judgments of church membership? The actual classifications show us that the clinicians were *not* very accurate. The percentages of correct identification for the individual judges ranged from .53 to .56 (chance level 50%). Taking the 43 cases on which all four judges agreed, the percentage correct was still only .58 (chance level 51%). The results indicate that the clinicians' tendency to link serpent handling with psychopathology was *not* in agreement with the

Table 11-3 Relationship between actual church membership and diagnostic MMPI classification. Only for cases on which 3 out of 4 judges agreed on the category ($N = 75$)

Actual church membership	MMPI classification				
	Normal	Neurotic	Behavior disorder	Psychotic	Total
Conventional denomination	22	10	4	4	40
Serpent-handling sect	22	4	5	4	35
Total	44	14	9	8	75

actual state of affairs. This can be seen in Table 11-3, which groups the profiles horizontally according to the subject's actual membership. Table 11-3 is based on the 75 cases on which three out of four judges agreed with respect to diagnostic category. From the table it can be seen that the abnormal profiles are not actually concentrated in the serpent-handling group. On the contrary, there is a somewhat larger percentage of abnormal profiles, particularly "neurotic" ones, in the conventional denomination.

On the basis of these results, we are inclined to conclude that personality evaluations of individuals practicing "unusual" forms of behavior may be adversely influenced by assigning considerable weight to incorrect preconceptions concerning the meaning of these behaviors. We base this conclusion on the inference that the information concerning the religious practices of the serpent-handling group was primarily responsible for the systematic error in classification. The use of "blind" interpretation (which will be discussed in a later section) may sometimes provide a more adequate test of both the clinician's and the instrument's potential for personality description and classification.

Descriptive Analysis of the MMPI Data

It appeared desirable not to limit the analyses to correlates of church membership but also to consider the possible effects of sex and age differences. The sample was, therefore, subdivided into eight subgroups through the simultaneous use of the three dichotomies: serpent handlers versus conventional denomination, males versus females, and old versus young subjects. Three-way analyses of variance of the MMPI scores were carried out using church membership, sex, and age as factors. Prior to the analyses the subgroups were made equal in size (10 subjects in each) by eliminating *S*s whose ages would reduce the similarity in age distribution among subgroups of the same age level. Through this elimination, which was based on age only and did not involve any consideration of the MMPI profile, the size of the total sample was reduced to 80. Next, using the scores of this sample of 80, separate analyses were carried out on the validity scales *L*, *F*, and *K*) and the nine clinical scales (*Hs*, *D*, *Hy*, *Pd*, *Pa*, *Pt*, *Sc*, *Ma*, and *Si*). *K*-corrected *T* scores were used for the analysis.

In addition, eight of the clinical scales (*Hs*, *D*, *Hy*, *Pd*, *Pa*, *Pt*, *Sc*, and *Ma*) were subjected to a supplementary analysis. These analyses differ from the previous one in that they were not conducted on *T* scores but on what we have called "rank scores." The rationale and derivation of the rank scores require a few words of explanation. Clinicians have long emphasized the diagnostic importance of the "shape" of an MMPI profile; that is, they believe it is important to evaluate the elevation of any given scale *relative* to elevations on other scales. The use of the familiar MMPI code types illustrates this emphasis on profile shape. The rank scores are comparable to code typing in that they also express relative elevation, but differ because they permit a more sensitive quantitative analysis. The derivation of the rank scores was as follows: Each *S*'s individual profile was inspected, and his *T* scores (*K*-corrected) on each of the eight clinical scales used were ranked in order of magnitude. The rank order of the individual's *T* score on a given scale constituted his rank score on that particular scale. For example, if a subject received his highest score on the *Hy* scale, then his rank score on this scale would be 1.[3] The rank scores on each scale were subjected to the same three-way analyses of variance as the *T* scores.

The results of the analysis of the *T* scores for the eight subgroups on the 12 MMPI scales are shown in Table 11-3. The average *T* scores for the various groups are shown, and significance levels for the analysis of variance are shown in the right-hand column. The corresponding analysis, using rank scores, is shown in Table 11-4. One should keep in mind that in this table the lower the number the higher the score.

The combined results presented in Tables 11-4 and 11-5 may be summarized as follows: Comparison of the two church groups shows that the serpent handlers obtained higher average scores than the conventional denomination on the *Pd* and *Ma* scales and that the conventional denomination had higher averages on the *K* and *Hy* scales. Several large age differences were found. The older group scored higher on *L*, *Hs*, *D*, *Hy*, and *Si*. The younger group scored higher on the *Ma* scale. A sex difference was also found; females scored higher on the *Si* scale than males.

The necessity of taking age into account in the comparison of the two churches is evident from the significant interaction of age and church membership on the *D* scale. This interaction is due to the very high *D* scores of the old members, male and female, of the

[3] The evaluation of profile shapes and of profile similarity (as expressed in *Q* correlations) can lead to problems when the direction of scoring adopted for the scales that make up the profile is chosen arbitrarily. In the present analysis of rank data direction is consistent: The "high end" of the scales is associated with psychopathology. More extensive discussions of the problem of "direction of measurement" have been presented elsewhere (Howard & Diesenhaus, 1967; Tellegen, 1965).

Table 11-4 MMPI *T*-score averages of subgroups in the two churches

Scale	Conventional denomination				Serpent handlers				Results: Analyses of variance
	Females		Males		Females		Males		
	Young	Old	Young	Old	Young	Old	Young	Old	
L	47	53	49	54	51	53	48	57	Age $< .005$
F	57	57	57	60	60	62	64	59	n.s.
K	51	52	54	52	44	47	44	50	Church group $< .005$
Hs	54	64	52	67	52	58	50	62	Age $< .0005$
D	51	73	54	72	54	58	56	66	Age $< .0005$ Church $\times$ age $< .01$
Hy	57	65	55	62	53	53	52	58	Church group $< .05$ Age $< .01$
Pd	60	60	64	66	61	68	68	68	n.s.
Pa	63	57	58	57	58	59	57	60	n.s.
Pt	59	68	61	66	57	61	61	60	n.s.
Sc	57	61	62	63	60	61	60	61	n.s.
Ma	57	51	58	53	57	54	67	59	Age $< .05$
Si	56	67	52	65	60	62	54	58	Age $< .0005$ Sex $< .05$
Mean age	21	48	21	51	22	49	21	52	
Age range	16–32	38–60	17–29	39–68	16–31	39–59	16–29	41–67	

Table 11-5 MMPI rank-score averages of subgroups in the two churches

Scale	Conventional denomination				Serpent handlers				Results: Analyses of variance
	Females		Males		Females		Males		
	Young	Old	Young	Old	Young	Old	Young	Old	
Hs	5.6	4.0	6.1	3.3	6.2	5.2	6.3	4.6	Age $< .001$
D	5.3	2.0	5.4	2.4	5.2	5.0	4.3	3.4	Age $< .0005$ Age $\times$ Church $< .01$
Hy	4.2	3.8	5.0	4.7	5.2	5.5	6.0	6.1	Church group $< .01$
Pd	3.8	5.1	3.2	3.7	3.1	2.5	2.2	2.3	Church group $< .005$
Pa	2.9	6.3	4.9	6.2	4.4	4.4	5.5	5.1	Age $< .025$ Age $\times$ Church $< .01$
Pt	4.2	3.0	3.3	4.1	4.3	3.8	4.2	4.9	n.s.
Sc	5.1	5.4	4.1	5.1	3.9	4.2	4.6	4.8	n.s.
Ma	5.0	6.6	4.3	6.8	3.9	5.6	3.1	5.0	Church group $< .025$ Age $< .001$

conventional denomination. A second interaction involved the *Pa* scale and was produced by the rank scores (Table 11-5). However, inspection of the averages on this scale, shown in Tables 11-4 and 11-5, shows an irregular pattern; the interdependence of rank ("ipsative") data suggests that this particular interaction might be more safely accounted for in terms of the findings on other scales.

Interpretative Analysis of the MMPI Data

The next analysis is specifically concerned with the psychological significance of the statistical findings reported in the previous section. To be reported are the "blind" profile interpretations that were provided for us by three experienced clinicians. The three psychologists who cooperated in this part of the study had neither participated in the earlier profile sorting nor were they aware of the nature of the study. Each of the clinicians was given a set of mean MMPI profiles representing the *T*-score averages of the young and old members of both church groups. (In this and all other material given to the judges, the two church groups were consistently referred to only as "church A" and "church B.") The judges were also given a summary of statistical differences between the subgroups (reported in Tables 11-4 and 11-5). Finally, the judges were given a statement describing the *common* geographical, socioeconomic, and cultural backgrounds of the two church groups. This information was given in order that the clinicians would be in a position to formulate relevant and specific interpretative statements about the groups rather than be limited to generalities. Thus it is only in a more restricted, but, we believe, more meaningful sense, that we may speak of "blind" interpretation. The judges were *not* given information concerning the contrasting religious practices of the two church groups in order to prevent the misconceptions that had entered into the profile sortings reported earlier.

In formulating their interpretations, the clinicians were not asked to adhere to a rigidly specified format. It was suggested, however, that they comment on age differences as well as church group differences. All three clinicians responded with quite detailed and interesting interpretations. We will cite extensively from their reports and will attempt to present in an integrated manner what we consider to be the most important portions. First we will cite the clinicians' inferences regarding the two church groups, then their comments comparing the two age groups, and third interpretations of the observed interaction between age and church membership.

With respect to church group differences, the clinicians noted the relatively higher average scores for the conventional group on the *K* scale and the *Hy* scale, and, therefore, assumed that members of the conventional group would be relatively more defensive, more disposed to deny emotional discomfort, and more inclined to see themselves as persons who have things "under control." Thus clinician A sees members of the serpent-handling sect as "more willing to admit bad things about themselves."[4] Clinician B considers members of the conventional denomination "somewhat more reserved, 'defensive,' and inclined to general attitudes of sublimation and denial" than snake handlers. Clinician C says of the members of the conventional denomination that they "attribute to the self more stability and integration" than is true for the snake-handling sect. Pursuing this line of thought, this clinician expects that members of the conventional denomination tend to "assume more personal responsibility for adequacy and achievement, or lack of it," while the serpent handlers "would be more likely to see themselves 'in the hands of fate,' buffeted by external forces, and at the mercy of those more powerful."

Also taken into account were the differences between the two church groups on the *Pd* and the *Hy* scales. As reported earlier, the serpent handlers had higher average rank scores on both these scales than the members of the conventional denomination. Consequently, the clinicians tended to regard the serpent handlers, compared to the members of the other church, as more active, less inhibited, more "extraverted" (in the Eysenckian rather than Jungian sense). Thus, clinician A remarks that members of the snake-handling sect "appear to be more energetic, uninhibited, outgoing" and "more impulsive and spontaneous" than members of the conventional denomination. Clinician A further remarks that if a psychiatric label had to be selected, the mean profile of the serpent handlers would be most suggestive of personality or character disorder (rather than neurosis or psychosis). Clinician B remarks in the same vein that the data would be in line with the notion that the personalities of the serpent handlers tend to be "somewhat more aggressive, spontaneous, exhibitionistic."

Interesting inferences were made concerning the religious services of the two church groups. Clinician A suggests that the members of the conventional denomination "might be more concerned with ritual and form," while the services of the serpent handlers might be distinguished by "more activity and social interaction." Clinician B similarly surmises that services of the conventional denomination "are relatively

[4] The three clinicians will be referred to as clinicians A, B, and C. The two churches were known to the clinicians only as churches A and B. However, in the text the actual church designation will be used for clarity and convenience.

more structured, ritualized, and controlled, especially with regard to emotional expression" and suggests that, on the other hand, the services of the snake handlers might be characterized by "more frequent spontaneous expression of faith as in public 'witnessing' and 'confession,' " in short, by "a church atmosphere which encourages active emotional display." Clinician B goes on to suggest that among the members of the conventional church "religious life as overtly expressed is relatively restricted to activities in the church proper," while by contrast he would expect in the case of the serpent-handling sect "such things as table graces and family prayers" to be more likely. By way of summary, this clinician describes the religious orientation of the conventional group and the serpent-handling sect, respectively, as "Episcopalian-like" and "Baptist-like," adding that the members of the conventional church "represent a group probably with a somewhat better level of education, income, etc."

Turning now to the age factor, we saw earlier that substantial differences were found between the two age groups on a number of scales. The clinicians took due note of these differences. Clinician C points out, first of all, that the direction of the differences seems "consistent with clinical expectations regarding aging." Clinician B similarly notes that "the old members of both churches are more like older people generally, and young people of both churches are more like young people generally." As far as the meaning of these differences is concerned, clinician C interprets it as indicating that the "old group reports more somatic symptoms, is less extroverted and energetic, and more rigid than the young group."

Of more special interest to the clinicians than the overall age difference was the evidence that this difference is not the same in the two church groups, as specifically indicated by the significant interaction between church groups and age groups on the D scale. The averages of the subgroups on this scale, shown in Tables 11-4 and 11-5, reveal that the interaction is largely the result of the particularly high average scores (more than two standard deviations above the normative mean) of the older male and female members of the conventional church group. The clinicians acknowledged this state of affairs, first of all, by describing the older members of the conventional church as a particularly depressed and unhappy group. As clinician C puts it, the older members of the conventional church as a group "seem dysphoric, insecure, and quite withdrawn." Clinician B believes that, compared with the serpent handlers, the members of the conventional church are "more susceptible to depression, worry, and anxiety with advancing years."

The greater contrast between young and old in the conventional church group inspired hypotheses concerning differences between the two churches as social units. These hypotheses essentially reflect a belief that the conventional church group, compared with the snake-handling sect, is less cohesive, is more affected by the disrupting influences of outside forces, and that its impact on the members is less pervasive. For example, clinician C remarks that it is easier to rationalize the young and old serpent handlers "as belonging to the same group, sharing the same attitudes and outlook," than is the case in the conventional church. Clinician C in this connection suggests "as a wild hypothesis" that the more marked change in MMPI pattern with age in the conventional church "hints of more impact of cultural and technological change" on this group than on the serpent handlers. Clinician B, focusing on internal factors, believes that the older members of the conventional church show such marked depression because they derive less comfort and security from their faith and are more likely to suffer from a sense of isolation than their counterparts in the snake-handling sect. This problem, clinician B believes, might be explained by the apparently more reserved emotional climate prevailing in the conventional church, a climate which is seen as less conducive to "open and public identification" and as lowering the probability of "strong group identification." This same clinician also speaks of the contrasting roles believed to be played by the young members of the two church groups. On one hand, the atmosphere of the conventional denomination is seen as more "intellectual" and controlled so that one would expect its younger members to play "a relatively less participant role." In contrast, the services of the serpent-handling church are believed to be not only less "programmed" and more spontaneous but also more conducive to equal participation by young and old. Clinician A expresses very similar views on the differences in cohesiveness between the two churches. This clinician, for example, speculates that in the serpent-handling church the younger generation has "an easier time identifying" with the older generation than is true for the conventional church.

Objective Evaluation of the Clinical Interpretations

Although the explicitness and congruence of the preceding clinical interpretations appeared rather impressive, it was felt that the main features of the interpretative pictures might stand out even more clearly if some of the observations made by the three clinicians were subjected to quantification. As a final step in the analysis, the individual MMPIs were systematically rated on those psychological dimensions that were most prominent in the qualitative interpretations of the group profiles.

The rating dimensions were selected as follows: First, all trait descriptions or labels occurring in any of the interpretations were typed on separate cards. Next, two of the authors (JNB and AT) independently formed clusters of traits that were equivalent or closely related. After comparing and discussing their groupings, they jointly arrived at eight clusters. They then chose for each of the clusters the representative trait names shown in the far left-hand column of Table 11-6. A rating scale also had to be selected. The one adopted is a modified version of a scale constructed by Lorr, Klett, and McNair (1963) and provides for the following ratings: 0—absence, 1—very slight, 2—a little, 3—mild degree, 4—moderate degree, 5—quite a bit, 6—distinct, 7—marked degree, and 8—extremely high degree.

Four additional experienced clinicians, not acquainted with the study, were asked to rate 40 individual MMPI profiles on the eight dimensions. The total sample of 80 MMPI profiles was distributed so that each MMPI profile was rated by two judges. After the judges had completed their tasks, the two ratings obtained for each individual MMPI were averaged, and analyses of variance were conducted for each of the eight dimensions. The subgroup averages and the results of the analyses of variance are shown in Table 11-6.

An inspection of the results reveals good agreement with the interpretations summarized in the preceding section. The snake handlers were judged more frank and more willing to admit shortcomings than members of the conventional denomination (rating scale A); snake handlers were also seen as having more problems associated with impulsivity or character disorder (rating scale E). The differences between young and old are also quite evident, with the younger subjects being rated as less depressed and pessimistic (scale B), more energetic and active (scale C), more emotionally demonstrative (scale D), less somatically preoccupied (scale G), and less troubled by feelings of inferiority and inadequacy (scale H). There is again the interaction between age group and church denomination on the trait of depression and pessimism (scale B) due to the particularly high average ratings of the older members of the conventional church group. The ratings disclose an additional interaction, not found in the early analyses, between sex and age group on scale E suggesting that problems of impulse control and character disorder are most prominent among younger males in both church groups.

In summary, it appears that the ratings of the individual profiles, in supplementing qualitative description with quantitative results, in-

Table 11-6 MMPI rating averages of subgroups in the two churches

Trait	Conventional denomination				Serpent handlers				Results: Analyses of variance
	Females		Males		Females		Males		
	Young	Old	Young	Old	Young	Old	Young	Old	
A. Frankness; willingness to admit shortcomings	3.8	4.1	3.4	3.6	5.1	3.6	5.5	4.1	Church group < .025 Church × age < .005
B. Pessimism; depression	1.8	5.1	1.8	5.0	2.3	2.5	2.1	4.2	Age < .0005 Church × age < .01
C. Energy; activity	4.1	2.5	4.2	3.0	4.2	3.4	5.5	3.5	Age < .005
D. Emotional exhibitionism; demonstrativeness	3.6	2.5	4.3	3.1	3.6	3.7	4.4	3.5	Age < .025
E. Problems of impulse control; character disorder	2.4	2.1	3.6	3.1	3.2	3.3	4.4	3.5	Church group < .05 Sex < .05 Sex × age < .025
F. Guilt proneness; rigid superego	3.5	4.3	2.6	4.0	2.8	2.9	2.7	3.8	n.s.
G. Hypochondriacal concerns	2.5	4.2	1.7	4.8	1.9	2.6	1.6	3.9	Age < .0005
H. Feelings of insecurity and inadequacy	3.8	4.9	2.7	5.0	3.7	3.4	3.1	4.6	Age < .025

deed highlight many of the points contained in the interpretation of the group profiles.

COMMENTS AND CONCLUSIONS

Our detailed analysis of the psychometric data should not obscure the fact that data of this nature can only fulfill a supplementary function. One cannot rely solely on the MMPI, particularly when one's subcultural research extends the use of the assessment device to a population that differs importantly from the samples on which most of the information concerning the test's validity was collected. It is necessary, therefore, to compare the test findings with other data. Any demonstration of agreement between the MMPI and other sources would add to one's confidence that the test measures what it was found to measure in its original setting. The limitations of the present study preclude comparisons of this nature except on one particular issue. The comparison in question concerns the religious practices of the two church groups. Descriptions of these practices, based on direct observation, had been obtained prior to the analysis of the MMPI data. These descriptions—summarized in the "Method" section—characterized the services of the serpent handlers as unstructured, spontaneous, and emotionally expressive, with no fixed roles assigned to particular individuals. In contrast, the services of the conventional group were described as highly structured and tightly scheduled, with stable role playing. The reader may already have noted that the "blind" interpretations of the three clinicians contain passages that are quite similar to these descriptions: The clinicians inferred that the serpent handlers' services were spontaneous and emotionally demonstrative; on the other hand, they expected the services of the conventional group to proceed in a more structured and ritualized manner. We would not argue, of course, that in this instance the MMPI data were greatly needed to "confirm" the field observations. Rather, we would view the independent observations as upholding certain MMPI-based conclusions, thus generally bolstering our confidence in the usefulness of the instrument in this setting. But the interpreted test data also contributed by linking in a psychologically understandable way the contrasting religious practices of the two groups with certain psychological differences related to the Pd and Ma scales.

It is perhaps not superfluous to point out also that our findings might have been different had we studied a different but comparable pair of church groups and that generalizations from our results are, therefore, tentative.[5] Likewise, since the present study is a correlational one, any causal inferences concerning the impact of certain personality characteristics on the social environment and vice versa are in need of further confirmation.

Turning to a different issue, we remind the reader that the preceding analyses and interpretations focused primarily on *differences* between the various subgroups and did not call attention to one other important aspect of our MMPI data, namely, the overall *elevation* of the T scores in both samples. Table 11-4 shows that on the eight clinical scales, 32 out of 64 T-score averages are 60 or higher, that is, one standard deviation or more above the normative mean. Table 11-3, furthermore, shows that of 75 profiles only 44 were classified "normal," while 31 were placed in one of three psychiatric categories with both church groups contributing substantially. These results require some comment. Taken at face value, they suggest a high incidence of psychopathology in both churches. Additional information would be needed, however, before one could reach a definite conclusion. For example, one would like to know how deviant the MMPIs of our present two samples are compared with a *local* normative group of unselected individuals. But this would not be enough; again, data from sources other than the MMPI would be needed. For example, an MMPI comparison of two local groups independently (if crudely) classified as "psy-

[5] The following reaction by Reverend Jerry Butcher to an earlier draft of this paper is an informal but informative comment on the issue of generalization:

> My experience as a minister to the "middle–upper middle" strata of mid-western culture (ten years now) would seem to confirm the results of your study. I wonder if those personality patterns would be much different in, say, a conventional . . . Church in Ohio over against a radical Baptist or Holiness Church? (or in Minnesota!)
>
> The high number of "neurotic" members in the conventional church is not too surprising. Pessimism among the elder members of both seems quite true to the pattern I have found as a pastor. I think Clinician B's theory that the climate in the conventional church is less conducive to "open and public identification," and that there is a lack of "strong group identification" in the conventional church is quite sound. We in the institutional Church have recognized this to be among our chief problems for quite some time, especially with regard to the aged.
>
> It was quite interesting also to see the difference free emotional expression in worship seems to have on a church over against the more rigid forms of the conventional church. I don't think my congregation is ready yet for "snake handling" but many pastors in the conventional churches are experimenting with "unconventional" methods of worship (for example: lay preaching, liturgical jazz, glossolalia, etc.).
>
> I think this study is relevant to the Church's position as a social institution in our culture.

chiatric" versus "normal" would shed some light on the psychopathological implications of our present test results. At this point no such information is available. The conclusion that both church groups show a high incidence of psychopathology remains, therefore, tentative.

What light do the data shed on La Barre's hypothesis concerning serpent handling and serpent handlers? Although our results do not permit a detailed evaluation of La Barre's views, it appears that some of our findings are at least relevant. Our data indicate perhaps more explicitly than does La Barre's monograph that individual predispositions may account in part for the fact that only certain members of a subculture become serpent handlers. To us, the psychometric data also suggest that the traits predisposing toward membership in the serpent-handling sect are more closely related to impulsivity and emotional expressivity than to intensified neurotic conflicts of the kind elaborated by La Barre on the basis of the serpent-handling "symptom." Putting it somewhat differently, if we had to identify a major differential personality factor facilitating participation in the serpent-handling cult, we would point to "extraversion" rather than to "neuroticism" (using Eysenck's broad taxonomy, Eysenck, 1953). We recall here La Barre's own factual accounts, particularly his description of the repeated conflicts between serpent handlers and local authorities described in one place as "an amiable kind of cat-and-mouse game with the police." This description points to a penchant for nonconformity and for stirring up excitement on the part of the serpent handlers which actually is quite consonant with the extraversion construct. Greater "psychological youthfulness" is what seems to distinguish the serpent handlers from the conventional church group, a contrast further enhanced by MMPI results suggesting that older members of the conventional church group have many more depressive symptoms than older members of the serpent-handling sect. From the present perspective, the occasional enactment of the serpent-handling ritual by a few members would not in and of itself explain the appeal of the cult for its members. Rather, one would expect the serpent handler to value his church and its religious services (which assign such an important role to spontaneous expression in testimony, singing, and dancing) as more generally providing a variety of opportunities for pleasurable, exciting, and significant emotional experiences. That too much emphasis on the deviancy rather than on the extraverted nature of these practices can lead even experienced clinicians astray was suggested by the results reported in our section on "clinical preconceptions."

In summary, we believe that the use of a psychometric instrument in this subcultural study resulted in relevant additional information. Certain MMPI differences between subgroups were identified, and clinical interpretations were obtained suggesting that these differences had distinct psychological implications. A similar psychometric approach could also prove to be of value in future studies of this nature.

REFERENCES

Eysenck, H. J. *The structure of human personality.* London: Methuen, 1953.

Howard, K. I., and Diesenhaus, H. I. Direction of measurement and profile similarity. *Multivariate Behavioral Research,* 1967, **2,** 225–237.

La Barre, W. *They shall take up serpents: Psychology of the Southern snake-handling cult.* Minneapolis: University of Minnesota Press, 1962.

Lindzey, G. *Projective techniques and cross-cultural research.* New York: Appleton-Century-Crofts, 1961.

Lorr, M., Klett, C. J., and McNair, D. M. *Syndromes of psychosis.* New York: Macmillan, 1963.

Tellegen, A. Direction of measurement: A source of misinterpretation. *Psychological Bulletin,* 1967, **63,** 233–243.

Chapter Twelve

The Regional Localization Hypothesis and Personality Changes Associated with Focal Cerebral Lesions and Ablations

Manfred J. Meier
University of Minnesota

The clinical recognition of behavioral changes associated with frontal lobe lesions contributed to the development of psychosurgical procedures in the treatment of selected severe personality disturbances (Freeman & Watts, 1942; Moniz, 1936). Personality changes observed after prefrontal leucotomy and topectomy gave impetus to investigations of the effects of discrete cerebral lesions on personality functioning and to the determination of the empirical validity of a regional cerebral localization hypothesis with respect to personality changes (Andersen, 1949). Since these studies have related localized structural variables to changes in personality function, some discussion of these structural dimensions and their major behavioral correlates might facilitate any evaluation of the implications this literature may have for a regional localization hypothesis. With the exception of a few studies involving psychological tests derived from Eysenck's theory of personality (Meyer, 1960, p. 552), the MMPI was utilized in most investigations for measuring personality changes resulting from or associated with structural lesions of the brain. This review will attempt to integrate the findings of relevant research with the MMPI into current conceptualizations of the regional localization of brain function in man.

This reviewer was supported in part by Research Career Development Award NB-K3-18,539 and in part by grants NB-03364 and NB-04954 from the National Institute of Neurological Diseases and Blindness of the United States Public Health Service.

SOME STRUCTURAL AND BEHAVIORAL RELATIONSHIPS

It is beyond the scope of this paper to review the evidence for regional equipotentiality or localization of brain function. An excellent review of the major findings and methodological issues involved in establishing behavioral correlates of focal brain lesions is available elsewhere (Meyer, 1960). Most of the research in this area has involved the assessment of sensorimotor, perceptual, and intellectual deficits associated with focal cerebral lesions along two general structural dimensions of the cortex: laterality and caudality. Many of these investigations have been concerned with establishing functional asymmetries between the cerebral hemispheres in relation to verbal-performance IQ discrepancies on the Wechsler Adult Intelligence Scale (WAIS) or earlier versions of the test (Andersen, 1951; Meier & French, 1966; Meyer & Yates, 1955; Reitan, 1955). Although the resultant findings have not been unequivocal (Meier, 1966; Smith, 1966), it has been reasonably well established that the dominant cerebral hemisphere, or left hemisphere in persons with clear right-body-side preferences, primarily subserves verbal intellectual functions, while the right, or nondominant, cerebral hemisphere mediates the integration of visuospatial and temporal-spatial relationships. Thus, the major behavior correlate of structural lesions along the interhemispheric laterality dimension in man appears to involve differential changes in verbal and visuospatial functions.

Similarly, numerous higher-order behavioral changes have been correlated structurally with topographical variation in lesion localization along the cephalocaudal dimension of the cerebral cortex. For example, the prefrontal areas have been implicated in planning and foresight abilities (Mettler, 1949; Smith, 1960), ability to shift from one solution to the other (Milner, 1964), and in setting a luminous line to the vertical under visuopostural conflict conditions (Teuber & Mishkin, 1954). Lesions of the anterior and middle temporal lobe have been associated with deficits in complex visual and auditory functioning (Kimura, 1961; Meier & French, 1965b; Milner, 1958), while posterior temporal-parietal lesions have been shown to produce impairment of somesthetic discrimination (Teuber, 1962), more conspicuous intellectual deficits (Weinstein, 1962), and a wide range of well-known aphasic, agnostic, and apraxic disturbances. These differential outcomes for left- and right-sided lesions, depending in turn upon their location along the cephalocaudal dimension, reflect an interaction between lesion laterality and caudality in the determination of changes in function. Any search for functional interpretations of anatomic locus variables must accommodate the interactions between these dimensions.

NEUROPATHOLOGICAL FACTORS RELATED TO PERSONALITY CHANGE

The above considerations serve to highlight the kinds of relationships between selected anatomic and perceptual or intellectual variables which have emerged in neuropsychological research. Although investigative emphasis has been placed upon the determination of cognitive changes associated with cerebral lesions, some efforts have been directed toward the objective establishment of personality correlates of lesion localization. The early efforts to measure such correlates with the MMPI proceeded from consideration of the laterality and caudality dimensions. Insofar as lesion laterality had been shown to be associated with verbal-performance IQ discrepancies on the Wechsler-Bellevue II (Andersen, 1951) and not with personality differences, it was predicted that lesion localization along the cephalocaudal dimension might be related to different personality changes in patients with anterior as compared with posterior location of the lesion (Andersen & Hanvik, 1950; Friedman, 1950; Williams, 1952). More recent MMPI research has involved pre- and postoperative assessment of patients who underwent unilateral temporal lobectomy for the treatment of intractable temporal lobe seizures (Meier & French, 1964, 1965a, 1965c). These later studies attempted to expand the conceptual base, in anatomical terms, for generating predictions about variation in personality by examining the relationship between personality variables, vertical localization, and bilaterality of the lesion as well.

EARLIER MMPI RESEARCH: CAUDALITY AND PERSONALITY CHANGE

Prompted by reports of clinical reduction of anxiety and related changes following prefrontal leucotomy, Andersen (1949) obtained serial MMPI data from a severe psychoneurotic patient before and over a period of days after operation. Although some decline was noted on the *D* and *Pt* scales the day following the operation, scale elevations returned to preoperative levels over the subsequent 10 days. This study is perhaps noteworthy for the failure to demonstrate, in a single case, the emergence of profound personality change on the MMPI after surgery, even though the patient was considered to have undergone major changes clinically in the direction of increased indifference, apathy, carelessness of dress, and giddiness. Although the patient apparently recovered from these behavioral alterations during the period of serial MMPI testing, such recovery was not clearly reflected in the minor scale elevation changes seen.

In a more extensive study of MMPI changes following prefrontal leucotomy (Vidor, 1951), statistically significant declines were reported on the *D* and *Pt* scale scores and on the time required to do the test. The preoperative mean profile without the *K* correction (2′87654-319/) shifted downward postoperatively (′64285-7913/) suggesting a reduction of anxious, depressive, and schizoid symptomatology. In a similar study of 25 schizophrenic patients (Ruja, 1951), no significant scale changes were found over a six-month pre- to postoperative interval. These equivocal effects of prefrontal lobotomy on MMPI scale change do not provide sufficient information to have definitive implications for personality functioning and the frontal lobes. It might be tentatively concluded that prefrontal leucotomy may have (1) little effect on psychopathological changes in ideation in schizophrenic patients and (2) some effect on preexisting affective disorders in reducing anxiety, depression, and obsessive-compulsive characteristics as measured by the MMPI. These conclusions would stand in general agreement with the work of the British investigators (Crown, 1952; Petrie, 1952) who observed decreases after prefrontal leucotomy in neuroticism and introversion as measured by performance tests derived from Eysenck's dimensions of personality (Willett, 1960).

The more extensive earlier MMPI studies were not done with leucotomized patients and, therefore, did not include pre- to postoperative evaluation of personality change. Instead, focal cerebral lesion samples were built cross-sectionally on the basis of neurosurgical and x-ray criteria of focal involvement primarily in patients with brain tumors and penetrating missile wounds. Thus, these patients were not selected for personality disturbances and were assumed to have been free of such disturbances before lesion to the brain occurred. Andersen and Hanvik (1950) reported MMPI differences between 16 frontal and 27 parietal lobe lesion patients in a preliminary attempt to establish an empirical relationship between personality changes and lesion caudality. Parietal lobe lesions were associated with higher elevations on the *F*, *D*, *Pt*, and *Sc* scales, while the frontal subjects' scores were higher on *K*. The mean composite code (Welsh, 1948) for the frontal lobe lesion patients (′3-18 4276 95/0) reflected a higher incidence of normal and hysteroid code types in that group. By contrast, the composite code (12′378-946 0/5) was related to a greater number of abnormal profiles, particularly with depressive, hypochondriacal, and anxious configurational characteristics, in the parietal lobe group. Thus, the two groups differed in both type and severity of personality changes associated with lesion location along the cephalocaudal dimension. Corresponding differences were not present in intellectual functioning. Intellectual differences were instead related to lesion laterality; left-hemisphere lesions produced relatively greater verbal IQ deficits and right-hemisphere lesions greater performance IQ deficits (Andersen, 1951).

Friedman (1950) extended this investigation with a series of similarly selected frontal and parietal lobe lesion patients. His parietal lobe group showed significantly greater elevations than the frontal group on *F, Hs, D, Hy, Pt, Sc,* and *Si* scale scores. Conversely, the frontal lobe group scored higher than the parietal lobe group on the *K* scale only. Mean MMPI profiles confirmed the Andersen and Hanvik finding of a hysteroid or conversion reaction code type in the frontal group ('-381 475962/0) that was well within normal limits of variation. The mean composite profile of the parietal lobe group was grossly elevated (2187'3-09645/) and was consistent with depressive, hypochondriacal, anxious, and schizoid features in this group. MMPI rank means provided even sharper contrasts between these code types; and, again, no differences emerged as a function of lesion laterality. Subsequent item analysis, utilizing a 3% significance level for item selection, yielded a Parietal-Frontal (*Pf*) scale consisting of 32 items. These items, responded to in the psychopathological direction more often by the parietal lobe group, appeared to reflect difficulties in reading, depression, anxiety, somatic preoccupation, social sensitivity, sleep disturbances, judgmental changes, and inadequacy feelings. Group separation, using a cutting score between 11 and 12 raw score points, exhibited an overlap of only three cases of parietal lobe patients which were misclassified as frontal lobe patients. In a cross validation on new groups (8 frontal lesions; 13 parietal lesions), group separations showed attrition to 67% correct identification.

Although Friedman was particularly interested in clinical application of the *Pf* scale, the utility of the scale is questionable since it can be applied only after the lesion has been detected on some other basis and since it would not be expected to differentiate anxious and depressed patients with nonorganic disorders from patients with parietal lobe lesions. The *Pf* scale is perhaps noteworthy as a point of departure in assessing parietal lobe-related personality changes, whatever their ultimate origins in physiological changes due to neuronal destruction or as secondary reactions to somatosensory deficits and other readily discernible neurological symptoms arising from parietal lobe lesions.

Additional evidence of a relationship between MMPI variables and cerebral localization along the cephalocaudal dimension was provided by the construction of the Caudality (*Ca*) scale (Williams, 1952). Utilizing identical selection criteria, Williams added 20 frontal, 20 parietal, and 20 temporal lobe lesion patients to Friedman's frontal and parietal lobe samples. The combined frontal lobe group exhibited a mean profile without slope and a moderate elevation on the *Sc* scale, while the enlarged parietal lobe group showed the characteristic affective disturbance profile with elevations on the *D* and *Pt* scales. The temporal lobe group mean profile resembled that of the patients with parietal lobe lesions except for an additional but secondary elevation on the *Sc* scale mean. Thus, the temporal lobe group MMPI characteristics, although consistent with expectation for profile type and degree of elevation, could be inferred to reflect indications of subtle ideational disturbances resembling those suggested in the *Sc* elevation of the frontal lobe group. This apparent commonality between the frontal and temporal lobe groups was expressed in the failure of the *Pf* scale to differentiate the temporal from the frontal lobe group with the original cutting score. By contrast, the *Pf* scale continued to differentiate between the new frontal and parietal samples suggesting the scale's specific sensitivity for involvement in those regions. In order to increase the sensitivity of the *Pf* scale to frontal-temporal differences, Williams conducted additional item analyses in a double cross-validation design by comparing response frequencies of the combined parietal and temporal patients with those of the frontal lobe group. Utilizing the gross median (raw score = 11) of the resulting 37-item scale (*Ca*), he failed to identify 6 temporal, 12 parietal, and 10 frontal lobe cases for an overall accuracy of 76% in differentiating the frontal from the posterior lesion group. Although these items contributed to all the clinical scales, greatest overlap occurred with the *D*, *Pt*, *Hy*, and *Sc* scales. By increasing the sensitivity of the *Ca* over that of the *Pf* scale to temporal lobe lesions, the *Ca* scale could be construed to tap behavioral changes associated with the caudality dimension generally rather than with parietal and frontal localization specifically.

THE LOCALIZATION HYPOTHESIS: CAUDALITY, VERTICALITY, AND BILATERALITY

Although neither of the above investigators unequivocally concluded that the MMPI differences between patients with anterior and those with posterior cerebral lesions were a direct outcome of intrinsic localized anatomical and physiological changes in the cerebral cortex, their findings could be viewed as supporting a regional localization hypothesis for the expression of motivational-emotional changes in behavior as measured by the MMPI. Such a conclusion would appear to be contingent upon the substantive fulfillment of a number of underlying assumptions with respect to the relationship between lesion caudality and personality change.

First, it seems reasonable that personality changes, in order to reflect intrinsic neural substrate factors, should emerge independently of conspicuously debilitating and incapacitating sensorimotor deficits. Otherwise, differences in personality functioning between the representative caudality criterion groups might merely reflect reactions to differences in the adjustive implications resulting from differential neurological deficit. As a consequence of the interpersonal and vocational complications introduced by somatosensory and upper motor neuronal involvement, such deficits could realistically be expected to elicit depressive and apprehensive reactions to loss in function. It is well known that parietal lobe involvement produces more severe sensorimotor deficits than does any other region of the cerebral cortex (Baker, 1958). Moreover, the prefrontal and anterior temporal areas are often associated with a relative absence or equivocal expression of sensorimotor findings (Baker, 1958). For these reasons, the higher elevations on the *D* and *Pt* scales of the MMPI among patients with parietal lobe lesions may constitute an affectively reactive epiphenomenon rather than direct expression of neuronal changes. This interpretation seems yet more credible when consideration is given to the fact that the patients with frontal lobe lesions in both the Friedman and Williams studies failed to exhibit MMPI elevations of definitive psychopathological magnitude. As a group they showed only mild hysteroid features and a secondary elevation on the *Sc* scale. Similarly, the *Pf* scale failed to differentiate the patients with temporal lobe from those with frontal lobe lesions until additional analyses increased the sensitivity of the extended *Ca* scale.

A second assumption underlying a regional localization hypothesis for the caudality dimension and personality changes would seem to require that the physiological mechanisms underlying pathological changes in motivational-emotional behavior patterns are functionally organized along the cephalocaudal axis of the cerebral cortex. However, neurophysiological and neuropsychological investigations into the temporal lobe and associated deeper structures of the limbic system in animals have adduced evidence for the functional organization of emotional and motivational patterns of behavior along the vertical axis of CNS structure (Bard & Mountcastle, 1948; Brady, 1958; Kluver & Bucy, 1938; MacLean & Delgado, 1953; Olds, 1958; Ruch, 1965). Anatomically, it has become apparent that efferent projections from the hippocampus and cingulate cortex lead to the midbrain reticular formation that interconnects reciprocally with the nonspecific intralaminar nuclei of the thalamus (Johnson, 1953). These nuclei have been shown to interact anatomically with limbic system structures in an ascending and descending manner (Nauta, 1953, 1956) and, along with the midbrain reticular formation, project to the neocortex (Morison & Dempsey, 1942; Moruzzi & Magoun, 1949). Moreover, the limbic system, in addition to the temporal pole and deeper subcortical structures, consists of portions of the frontal lobe, specifically the orbital frontal surface and the cingulate cortex (Cajal, 1909; Lorente de No, 1934). This system, therefore, includes both frontal and temporal components, as well as the hippocampus, amygdala, and insula, to form a vertically organized system whose complex interrelationships are maintained through the uncinate fasciculus (Kendrick & Gibbs, 1958). Since both frontal and temporal lobe structures are involved, an anatomical distinction between the orbital frontal and related temporal lobe structures seems arbitrary and in contradiction to the known cytoarchitectural facts. For this reason, it might be more meaningful to seek a regional explanation of personality changes associated with lesions of the central nervous system by considering structural changes along the verticality and bilaterality dimensions rather than the caudality dimension of topographical lesion distribution.

PERSONALITY CHANGES AND LIMBIC SYSTEM LESIONS IN MAN

Clinical Context

The introduction of unilateral temporal lobectomy for the treatment of intractable psychomotor seizures has provided a basis for a preliminary exploration of this hierarchical conceptualization of the central nervous system in the determination of personality disturbances in man. It was felt that the incorporation of the verticality and bilaterality dimensions as possible correlates of personality change followed directly from the extensive animal literature implicating the limbic system and might be anchored empirically in those anatomical and electrophysiological criteria which are used in the neurological-neurosurgical setting to make and implement operative decisions (Meier & French, 1961).

Before considering this investigative context in more specific detail, it might be pertinent to review briefly the clinical manifestations of psychomotor seizures (Baker, 1958). Such seizures are associated with irritative foci usually due to old atrophic lesions in the limbic system and are characterized variously by special sensory or visual aura, cardiorespiratory sensations, psychical manifestations of an illusory or hallucinatory nature, dreamy states, mood changes, and automatisms. Automatisms may vary in content from benign manifestations such as fumbling with clothing or walking in a trance to unprovoked destructive behavior. Although consciousness is not lost, it is altered sufficiently to produce amnesia for the episode. Psychomotor seizures are considered the most difficult among the seizure disorders to control with anticonvulsant medication. Clinical confirmation of the location of the irritative epileptogenic focus, with a view to possible neurosurgical removal of the abnormally discharging tissue, is provided by electroencephalographic recordings to determine the corroborating presence of focal spike discharges over the anterior temporal lobes. Since seizure-related limbic system structures are often deep, special activating techniques (sleep, Metrazol) and electrode placements (sphenoidal, nasopharyngeal) may be necessary to elicit the focus. The decision to remove the underlying tissue usually depends on serial EEG confirmation of a spike focus along with poor seizure control clinically. This spike focus is monitored by depth electrocorticography at operation to confirm more directly the presence of an irritative focus before ablation (French, Brown, Ogle, & Johnson, 1956).

Clinical observations and isolated attempts to document systematically a significant incidence of personality disturbances among psychomotor epileptics have been reported (Tizard, 1962). In addition, a few studies have attempted to relate temporal lobe EEG classifications to some external criteria of personality functioning such as ratings of aggressiveness, neurotic case history manifestations, and Rorschach patterns (Grunberg & Pond, 1957; Nuffield, 1961). As Tizard (1962) pointed out, interpretation of these findings has been complicated by utilization of nonrepresentative samples, imprecise neurological criteria, failure to control for intellectual level, loose clinical and EEG criteria for patient selection, and absence of histological or neurosurgical criteria.

Predictions of MMPI Changes

Recent investigations of MMPI changes associated with limbic system lesions and ablations have provided some enlargement of the earlier MMPI data and some preliminary findings bearing upon the functional organization of personality changes along the verticality and bilaterality dimensions (Meier & French, 1964, 1965a, 1965c). In an attempt to examine the regional localization hypothesis in the context of limbic system involvement, it was predicted that (1) clinically established psychomotor epileptics with clear-cut corresponding electroencephalographic and electrocorticographic confirmation of discharging epileptogenic foci would show conspicuous indications of personality disturbance as measured by the MMPI; (2) bilateral EEG abnormalities, particularly bitemporal independent spike foci, would be associated with MMPI indications of personality changes to a greater extent than would unilateral EEG abnormalities; and (3) neurosurgical removal of the tissue generating the predominant epileptogenic focus would be associated with declines on the MMPI scales, particularly in patients with greater preoperative MMPI indications of personality disturbance. The first prediction was made on the assumption that limbic system involvement in man reflects structural and physiological changes in a major motivational-emotional system along the vertical axis, analogous to those reported in the animal literature; the second was derived from observations, implicating the bilaterality dimension, of profound behavior changes in monkeys following bilateral temporal lobectomy and amygdalectomy (Kluver & Bucy, 1938); and the third prediction was suggested by an anticipated general reduction in abnormal electrophysiological limbic system discharges after temporal lobectomy.

Clinical Criteria and Samples

The series of patients in these studies consisted of 72 patients referred for temporal lobectomy after preliminary screening in the Neurology and Neurosurgery Outpatient Clinics of the University of Minnesota Hospitals. The criteria for unilateral temporal lobectomy included poorly controlled psychomotor seizures, serial confirmation of a temporal lobe spike focus over one or both temporal lobes with scalp and/or nasopharyngeal recording electrodes, and corroboration of an excisable epileptogenic focus with depth electrodes at the time of surgery. Of these 72 patients, 53 underwent unilateral temporal lobectomy, 40 were available for pre- to postoperative follow-up evaluations, and 19 served as nonoperated controls. This reduction in sample size reflected factors inherent in follow-up research, i.e., geographic dispersion, death, uncooperativeness, subsequent institutionalization, and inability to obtain leave from work. Fulfillment of the clinical and EEG criteria for unilateral temporal lobectomy was determined by an interdisciplinary team independent of psychological test data. The 19 nonoperated patients were collected later in the course of these investigations when it became apparent that bitemporal EEG spike foci preoperatively were associated with minimal reduction in seizure frequency postoperatively and, therefore, became a contraindication to surgery. This group provided a nonoperated control as well as a replication group for determining the relationship between EEG spike foci and personality change.

Operative Procedure

At the time of surgery, a craniotomy flap was turned to expose the temporal lobe and parts of the occipital, parietal, and frontal lobes. Extensive electrocorticographic scanning and plotting of the exposed cortex were done in an attempt to define as closely as possible any abnormal electrical discharge. After confirmation of a well-delineated, circumscribed temporal lobe focus was established, resection of that portion of the temporal lobe was performed in an *en bloc* fashion. Resection was carried perpendicular to the surface of the brain, through the lateral ventricle and then through the hippocampus to the medial aspect of the lobe with the insula being completely exposed. Attempts were made to keep the character of the excision relatively constant from patient to patient. In most instances the posterior margin of the resection was 7 to 9 centimeters from the tip of the temporal lobe. Electrodes were then reapplied and electrographic recordings made along the margin of the excised area. When necessary, further excision was made until no electrical abnormalities were evident.

MMPI and Preoperative EEG

In addition to the validity and clinical scales of the MMPI, the *Ca* scale and an Index of Psychopathology (*Ip*) were included for analysis. The development of *Ip* constituted an effort to quantify the concept of "degree of psychopathology" as applied clinically to psychopathological MMPI profile configurations obtained from inpatient psychiatric samples (Sines & Silver, 1963). *Ip* provides a measure, based on weighted fractions of the *Pa* and *Sc* scale scores, that correlates highly with values assigned along a 10-point continuum of rated "degree of psychopathology" when the entire profile was used as a basis for judgment by experienced interpreters of the test.

EEG classification into unilateral and bilateral temporal lobe abnormality subgroups was based upon consistency in the distribution of such foci in at least two consecutive EEG tracings in the six-month period before operation. A third classification within the bilateral EEG abnormality group involved the presence in these tracings of bitemporal independent spike foci. The EEG criterion for this grouping required the appearance of a well-defined spike focus arising over each temporal region without contiguity of discharge and with apparent differences in the structural characteristics such as buildup, amplitude, and afterdischarge. Each patient served as his own control for the various analyses of pre- to postoperative MMPI scale score and *Ip* change.

Division of the total preoperative sample into subgroups in which a left as compared to a right temporal lobe excision was performed failed to reveal significant mean differences on any of the MMPI variables. This was consistent with previous findings of an absence of variation in personality functioning as a function of lesion laterality. Characteristically the preoperative means of both groups fell above the normative mean of 50 to yield a fairly well elevated Welsh composite profile ('827913-4650/). The bilateral EEG abnormality group composite profile (8'276 1 430-95/), however, exhibited significantly higher elevations on the *F, D, Pa, Sc, Ca,* and *Ip* measures when compared with the unilateral EEG group ('98-372 1 45 60/). Further comparison of the bitemporal independent EEG spike foci group (8' 67 24 391-0/5) with the remaining bilateral abnormality group ('81-920345-76/) revealed the most extensive subgroup MMPI differences. This was evidenced by significantly higher elevations on the *D, Hy, Pd, Pa, Pt, Ca,* and *Ip* scale means of the bitemporal EEG spike foci group (Meier & French, 1965b).

For the 40 patients followed one year after operation, the postoperative composite profile ('8972-341650) reflected significant pre- to postoperative reduction on the *Pa, Ca,* and *Ip* means as well as an increase on the *K* scale mean for the group as a whole. Some subtle laterality differences were suggested by selective declines on the *Pa* and *Si* scales after left and on the *Sc* scale after right temporal lobectomy. By far the greatest preoperative MMPI elevation (8762'40139-5/) and postoperative scale mean reductions (8'2764319-05/) were observed in a group of 12 patients available for follow-up evaluation with independent bitemporal EEG spike foci. This group underwent significant declines on the *Pa, Pt, Si, Ca,* and *Ip* mean. The composite of the total bilateral group (8′7621340-95/) was somewhat less elevated and exhibited pre- to postoperative reductions on the *Ca* and *Ip* means with an increase on the *K* scale means. The less pathological preoperative composite (′987-3214560/) profile of the unilateral group changed in a downward direction generally with significant declines on the *Ma* and *Ca* scale means. Both the pre- and postoperative composite profile (′9-8723456/0) for the unilateral EEG group approached the accepted MMPI criteria for normality. The one-year later test to retest MMPI mean changes of the nonoperated control group were generally in an upward direction and did not reach acceptable levels of confidence. This group, consisting of patients with bitemporal independent EEG spike foci, showed a preoperative composite profile (2′8743 019-65/) with changes in an increasingly schizoadaptive direction one year later (82′43 17 960-5/).

It seemed clear that the MMPI characteristics of these temporal lobectomy groups resembled those observed in patients with posterior more than anterior focal cerebral lesions in the earlier MMPI investigations of test-lesion relationships. However, most subgroups showed sizable elevations on the *Sc* scale, similar to those previously observed among patients with anterior lesions as well. Treating the temporal lobe sample as a posterior lesion criterion group, a partial cross validation of the *Ca* scale yielded some interesting outcomes (Meier & French, 1964). Utilizing Williams's *Ca* validation group cutting point, 31 of 40 of the follow-up temporal lobectomy group produced scale elevations above the cutting point and, therefore, would have been validly classified as a posterior lesion group in almost 80% of the cases, essentially equivalent to the predictive efficiency of the original cross validation for the scale. However, application of the same cutting point to the *Ca* scale distribution one year after operation resulted in chance level group separations with approximately half scoring above and half below the cutting point. This loss in predictive efficiency, resulting from related declines in *Ca* scale scores, occurred within all subgroup classifications with the exception of the nonoperated control subjects who continued to score above the cutting point in 16 of 19 cases (83%). Scale changes suggested a direct relationship between presence of an electrographic discharging focus and the personality characteristics measured by the *Ca* scale. These personality characteristics, as judged from the scale items, included anxiety, depression, guilt feeling, social withdrawal, feelings of inadequacy and isolation, somatic concern, schizoid interpersonal features, and schizophrenic-like ideational disturbances.

CONCLUSIONS AND IMPLICATIONS

Predictions generated from the regional localization hypothesis, modified to incorporate recent neuroanatomical and neurophysiological developments involving vertical organization of the limbic system and the anticipated effects of bilateral temporal lobe lesions, were generally confirmed by these later studies. Psychomotor epileptics with electrographic-discharging epileptogenic foci in the anterior temporal lobe showed MMPI indications of personality disturbance similar to those seen in patients with posterior focal cerebral lesions in previous research. Since these test indicators were more frequently associated with bilateral EEG abnormalities, especially with bitemporal EEG spike foci, it seemed likely that intrinsic pathophysiological variables affecting limbic system function could have been contributing to personality change. This conclusion was supported further by observation of MMPI scale reductions following neurosurgical removal of the pathophysiologically discharging focus, particularly in patients with bitemporal EEG spike foci and associated abnormal preoperative elevations on scales designed to measure affective and schizoadaptive personality characteristics. The finding of a pre- to postoperative reduction from high to chance levels in *Ca* scale efficiency for localizing the temporal lobe patients as a posterior lesion group also suggested a direct causal relationship between a limbic system pathophysiological-discharging focus and personality disturbances. Thus, the data were consistent with recent comparative neuropsychological research implicating the temporal lobe and the paleocortical structures of the limbic system in generating emotional-motivational patterns of behavior.

Although consistent with a regional localization hypothesis emphasizing the contribution of the limbic system to personality disturbances, the results cannot be unqualifiedly interpreted as a direct behavioral expression of limbic system involvement in man. The possible confounding of a number of variables with direct pathophysiological effects should be acknowledged. First, the presence of bitemporal independent spike foci implies greater chronicity of the pathophysiological process and, therefore, longer exposure to any secondary environmental stress associated with clinical manifestations. This chronicity factor was suggested by investigations of the genesis of bitemporal independent spike foci in monkeys after implantation of alumina gel in one temporal lobe (Morrell, 1959). Initially, a spike focus emerged at the site of implantation. Over time, a secondary, or mirror, focus, which discharged contiguously in time and showed recognizably similar morphological characteristics as the parent focus, developed in the homotopic temporal lobe. After weeks or months, this focus evolved into an independent spike focus by discharging discontiguously relative to the primary focus and manifesting recognizably different amplitudes and after discharges. These secondary alterations in firing could develop in response to neurohumoral alterations at synaptic sites in the dendritic membranes subjected to prolonged synaptic bombardment from the primary lesion (Guerrero-Figueroa, Barros, Heath, & Gonzalas, 1964). Such changes have been shown to appear in minutes in the frog (Wilder & Morrell, 1967) and over years in man (Hughes, 1966). Thus, rate of appearance, predictability, and differentiatability of the secondary focus have been shown to vary negatively with phylogenetic level and degree of CNS maturation. Although some patients in this series probably have had bitemporal spike foci from an early age and even before onset of seizures, others were observed to develop such foci over a period of years of serial electrographic follow-up. These considerations make it difficult to disentangle the effects of prolonged bitemporal pathological variables and extended situational stress factors associated with a history of seizures. The electrophysiological data on genesis of secondary epileptogenic foci data could be used to argue for and against both a pathophysiological and a situational explanation of relationships between MMPI scale elevations, preoperative bitemporal EEG spike foci, and neurosurgical removal of the primary discharging focus.

The requirement of poorly controlled seizures for temporal lobectomy partially obviated the cogency of a purely situational account of the preoperative MMPI data, but pre- to postoperative changes in seizure frequency might have facilitated some of the postoperative improvement in personality function. However, reductions in seizure frequency were observed less frequently in patients with bitemporal spike foci, the group in which the most dramatic pre- to postoperative MMPI changes appeared. The hospital charts revealed no definitive empirical relationships between seizure frequency and MMPI change, but chart data are admittedly marginal in reliability where the recording of seizure-related clinical phenomena is concerned. Prolonged environmental effects can be measured only indirectly through careful documentation of life history variables, frequency of seizures, age at onset, and interpersonal response to seizures; but precise and objective measures of these variables are not readily obtainable. Where independent variables are sampled, as in these studies, such selective effects, operating outside the boundaries of surveillance and control in the clinical setting, could have been confounded with direct neurosurgical effects and the pathophysiological influences implied in the

EEG correlates of personality disturbance. Although these considerations detract from the evidence provided by these findings for the regional localization hypothesis, statement of the hypothesis in terms of a postulated contribution of the vertically organized limbic system in the generation of motivational-emotional behavior disturbances in man would seem worthy of continued investigation.

REFERENCES

Andersen, A. L. Personality changes following prefrontal lobotomy in a case of severe psychoneurosis. *Journal of Consulting Psychology,* 1949, **13,** 105–107.

Andersen, A. L. The effect of laterality localization of focal brain lesions on the Wechsler-Bellevue subtests. *Journal of Clinical Psychology,* 1951, **7,** 149–153.

Andersen, A. L., and Hanvik, L. J. The psychometric localization of brain lesions: The differential effect of frontal and parietal lesions on MMPI profiles. *Journal of Clinical Psychology,* 1950, **6,** 177–180.

Baker, A. B. *An outline of clinical neurology.* Dubuque, Iowa: Wm. C. Brown, 1958.

Bard, P., and Mountcastle, V. B. Some forebrain mechanisms involved in expression of rage with special reference to suppression of angry behavior. *Research Publication of the Association of Nervous and Mental Disorders,* 1948, **27,** 362–404.

Brady, J. V. The paleocortex and behavioral motivation. In H. F. Harlow and C. N. Woolsey (Eds.), *Biological and biochemical bases of behavior.* Madison: University of Wisconsin Press, 1958. Pp. 193–235.

Cajal, S. R. *Histologie du système nerveux de l'homme et des vertèbres.* (Trans. from the Spanish by L. Azouley.) Paris: Maloine, 1909. 2 vols.

Crown, S. An experimental study of psychological changes following prefrontal lobotomy. *Journal of General Psychology,* 1952, **47,** 3–41.

Freeman, W., and Watts, J. *Psychosurgery.* Springfield, Ill.: Charles C Thomas, 1942.

French, L. A., Brown, I. A., Ogle, W. S., and Johnson, S. Temporal lobe epilepsy: Its clinical manifestations and surgical treatment: I. A preliminary report. *Medicine,* 1956, **35,** 425–459.

Friedman, S. H. Psychometric effects of frontal and parietal lobe brain damage. Unpublished doctoral dissertation, University of Minnesota, 1950.

Grunberg, F., and Pond, D. A. Conduct disorders in epileptic children. *Journal of Neurology, Neurosurgery, and Psychiatry,* 1957, **20,** 65–68.

Guerrero-Figueroa, R., Barros, A., Heath, R. G., and Gonzalas, G. Experimental subcortical epileptiform foci. *Epilepsia,* 1964, **5,** 112–139.

Hughes, J. R. Bilateral EEG abnormalities on corresponding areas. *Epilepsia,* 1966, **7,** 44–55.

Johnson, F. H. Neuro-anatomical tracts considered as correlates of the ascending reticular activating system in the cat. *Anatomical Record,* 1953, **115,** 327–328. (Abstract)

Kendrick, J. F., and Gibbs, F. A. Interrelations of mesial temporal and orbital frontal areas revealed by strychnine spikes. *Archives of Neurology and Psychiatry,* 1958, **79,** 518–524.

Kimura, D. Some effects of temporal-lobe damage on auditory perception. *Canadian Journal of Psychology,* 1961, **15,** 156–165.

Kluver, H., and Bucy, P. C. An analysis of certain effects of bilateral temporal lobectomy in the rhesus monkey, with special reference to "psychic blindness." *Journal of Psychology,* 1938, **5,** 33–54.

Lorente de Nõ, R. Studies on the structure of the cerebral cortex: II. Continuation of the study of the ammonic system. *Journal of Psychology and Neurology,* 1934, **46,** 113–117.

MacLean, P. D., and Delgado, J. M. R. Electrical and chemical stimulation of frontotemporal portion of limbic system in the waking animal. *Electroencephalography and Clinical Neurophysiology,* 1953, **5,** 91–100.

Meier, M. J. Behavioral correlates of acute cerebral infarctions. Presented at the National Institute of Neurological Diseases and Blindness Conference on Collaborative Cerebrovascular Research, Honolulu, 1966.

Meier, M. J., and French, L. A. Progress Report to the National Institute of Neurological Diseases and Blindness, Grant B-1158, 1961.

Meier, M. J., and French, L. A. Caudality scale changes following unilateral temporal lobectomy. *Journal of Clinical Psychology,* 1964, **20,** 464–467.

Meier, M. J., and French, L. A. Changes in MMPI scale scores and an index of psychopathology following unilateral temporal lobectomy for epilepsy. *Epilepsia,* 1965, **6,** 263–273. (a)

Meier, M. J., and French, L. A. Lateralized deficits in complex visual discrimination and bilateral transfer of reminiscence following unilateral temporal lobectomy. *Neuropsychologia,* 1965, **3,** 261–272. (b)

Meier, M. J., and French, L. A. Some personality correlates of unilateral and bilateral EEG abnormalities in psychomotor epileptics. *Journal of Clinical Psychology,* 1965, **21,** 3–9. (c)

Meier, M. J., and French, L. A. Longitudinal assessment of intellectual functioning following unilateral temporal lobectomy. *Journal of Clinical Psychology,* 1966, **22,** 22–27.

Mettler, F. A. (Ed.) *Selective partial ablation of the frontal cortex.* New York: Hoeber, 1949.

Meyer, V. Psychological effects of brain damage. In H. J. Eysenck (Ed.), *Handbook of abnormal psychology.* New York: Basic Books, 1960. Pp. 529–565.

Meyer, V., and Yates, A. J. Intellectual changes following temporal lobectomy for psychomotor epilepsy. *Journal of Neurology and Psychiatry,* 1955, **18,** 44–52.

Milner, B. Psychological defects produced by temporal lobe excision. *Re-*

search Publication of the Association of Nervous and Mental Disorders, 1958, **36**, 244–257.

Milner, B. Some effects of frontal lobectomy in man. In J. M. Warren and K. Akert (Eds.), *The frontal granular cortex and behavior*. New York: McGraw-Hill, 1964. Pp. 313–331.

Moniz, E. Prefrontal leucotomy in the treatment of mental disorder. *American Journal of Psychiatry*, 1936, **93**, 1379–1385.

Morison, R. S., and Dempsey, E. W. A study of thalamo-cortical relations. *American Journal of Physiology*, 1942, **135**, 281–292.

Morrell, F. Secondary epileptogenic lesions. *Epilepsia*, 1959, **1**, 538–560.

Moruzzi, G., and Magoun, H. W. Brain stem reticular formation and activation of the EEG. *Electroencephalography and Clinical Neurophysiology*, 1949, **1**, 455–473.

Nauta, W. J. H. Some projections of the medial wall of the hemisphere of the rat's brain (cortical areas 32 and 25, 24 and 29). *Anatomical Record*, 1953, **115**, 352. (Abstract)

Nauta, W. J. H. An experimental study of the fornix system in the rat. *Journal of Comparative Neurology*, 1956, **104**, 247–271.

Nuffield, E. J. A. Neurophysiology and behavior disorders in epileptic children. *Journal of Mental Science*, 1961, **107**, 438–457.

Olds, J. Adaptive functions of paleocortical and related structures. In H. F. Harlow and C. N. Woolsey (Eds.), *Biological and biochemical bases of behavior*. Madison: University of Wisconsin Press, 1958. Pp. 237–262.

Petrie, A. *Personality and the frontal lobes*. London: Routledge, 1952.

Reitan, R. M. Certain differential effects of left and right cerebral lesions in human adults. *Journal of Comparative and Physiological Psychology*, 1955, **48**, 474–477.

Ruch, T. C. Neurophysiology of emotion. In T. C. Ruch, H. D. Patton, J. W. Woodberry, and A. L. Towe (Eds.), *Neurophysiology*. Philadelphia: Saunders, 1965, pp. 508–522.

Ruja, D. H. Personality changes following prefrontal lobotomy in 25 schizophrenic patients. *American Psychologist*, 1951, **6**, 499.

Sines, L. K., and Silver, R. J. An index of psychopathology (*Ip*) derived from clinicians' judgments of MMPI profiles. *Journal of Clinical Psychology*, 1963, **19**, 324–326.

Smith, A. Changes in Porteus Maze scores of brain-operated schizophrenics after an eight-year interval. *Journal of Mental Science*, 1960, **106**, 967–978.

Smith, A. Certain hypothesized hemispheric differences in language and visual functions in human adults. *Cortex*, 1966, **2**, 109–126.

Teuber, H. L. Effects of brain wounds implicating right or left hemisphere in man: Hemisphere differences and hemisphere interaction in vision, audition, and somesthesis. In V. B. Mountcastle (Ed.), *Interhemispheric relations and cerebral dominance*. Baltimore: Johns Hopkins Press, 1962. Pp. 131–157.

Teuber, H. L., and Mishkin, M. Judgment of visual and postural vertical after brain injury. *Journal of Psychology,* 1954, **38,** 161–175.

Tizard, B. The personality of epileptics: A discussion of the evidence. *Psychological Bulletin,* 1962, **59,** 196–210.

Vidor, M. Personality changes following prefrontal leucotomy as reflected by the MMPI and the results of psychometric testing. *Journal of Mental Science,* 1951, **97,** 159–173.

Weinstein, S. Differences in effects of brain wounds implicating right or left hemispheres: Differential effects on certain intellectual and complex perceptual functions. In V. B. Mountcastle (Ed.), *Interhemispheric relations and cerebral dominance.* Baltimore: Johns Hopkins Press, 1962. Pp. 159–176.

Welsh, G. S. An extension of Hathaway's MMPI profile coding system. *Journal of Consulting Psychology,* 1948, **12,** 343–344.

Wilder, B. J., and Morrell, F. Secondary epileptogenesis in the frog forebrain. *Neurology,* 1967, **17,** 1041–1057.

Willett, R. A. The effects of psychosurgical procedures on behavior. In H. J. Eysenck (Ed.), *Handbook of abnormal psychology.* New York: Basic Books, 1960. Pp. 566–610.

Williams, H. L. The development of a caudality scale for the MMPI. *Journal of Clinical Psychology,* 1952, **8,** 293–297.

Chapter Thirteen
Invasion of Privacy: How Legitimate Is the Current Concern over This Issue?

W. Grant Dahlstrom
University of North Carolina

Only future historians of our profession will be able to give the proper answer to this query, but I should like to venture a partial answer from our limited perspective. The current concern that the use of psychological tests make unwarranted intrusions into the lives and interests of our citizens is out of proportion in relation to the actual risks that these instruments and methods now pose, and it is off target because the real issues posed by the increased precision and relevance of psychotechnology are being neglected. I should hope that, once aroused by the false issues of invasion of privacy by test methods, people will turn their attention to the legitimate issues involved in proper control over human behavior.

The underlying issue, which is the more pressing and by far the more deserving of our attention, was clearly grasped by J. Robert Oppenheimer and summed up succinctly in his invitational address to the convention of the American Psychological Association meeting in San Francisco in 1955:

> In the last ten years the physicists have been extraordinarily noisy about the immense powers which, largely through their efforts, but through other efforts as well, have come into the possession of man, powers notably and strikingly for very large-scale and dreadful destruction. We have spoken of our responsibilities and of our obligations to society in terms that sound to me very provincial, because the psychologist can hardly do anything without realizing that for him the acquisition of knowledge opens up the most terrifying prospects of controlling what people do and how they think and how they behave and how they feel. This is true for all of you who are engaged in practice, and as the corpus of psychology gains in certitude and subtlety

> and skill, I can see that the physicists's pleas that what he discovers be used with humanity and be used wisely will seem rather trivial compared to those pleas which you will have to make and for which you will have to be responsible. [1956, p. 128]

Utilization of psychological knowledge is the core of the legitimate issue in this controversy; proper and constructive application of an increasingly precise psychotechnology is the basic problem which should be confronted. Psychological tests, as the most visible aspect of this growing psychotechnology, have received most of the attention, disproportionately and undeservingly. This displacement from the whole area to one specific technique is unfortunate but not so unfortunate as the kind of response that has been generated to the problem. Exaggerated concerns with these issues have led to proposals of extensive legislative restrictions to solve problems best resolved by administrative decisions and policy changes.

Some agencies have been led to set up censorship boards to keep the topics covered in basic research instruments innocuous (e.g., the Internal Clearance Committee in the Bureau of Research of the U.S. Office of Education—Willingham, 1967). Some proposed solutions envision serious restrictions upon the activities of professional psychologists in carrying out their services and even dictate patterns of interprofessional relationships in some governmental agencies (i.e., between psychologists and psychiatrists). Where we would hope for statesmanship with forward-looking and constructive proposals, we have instead found bandwagon politics and circus-arena legislative hearings. In spite of the best efforts of the committees of both houses of Congress to find new cases to document their claims of widespread abuses of personality testing, the factual yield was amazingly small (Brayfield, 1965). Yet the battles in the headlines and the efforts to introduce restrictive legislation go on as if the findings had uncovered evidence of massive misuse of personality questionnaires and instruments. As a result, many legitimate psychological applications will, in all likelihood, be blocked by crippling laws, and even more importantly, much needed research to improve and perfect our techniques will be stymied.

Are there abuses? Of course there are. Any realistic appraisal of human affairs must acknowledge that there are some individual instances of malpractice in any profession. Psychological practice is no exception. Neither is it a field of charlatans and miscreants. The profession of psychology has operated under codes of professional conduct for many decades (Moore & Hoch, 1967). These codes are designed to protect the clients, the students, and the research subjects of psychologists in many different areas of endeavor: school psychology, clinical and counseling practice, professional training, and laboratory and field research. They are explicit, cogent, and enforceable; they are also under continuous revision. Through the efforts of ethics committees of our professional organizations, these codes are being applied now and are being perfected for more effective application in the future. These codes of professional conduct are also backed up by licensing and certification provisions for psychological practice in almost every state in the country. Little has been said in the public debates about these efforts of psychologists to police themselves or the soul searching that has always gone on in professional associations about professional conduct and ethical issues. Many critical articles have decried psychologists' lack of concern with these issues without giving proper recognition to this vigorous endeavor in our profession for self-control and self-policing (Westin, 1967).

What are the legitimate issues? Some of the heated arguments about the invasion of privacy by means of personality tests have arisen from a serious misunderstanding of three persistent and perplexing problems in the application of psychological methods to personnel decisions, particularly governmental personnel actions. First of all, there are recurring difficulties in disentangling institutional decisions and individual decisions (in the terminology of Cronbach & Gleser, 1965). There is also an inherent ambiguity in the notion of invasion of privacy that leads to serious difficulties in communication about this problem. Lastly, there is a recurrent misunderstanding about the constraints involved in taking a psychological test which bears directly upon the issue of this controversy.

The first difficulty comes down to the issue of who is the client being served by a given psychologist—a particular individual or an institution? In private practice, the answer is usually relatively simple: The psychologist is hired to serve the best interests of his patient, client, or customer. Even here, of course, the psychologist must also operate in such a way as to serve his profession, his community, and his society as well. There is generally no conflict; but on occasion some very difficult decisions may confront him, e.g., when he finds that a persistent firebug has sought his services for help in controlling himself and reveals to him some as yet undetected fire-setting actions. Similarly, when a psychologist works for a private company and screens applicants for potential hiring, the psychologist's loyalties are to the company and not to the individuals being screened. Although the situation may occasionally generate comparable ethical dilemmas, as when a person badly in need of a job may be passed over because he is not the best one for the needs of the company, by and large the loyalties of the psychologist are unambiguous in these two kinds of professional activity. But, since the psychologist is apt to use psychological tests in both contexts, the attitudes generated in the general public toward these instruments become quite mixed. In private practice, the psychologists may use a test to discover some aspects of the client that the individual himself does not know or does not fully appreciate, this information then being shared with the client to help him make more informed and accurate decisions about himself, his career, or other aspects of his personal future. In the other situation, however, the psychologist employs the test to discover aspects of the applicant which will be used to make some decision to enhance the welfare of the institution. The outcome of the decision may also lead to the betterment of the applicant, but it often does not. One result of this dual role of tests in the hands of psychologists is an intense ambivalence of feelings on the part of the general public about tests. Although this outcome is understandable, it is nevertheless unfortunate. It may also be unavoidable, as physicians have found in the persistent ambivalence with which hypodermic needles and scalpels are viewed by the general public; but there is no corresponding legislative pressure now to outlaw the use of needles and scalpels in the practice of medicine.

Another result of this dual role of psychologists in serving both individual and institutional clients is some feeling that all decisions of this sort should be resolved in favor of the individual; the institutional interest should always yield to the individual's welfare. Consider the following concern:

> Most troubling of all is the question as to whether it is ethical for psychologists to consider the employer (or school) their client, and the individual applicant or employee or student as merely a subject, from whom they pump as much as possible of what the employer wants to know and in whom they seek whatever qualities the employer deems desirable. (Goldman, 1963)

From this point of view, a psychologist is ethically wrong to serve any client but an individual and would be in moral jeopardy in any activity where his methods are used to serve a group, even so small a group as a married couple whom he sees for marital counseling where his loyalties could conceivably be divided! A more reasonable view would seem to be that any organization that exists to serve legitimate functions can be a client for a psychologist for whom he can ethically apply his methods in service to further those legitimate ends. In doing so, the psychologist will then seek to gather necessary data to serve that agency's best interests. The quotation above from the *Personnel and Guidance Journal* should properly be reworded to substitute "what the employer needs to know" for "wants to know" and "whatever qualities the employer deems necessary" for "deems desirable." As it stands, the statement reads as if the psychologist in an agency's employ has no discretion about what he covers in his battery and what he recommends in his reports. The point here is that there are important and legitimate requirements of our governmental institutions, business organizations, and medical facilities that must be served and can often best be served by applying personality tests to improve the accuracy of the personnel decisions or therapeutic programs. It is reasonable and proper to use tests to study job applicants, employees who are candidates for promotion, or patients in need of treatment. The qualifications and suitability for certain positions, in or out of government, have increasingly come to involve various characteristics of personality and temperament, often far outweighing the importance of particular skills, special educational backgrounds, or even experience in other jobs. These variables have proven to be important in the selection of astronauts; it is not surprising that they also prove to be important in other governmental positions as well.

Proper evaluation of applicants for positions or promotions, then, involves asking them to go through procedures not so much for their own welfare as for the welfare of the agency and its mission. The individual's privacy may be invaded thereby through the actions of a governmental agency, but this is neither new nor inherently dangerous. The Bureau of Internal Revenue and the Bureau of the Census already have methods of invading the privacy of every American family, annually or decennially. These agencies do so pursuant to their own missions, missions which are of ultimate benefit to all American citizens. The most important point for this issue under discussion, however, is that they carry out these invasions of the privacy of individual citizens with proper safeguards and assurances against any misuse of the information that their methods glean from tax returns or census interviews. What is needed in the introduction of psychological methods to improve upper-level governmental personnel decisions is a set of adequate safeguards, not a set of legal blocks. Patterns of administrative control, clarification of policies about personnel records and who has access to data in files, together with penalties for violation of these provisions, would appear to be much more constructive solutions than legal proscriptions against the kinds of test devices to be used or the content of the inquiries to be made in any personnel decisions.

A second kind of misunderstanding that beclouds this general discussion and makes it particularly difficult to come to grips with the delicate decisions involved in the institutional-versus-individual dilemma described above stems from different interpretations of the phrase "invasion of privacy." One set of meanings centers about the issue of confidentiality: Are certain facts about a person that he would prefer to keep secret in danger of being revealed to someone who could then use them against him? At this level of discourse, clear and definitive answers can be given about the number and variety of effective safeguards that can be erected to guarantee confidentiality of material given to a psychologist by his client. Ethical constraints, physical protection of data in files by coding of names and by limiting access, as well as vigorous efforts to establish legal controls, such as privileged communication of confidences given by clients in their talks with psychologists, are all directed toward assuring individuals being served that there will be no breach of confidentiality. Obviously, however, these assurances can only be given by a psychologist to his own client. When the person being tested is not the psychologist's client but is an applicant for a position in the agency for which the psychologist is working, then these assurances of confidentiality cannot and should not be given to the subject under study.

When some people face the issue of invasion of privacy, however, they are not focusing upon issues of confidentiality as much as upon what may be termed ruptures in their need for inviolacy. For them it is not so much that someone else, such as a professional psychologist, may learn something they want to keep private but rather that another person has imposed upon them in some significant way. Busy and intent upon their own pursuits, they consider any intrusion upon their activities as a violation of their private pattern of living. They have a strong wish to remain inviolate, in the terms of Murray (1938). This desire, of course, is by no means restricted to freedom from intrusion by psychological inquiries such as tests or investigations by opinion pollsters but applies as well to interruptions of their activities by such entertainment gimmicks as "Candid Camera" or "People Are Funny." Following Murray's analysis of this need, however, it should be clear that people differ very widely in the extent to which they feel this need or require this freedom from intrusions from any source whatever. For some, this desire is central to their whole way of life; they would probably be incredulous that anyone would feel any differently. For others, many others, this feeling is itself so alien that they welcome any kind of overture from whatever source. Witness the surprise of field investigators in urban poverty areas who expected to be rejected and, perhaps, even attacked when they brought out their tape recorders only to find to their great relief that most of the residents crowded about eager to tell someone, anyone, about their living conditions (Clark, 1965). In between are many people who, although sensitive to unwarranted intrusions into their private lives, are willing to open their defenses of reserve and social distance to legitimate and reasonable requests. Has there ever been a violation of confidentiality of a subject who served as a control normal in the derivation of the MMPI for Hathaway and McKinley or as an informant for the Kinsey survey of American sexual behavior? These thousands of subjects were willing to abrogate their personal reserve to permit this kind of invasion of their private lives for highly worthwhile scientific enterprises.

I suspect that the people who are most concerned about personal inviolacy of the sort I have described are the upper-socioeconomic-level writers, lawyers, and members of the legislature. They are raising these issues and pressing heavily for prohibitions and legal restrictions on psychological tests and questionnaires, while the people that they are striving to protect, the rank and file of American citizens, are much less concerned about either the procedures or the purposes of psychological investigations. This would certainly be a reasonable inference from the distribution of the values of the K scale in the general population and the test-taking attitudes and feelings about self-revelations that are correlates of that scale of the MMPI (Dahlstrom & Welsh, 1960). It should be clear, if this is a valid distinction, that, although some people will be satisfied about invasion of privacy issues as soon as guarantees of confidentiality have been established, other people will still object vigorously to any proposal of self-exposure, be it for their own good, to get a better job, or to further scientific understanding of human nature.

The third persistent difficulty that hinders full and adequate discussion of these issues is a set of misunderstandings about psychological testing and the pressures that it involves for the test subject. Some writers have described tests in a way that gives the impression that they are some inhuman process of extracting information against a sub-
any test in existence today requires the *voluntary* participation of the
ject's will and beyond his control. Far from such an inexorable process,

test subject to provide a sample of his spontaneous behavior. Although there are psychological techniques that require relatively little behavior, such as some of the polygraphic procedures, or no conscious cooperation, such as the unobtrusive measures described by Webb, Campbell, Schwartz, and Sechrest (1966), this is not true of psychological tests. Each test session constitutes a special social contract between the examiner and the test subject; unless the subject fulfills that contract, the examiner has nothing on which to base his conclusions. Some of the better tests contain explicit checks on whether the test subject has cooperated in his part of the bargain, but these too work to the test subject's advantage minimizing the risk of unwarranted inferences from an inappropriate behavior sample. (This is particularly important when the examiner is testing more than one subject at a time and cannot make the needed observations to assure himself that all his subjects understood the procedures and instructions and were able to comply with the test instructions.) This basic necessity for full, conscious, and voluntary cooperation should itself be reassuring to people who are fearful that psychological tests constitute a serious threat to civil liberties or personal privacy. No one can be tested who does not agree to be tested.

In a statement prepared for the hearings of the Senate Judiciary Committee's Subcommittee on Constitutional Rights (under the chairmanship of Senator Sam J. Ervin) during the summer of 1965 (Brayfield, 1965), Earl Baughman and I tried to indicate that proper use of psychological tests required that they be administered and interpreted by individuals who are professionally qualified and competent. Part of this argument rests on the understanding that completing a psychological test involves a contract between the test subject and the psychologist. This contract differs in important ways from the completion of (often quite similar) governmental forms and anamnestic questionnaires. Contrast, if you will, the affidavits one makes in filling out the standard Form 57 for government employment with the instructions for completing a personality inventory like the MMPI. The applicant swears that the data that he has given are "true, complete, and correct to the best of my ability" and risks a heavy fine or imprisonment if he is detected in some significant falsification. On the MMPI, on the other hand, he is instructed: "Remember to give your own opinion of yourself." The approach is entirely different, and it takes a skillful and knowledgeable psychologist to make it entirely clear to the client that he is entering into a different kind of contract when he takes the tests from what he may have been used to operating under in routine government personnel procedures.

Both the inquiries of the Subcommittee on Constitutional Rights and the House Subcommittee on Invasion of Privacy (under the chairmanship of Congressman Cornelius E. Gallagher) sought to document the extent of the violations in the use of psychological tests of the privacy of employees of various federal agencies; both failed to document their case that there was a deliberate and widespread *misuse* of tests (Brayfield, 1965). Both committees also failed to appreciate the special area of competence of the professional psychologist and the need to preserve his right to choose the instrument or appraisal method that he deems most appropriate for the evaluative questions being posed. The overall effectiveness or level of contribution of psychology as a profession can and should be studied, in and out of the government service, just as the overall effectiveness of the contributions of medical scientists and aeronautical engineers should be occasionally reappraised. The competence and ethical integrity of any particular psychologist may also be a legitimate area of inquiry from time to time by governmental bodies. But there is a region of professional decisions within which neither inquiry nor legislation is appropriate: the range of choices of techniques and instruments available to the professional psychologist for settling particular professional questions. Legislation cannot be used to control the choice of scalpel or syringe by the surgeon, yet laws now being proposed attempt to legislate the patterns of professional practice by qualified psychologists.

Both scientific study of human behavior and application of the findings of these inquiries by professional psychologists to enhance an individual's well-being or the public's welfare are legitimate and honorable activities. There is no conspiracy against individual liberties or personal freedom in the present-day practice of psychology. Psychologists have long been aware of the potentialities and responsibilities inherent in the knowledge that they are accumulating, and they have been effective in transmitting this awareness to new generations of research psychologists and professional practitioners.

Critics such as Orville G. Brim (Willingham, 1967) claim that the present-day reaction against the use of psychological tests is something new to psychologists:

> It's very difficult to really conclude that society does not want some of the knowledge which it is possible for us to produce, if the cost involves giving up of values of personal dignity and privacy. You cannot say that knowledge is an end in its own right in this sense. It is not, because the majority of the people in society do not want to pay that price. . . . So behavioral scientists are surprised and essentially caught with no rationale

and no ethics and no philosophy to guide their own mode of balancing this value conflict. (Willingham, 1967, p. 30)

This strikes me as another form of the all-too-familiar anti-intellectual position against a basic science of human behavior. In Brim's statement above, for example, who is speaking here for "society," and on what grounds can it be concluded that this kind of psychological research and service is opposed by the "majority of the people"? Psychologists, like all social scientists, have been willing and able to work within a framework of social and cultural taboos in the pursuit of their investigative goals. It is shameful to impute "no ethics and no philosophy" to an entire scientific discipline or to accuse it of being naïve in respect to the power of anti-intellectual reactions against both their methods and their findings. The psychological profession deserves better from its critics, whether they are in some allied discipline or in the field of psychology itself.

REFERENCES

Brayfield, A. H. (Ed.) Testing and public policy. *American Psychologist,* 1965, **20,** 857–1005.

Clark, K. B. *Dark ghetto: Dilemmas of social power.* New York: Harper & Row, 1965.

Cronbach, L. J., and Gleser, G. C. *Psychological tests and personnel decisions.* (Rev.) Urbana: University of Illinois Press, 1965.

Dahlstrom, W. G., and Welsh, G. S. *An MMPI handbook: A guide to use in clinical practice and research.* Minneapolis: University of Minnesota Press, 1960.

Goldman, L. Review of M. L. Gross, *The brain watchers. Personnel and Guidance Journal,* 1963, **41,** 824–825.

Moore, B. V., and Hoch, E. L. (Eds.) *Casebook on ethical standards of psychologists.* Washington, D.C.: American Psychological Association, 1967.

Murray, H. A. (Ed.) *Explorations in personality.* New York: Oxford University Press, 1938.

Oppenheimer, J. R. Analogy in science. *American Psychologist,* 1956, **11,** 127–135.

Webb, E. J., Campbell, D. T., Schwartz, R. D., and Sechrest, L. *Unobtrusive measures: Nonreactive research in the social sciences.* Chicago: Rand McNally, 1966.

Westin, A. F. *Privacy and freedom.* New York: Atheneum, 1967.

Willingham, W. W. (Ed.) Invasion of privacy in research and testing. *Journal of Educational Measurement,* 1967, **4,** Supplement, 1–31.

Comments on the Invasion of Privacy Issue

Paul E. Meehl
University of Minnesota

I do not know nearly as much about this controversy as Professor Dahlstrom does on the factual side, and I have no knowledge that our colleagues are engaging in many unethical uses of the MMPI. We have all heard stories about individual episodes and anecdotes about the way a dean or someone uses the instrument that make us a bit nervous.

But it is important to stress that, after we have done our best to refute some of the erroneous arguments advanced by uninformed persons and have pointed out what is wrong with those arguments, we still do face some real problems.

Let me first discuss the need for communication improvement. For example, a local TV commentator mentioned several MMPI items and said, "Now isn't this absurd, that anyone would get hired because he says, 'I like Lincoln better than Washington'?" Now as I view it this type of criticism is partly a problem of effective social communication and education. I think we could get it across to the average person that, even though some of the MMPI items seem a little strange, the resulting pattern of responses provides a valid description of personality.

My recollection of the Wasserman test is that they take the heart of a calf and grind it up and dissolve it in alcohol. What is done in running a Wasserman sounds like an "eye of newt and toe of frog" kind of business, and they do not hire people to be railroad engineers if they get too much sedimentation or something in this mess of sludge. Our TV critic might say about this procedure, "What kind of witchcraft are these MDs perpetrating?" And then we tell him, "You know what that procedure is? It's the Wasserman test, and it has a validity of 96%."

We have not worked as hard on community relations as we should have, with the result that uninformed people draw conclusions which they would not draw if they had as much as 30 minutes of careful indoctrination by a psychologist with educational intent.

The validity of the empirical method can be conveyed without tipping our hand and telling about all the items. We can use examples of items in order to explain the test. Give the layman a little theory, such as we give the beginning psychology class—a description of empirical keying, what a trait is, and so on. In fact, we can even use the layman's biases in this respect. In presenting these ideas to some not highly educated lay relatives of mine, I have geared the discussion to their prejudices against psychological theorizing. I say to them, "Well, we make these tests by gathering facts. We are not merely armchair-professors theorizing; we find out, like the insurance companies do, how certain types of people answer the items." And they get the message.

After we have taken account of the public image we have presented, recognizing that we always will have a few kooks about whom we can do nothing—the people who write in and say, "Too many people are trying to find out things no one should know about and besides I'm against fluoridation, communism, and perversion"—we must consider the important (and intrinsically interesting) ethical and political issues involved in the use of tests such as the MMPI. After we subtract the kook variance and the uninformed variance, there is a valid component of variance left. These questions of "politics" (in the broad sense of the word, including freedom, human rights, the open society, and the invasion of privacy) have some legitimate weight and meaning, and perhaps we have not thought as deeply about them as we should. (As a footnote, I would say that this is a reflection of the phenomenon one observes generally in the social sciences, namely, that social scientists are not "hep" when it comes to thinking about ethical issues or axiology generally. A student is very articulate when you ask him about the analysis of covariance or Freud's theory of libido development; if you ask him to talk for five minutes about an ethical judgment, he either dissolves into a welter of anxiety or moves into the cliche circuit and acts as though the thought never entered his mind that he could reason about ethical matters. People, at least educated people, used to have a modicum of dialectic skill with and information about these questions, whereas now most of us are unable to take hold of an ethical problem. We don't have any rubrics, we don't have any canons, we act as though we never read a book on the theory of casuistry—like the Jesuits' 1,500-page volumes on when you can lie about things, or when is a lie really a lie, etc.) What I am suggesting is that there are some valid ethical dilemmas about the use of the MMPI; and my hunch would be that we as psychologists do not have all the necessary skills to deal with them. We need logicians, professors of ethical theory, lawyers, and political theorists to help us. Not that we would accept their opinions completely, but we ought at least to learn their methods and theories.

It seems to me that there is a set of factual issues which is distinguishable from the ethical-political issues. For instance, Dr. Dahlstrom alluded to the question, What exactly do people object to about the MMPI? Is it mainly that a certain *inference concerning a trait* might be made from the test? Or is it the fact that one is *required to reveal a specific item content?* I don't know, and I suspect nobody knows, what most people find objectionable. Consider those administrators or lawyers or members of the Senate who object to giving the MMPI when hiring personnel. What do they find objectionable? Is it that no one should have the right to *infer* that an applicant has, say, a little impulsivity with his 49′ multiphasic? Is that what bothers them? Or is it that the applicant was forced to *say,* "If I had a chance to get into a movie without paying, I would probably do it." Recently I was talking to my brother-in-law (who knows nothing about psychology), who had to take the MMPI when he went to work for Northwest Orient Airlines as a flight engineer. Somewhat to my surprise, he did not care that they might infer that he had certain personality traits. He said, "I figure if I go in to be interviewed for a job, the psychologist will notice things about me. I realize that you often spot things that I don't even see—like how a person scratches a match or places his feet. This is your field, you're an expert. So if you interview me for Northwest Orient Airlines, you will be doing your best expert job. Nothing wrong with that at all. Why should they hire me if I'm a nut and you can spot it? So I figure I'd go to the personnel man, and he'd probably see something. I'd give myself away, and I couldn't hide it even if I wanted to." I tried the approach (not fully believing it!) of "I don't see why it's worse to discover it with the test than with the man." But he said, "I don't know whether I would go into a movie without paying. That's not the point. They have no right to inquire. They have no right to know whether I *say* I would." I asked, "Well, have you?" And he said, "No, I haven't and I wouldn't, but that's not the point. They have no right to *know* that." We need to know more about objections of this nature, objections about certain *item content,* where a person's concern is not so much confidentiality but Murray's "need inviolacy." The feeling I got from him was that

"No one has the right to ask me about this particular matter in order for me to be a flight engineer."

We could say that he does not have to answer the question; but if he does not answer it, he leaves it in the "cannot say" category. My brother-in-law feels that if he cannot say whether he would go to a movie without paying, anyone looking at this would think that there was some funny reason for his leaving that item unanswered—rather like "taking the Fifth Amendment" to refuse a question. My point is simply that there is a class of interesting and important factual issues which people complain about in the test. Perhaps we should find out what the effect of a little elementary information would be (for example, how we use the MMPI items and how we determine the scoring) on the complaints of a person of average intelligence but not sophisticated in the social sciences. We should know the answers to those factual questions better than we do. But I would distinguish these issues from a set of issues that are *not* "factual," at least in the usual sense, namely, the ethical-political issues.

One of the first things we should discuss with people who know something about theories of ethics, law, theology, or political theory is *whether there are any almost-absolute rights being violated here.* Assume that Sidney Hook is correct in saying, "There isn't any such thing as an *absolute* right." For instance, the notion of an absolute freedom of speech, he says, is something that Justice Black just never thought through; it is a crazy idea. I agree with Sidney Hook and will use the phrase "quasi-absolute." By quasi-absolute, I mean there are some kinds of things which we, in a democratic society with an Anglo-Saxon ethic concerning politics, consider damn-near absolute. A quasi-absolute right is one which we take to be so fundamental, so rock-bottom, so precious, so highly valued in our ethos that only the very *strongest* kinds of counterconsiderations will be allowed to prevail against it. Thus, free speech is a right we allow to be countervailed by the danger of hollering "Fire" in a crowded theatre and by civil actions for libel, etc. But the countervailing "cutting score" is set extremely high. Again, this right is so fundamental that we do not (even in an emergency) think it is proper to use torture to get a human being to say, "Yes, I committed such and such a crime." In many societies, including Western Christian culture until rather recently, torture was standard operating procedure as part of the state's method of investigating crimes. The French monarchy had a king's assassin; everybody knew there was such a person—I believe his identity was even known—and he was provided for in the budget. The King of France would say, "Look, the Duke of So-and-so is writing too many pamphlets; get him, see?" And that was it. Now, we would say that will not do. Our conception is that no matter *how* bodacious, *how* obstreperous or obnoxious somebody is, it should not be legitimate for the executive in our society to have him killed.

I cite these extreme examples not to make an analogy but merely to set your switches to this effect: that we *do* have a few rights we consider quasi-absolute, maybe not completely, but nearly so. We say, for instance, that there are some means which are so intrinsically illicit that *no* end will justify their use. That list of forbidden means may be rather small, but we do have such a list. Now, a question: Does the MMPI ask people to reveal facts about themselves in a format, in a setting, and under a kind of pressure that violates the quasi-absolute form of freedom in our society? For instance, complaints regarding the many sex items are often unjustified; but there are some "unusual sex practices" items on the MMPI which if answered affirmatively would constitute a confession to a crime that is punishable by Minnesota law. (For example, the item "I have engaged in unusual sex practices" is probably taken, by most persons, to include sex practices which we psychologists know to be not so very "unusual." But they are, in most states, violations of the criminal law, often having very heavy penalties attached. It is hardly paranoid for a person to resist, and resent, questions which refer to behavior that could (if the county attorney chose to take an interest in it) put him in prison for 20 years! And we know that MMPI files are sometimes maintained on high security, sometimes (more often, I fear) not.

Now let me play the other role for a moment. Consider the use of the MMPI for selecting Northwest Orient Airlines electrical inspectors. The psychopathic component on the MMPI is largely validated in a psychiatric context. For the moment, pretend that no studies of behaviors like accident-proneness or goofing off in school had ever been done. Under these circumstances, I would say there is an ethical problem in industry—when you extrapolate the behavior domain into a new context. Whether it is illicit to use the instrument under these circumstances is dependent upon the sensitivity of the job. If the job is one which affects whether airplanes crash, then I would say, "Look, if you are an industrial psychologist using the MMPI in the airline industry, you ought to try to validate it. But, even before you validate the instrument, if a high degree of judgment and responsibility is required in the position for which you're screening and if your selection ratio is running reasonably small, then you should give a Mult. If it's a matter of selecting a shoe salesman, eliminating the 49's isn't that important. But, when I fly, I would feel more comfortable knowing that some screening of the crew, even with imperfect tests, has been done—I would prefer not having 49's at the helm."

In summary, we have two main problems in addition to the purely political, public image, and community educational. The first problem is empirically researchable. What is it that people, once they are adequately informed, mainly object to? The second problem, more one of conceptual analysis, is do their (informed) objections have merit from the legal, ethical, philosophic, or theological standpoint? For this second problem, the psychologist needs help from experts in those other domains.

Appendix A
Interpretative Manual to the MMPI

Robert C. Carson
Duke University

INTRODUCTION

This manual, an outgrowth of experiences gained at the University of Chicago with an earlier edition, represents an attempt to provide in brief and readily available form a source of interpretative hypotheses for the clinical use of the Minnesota Multiphasic Personality Inventory. It is intended for the clinical student whose experience with the test in a clinical setting is in the beginning stages. I have, therefore, attempted to select for presentation only those aspects of MMPI interpretation which may be regarded as fundamental. As with any clinical psychological instrument, skill in the use of the MMPI is gained only through continued experience with it in a clinical setting.

This manual assumes that the reader is familiar with the content, structure, and development of the MMPI as a psychometric instrument. Familiarity with the standard test manual (Hathaway & McKinley, 1951) is a minimal requirement. Persons seeking a more advanced knowledge of the test, and this should include all who plan to use it extensively in clinical work, are strongly urged to familiarize themselves with the material contained in two volumes by Welsh and Dahlstrom (1956, 1960). Although the basic rationale is not very complicated, the test's usefulness is greatly enhanced if the user has a detailed knowledge of its characteristics including the item components of the various scales.

A general word of caution is appropriate at the outset. The highly mechanized and "objective" appearance of an MMPI profile often tempts people to abandon their usual approach in evaluating clinical data and to adopt a kind of rigidly psychometric—sign—actuarial method of interpretation; indeed the MMPI has enjoyed great esteem among some psychologists on the basis of its being peculiarly suited for such treatment. However, most clinicians who regularly use the MMPI in clinical practice see this as being, at best, a relatively barren procedure. At its worst, from the point of view of the individual case, it is productive of sometimes serious diagnostic errors. The naïve application of quantitative formulas for determining clinical decisions is an especially hazardous pitfall for beginners in MMPI work.

The material of this manual represents a synthesis of ideas derived from a number of sources in addition to those recommended above. I have drawn extensively from the work of Cuadra and Reed and from Leary (1957). A number of clinical psychologists have kindly provided comments and encouragement on the earlier version of the manual, and many of their suggestions are incorporated in the present revision. I am particularly indebted in this regard to Drs. Starke R. Hathaway and William Schofield of the University of Minnesota, Drs. Charles Dicken and Morton A. Lieberman of the University of Chicago, and to my colleague at Duke University, Dr. John Altrocchi.

INTERPRETATION: THE VALIDITY SCALES

The standard MMPI profile includes four scales whose original purpose was to provide the clinician with a frame of reference for interpreting the "clinical" scales. In practice, each of these four scales has been found to have psychological correlates no less important clinically than those of the clinical scales, and their original function as validational devices has been all but overshadowed by their utility in providing information on certain crucial dimensions of personality.

The ? Scale

This is not a scale in the usual sense, consisting simply of the number of items to which the individual has not answered "true" or "false." No significance is attached to raw scores of 30 or below, but in those fairly rare cases in which the score exceeds 30, and especially where it approaches 100 or more, it becomes essential to take into account its attenuating effect upon the clinical profile and to attempt to discover the source of the individual's "cannot say" propensity. Generally speaking, if reading difficulties can be ruled out, moderate ? elevations are indicative of obsessional processes, often with elements of extreme intellectualization and not infrequently involving highly idiosyncratic interpretation of items. One familiar manifestation of this type of process is seen in the legalistic overcautiousness of some paranoid patients who, if permitted, may leave unanswered the majority of the items. Individuals who are severely impaired psychiatrically often have markedly elevated ? scores simply on the basis of being unable to perform the decision-making task.

Many patients with high ? scores can be persuaded to respond in a definitive way to the neglected items, and it is a good idea to make the attempt routinely. Failing this, it is often instructive to score all neglected items in the significant direction and to compare the profile derived on this basis with the original, noting particularly any occurrences of incongruity which might result from a nonrandom selection of items left unanswered.

The *L* Scale

The *L* scale consists of 15 items selected on the basis of "face" validity to identify persons who attempt to give an overly perfectionistic view of themselves. The items refer to attitudes and practices which have a very positive valence culturally but which are actually found—if they occur at all—only in the most conscientious persons. Item example: "I do not read every editorial in the newspaper every day" (scorable F).

A raw score of 5 or more is suggestive of excessive rigidity, if not of conscious deception, if it cannot be explained on the basis of occupation (e.g., clergy) or naïveté associated with a culturally limited background. In the general population, scores above 6 occur with persons who, for one reason or another, have pathologically intense needs to present a good front; it is interesting that high scores have been found actually to predict underachievement. The scale often does not detect deception in sophisticated individuals; and, in fact, a high score in an individual of mature background may be associated with judgment deficiencies and should be further investigated in this light.

The *F* Scale

The *F* scale consists of 64 items that were answered almost always in the same direction by the normal standardization group. Content varies widely. Item examples: "Everything tastes the same" (T), "I believe in law enforcement" (F). *T* scores above 80 suggest the following possibilities: (1) error by the examiner in scoring the test; (2) failure of the patient to understand the items; (3) lack of cooperation, the patient having purposely responded in a random and haphazard fashion; (4) distortion due to confusion, delusional thinking, or other psychotic processes; or (5) distortion due to the wish to put oneself in a bad light or falsely to claim mental symptoms. (See below under *F-K* index.)

With the *T* score above 80, the examiner should entertain the hypothesis that he has an invalid profile and should attempt to check this out by considering the characteristics of the remainder of the profile and (with the booklet form) the patient's responses to repeated items from the standpoint of intratest consistency. *T* scores in the range of 65 to 80 are indicative of unusual or markedly unconventional thinking and frequently appear in sullen, rebellious personalities of the schizoid, antisocial, or "Bohemian" type. Young people struggling with problems of identity and the need to define themselves by exhibiting nonconformity (the beard and sandals set) frequently score in this range on *F*. The profile in such cases is usually a valid one. Occasionally individuals who are intensely anxious and pleading for help may get *F* scores somewhat above 80 that are bona fide and do not represent psychotic distortions; in such cases the profile will be markedly elevated but interpretable. *F* appears to be positively correlated with severity of illness in a clinic population. Individuals having moderately elevated *F* scores are likely to be described as moody, changeable, dissatisfied, opinionated, talkative, restless, and unstable. Low scorers are often described as sincere, calm, dependable, honest, simple, conventional, moderate, and as having narrow interests.

The *K* Scale

The *K* scale consists of items selected on the basis of their ability to identify "false negative" cases; there are 30 items, of which 24 have been found to be highly correlated with Edwards' Social Desirability factor. The scale in its present form is the product of long efforts to devise empirically a scale to measure guardedness or defensiveness in test-taking attitude. In this sense, *K* is seen as a "suppressor variable." It measures approximately what *L* was intended to measure, but it does so in a much more subtle and effective manner. *K* is used as a correction factor for some of the clinical scales. Item example: "Often I can't understand why I have been cross or grouchy" (F).

High *K* scorers are people who cannot tolerate any suggestion that they are insecure, that they have difficulties in social relations, or that they may not have their lives well ordered and controlled. They are intolerant and unaccepting of unconventional or nonconformist behavior in others. Markedly concerned about their own social stimulus value, they are nevertheless relatively without insight concerning their effect upon others. In a clinical situation they show much hesitance and a great desire to ensure confidence and approval. Moderate elevations on K are found in people described as enterprising, ingenious, resourceful, sociable, reasonable, enthusiastic, and as having wide interests. Some elevation is seen as desirable prognostically ($T = 55$ to 65), and successfully treated patients appear to show some rise on K; in this high average range it suggests adaptiveness and the availability of ego resources. High K is associated with low expectancy of delinquency in adolescents, especially females. Generally speaking, prognosis tends to be poor with extreme scores in either direction. A low K is usually accompanied by caustic manners, suspicion of the motivations of others, and exaggeration of the ills of the world. Low K scorers have been described as awkward, cautious, peaceable, high strung, cynical, dissatisfied, and individualistic. In terms of the K correction on other scales, one should be aware that the patient who gets an elevation on scale 8 by virtue of his having a high K is not the same kind of person as the one who gets a high 8 by claiming or admitting 8-type problems and symptoms.

The F-K Index. The ratio of F to K has been used as an indication of "faking," good or bad, and somewhat more successfully in the latter case than in the former. When F minus K (in terms of raw score) is positive and greater than 11, it is suggestive of a conscious attempt to look bad or to exaggerate illness (malingering), particularly if the absolute scores on the two scales are low. When the index is negative and exceeds 12, it suggests a deliberate effort to look good and to deny emotional problems.

INTERPRETATION: THE CLINICAL SCALES

General Interpretative Comments

Dimensions of Variation. MMPI profiles may be conceived of as varying on three dimensions: elevation, scatter, and shape.

Elevation: Historically, the first of these, elevation, was understandably emphasized as being of prime importance. More recently, however, clinicians have tended to deemphasize elevation, and for good reasons. The reader will note in what follows a frequent failure to specify absolute T-score ranges within which particular interpretative hypotheses may apply. This seeming vagueness is purposeful and stems from a recognition that the "meanings" of the various clinical scales are to a considerable extent a relative matter. Within limits a scale may be considered "up" or "down" to the extent that the score deviates from other scores in the profile. Although it would obviously be absurd to discount the general significance of elevation, interpretative precision is primarily a function of the examiner's knowledge of profile configurations.

Slope: A word should be said about slope as an important configurational characteristic of the total profile. In general, the clinical profiles of psychoneurotic persons tend to slope downward from left to right, while those of psychotics tend to slope in the opposite direction. Individuals with character problems tend to have profiles with peaks confined to the middle scales with a dropping off at either end. These are, of course, merely modal observations and must be used cautiously.

Scatter: Profile scatter has usually been discussed in connection with what MMPI workers refer to as "phasicality" which means approximately the same thing. In general, low scatter profiles give us less information than do profiles in which there is marked interscale variability. Beyond this rather banal observation, I have not been impressed with scatter as being in itself an important variable in interpretation.

Scale 1 (*Hs*)

This scale contains 33 items of a fairly obvious nature having to do in the main with bodily function and malfunction. The complaint items tend to be vague and nonspecific. Although scale 1 rises slightly with physical disease, it is mainly a "character" scale, and physically ill patients generally score higher on scale 2. Scale 1 is a gross index of something related to optimism-pessimism. High scorers are sour on life, whiny, complaining, and generally handle their hostile feelings by making those around them miserable. Frequently they use somatic complaints to control others. They tend to be cynical and defeatist, especially as regards others' efforts to help them. They are highly skilled in frustrating and infuriating physicans, of whom they often engage a great number in succession. Elevation is associated with poor progress in psychotherapy. Even persons having moderate elevations on scale 1 tend to be seen as unambitious, lacking in drive, stubborn, and narcissistically egocentric; they appear readily to develop a paranoid posture when pressured. In contrast, persons scoring low on scale 1 are described as alert, capable and responsible. Effectiveness in living is suggested by a low 1.

Relations with Other Scales. Elevations on scales 1 and 3 with an intervening valley at scale 2 form what has come to be called the "conversion V." Persons exhibiting this pattern are characterized by an extreme need to interpret their problems in living in a way that is both "rational" and socially acceptable. Many of them develop somatic displacements that permit a localization of the difficulty outside of the personality; others develop psychological symptoms of a highly "reasonable," socially acceptable type. In any case, the real function of the symptom is obscured by hysteroid operations.

In general, an accompanying elevation on 3 attenuates the overtly pessimistic, complaining attitudes of the high 1 person, and where 3 is higher the operation of denial may even permit expressions of optimism.

With very high scores on scale 8, an elevation on scale 1 is often associated with somatic delusions.

With elevations on scales K, 1, and 3, and especially if F, 2, 7, and 8 are down, the individual is likely to be extremely defensive, presenting himself as exceedingly "normal," responsible, helpful, and sympathetic. Such persons are very threatened by any suggestion of weakness or unconventionality in themselves. Often they are markedly organized around ideals of service and contribution to others at the level of overt behavior. They do not tolerate well the role of "patient."

Scale 2 (D)

Scale 2 consists of 60 items relating to matters such as worry, discouragement, self-esteem, and general outlook. Scale 2 is the most frequent peak in the profiles of psychiatric patients. It tends to be fairly unstable, being highly sensitive to mood changes, and its meaning tends to vary depending upon the characteristics of the remainder of the profile. In general, it is the best single—and a remarkably efficient—index of immediate satisfaction, comfort, and security; it tells something of how the individual evaluates himself and his role in the world. High 2 people tend to be silent and retiring, perhaps withdrawn, and are seen by others as aloof, evasive, timid, and more or less inhibited. Low 2 people are active, alert, cheerful, and outgoing and are likely to be seen by others as enthusiastic, self-seeking, and perhaps given to self-display. Occasionally one sees a profile in which 2 is the only elevated scale. Usually this will be a so-called reactive depression, even when the person may deny depressive feelings; particular attention should be given to a cautious evaluation of the suicidal risk.

Relations with Other Scales. Elevation with scales 1 and 3 is modal in the psychoneuroses (the "neurotic triad"), in some forms of which there is an additional spike on 7. With increasing experience the examiner will be able to arrive at quite precise diagnostic formulations within the class of neurotic illnesses by attending to the patterning of scores on scales 1, 2, 3, and 7.

Peaks on 2 and 7 are exceedingly common in psychiatric patients, reflecting the self-devaluation, intropunitiveness, tension, and nervousness characteristic of this group as a whole. Some 2–7 elevation is considered desirable in candidates for psychotherapy, since this usually indicates internal distress with motivation for change, as well as some introspective bent. Extreme elevations, however, often mean that the individual is so agitated and worried that he cannot settle down to the business of psychotherapy, and other forms of therapeutic intervention become necessary.

When elevations on 2 and 7 are accompanied by an elevation on 3, the individual is likely to present docile, markedly dependent interpersonal behavior with a tendency to inspire nurturant and helpful attitudes in others. The poignant helplessness of these persons not infrequently causes even experienced therapists to engage in nonfunctional protective maneuvers. Clinically, this type of problem is usually seen in the context of an anxiety or phobic reaction of relatively severe proportions.

Schizoid and schizophrenic conditions are nearly always accompanied by some elevation on 2. In such cases, the disaffiliation and sullen distrustful anger of the schizoid will also be present in elevations on *F*, 4, and 8.

Note on Suicide. There is no "suicidal profile" that has any real clinical utility. The processes measured by scales 2, 4, 7, and 8 appear to act in some way as "excitors" or "releasers" of suicidal behavior; but predictive statements based upon these relationships will inevitably produce an intolerably high false positive rate.

Scale 3 (*Hy*)

Scale 3 consists of 60 items, most of which fall into two general types: (1) rather specific somatic complaints and (2) items that deny any emotional or interpersonal difficulty. In normal subjects these two clusters show no tendency to occur together; in persons organized around hysteric operations, they seem to be closely associated. High 3 people are very likely to be extremely naïve and self-centered in outlook. They are very demanding of affection and support and endeavor to get these by indirect but obtrusively manipulative means. Often they are highly visible and rather uninhibited in social relations; but such relations are carried on at a superficial, immature level. Some high 3 people act out sexually and aggressively in blatant fashion with convenient and often incredible inattention to what they are doing. They are, on the whole, people blandly without insight. Because they have strong needs to be liked, their initial response to treatment is apt to be enthusiastic. Sooner or later, however, they become intolerant of the inevitable challenges to their defenses, frequently make impossible demands on the therapist, and become generally resistive, often complaining that they are being mistreated, that the therapist does not understand them, etc. The person with an elevated 3 is unlikely to be seen as psychotic, regardless of what shows on other scales; the examiner should, therefore, be very wary about diagnosing psychosis when 3 is clearly elevated. Little of a reliable nature is known about low 3 people, but many of them seem to be socially isolated, cynical, and generally misanthropic.

Relations with Other Scales. The neurotic triad and conversion V configurations have already been considered. Elevations on K and 3 when F and 8 are low are characteristic of affiliative, constrictedly overconventional people. These individuals show prominently in their relations with others an exaggerated striving to be liked and accepted. Characteristically they maintain an unassailable optimism and emphasize harmony with others, if necessary at the expense of internal values and principle. They are likely to become extremely uncomfortable in, and, therefore, to avoid, situations demanding angry response, independent decision, or the exercise of power. When such persons do show up in the clinic, which is infrequent, they are most resistant to considering that their difficulties may result from emotional conflict. It is also a remarkable fact that even in the face of catastrophic failure they often resolutely maintain that "things are going fine"; defeated feelings seem to be intolerable to these people.

Scale 4 (*Pd*)

The 50 items in this scale deal in the main with general social maladjustment and absence of strongly pleasant experience. These include complaints against family, feelings of having been victimized, boredom, and feelings of alienation from the group—of not being in on things. High 4 people are generally characterized by angry disidentification with recognized conventions; their revolt may be against family or society or both. Many high 4s exhibit an apparent inability to plan ahead, if not a reckless disregard of the consequences of their actions, and unpredictability is a feature of their behavior. Usually social relationships are shallow; the individual rarely develops strong loyalties of any kind. These people sometimes make a good impression at first, but on longer acquaintance their essential unreliability, moodiness, and resentment become apparent. They may justify their disregard of convention on the basis of being "above" mere propriety, reflecting the high value many of them place on themselves. High 4 is associated with inability to profit from experience, including psychotherapy; in adolescent delinquents with 4 peaks, therapy appears to be less effective in producing changes than does increasing age. Low scorers on 4 tend to be conventional, rigid, and overidentified with social status; frequently they manifest very low levels of heterosexual aggressiveness.

Relations with Other Scales. Some elevation on 4 is a fairly stable feature in character disorders and the psychoses, reflecting a component of brooding resentment. A peak on 4 in the presence of a low 2, even when 4 is only moderately elevated, indicates an especially low probability of significant personality change occurring.

Elevation on scales 4 and 9 are frequent in the behavior disorders. Such a pattern is nearly always associated with some form of acting out behavior. The individual exhibits an enduring tendency to get into trouble with his environment, usually only in a way that damages his own or his family's reputation; antisocial and criminal acts are not uncommon, however. Arousal seeking and an inordinate need for excitement and stimulation characterize the 4-9 group as a whole.

When clear elevations on 4 and 9 are accompanied by a clear elevation on 6 as well, serious concern is warranted in regard to aggressive behavior. This is especially true if scale 8 is also elevated. This pattern has been observed often in persons exhibiting sudden violence.

Peaks on 4 and 6 identify angry, sullen people who utilize excessively a transfer of blame mechanism. Typically they are rigidly argumentative and difficult in social relations, frequently being seen as obnoxious. They are poor candidates for treatment.

The foregoing is less true if scale 3 is also elevated. In general, elevations on both 3 and 4 identify markedly immature persons who tend outwardly to be conformists and who discharge their hostile rebellious feelings in indirect ways. Many of these people, for example, establish enduring relationships with marginal, acting-out individuals, thereby vicariously gratifying their own antisocial tendencies. The 3-4 pattern suggests fertile soil for dissociative phenomena.

When elevations on *F*, 4, and 8 occur in the presence of a low 2, this is usually an aggressive, punitive individual who is most comfortable when inspiring anxiety and guilt in others. Often such individuals drift into roles in which such behavior is socially sanctioned, or at least not manifestly condemned, e.g., the law enforcer, the overzealous clergyman, the school disciplinarian. The behaviors expected here range all the way from stern, punitive, cold disapproval to clinical sadism. When these individuals find themselves in situations in which their guilt- and fear-provoking operations are blocked, they are likely to feel unprotected, anxious, and uncomfortable. Many individuals diagnosed clinically as sociopaths exhibit this configuration.

Scale 5 (*Mf*)

Scale 5 contains 60 items having to do with interests, vocational choices, aesthetic preference, and an activity-passivity dimension. The same scale is used for both sexes and is merely scored in the opposite direction for females. It was originally intended to measure masculinity-femininity but is far from being a pure measure of this dimension; it is, for example, definitely correlated with education and intelligence, and interpretative statements should take this correlation into account. An elevation on scale 5 is never in itself sufficient reason to diagnose homosexuality, overt or "latent." Moreover, homosexuals who wish to conceal their inversion appear able to do so with relative ease insofar as this scale is concerned.

In general, scale 5 is a measure of sophistication and aesthetic interest. Clear elevations are suggestive of nonidentification with the culturally prescribed masculine or feminine role. For males, high scorers tend to be relatively passive individuals; some are definitely effeminate in manner. These men are seen as imaginative and sensitive and tend to have a wide range of interests. Low 5 males are easygoing, adventurous, perhaps somewhat "coarse." In some low 5 scorers, there is an element of compulsive masculinity; the individual's efforts to appear masculine seem overdone and inflexible, often taking the form of exhibitionistic display of physical strength and endurance. Not surprisingly, if such people enter treatment they are usually found to have very disturbing questions concerning their own identity and maleness.

For females, high scorers tend in general to be aggressive, dominating, and competitive; they are found in large numbers in activities and occupations that are traditionally male. These women are typically confident, spontaneous, and somewhat uninhibited in those areas of living in which heterosexual implications are absent; they become anxious in situations in which they are expected to adopt a feminine sexual role. Their interests tend toward the mechanical and scientific. Some elevation on *Mf* may be considered normal in girls in their middle to late teens and in women from atypical cultural backgrounds. Low 5 females are passive, submissive, yielding, and demure—sometimes to the point of representing living caricatures of the feminine stereotype. Women who achieve extremely low *T* scores are usually highly constricted, self-pitying, and faultfinding; they seem unable to tolerate pleasant experiences.

Relations with Other Scales. Males: Elevation on 4 and 5 is a not uncommon configuration and indicates a Bohemian type of character (lately, "hippie") who leaves little doubt as to his nonconformity. Such people delight in defying and challenging convention and by their general behavior and appearance so indicate. Many overt homosexuals exhibit this pattern and are often not in the least reticent about discussing their sexual behavior with anyone who seems interested. The foregoing comments may not apply where the profile shows other peaks as well or where it is generally elevated. A *low* 5 with a high 4 points to a tendency toward flamboyant masculinity, as previously described; in teenagers this is often manifested as delinquency.

Females: A high 5 together with a high 4 is found among women who are rebelling against the female role. Generally speaking, the high 5 woman's behavior becomes more clearly deviant with increasing elevation on 4. Women whose profiles show a low 5 with an elevation on 4 are hostile, angry people who, however, are unable to express such feelings directly. Instead they resort to various masochistic operations that provoke other people to anger and rage, often taking satisfaction in pitying themselves because they have been mistreated; there is often an accompanying elevation on 6 that reflects the degree to which the transfer of blame elements in this pattern become involved in a generalized paranoid posture. These women are often extremely adroit in eliciting rage, and this is likely to create special problems in therapeutic management.

Some people exhibit a related kind of behavior as a way of life. They present themselves to others as weak, inferior, guilty, and submissive. They are markedly self-effacing and shun any outward appearance of strength or pride. They invite others to be patronizingly superior and deprecating and appear to feel least uncomfortable in relationships when they are receiving such treatment. In many ways this is the syndrome of the intellectual ("egghead") in American culture; the inveterate "clown" is another example. Ambivalence, immobility, and a sense of failure are characteristic. The clinical extreme of this form of behavior is the psychotic depressive reaction. On the MMPI, these people have a configuration involving elevations on scales 2, 7, and (often) 4. In males, there is in addition a clear elevation on 5; in females, there is a valley on 5.

Scale 6 (*Pa*)

Scale 6 consists of 40 items that tap such processes as sensitivity, being easily hurt, moral virtue, rationality, denial of suspiciousness, and complaints about others' shortcomings. This is one of the poorer MMPI scales, at least from the viewpoint of performing its intended function of detecting paranoid thinking. Many people who are clinically extremely paranoid show no elevation at all. It is true, however, that persons who do get definite elevations on scale 6 can nearly always be demonstrated to have paranoid ideation, if not frank delusions. To a lesser extent this is also true of persons who get extremely low scores on scale 6. The latter apparently are identified by virtue of being *too* cautious in what they say about themselves. Moderate elevation on 6 ($T = 60$ to 70) suggests an individual who adopts an intropunitive role outwardly but who expresses hostility by "arranging" events in which others are victimized (the "What did I do wrong?" syndrome). In general, high 6 scorers tend to be suspicious and brooding, to harbor grudges, and usually to feel that in some way they are not getting what is coming to them. In treatment they are rigid and rationalistically argumentative. With an elevated 6 it is frequently useful to look at the person's responses to individual items in the scale to differentiate between general characterological paranoia and the presence of clearly delusional thinking. Low 6 scorers tend to be stubborn and evasive, often feeling that dire consequences will follow upon their revealing themselves in any way. There may be, then, little essential difference between high and low scorers on 6; this, of course, leaves unexplained why they differ in their responses to the items in this particular scale.

Relations with Other Scales. Definite elevations on scales 6 and 8, regardless of the configuration of the profile as a whole, are usually indicative of paranoid schizophrenia.

Sometimes a moderate elevation on 6 occurs with an elevation on 3. This will usually be an individual who is blandly repressive in regard to hostile and aggressive impulses. Such individuals deny suspicious and competitive attitudes and comfort themselves by consciously perceiving the world in naïvely positive and accepting terms. They are, however, hard to get along with on more than a casual basis, since their underlying hostility, egocentricity, and ruthless power operations are likely to be apparent to a degree that is inversely proportional to social distance.

The relationship between 6 and 4 has already been discussed.

Note on Paranoid Conditions. The examiner working in a clinical setting may occasionally have an individual referred for examination for what appears to be good cause in terms of suspected psychopathology but who nevertheless achieves a perfectly "normal" profile, validity scales included. In a very large proportion of such cases this will turn out to be some form of paranoid disorder.

Scale 7 (*Pt*)

Scale 7 consists of 48 items relating to anxiety symptoms, inability to resist, irrational fears, and self-devaluation. This scale is a general measure of anxiety and ruminative self-doubt. High scorers tend to be obsessionally worried, tense, indecisive, and unable to concentrate. Low scorers are usually relaxed, self-confident, and secure. Individuals having marked elevations on this scale almost always exhibit extreme obsessionalism, but this must be differentiated from the so-called compulsive defense system. Many rigidly compulsive people show no elevation at all, presumably because their rigid organization wards off any feelings of insecurity, concern about their own worth, etc.

Relations with Other Scales. The clinically very common 2-7 profile was discussed in connection with scale 2.

Scales 7 and 8 are highly correlated, but important implications concerning diagnosis and prognosis depend upon their relative heights.

When 7 is higher than 8, regardless of the height of 8, the situation tends to be more benign than when the reverse is true; the individual is still fighting his problems and defending himself with some effectiveness against the development of more fixed patterns of disturbed thought and behavior. When both scales are elevated above 75 and when 8 is relatively higher, this is often an established schizophrenic psychosis, especially if the neurotic triad is relatively low; even in those cases in which psychosis can be ruled out, the problem is likely to be a very refractory one, e.g., a severe, alienated character disorder.

Scale 8 (*Sc*)

Scale 8 contains 78 items dealing with social alienation, isolation, complaints of family alienation, bizarre feelings, influence of external agents, peculiar bodily dysfunction, and general dissatisfaction. The examiner should be wary of an understandable tendency to interpret scale 8 too narrowly. It was developed on schizophrenic individuals, and it is extremely valuable in the diagnosis of schizophrenic illness. It is necessary to point out, however, that a limited conception of this important scale will needlessly restrict its range of usefulness and encourage a disregard of available and potentially very enlightening information.

High scorers on 8 almost always feel alienated, misunderstood, and peculiarly not a part of the general social environment. They have fundamental and disturbing questions about their own identity and worth. They are somehow confused about how one goes about the business of being a socialized human being; many of these persons feel that they are hopelessly lacking something fundamental which is the key to successful relations with others. Among high 8s there are many painfully withdrawn people who have little or nothing in the way of social relationships and who occupy themselves excessively with private autistic fantasy. Even with moderate elevations there is usually some difficulty in thinking and communication. These people seem to be in contact and seem to be talking sense, but one is vaguely aware that he is really not understanding very well what it is they are saying; they appear habitually to avoid making unequivocal statements. A high score on 8 makes the prognosis for short-term psychotherapy relatively poor. It should be noted that patients who are clinically most schizophrenic get T scores in the 80 to 90 range. Agitated neurotics, prepsychotics, and so-called pseudoneurotic schizophrenics score highest on 8.

Relations with Other Scales. The basic schizoid configuration involving elevations on *F*, 2, 4, and 8 and the important relationships between 7 and 8 have been described above.

Something further should be said about the person with peaks on both 4 and 8, a not infrequent combination. Typically such a person's problems stem from the early establishment of an attitude of distrust toward the world. These are people who, as children, acquired a set to perceive other people as hostile, rejecting, and dangerous. They also learned, however, that they could protect themselves and alleviate to some degree their painful anticipations of hurt by striking out in anger and rebellion. The pattern is continued into adulthood, the person being so rebellious and angry that his social behavior continually reinforces his alienation from the group. Intervention into this vicious circle by way of psychotherapy is an extremely difficult operation.

When 8 and 9 are elevated together, it usually identifies an individual who handles his inability to relate, or his fear of relating, by distractability operations. The 8-9 pattern appears to be associated with a highly malignant psychopathological process, and its occurrence should be viewed with extreme seriousness even where elevation is only moderate. These people are very difficult to work with psychotherapeutically because they cannot permit a focalization of issues; they never settle on anything long enough to allow a real coming to grips.

Scale 9 (*Ma*)

Scale 9 contains 46 items having to do generally with expansiveness, egotism, and irritability. High scorers are warm, enthusiastic, expansive, generally outgoing, and uninhibited. They tend to become easily offended, however, and may be seen as tense and hyperactive. Many of these people have an unusual capacity for sustained activity and effort. *T* scores in the range of 60 to 70 suggest a pleasant outgoing temperament. Above this, there is increasing likelihood of maladaptive hyperactivity, irritability, and insufficient inhibitory capacity. Low scorers often exhibit listlessness, apathy, and lack of drive; almost always they are people lacking in self-confidence and a normal degree of optimism regarding the future. A very low score on 9 suggests serious depression even when scale 2 is not markedly elevated.

Relations with Other Scales. Although scales 2 and 9 are negatively correlated, the relationship is far from perfect, and one occasionally sees profiles with elevations on both. This seemingly contradictory pattern suggests three possibilities: (1) an agitated state in which the individual is painfully aware of intense pressure from hostile and other ego-alien impulses; (2) a condition of introspective preoccupation and heightened narcissistic self-absorption (this is occasionally seen in disturbed adolescents with "identity" problems); and (3) the presence of an organic brain lesion.

When 2 and 7 are down, a moderately elevated 9 frequently identifies an individual whose security operations are organized around interpersonal power or narcissistic competitiveness. It is useful to distinguish the two, and *K* is sometimes helpful here. *K* is often elevated with 9 in managerial, autocratic, power-oriented individuals whose compulsive energy and planful organization provoke a somewhat overwhelmed deference and submission in others. These people often make excellent administrators, possibly because ambiguity, uncertainty, and indecision are intolerable to them. They insist upon being informed and feel most uncomfortable in situations in which they are not. As might be expected, they do not as a rule respond productively to the typical psychotherapeutic situation.

K is not usually elevated with 9 in competitive, narcissistic personalities. These individuals organize their lives around competitive self-enhancement and tend to be extremely threatened whenever in a situation in which submissiveness or dependence are expected. They depend for their self-esteem on demonstrations of weakness in others and strength in themselves, and they exact a grudging, envious submission and respect from those with whom they interact. In women this frequently manifests itself in an exhibitionistic emphasis on physical attractiveness (the "Hollywood" syndrome). If such a person enters psychotherapy the therapist may be treated to endless—and often quite fascinating—orgies of self-display, but his chances of having a successful therapeutic experience are not great.

Scale 0 (*Si*)

This is one of the "additional" MMPI scales. Its development was somewhat different from that of the other scales of the standard clinical profile in that the criterion instrument did not involve a psychiatric syndrome. The items deal mainly with social participation. This scale provides a fairly gross, but sometimes quite useful, index of comfort in interpersonal relationships. High scorers tend to be withdrawn, aloof, and anxious in contact with people. Scores above 70 will on rare occasions identify a schizoid factor in well-controlled, socialized psychotic personalities when this is missed by other scales. Low scorers on 0 are sociable, warm people. Extremely low scores suggest a certain flightiness and superficiality of relationships; these hail-fellow-well-met individuals have well-developed social techniques and very many social contacts, but they do not establish relationships of real intimacy.

REFERENCES

Cuadra, C. A., and Reed, C. F. An introduction to the MMPI. (Mimeographed and privately distributed.)

Dahlstrom, W. G., and Welsh, G. S. *An MMPI handbook: A guide to use in clinical practice and research.* Minneapolis: University of Minnesota Press, 1960.

Hathaway, S. R., and McKinley, J. C. *The Minnesota Multiphasic Personality Inventory manual.* (Rev. ed.) New York: The Psychological Corporation, 1951.

Leary, T. *Interpersonal diagnosis of personality.* New York: Ronald Press, 1957.

Welsh, G. S., and Dahlstrom, W. G. (Eds.) *Basic readings on the MMPI in psychology and medicine.* Minneapolis: University of Minnesota Press, 1956.

Appendix B
Comparison of MMPI Studies of Parents

(This material accompanies Chapter 8.)

A. Jack Hafner
Marian D. Hall
James Neal Butcher
Wentworth Quast

Author	Subjects	Method	Scale differences	Results
Adrian, R. J. (1957)	124 parents of disturbed children 124 PTA parents	D^2 and *LDF* were employed to yield optimum combination of MMPI scores for differentiation of clinic and PTA parents.		Clinic parents' profiles were more aberrant. Moderate or marked dissimilarity in the MMPI profiles for husbands and wives appeared to be associated with poor child adjustment. Judges were able to differentiate the groups significantly in MMPI sortings.
Adrian, R. J., Vacchiano, R. E., and Gilbart, T. E. (1966)	1. 62 parents of maladjusted children 62 PTA parents	D^2 and *LDF* were used to yield optimum combination of MMPI scores for differentiation of clinic and PTA parents. Fisher-Behrens *d* test between scale means.	Clinic mothers > Control mothers *L* .01 *F* .01 *Hs* .01 *D* .01 *Hy* .01 *Pd* .01 *Pa* .01 *Pt* .01 *Sc* .01 *Si* .01	MMPI maximally discriminated parents of adjusted and maladjusted children. Discrepancies within the clinic group were greater than within the PTA group.

		Clinic fathers >	Control fathers	
		F	.01	
		Hs	.01	
		D	.05	
		Pd	.01	
		Pt	.01	
		Sc	.01	
		Si	.05	
		Discrepancy-clinic >	Control couples	
		L	.01	
		F	.01	
		Hs	.01	
		D	.01	
		Hy	.01	
		Pt	.01	
		Sc	.01	
2. 192 accepted adoptive applicants, 144 rejected adoptive applicants.	*LDF* weights obtained above were applied to prospective adoptive groups.			Classification based on application of *LDF* equation to two groups of adoptive applicants revealed little agreement with the independent decision of the adoptive agencies.

Author	Subjects	Method	Scale differences	Results
Anderson, L. (1968)	23 fathers and 23 mothers of "aggressive" preadolescent boys. 29 fathers and 29 mothers of "neurotic" preadolescent boys. All subjects married and living together. 50 fathers and 50 mothers of "normal" boys.	Multivariate analysis, all groups combined. Mothers and fathers analyzed separately by frequency of high and low points in individual profiles, inspection of group mean profiles, and by an analysis of configural differences between the *Hy*—*Pd* and *Pd*—*Mf* scale scores.	Multivariate analysis Experimental parents > Controls *Hs* .05 *D* .01 *Hy* .001 *Pd* .001 "Aggressive" parents > "Neurotic" parents *Hs* .001 *Pd* .01 *Pt* .01 *Sc* .001 *Ma* .01 "Neurotic" parents > "Aggressive" parents *K* .001	Parents of "aggressive" boys much higher on *Pd* than fathers of either "neurotic" boys or controls. Also high on *Sc* and *Pt*. Fathers of "aggressive" boys higher on *Pd* than *Hy* in configural analysis, while fathers of "aggressive" boys higher on *Pd* than *Mf* than either fathers of "neurotic" boys or control fathers. Mothers of "aggressive" boys lowest on *Mf*, highest on *Pd*, but no marked group differences in the mothers.

			High points	
			"Neurotic" fathers > "Aggressive" fathers	
			K .01	
			"Aggressive" fathers > "Neurotic" fathers	
			Pd .001	
			Low points	
			"Aggressive" mothers < "Neurotic" mothers	
			Mf .05	
			Configural analysis	
			Hy—Pd: "Aggressive" fathers < "neurotic" fathers < control fathers	
			Pd—Mf: "Aggressive" fathers > "neurotic" fathers > control fathers	
Boveng, T. (1963)	Parents of 27 learning inhibition (*LI*) boys. Parents of 25 "normal" boys.	*t* test and high-point codes.	*LI* fathers > *C* fathers *Pd* .005 *D* .05 *LI* fathers > *C* mothers *F* .05 *LI* mothers > *C* fathers *K* .05	*LI* parents had twice as many scales $T \geq 70$. *LI* mothers had twice as many low-point 5 scales as control mothers. Lack of significant difference between *LI* and *C* mothers may be the result of unusual maladjusted *C* mother group (mean high point for *C* mothers = 76).

Author	Subjects	Method	Scale differences	Results
Burian, G. J. (1957)	60 mothers and fathers of disturbed (inpatient) children and normal parents from the Goodstein and Dahlstrom sample and from the Hathaway-Meehl normative data.	*t* tests and frequency of initial scale in the high point code.	Clinic parents > controls *L* *F* *Hs* *D* *Hy* *Pd* *Pa*	Scales *Hy*, *Pd*, and *Pa* appeared more frequently as high point among clinic parents than among controls.
Butcher, J. N. (1966)	40 mothers and 35 fathers of "externalizing" adolescent boys 14 mothers and 11 fathers of "internalizing" boys	"Externalizing" and "internalizing" boys were selected by presenting symptoms and behavior from three clinics using an objectively derived checklist. Parents who had taken the MMPI were used in the analysis.		Fathers of "externalizing" boys showed significantly greater elevation on the *Pd* scale than fathers of "internalizing" boys. 37% of externalizing fathers had *Pd* scores over $T =$ 70, while no fathers of internalizing boys had *Pd T* scores over 70. The mothers of internalizing boys appeared more neurotic. They had more

				frequent elevations on *Hs, D, Hy, Pa,* and *Si* than mothers of externalizing boys.
Butcher, J. N., and Messick, D. M. (1966)	29 fathers, 27 mothers (volunteers) of 8th-grade boys.	Peer and teacher ratings placed boy in high, middle, low aggression group. *d** measure of dissimilarity used to compare parent-child profile.		Children in middle aggression group more like parents than either extreme group. High aggression boys more like father, least like mother. Low aggression boys more like mother than father.
Erickson, M. T. (1966)	12 mothers, 11 fathers of 12 emotionally disturbed children (*E*). 12 mothers, 12 fathers of 12 organically retarded children (*O*). Control — MMPI normative group	*t* tests	*E* mothers > Controls *D* *Hy* *Pd* *Mf* *Pa* *Pt* *O* mothers > Controls *Hy* *Pd* *Pa* *Ma* *E* + *O* mothers > Controls *Hy* *Pd* *Pa*	Parents of *E* and *O* children have similar MMPI profiles. Both groups are more deviant than controls. MMPI parent profiles not useful in differential diagnosis of children.

Author	Subjects	Method	Scale differences	Results
			E fathers > *O* fathers	
			Hy	
			E fathers > Controls	
			Hy	
			Pd	
			Mf	
			O fathers > Controls	
			D	
			Pd	
			Mf	
			Ma	
			E + *O* fathers > Controls	
			Pd	
			Mf	
Goodstein, L. D. (1956)	Parents of 50 stutterers and Goodstein-Dahlstrom data.	*t* tests and high-point codes	Follow-up < Experimental *Ma* .01 Follow-up < Control *Pd* .01 *Ma* .01	Follow-up sample not more adjusted than previous one. Degree of parental pathology as measured by MMPI is not related to severity of stuttering.
Goodstein, L. D. (1960)	175 families of child with cleft palate. PTA parents as control.	*t* tests and high-point codes	Experimental > Control *L* .01 *A* .01 Control > Experimental *K* .01 *Pd* .01 *Sc* .01	Differences that were obtained were considered to be a function of sampling problem and socioeconomic level.

Goodstein, L. D. (1960)	175 families of child with cleft palate.	Testing relationships between ratings of parents' adjustment, MMPI, and other clinical variables: age, type of cleft, child's social adjustment, handling.		Ratings of parental adjustment based on MMPI of little help in understanding parents of children with cleft palate.
Goodstein, L. D., and Dahlstrom, W. G. (1956)	200 parents of stutterers and 200 parents of nonstutterers.	*t* tests and high-point codes	Experimental > Control *A* .01 Control > Experimental *K* .05 *D* .01	Children of experimental parents with *T* scores $\geq$70 rated as having significantly *less* severe stutter than children of other experimental parents. The two groups were not significantly different.
Goodstein, L. D., and Rowley, V. N. (1961)	50 parents of disturbed children broken into 4 groups: S Schizophrenic AO Acting out PT Personality trait N Neurotic	*t* tests between fathers *t* tests between mothers *t* difference between 4 experimental groups for fathers *t* difference	Experimental > Control fathers *Hs* .05 *D* .05 Experimental > Control mothers *D* .05 *Hy* .05 *Pa* .05	Parents of disturbed children more maladjusted than parents of normals, but not as maladjusted as those who seek help for themselves.

Author	Subjects	Method	Scale differences	Results
	50 control parents	t = difference between 4 experimental groups for mothers.	No significant difference among fathers. Mothers: (all at .05 level) AO > PT: *D, Hy, Pd* AO > N : *Pd* N > PT: *D, Hy* PT > N : *Ma* PT > S : *Mf* S > PT: *Pd* S > N : *Pd*	
Grossman, D. J. (1952)	42 parents of stutterers and 42 parents of nonstutterers.	"Pattern analysis" of MMPIs. Analysis of variance.		A statistically significant analysis of variance indicates that stutterers' parents interpret MMPI items "more atypically" than nonstutterers' parents.
Hall, M. D. (1963)	27 parents of learning inhibition (*LI*) boys. Control group from MMPI standardization sample.	t tests between raw scores	Mothers > Controls *K* .002 *D* .10 *Hy* .002 *Pd* .002 *Pa* .02 *Pt* .05 *Si* .10	

			Fathers > Controls *K* .10 *D* .02 *Hy* .002 *Pd* .002 *Mf* .002 *Pt* .05 *Ma* .10	
Hanvik, L. J., and Byrum, M. (1959)	96 male and 156 female parents of children seen at child guidance clinic.	Plotting *T* scores and using clinical interpretation. Coding profiles by ranking methods.		Both males and females tend to score above average on *Hy, Pd, Pa, Pt* and *Sc* (particularly *Hy* and *Pd*). Low *Mf* in mothers with *Hy* as highest scale is associated with "rebelliousness" in children.
Kalhorn, J. (1947)				High- and low-scoring mothers on MMPI both differed from average in parent behavior, primarily on indulgence.

Author	Subjects	Method	Scale differences		Results
L'Abate, L. (1960)	42 parents who brought child to clinic together. 27 mothers who brought child without husband. 98 control parents.	*t* tests	All		Mothers who brought sons to clinic alone seemed more disturbed than mothers who came with husbands. Boys accompanied only by mothers appeared more maladjusted than those who came with both parents.
			Experimental mothers ($N = 48$) >	Control mothers ($N = 49$)	
			Cannot say	.05	
			Hs	.05	
			D	.05	
			Hy	.05	
			Pt	.05	
			K	.05*	
				* control group higher.	
			Mothers without husbands >	Mothers with husbands	
			D	.05	
			Pt	.05	
			Experimental fathers >	Control fathers	
			Cannot say	.01	
			Pa	.05	
			Sc	.05	
Lauterbach, C. G., London, P., and Bryan, J. (1961)	1. 110 parents of child guidance children; 64 male, 46 female. 2. Goodstein-	*t* tests	CG fathers >	CG mothers	CG parents higher than normal parents but lower than VA neurotics.
			Ma	.05	
			CG mothers >	CG fathers	
			L	.05	
			Sc	.05	

Dahlstrom's normal subjects and stutterers.	CG parents >	Normal parents
	Hs	.01
	Hy	.01
	Pd	.01
	D	.05
	Pa	.05
	Sc	.05
	CG parents >	Stutterers' parents
	L	.001
	Hs	.001
	Hy	.001
	Pd	.001
	Sc	.05
3. Hovey's 3 groups of VA patients: a. Dissociative conversion b. Somatization c. Anxiety reaction	VA Dissoc-conver >	CG parents
	Hs	.05
	D	.05
	Hy	.05
	Ma	.05
	Pa	.05*
		*CG parents higher
	VA somatization >	CG parents
	Hs	.001
	D	.001
	Hy	.001
	Pt	.001
	Ma	.001

Author	Subjects	Method	Scale differences	Results
			VA anxiety reaction CG > parents All scales .001	
Lauterbach, C. G., Vogel, W. and Hart, J. (1962)	24 families; father, mother, adolescent "problem" son.	*t* tests between sons, mothers, and fathers Rhos were obtained between pairs of profiles F-M-S. One *R* of parents related to child pathology	Son > Mother *F* .01 *K** .01 *D* .05 *Pd* .01 *Mf* .01 *Pa* .01 *Pt* .01 *Sc* .01 *Ma* .01 *Sons lower.	Sons showed more pathology than parents. Correlations (identification) were much smaller than Sopchak obtained with normal families. Parents of disturbed sons are less similar to each other than are normal parents.
			Son > Father *F* .01 *K** .01 *Pd* .01 *Mf* .05 *Pa* .01 *Pt* .01 *Sc* .01	No significant relationship between amount of identification of parent pairs and the degree of son's pathology.
			Son > Father *Ma* .01 *Si* .05 *Sons lower.	Disturbed sons less like parents than normal sons.

			Father > Mother		
			Mf	.01	
			Significant rhos:		
			F-S: *Pa* $r = -.48$	.05	
			M-S: *Hy* $r = .58$	.01	
Liverant, S. (1959)	108 parents of N.C. patients. 108 parents of Iowa normal subjects.	*t* tests between experimental and control fathers	Experimental > father	Control father	26% of experimental fathers and 15% of control fathers had one scale $T \geq 70$.
			Hs	.01	
			D	.01	
			Hy	.01	
			Pt	.05	
		t tests between experimental and control mothers	Experimental > mother	Control mother	22% of experimental mothers and 9% of control mothers had one scale $T \geq 70$.
			F	.05	
			*K**	.01	
			D	.01	
			Hy	.05	
			Pd	.01	Neither parent had a high frequency of any code type.
			Pa	.05	
			Pt	.05	
			A	.01	
			*Control group higher.		
			Experimental > father	Experimental mother	
			Hs	.05	
			Mf	.05	
			Ma	.05	
			Experimental > mother	Experimental father	
			Pa	.05	
			A	.05	

Author	Subjects	Method	Scale differences	Results
			Control father > Control mother *Mf* .05 *Ma* .05	
		Experimental group split into 4 subgroups: 1. Schizophrenic (S) 2. Acting out (AO) 3. Physical complaint (PC) 4. Neurotic (N) *t* tests among parents of different groups Chi-square on number in each group with $T \geq 70$.	Mothers: S > AO *Mf* .05 Fathers: S > AO *Mf* .05 S > PC *Mf* .05 N > AO *Mf* .05 N > PC *Mf* .05 AO > S *Pd* .05 PC > N *D* .01 N > PC *Ma* .05	S and N mothers combined were less severely disturbed than AO and PC mothers (.05). Support for impression that parents of disturbed children are themselves significantly more maladjusted than parents of nondisturbed. However, experimental parents more like "normal" parents than like adults who seek help themselves.
Loeb, J., and Price, J. R. (1966) *Part I*	Continuously married parents: 44 mothers, 19 fathers (M). 44 divorced or	*t* tests, high-point codes. Chi-square, critical ratios on high-point codes and fre-	DS mothers > M mothers *F* .01 *Pd* .001 *Sc* .05 *Ma* .05	55% DS mothers, 32% M mothers had profile with one scale $T \geq 70$ ($p < .05$).

separated mothers (DS).	quency of $T \geq 70$.	R mothers > M mothers		49% of DS had *Pd* as high point, 38% of M had *Hy* as high point ($p < .001$) 1. Most frequent two-point codes for DS: 46 and 43. 2. Most frequent two-point code for M: 31.
26 remarried mothers (R).		*Pd*	.01	No significant differences between DS group and R group of mothers.
19 divorced, separated, or remarried fathers (DSR).		DSR fathers > M fathers		50% of R group mothers had elevated records: Most frequent high point being *Hy*, next most frequent was *Pd*.
		Pd	.001	47% of DSR group of fathers had elevated clinical scales compared to 32% of M group of fathers.
		Pa	.05	DSR fathers' most frequent high point was *Pd* (50%), M fathers' was *Hy* (29%).

Author	Subjects	Method	Scale differences	Results
Part II	44 (29 boys, 15 girls) children of continuously married mothers. 44 (29 boys, 15 girls) children of divorced and separated mothers.	Children rated on aggressiveness according to parental and school reports.		Children of divorced and separated parents had more problems including aggressive or acting-out behavior (64%) than children of continuously married parents (23%) ($p < .001$). 10 out of 15 daughters of divorced and separated women were rated aggressive, whereas only 1 of 15 daughters of continuously married women was rated aggressive. *Pd* scores of mothers in each of two marital status groups were not found to be related to aggressiveness of their children.

Marks, P. A. (1961)	48 clinic cases. Validation findings reduced this to 42: 42 mothers, 42 children, 32 fathers. Control group consisted of 315 females and 226 males.	*t* tests and high-point codes	Clinic mothers >	Controls	Abnormal scores occur in 50% of clinic mothers' profiles as compared with 14 and 75% among normal and psychiatric groups, respectively. Five high-point code patterns (13-31, 24-42, 20-02, 34-43, 9) comprise 70% of all profiles in the clinic mother samples. Abnormal scores occur in 44% clinic mothers' profiles as compared with 15 and 75% among normal and psychiatric groups, respectively. Four high-point code patterns (13-31, 20-02, 4, 59-95) comprise 85% of all profiles in the clinic father samples.
			K	.01	
			Hs	.05	
			D	.05	
			Hy	.05	
			Pd	.01	
			Pa	.01	
			Pt	.01	
			Sc	.05	
			Si	.05	
			Clinic fathers >	Controls	
			K	.05	
			Hs	.05	
			D	.01	
			Hy	.01	
			Pd	.01	
			Mf	.05	
			Pt	.01	
			Sc	.05	

Author	Subjects	Method	Scale differences		Results
Sopchak, A. L. (1952)	78 male, 30 female college students.	4 administrations of MMPI with different instructions:	Father and son	significant *r*s	
		A–standard	*Mf*	.01	
		B–as father would reply	*Pa*	.01	
		C–as mother would reply	*Pt*	.01	
		D–as most people would reply	*Sc*	.01	
		Identification scores and correlations	*Hy*	.01	
			Mother and son	significant *r*s	
			Pt	.01	
			Sc	.01	
			Hy	.01	
			D	.05	
			Most people and son		
			Mf	.01	
			Sc	.01	
			Hy	.01	
			D	.05	
			Pa	.05	
			Father and daughter		
			Mf	.01	
			Pt	.05	
			Sc	.05	

			Mother vs. daughter no significant correlations	
Sopchak, A. L. (1958)	25 male and 25 female college students and their parents.	Spearman correlations between student and parent MMPIs	Male and father *Hy* .05 *Pd* .05 *Pa* .05 *Pt* .05 *Sc* .05 Male and mother *Pa* .05 *Pt* .01 *Sc* .05 Female and father *D* .05 *Pa* .05 *Pt* .01 Female and mother All clinical scales significant at .01 level	Males identify more with father and females identify more with mother.

Author	Subjects	Method	Scale differences	Results
Stennett, R. G. (1966)	826 members of 230 "troubled families."	CTP used with children up to 13 yrs; MMPI with older *S*s. "Level" scores computed for both CTP and MMPI.		1. 10% of families had level 1 ($T \geq 70$) and 35% had level 2 ($T = 50$ to 69) MMPI scores; i.e., the referred patient is basically an emissary from a troubled family. 2. There is a small but significant correlation in the level of psychopathology between the parents of troubled families. 3. No support for the hypothesis that the parents in these families have either complementary or conflicting personality characteristics to a greater or lesser degree than would be expected by chance.

Toms, E. (1955)	Mothers of 30 paranoid schizophrenic veterans. Mothers of nonhospitalized veterans as controls.	Shipley-Hartford, TAT and MMPI. *t* tests Profiles tested for homogeneity using Sullivan and Welsh techniques.		Mothers of schizophrenics do not exhibit specific personality traits that distinguish them from control mothers although they do appear more maladjusted than control mothers.
Vogel, W., and Lauterbach, C. G. (1963)	24 families (father, mother, adolescent son) in therapeutic contact. 85 control adolescents from Droppleman and Schafer data.	Tested relationship between adolescent's personality ratings of parents and adolescent's adjustment. Rank order correlation between each parent's MMPI and son's MMPI-defined degree of identification. Internalization ratio (*Hs, D, Pt*) and externalization ratio (*Hy, Pd, Ma*) computed for each.		With increasing psychopathology in son's MMPI, sons saw mother as more "controlling" and more "physically controlling." The higher the father's internalization ratio, the more their sons saw their mother as "controlling" and "hostile controlling."

Author	Subjects	Method	Scale differences	Results
Williams, J. (1951)	40 parents of cerebral palsied children. 40 control parents of non-cerebral palsied children.	Analysis of variance		Parents of cerebral palsied children do not differ from normal in personality integration.
Wolking, W. D., Dunteman, G. H., and Bailey, J. P. (1967)	312 mothers of male children, 233 fathers of male children, 143 mothers of female children, 105 fathers of female children, divided on basis of child's diagnosis: 1. Organic brain syndrome 2. Psychosis 3. Conversion reaction 4. Anxiety reaction 5. Behavior disorder 6. Mental deficiency	Multivariate analysis of differences of mean profiles for each group. *F* approximation to Wilks's lamba.		No difference among diagnostic groups for mothers or fathers of female children or fathers of male children. Some differences among mothers of male children, but magnitude too small to be useful.

Wolking, W. D., Quast, W., and Lawton, J. J. (1966)	538 mothers, 393 fathers of emotionally disturbed children. MMPI normative group as control.	*t* tests and high-point codes	Mothers > Control females All scales at .01 except *F* and *Mf* Fathers > Control males All scales at .01 except *L, F, Si* Clinic mothers: higher frequency of *D, Hy, Pd, Pa* high points. Clinic fathers: higher frequency of *D, Hy, Pd* high points.	Mothers with high *Hy — Pd* tend to have children with primary behavior disorders. Fathers of behavior disorders tend to have high *Hy — Pd*. Parents of disturbed have more pathology than Minnesota normals. Mothers' profiles did not vary with diagnosis, but fathers' profiles did tend to covary with diagnostic group.

Appendix C
Comparisons of MMPI Results for Acceptable and Unacceptable Psychotherapy Groups and Normal Subjects

(This material accompanies Chapter 9.)

James L. Jacobson

Robert D. Wirt

Scale	Acceptable		Unacceptable		t	Normal	
	$\bar{X}$	σ	$\bar{X}$	σ		$\bar{X}$	σ
Academic Achievement (*Ac*)	12.02	3.00	11.31	1.24	1.92	11.77	2.88
Adjustment to Prison (*Ap*)	16.64	3.30	17.52	3.69	2.14	14.49	2.98
Admission of Symptoms (*Ad*)	7.60	5.97	6.38	5.12	1.87	4.82	4.13
Aging (*Ag*)	68.76	10.57	65.64	9.90	2.60	62.67	9.19
Alcoholic Differentiation (*Ah*)	42.65	6.10	44.01	5.61	1.97	28.00	5.11
Alcoholism (Hampton) (*Al*)	53.61	12.83	52.86	13.12	.49	42.21	11.62
Alcoholism (Holmes) (*Am*)	31.89	5.16	33.90	5.08	3.32	20.29	5.02
Altruism (Mf_3)	5.14	2.00	5.15	2.05	.04	3.98	1.92
Amorality (Ma_1)	2.46	1.54	3.10	1.58	3.49	1.70	1.33
Anal Scale (*Anal*)	20.08	7.05	19.31	6.62	.95	19.11	6.17
Anxiety Reaction (*Ar*)	24.22	3.86	22.63	3.93	3.47	19.83	3.64
Attitude toward Others (*Ad*)	14.13	3.55	13.92	3.55	.51	13.06	3.14
Attitude toward Self (*As*)	13.91	3.92	13.42	3.92	1.07	14.34	3.33
Authority Problems (Pd_2)	5.45	1.43	5.96	1.52	2.94	3.50	1.52
Bizarre Sensory Experiences (Sc_3)	2.51	3.29	2.48	2.83	.09	2.36	2.38
Brooding (D_5)	2.92	2.00	2.77	2.03	.63	2.16	1.84
Caudality (*Ca*)	12.48	6.26	11.62	5.59	1.24	8.74	4.66
Choice of Nursing (*Nc*)	38.02	4.50	37.60	4.38	.81	33.12	4.47
Chronic Ulcerative Colitis (*CUC*)	10.99	9.42	9.21	7.66	1.76	9.25	6.38
Code 12 (Co_{12})	6.60	4.54	5.73	3.79	1.78	5.26	3.60
Code 13 Co_{13})	4.81	4.54	3.59	3.42	2.59	3.76	3.23
Code 21 (Co_{21})	10.93	6.79	10.09	5.70	1.13	8.57	5.62
Code 23 (Co_{23})	6.50	2.95	6.16	2.90	1.01	4.88	2.41
Code 27 (Co_{27})	12.59	8.24	12.18	7.34	.45	9.52	6.75

Code 31 (Co_{31})	6.24	2.27	5.79	2.24	1.73	5.52	2.01
Code 32 (Co_{32})	15.17	4.23	14.85	3.93	.66	12.61	4.47
Code 36 (Co_{36})	7.16	3.44	6.75	3.34	1.04	6.66	2.99
Code Type 4 (G_4)	79.78	17.76	81.31	15.23	.79	72.51	12.85
Code Type 9 (G_9)	57.10	10.39	58.67	9.21	1.36	54.19	7.31
Code Type 13 Hi 2 (G_{132})	94.97	22.41	92.44	21.73	.98	89.22	19.04
Code Type 27 (G_{27})	28.21	6.07	27.68	5.78	.76	23.09	5.22
Code Type 34 (Co_{34})	8.15	2.67	8.70	2.63	1.77	7.00	2.54
Code Type 34 (G_{34})	89.42	17.56	91.19	15.52	.91	82.18	15.07
Code Type 49 (G_{49})	37.46	6.09	38.97	5.17	2.27	35.37	4.95
Code Type 68 (G_{68})	24.53	13.98	24.15	12.66	.24	23.76	11.64
Code Type 78 (G_{78})	16.52	5.97	16.90	5.88	.54	11.90	5.15
Code Type 98 (G_{98})	22.73	4.57	24.05	4.52	2.46	20.25	4.45
Code Type 123 (G_{123})	34.57	6.56	34.09	6.07	.65	29.66	5.71
Code Type 137 (G_{137})	10.64	1.88	9.76	1.80	4.08	10.64	1.60
Code Type 138 (G_{138})	12.53	2.36	12.14	2.29	1.42	11.52	2.31
Code Type 139 (G_{139})	26.90	5.64	27.31	5.27	.63	25.13	4.35
Code Type 248 (G_{248})	14.68	2.79	15.91	3.16	3.51	11.85	2.55
Code Type 274 (G_{274})	31.53	5.89	32.49	5.06	1.48	22.94	4.26
Code Type 278 (G_{278})	47.44	17.80	45.38	16.87	1.01	34.67	14.70
Code Type 1234 (G_{1234})	44.98	7.62	45.59	7.39	.69	41.21	6.67
Code Type 1237 (G_{1237})	25.34	4.69	24.07	4.91	2.24	23.91	4.20
College Achievement (*Ae*)	13.88	2.68	13.81	2.92	.20	10.57	2.73
College Achievement, Female (*Af*)	27.52	5.08	25.23	5.32	3.74	24.34	4.40
College Counselee (*Cl*)	27.76	4.49	26.12	4.85	2.98	27.09	4.64
Competitor (*Cp*)	12.87	1.90	13.09	2.05	.95	12.07	1.74
Control (*Cn*)	25.68	4.78	26.85	4.75	2.09	22.19	4.51
Conversion Reaction (*Cr*)	52.13	9.49	50.86	9.85	1.11	52.91	8.56
Correction for Hypochondriasis (C_H)	16.61	7.17	16.70	6.50	.11	14.84	6.43

Scale	Acceptable		Unacceptable		t	Normal	
	$\bar{X}$	σ	$\bar{X}$	σ		$\bar{X}$	σ
Counselor Personality (*Cs*)	27.83	8.00	27.20	8.03	.66	24.63	7.23
Critical Items (*Cl*)	4.28	4.77	4.44	3.81	.31	3.59	3.63
Cynicism Factor (*Cy*)	3.58	2.30	3.42	2.38	.57	2.95	2.03
Defensiveness (Holroyd) (*Df*)	42.49	11.05	43.59	10.35	.88	35.06	10.72
Delinquency (*De*)	6.01	1.93	6.73	1.92	3.17	2.93	1.65
Delinquency (*Dq*)	13.11	4.45	15.02	4.81	3.50	7.91	3.62
Denial of Masculine Occupations (Mf_5)	3.94	1.88	3.55	1.80	1.80	1.93	.76
Denial of Social Anxiety (Hy_1)	3.36	2.06	3.49	1.90	.56	3.47	1.81
Denial of Symptoms (*Dn*)	14.18	5.39	14.14	5.14	.06	12.11	4.52
Dependency (*Dy*)	23.03	10.35	21.89	9.49	.98	18.27	8.85
Depression (*D*)	22.48	6.27	21.59	4.98	1.34	18.06	4.55
Depression and Morale Loss (*Ml*)	8.71	6.07	8.80	5.72	.13	7.10	5.23
Depressive Reaction (*Dr*)	23.47	3.74	22.43	3.66	2.38	23.67	3.32
Dissimulation (*Ds*)	11.80	8.18	12.12	7.76	.34	10.19	6.52
Dissimulation Revised (*Ds-r*)	6.87	5.10	6.99	4.81	.20	6.22	4.34
Dominance (*Do*)	13.85	3.60	13.92	3.31	.19	14.32	3.60
Dominance, Revised (*Do-r*)	8.28	2.58	8.40	2.34	.43	9.10	2.54
Ego Inflation (Ma_4)	2.50	1.66	2.60	1.61	.52	2.63	1.64
Ego Overcontrol (*Eo*)	13.07	3.40	11.70	3.68	3.29	8.54	2.99
Ego Strength (*Es*)	44.02	7.77	45.12	6.36	1.31	37.66	5.75
Emotional Alienation (Sc_{1B})	2.60	1.37	2.71	1.33	.70	2.17	1.09
Emotional Immaturity (*Em*)	14.35	6.78	14.35	6.55	.00	9.75	5.30
Epilepsy (*Ep*)	21.22	5.91	21.09	6.08	.18	13.64	4.58
Escapism (*Ec*)	16.13	4.92	17.57	4.44	2.62	10.21	3.70

Ethnocentrism (*Et*)	16.03	6.24	16.18	6.15	.20	15.29	5.68
Evaluation of Improvement (*Ev*)	19.97	11.74	19.49	11.12	.36	14.19	9.05
Familial Discord (Pd_1)	2.81	1.81	3.66	2.35	3.45	1.80	1.74
F (Confusion)	6.08	5.06	6.73	4.62	1.14	4.58	4.31
Female Masochism (*Fm*)	16.40	4.40	15.13	3.33	2.78	13.84	3.45
Feminine Occupational Identification (Mf_4)	5.76	3.07	6.24	2.98	1.34	1.15	.72
Femininity (*Fe*)	5.84	2.05	5.27	2.21	2.28	2.83	1.36
First Factor (*A*)	13.76	9.44	13.57	8.45	.18	11.27	7.39
Fourth Factor (*P*)	11.71	3.26	12.88	4.03	2.69	9.12	3.39
Fundamentalist Religiosity (*FRI*)	9.84	3.79	9.54	3.60	.68	8.18	3.80
General Maladjustment (*Gm*)	8.48	5.38	8.41	4.57	.12	4.79	3.73
General Personality Variance (*G*)	25.48	12.12	25.27	11.62	.14	23.67	10.99
Graduate School Potential (*Gr*)	8.54	2.77	8.49	2.69	.16	7.98	2.30
Headache Proneness (*Ha*)	9.91	4.00	9.64	3.51	.61	8.45	3.02
Health Concern Factor (*Hl*)	4.10	4.17	3.04	3.18	2.44	2.87	2.98
Honor Point Ratio (*Hr*)	9.38	2.91	9.63	2.81	.73	8.09	2.59
Hostility (*Ho*)	19.66	9.94	20.08	9.56	.37	21.27	8.54
Hostility Control (*Hc*)	8.75	4.49	8.73	4.41	.04	7.05	3.41
Hypochondriasis (*Hs*)	7.38	6.84	5.49	5.13	2.65	5.15	4.79
Hypoglycemia-neurosis (*Hn*)	9.99	2.81	9.42	2.33	1.87	6.39	2.25
Hypomania (*Ma*)	16.50	4.57	18.45	4.73	3.56	15.13	4.37
Hysteria (*Hy*)	22.36	6.66	20.96	6.09	1.86	17.32	5.33
Imperturbability (Ma_3)	3.20	1.76	3.61	1.78	1.95	3.43	1.73
Impulsivity (*Im*)	7.40	3.36	8.39	3.76	2.34	6.70	3.52
Inhibition of Aggression (Hy_5)	3.05	1.52	2.82	1.45	1.30	2.54	1.38
Inner Maladjustment (*In*)	41.02	25.45	40.20	23.01	.29	36.22	21.47
Intellectual Efficiency (*Ie*)	27.47	5.28	28.27	4.88	1.33	25.20	5.07
Intellectual Quotient (*Iq*)	40.52	7.58	41.33	7.10	.94	36.51	7.36
Iowa Manifest Anxiety (*At*)	17.10	9.68	16.03	8.94	.97	12.97	7.35

Scale	Acceptable		Unacceptable		t	Normal	
	$\bar{X}$	σ	$\bar{X}$	σ		$\bar{X}$	σ
Irregular Medical Discharge (*Id*)	19.20	7.19	19.48	6.99	.33	14.63	6.28
Jewish-Gentile Scale (*JGs*)	4.36	1.81	4.75	1.81	1.82	3.55	1.71
Judged Anxiety (*Ja*)	8.04	6.05	7.34	5.23	1.05	5.78	4.05
Judged Manifest Hostility (*Jh*)	14.17	6.82	15.73	7.09	1.90	15.03	6.54
Judging Complex Behavior (*Jc*)	26.57	4.29	26.31	3.71	.56	21.09	3.70
K (Validity)	14.84	5.38	15.12	5.42	.45	13.13	5.44
Lack of Ego Mastery, Cognitive (Sc_{2A})	1.64	2.15	1.50	1.70	.60	1.43	1.56
Lack of Ego Mastery, Conative (Sc_{2B})	2.75	2.41	2.90	2.36	.55	1.95	1.69
Lack of Ego Mastery, Defective Inhibition (Sc_{2C})	1.51	1.79	1.63	1.88	.55	1.43	1.53
Lassitude-Malaise (Hy_3)	3.90	3.11	3.75	2.81	.45	2.19	2.34
Latitude of Interest (*LI*)	35.86	7.41	37.98	7.68	2.38	20.52	3.88
Leadership (*Lp*)	31.50	8.55	32.27	7.63	.82	30.47	6.75
Lengthy Hospitalization (*Lh*)	19.53	3.08	19.55	2.91	.07	19.55	2.70
Lie (*L*)	4.22	2.38	4.00	2.06	.83	4.16	2.66
Low Back Pain, Functional (*Lb*)	11.05	2.67	10.59	2.63	1.47	8.60	2.30
Maladjustment Score (*MS*)	53.29	24.88	53.11	22.19	.07	38.92	20.05
Manifest Anxiety, Short Form (*At-s*)	7.00	4.52	6.94	4.50	.12	5.18	3.40
Masculinity-Femininity (*Mf-f*)	26.41	4.79	26.23	4.79	.32	16.45	3.18
Masculinity-Femininity (*Mf-m*)	23.44	4.78	23.55	5.14	.18	13.87	3.32
Masculinity-Femininity (*Mf′*)	14.74	3.89	14.95	3.83	.46	6.82	2.09
Mental Dullness (D_4)	2.99	2.65	2.99	2.50	.02	1.92	1.88
Minnesota State Prison Parole Predictions, Jacobson (*MSPP*)	7.58	2.64	8.59	2.32	3.45	4.37	2.00

Mult Intelligence Scale (*MI*)	16.77	4.43	16.76	4.35	.02	13.55	4.05
Naïveté (*Pa*$_3$)	4.58	2.64	4.51	2.62	.22	3.75	2.22
Need for Affection (*Hy*$_2$)	6.37	2.86	6.26	2.94	.32	4.93	2.45
Need for Treatment (*Nt*)	19.43	5.80	20.08	5.57	.97	14.55	5.13
Neurodermatitis (*Nd*)	7.61	1.53	7.74	1.32	.78	7.43	1.43
Neurotic Overcontrol (*No*)	5.40	2.81	5.09	2.88	.90	4.76	2.55
Neurotic Undercontrol (*Nu*)	13.19	5.44	13.74	5.41	.85	11.49	5.18
Neuroticism (*Ne*)	7.29	5.79	6.19	4.96	1.74	5.09	3.67
Neuroticism Factor (*Nf*)	9.18	5.36	9.38	5.14	.33	6.29	3.98
Normality (*N*)	30.26	9.78	29.52	9.72	.65	30.28	9.86
Obvious Depression (*D-O*)	10.22	5.99	9.75	5.21	.70	7.72	4.37
Obvious Hypomania (*Ma-O*)	6.35	3.31	7.24	3.69	2.16	5.83	2.85
Obvious Hysteria (*Hy-O*)	7.11	6.91	5.87	5.00	1.91	4.58	4.12
Obvious Paranoia (*Pa-O*)	4.15	3.50	3.86	2.84	.78	2.58	2.77
Obvious Psychopathic Deviate (*Pd-O*)	10.44	4.32	11.75	4.10	2.65	5.82	3.56
Oral Scale (*ORAL*)	13.61	4.98	13.85	4.59	.43	10.21	3.55
Originality (*Or*)	10.17	3.01	10.88	2.85	2.08	9.02	2.66
Overt Hostility (*Hv*)	5.31	1.78	5.53	1.87	1.02	5.17	1.64
Paranoia (*Pa*)	11.38	4.19	11.20	3.76	.38	8.58	3.42
Paranoia Factor (*Pk*)	1.68	2.58	1.55	2.04	.50	1.28	1.87
Paranoid Defensiveness (*PDF*)	25.01	7.06	25.36	7.54	.40	26.51	6.58
Paranoid Schizophrenia (*Pz*)	13.18	7.22	12.65	6.16	.67	12.18	5.82
Parietal-Frontal (*Pf*)	12.32	6.16	11.57	5.55	1.08	8.59	5.03
Patient-Normal Agreement (*PO*)	40.68	3.09	40.68	2.69	.00	34.95	2.95
Patient-Normal Disagreement (*PX*)	16.78	3.18	17.19	2.97	1.15	8.94	2.52
Pedophile (*Pe*)	8.32	2.90	7.89	2.47	1.36	4.08	2.10
Persecutory Ideas (*Pa*$_1$)	3.06	2.92	2.85	2.34	.69	1.91	2.16
Personal & Emotional Sensitivity (*Mf*$_1$)	6.13	2.74	6.03	2.85	.32	4.67	2.30
Pharisaic Virtue (*Pv*)	19.87	8.97	18.60	7.65	1.29	21.07	7.95

Scale	Acceptable		Unacceptable		t	Normal	
	$\bar{X}$	σ	$\bar{X}$	σ		$\bar{X}$	σ
Physical Malfunctioning (D_3)	3.55	1.63	3.35	1.30	1.17	3.09	1.44
Plus Getting Tendency (*PLUS*)	22.60	9.23	22.15	9.09	.42	19.71	8.36
Poignancy (Pa_2)	2.55	1.74	2.29	1.63	1.30	2.18	1.48
Positive Malingering (*Mp*)	14.29	4.26	14.08	4.09	.42	12.40	3.93
Posthospital Adjustment (*PHa*)	15.82	6.88	15.82	6.97	.00	12.43	5.96
Prediction of Change (*Pc*)	5.05	4.41	4.24	3.65	1.70	3.72	3.02
Prejudice (*Pr*)	12.08	6.15	11.81	6.39	.36	10.61	5.18
Preliminary Correction (L_6)	10.59	4.80	11.16	4.84	1.00	9.95	4.83
Preliminary Hypochondriasis (*H*)	13.98	9.50	11.63	7.37	2.35	10.08	6.57
Preliminary Prognosis (*Pp*)	12.96	5.84	13.42	5.62	.68	11.17	5.39
Premorbid History (*CHRCH*)	14.93	5.39	15.63	5.47	1.09	11.84	4.55
Prognosis for Electroshock Treatment (*Ps*)	20.29	7.97	21.45	8.09	1.23	16.86	7.16
Prognosis for Schizophrenia (*Pg*)	33.51	4.29	33.51	4.60	.01	29.95	4.27
Psychasthenia (*Pt*)	13.81	8.75	13.36	7.74	.46	10.88	7.76
Psychological Interests (*Py*)	4.18	1.33	4.38	1.25	1.33	4.14	1.09
Psychomotor Acceleration (Ma_2)	3.73	1.77	3.77	1.61	.16	3.67	1.39
Psychomotor Retardation (D_2)	6.87	1.60	6.50	1.80	1.83	5.71	1.75
Psychoneurosis (*Pn*)	14.24	6.18	14.00	6.12	.34	13.29	5.85
Psychopathic Deviate (*Pd*)	22.24	4.45	24.38	4.77	3.94	14.71	3.90
Psychotic Tendency Factor (*Pq*)	1.47	2.00	1.46	1.92	.04	1.81	2.00
Pure Correction (K')	9.15	3.32	9.63	3.43	1.20	8.43	3.32
Pure Depression (D')	12.06	2.45	11.93	2.32	.47	10.28	2.48
Pure Hypochondriasis (Hs')	2.03	2.15	1.46	1.86	2.38	1.59	1.74
Pure Hypomania (Ma')	10.22	3.44	11.13	3.29	2.31	10.36	3.34

Pure Hysteria (*Hy'*)	9.37	3.06	8.97	3.05	1.11	8.04	2.92
Pure Paranoia (*Pa'*)	4.32	1.78	4.20	1.78	.56	3.79	1.73
Pure Psychasthenia (*Pt'*)	3.47	2.55	3.27	2.15	.73	3.37	2.55
Pure Psychopathic Deviate (*Pd'*)	7.99	2.59	8.99	2.49	3.37	5.28	2.32
Pure Schizophrenia (*Sc'*)	4.03	2.93	4.31	3.05	.81	4.27	2.97
Pure Social Introversion (*Si'*)	21.45	7.11	19.20	6.90	2.74	18.35	5.78
Recidivism (*Rc*)	11.25	2.86	12.16	2.53	2.85	7.33	2.15
Religiosity (*Rel*)	8.03	3.37	7.50	3.23	1.38	8.17	3.64
Response Bias (*B*)	28.73	8.01	29.25	7.66	.56	29.86	7.62
Rigidity, Female (*Rg-f*)	5.21	1.49	4.53	1.56	3.76	5.19	1.51
Rigidity, Male (*Rg-m*)	5.27	1.34	4.67	1.52	3.56	5.24	1.46
Role Playing (*Rp*)	20.64	4.09	20.30	4.01	.72	17.95	3.79
Schizophrenia (*Sc*)	12.45	9.84	13.02	9.12	.50	10.32	7.67
Schizophrenia Conduct Disorder Differential (*Sk*)	12.04	3.64	12.52	3.99	1.06	8.75	3.37
Schizophrenia Correction (*Sx*)	9.33	1.68	9.23	1.69	.52	8.93	1.71
Second Factor (*R*)	15.94	4.52	14.57	4.38	2.60	11.59	3.91
Second Factor, Negative (*M*)	17.08	8.08	18.31	8.32	1.28	16.63	7.14
Self-alienation (Pd_{4B})	6.83	2.94	7.38	2.83	1.62	3.83	2.60
Self-sufficiency (*Sf*)	20.71	6.88	21.16	6.59	.57	22.06	6.19
Sex Differential (*Sd*)	17.71	4.30	17.05	4.20	1.30	8.82	2.91
Sexual Deviation (*Sv*)	41.25	10.38	40.03	8.89	1.08	32.27	8.82
Sexual Identification (Mf_2)	1.06	1.15	1.17	1.11	.81	1.08	1.01
Shyness Factor (*Sy*)	2.11	1.86	1.98	1.77	.62	1.94	1.69
Social Alienation (Pd_{4A})	6.98	2.82	7.51	2.85	1.60	4.64	2.73
Social Alienation (Sc_{1A})	4.04	2.81	4.39	2.75	1.06	3.48	2.32
Social Desirability (*So*)	66.60	9.31	67.07	8.48	.45	63.99	8.01
Social Desirability, Revised (*So-r*)	29.87	6.44	30.12	6.10	.33	27.81	5.03
Social Imperturbability (Pd_3)	7.08	2.80	7.68	2.55	1.91	7.66	2.46

Scale	Acceptable		Unacceptable		t	Normal	
	$\bar{X}$	σ	$\bar{X}$	σ		$\bar{X}$	σ
Social Introversion (*Si*)	28.60	9.85	25.90	9.17	2.41	24.66	8.01
Social Participation (*Sp*)	16.27	3.83	17.58	3.78	2.92	14.71	3.44
Social Presence (*Sr*)	14.57	3.31	15.35	3.33	1.99	14.87	3.01
Social Responsibility (*Re*)	18.04	4.19	17.05	4.10	2.02	17.63	3.81
Social Responsibility, Revised (*Re-r*)	12.57	3.02	11.95	2.91	1.76	13.48	2.97
Social Status (*St*)	19.70	4.22	20.60	3.55	1.97	15.39	3.91
Social Status, Revised (*St-r*)	10.36	2.85	11.03	2.75	2.03	8.34	2.74
Socioeconomic Status (*Ss*)	58.55	10.39	60.37	8.74	1.61	51.47	9.45
Somatic Complaints (Hy_4)	3.87	3.65	2.83	3.02	2.63	2.79	2.47
Somatization Reaction (*Sm*)	22.38	4.25	21.21	4.16	2.35	22.71	4.20
Stability of Profile, Female (*Sb-f*)	12.96	2.76	12.42	2.64	1.70	11.33	2.62
Stability of Profile, Male (*Sb-m*)	18.97	4.55	18.66	4.56	.59	17.26	4.43
Subjective Depression (D_1)	9.83	4.66	9.37	4.20	.89	7.55	3.25
Subtle Depression (*D-S*)	12.28	2.90	11.82	2.83	1.36	10.33	2.79
Subtle Hypomania (*Ma-S*)	10.15	2.69	11.21	2.40	3.53	9.30	2.60
Subtle Hysteria (*Hy-S*)	15.25	5.34	15.09	5.07	.25	12.74	4.53
Subtle Paranoia (*Pa-S*)	7.24	2.66	7.36	2.74	.35	6.00	2.28
Subtle Psychopathic Deviate (*Pd-S*)	11.80	2.74	12.62	2.80	2.53	8.89	2.52
Success in Baseball (*Ba*)	42.71	4.68	41.24	5.15	2.54	41.61	4.54
Teaching Potential (*Tp*)	66.82	17.23	66.77	15.92	.02	66.08	14.77
Test-taking Defensiveness (*Tt*)	13.51	3.47	12.94	3.38	1.40	12.85	3.20
Third Factor (*C*)	17.75	5.16	17.70	5.14	.09	13.63	4.24
Tired Housewife (*TH*)	12.73	5.95	12.09	5.52	.94	9.95	4.78

Tired Housewife and Worried Breadwinner Common Items (*T-B*)	7.42	3.07	7.09	3.01	.92	5.92	3.01
Tolerance (*To*)	18.62	5.88	18.89	6.05	.38	16.04	4.88
True Answer (*Ta*)	13.49	6.46	14.02	6.87	.67	12.79	6.23
Ulcer Personality (*Ul*)	48.03	8.79	46.72	8.86	1.26	42.72	7.42
Underachievement (*Un*)	11.17	2.00	11.43	2.02	1.09	10.23	1.78
Urethral-Phallic-Genital (*UPG*)	14.24	2.89	15.25	3.32	2.75	8.15	2.32
Work Attitude (*Wa*)	10.86	6.19	11.29	5.82	.60	10.15	4.85
Worried Breadwinner (*WB*)	14.12	4.18	13.55	4.01	1.18	9.30	3.81

Appendix D
Classification of MMPI Literature from 1959–1967

James Neal Butcher

The literature cited in this bibliography represents most of the work with the MMPI since (or just prior to) the publication of the Dahlstrom and Welsh *MMPI Handbook* in 1960. The references have been grossly categorized and indexed by content to provide the reader with a ready means of locating relevant material. The categories are arbitrary and primarily based on "face validity" of the titles. Some references could have been placed in more than one section, but to avoid repetition they are included only in what seemed to be the most relevant category. Although we have no doubt missed some relevant titles (particularly the MMPI derivatives) and have probably included a few tangential studies, we hope that this bibliography will be useful.

BIBLIOGRAPHY OF MMPI RESEARCH

I wish to thank Barbara Lindman Kassel for her conscientious examination of the *Psychological Abstracts,* the primary source of this bibliography. I am indebted also to a number of authors who provided me with references from other sources.

GENERAL GUIDES AND MANUALS

1. Carkhuff, R. R. *The MMPI: An outline for general clinical and counseling use.* Buffalo, N.Y.: Author, 1961, 53 pp.
2. Carkhuff, R. R., Barnett, L., Jr., and McCall, J. N. *The Counselor's handbook: Scale and profile interpretation of the MMPI.* Urbana, Ill: R. W. Parkinson, 1965, 72 pp.
3. Dahlstrom, W. G., and Welsh, G. S. *An MMPI handbook: A guide to use in clinical practice and research.* Minneapolis: University of Minnesota Press, 1960. 559 pp.

4. Drake, L. E., and Oetting, E. R. *An MMPI codebook for counselors.* Minneapolis: University of Minnesota Press, 1959, 140 pp.
5. Gilberstadt, H., and Duker, J. *A handbook for clinical and actuarial MMPI interpretation.* Philadelphia: Saunders, 1965, 194 pp.
6. Good, P. K., and Brantner, J. P. *The physician's guide to the MMPI.* Minneapolis: University of Minnesota Press, 1961.
7. Hathaway, S. R. MMPI: Professional use by professional people. *American Psychologist,* 1964, **19,** 204–210.
8. Hedlund, D. E. A review of the MMPI in industry. *Psychological Reports,* 1965, **17,** 875–889.
9. Kleinmuntz, B. Annotated bibliography of MMPI research among college populations. *Journal of Counseling Psychology,* 1962, **9,** 373–396.
10. Lanyon, R. I. (Ed.) *A handbook of MMPI group profiles.* Minneapolis: University of Minnesota Press, 1968.
11. Marks, P. A., and Seeman, W. *The actuarial description of abnormal personality: An atlas for use with the MMPI.* Baltimore: Williams & Wilkins, 1963.
12. Tellegen, A. The Minnesota Multiphasic Personality Inventory. *Progress in Clinical Psychology,* 1964, **6,** 30–48.

PSYCHOMETRIC CHARACTERISTICS

Alternate Forms

13. Bashaw, W. L. A comparison of MMPI profiles and validity scale scores obtained by normal and slide-projected administration. *Multivariate Behavioral Research,* 1967, **2,** 241–249.
14. Canter, A. The efficacy of a short form of the MMPI to evaluate depression and morale loss. *Journal of Consulting Psychology,* 1960, **24,** 14–17.
15. Urmer, A. H., Black, H. O., and Wendland, L. U. A comparison of taped and booklet forms of the MMPI. *Journal of Clinical Psychology,* 1960, **16,** 33–34.
16. Wolf, S., Freinek, W. R., and Shaffer, J. W. Comparability of complete oral and booklet forms of the MMPI. *Journal of Clinical Psychology,* 1964, **20,** 375–378.

Factor-analytic Studies

17. Anderson, H. E., Jr., Davis, H. C., Jr., and Wolking, W. D. A factorial study of the MMPI for students in health and rehabilitation. *Educational and Psychological Measurement,* 1966, **26,** 29–39.
18. Anderson, W., and Anker, J. Factor analysis of MMPI and SVIB scores for a psychiatric population. *Psychological Reports,* 1964, **15,** 715–719.

19. Baggaley, A. R., and Biedel, W. W. A diagnostic assembly of MMPI items based on Comrey's factor analyses. *Journal of Clinical Psychology,* 1966, **22**, 306–308.
20. Bendig, A. W. A factor analysis of personality scales including the Buss-Durkee Hostility Inventory. *Journal of General Psychology,* 1962, **66,** 179–183.
21. Bonner, R. E. Cluster analysis. *Annals of the New York Academy of Sciences,* 1966, **128,** 972–983.
22. Comrey, A. L. Comparison of two analytic rotation procedures. *Psychological Reports,* 1959, **5,** 201–209.
23. Comrey, A. L., and Soufi, A. Further investigation of some factors found in MMPI items. *Educational and Psychological Measurement,* 1960, **20,** 777–786.
24. Edwards, A. L., Diers, C. J., and Walker, J. N. Response sets and factor loadings on sixty-one personality scales. *Journal of Applied Psychology,* 1962, **46,** 220–225.
25. Eichman, W. J. Replicated factors on the MMPI with female NP patients. *Journal of Consulting Psychology,* 1961, **25,** 55–60.
26. Eichman, W. J. Factored scales for the MMPI. A clinical and statistical manual. *Journal of Clinical Psychology,* 1962, **18,** 363–395.
27. Finney, J. C. The MMPI as a measure of character structure as revealed by factor analysis. *Journal of Consulting Psychology,* 1961, **25,** 327–336.
28. Finney, J. C. Factor structure with the new set of MMPI scales and the formula correction. *Journal of Clinical Psychology,* 1966, **22,** 443–449.
29. Franks, C. M., Souieff, M. I., and Maxwell, A. E. A factorial study of certain scales from the MMPI and the STDCR. *Acta Psychologica, Amsterdam,* 1960, **17,** 407–416.
30. Gocka, E. F., and Marks, J. B. Second-order factors in the 16 PF test and MMPI inventory. *Journal of Clinical Psychology,* 1961, **17**, 32–35.
31. Gocka, E. F., and Mees, H. L. The representation of MMPI scales by MMPI factor scales. *Journal of Clinical Psychology,* 1960, **16,** 291–295.
32. Golin, S., Herron, E. W., La Vista, R., and Reineck, L. Factor-analytic study of the manifest anxiety, extraversion, and repression-sensitization scales. *Journal of Consulting Psychology,* 1967, **31,** 564–569.
33. Hartley, R. E., and Allen, R. M. The Minnesota Multiphasic Personality Inventory (MMPI) and the Edwards Personal Preference Schedule (EPPS): A factor analytic study. *Journal of Social Psychology,* 1962, **58,** 153–162.
34. Kassebaum, G. G., Couch, A. S., and Slater, P. E. The factorial dimensions of the MMPI. *Journal of Consulting Psychology,* 1959, **23,** 226–236.

35. Mees, H. L. Preliminary steps in the construction of factor scales for the MMPI. *Dissertation Abstracts,* 1960, **20,** 2905.
36. Shure, G. H., and Rogers, M. S. Note of caution on the factor analysis of the MMPI. *Psychological Bulletin,* 1965, **63,** 14–18.
37. Welsh, G. S. MMPI profiles and factor scales *A* and *R*. *Journal of Clinical Psychology,* 1965, **21,** 43–47.

Item Characteristics

38. Aaronson, B. S., and Rothman, I. A key-word index to the items of the MMPI. *Journal of Psychological Studies,* 1962, **13,** 121–151.
39. Anderson, H. E., Jr., and Bashaw, W. L. Further comments on the internal structure of the MMPI. *Psychological Bulletin,* 1966, **66,** 211–213.
40. Butcher, J. N., and Tellegen, A. Objections to MMPI items. *Journal of Consulting Psychology,* 1966, **30,** 527–534.
41. Chyatte, C., and Goldman, I. J. The willingness of actors to admit to socially undesirable behavior on the MMPI. *Journal of Clinical Psychology,* 1961, **17,** 44.
42. Duff, F. L. Item subtlety in personality inventory scales. *Journal of Consulting Psychology,* 1965, **29,** 565–570.
43. Gravitz, M. A. Frequency and control content items normally omitted from MMPI scales. *Journal of Consulting Psychology,* 1967, **31,** 642.
44. Hanley, C. The "difficulty" of a personality inventory item. *Educational and Psychological Measurement,* 1962, **22,** 577–584.
45. Harris, J. G., Jr., and Baxter, J. C. Ambiguity in the MMPI. *Journal of Consulting Psychology,* 1965, **29,** 112–118.
46. Jones, R. R. The relationships between item properties and scale reliability. *Dissertation Abstracts,* 1966, **26,** 4830.
47. Katzell, R. A., and Katzell, M. E. Development and application of structured tests of personality. *Review of Educational Research,* 1962, **32,** 51–63.
48. Lewis, J. W., and Caldwell, W. E. A psycholinguist investigation of verbal psychological tests. *Journal of General Psychology,* 1961, **65,** 131–144.
49. Pearson, W. O. The relationship between item difficulty and interitem correlation in the Minnesota Multiphasic Personality Inventory and the Guilford-Zimmerman Temperament Survey. *Dissertation Abstracts,* 1960, **20,** 4177–4178.
50. Perkins, J. E., and Goldberg, L. R. Contextual effects on the MMPI. *Journal of Consulting Psychology,* 1964, **28,** 133–140.
51. Rorer, L. G. The function of item content in MMPI responses. *Dissertation Abstracts,* 1963, **24,** 2566.
52. Rosen, A. Punched card methods for item analysis in the development

of structured personality scales. *Journal of General Psychology,* 1959, **61,** 127–135.

53. Stone, L. A. Subtle and obvious response on the MMPI. *Psychological Reports,* 1964, **15,** 721–722.
54. Walker, C. E. The effect of eliminating offensive items on the reliability and validity of the MMPI. *Journal of Clinical Psychology,* 1967, **23,** 363–366.
55. Wiggins, J. S. An MMPI item characteristic deck. *Educational and Psychological Measurement,* 1964, **24,** 137–141.
56. Wiggins, J. S. Substantive dimensions of self-report in the MMPI item pool. *Psychological Monographs,* 1966, **80,** 42 pp.
57. Wiggins, J. S., and Goldberg, L. R. Interrelationships among MMPI characteristics. *Educational and Psychological Measurement,* 1965, **25,** 381–397.
58. Wiggins, J. S., and Vollmar, J. The content of the MMPI. *Journal of Clinical Psychology,* 1959, **15,** 45–47.

MMPI in Relation to Other Instruments

59. Adams, H. B., Cooper, G. D., and Carrera, R. N. The Rorschach and the MMPI: A concurrent validity study. *Journal of Projective Techniques,* 1963, **27,** 23–34.
60. Barger, B., and Hall, E. The relationship of MMPI high points and PIT need attitude scores for male college students. *Journal of Clinical Psychology,* 1965, **21,** 266–269.
61. Barger, P. M., and Sechrest, L. Convergent and discriminant validity of four Holtzman Inkblot Test variables. *Journal of Psychological Studies,* 1961, **12,** 227–236.
62. Brenner, M. S. The relationship between TAT hostility and overt hostile behavior as a function of self-reported anxiety. *Dissertation Abstracts,* 1961, **22,** 637–638.
63. Crites, J. O. Ego-strength in relation to vocational interest development. *Journal of Counseling Psychology,* 1960, **7,** 137–143.
64. Dana, R. H. Objective TAT scores and personality characteristics: Perceptual organization. *Perceptual and Motor Skills,* 1960, **10,** 154.
65. Dana, R. H., and Hopewell, E. Repression and psychopathology: A cross-validation failure. *Psychological Reports,* 1966, **19,** 626.
66. Dunteman, G. H., and Bailey, J. P., Jr. A canonical correlational analysis of the Strong Vocational Interest Blank and the Minnesota Multiphasic Personality Inventory for a female college population. *Educational and Psychological Measurement,* 1967, **127,** 631–642.
67. Endicott, N. A., and Endicott J. The relationship between Rorschach

flexor and extensor *M* responses and the MMPI. *Journal of Clinical Psychology,* 1964, **20,** 388–389.
68. Gauron, E. F., and Adams, J. The relationship of the Edwards Personal Preference Schedule to the MMPI in a patient population. *Journal of Clinical Psychology,* 1966, **22,** 206–209.
69. Goldfried, M. R. Rorschach developmental level and the MMPI as measures of severity of psychological disturbance. *Journal of Projective Techniques,* 1962, **26,** 187–192.
70. Harrison, R. J. Predictive validity of some adjustment tests: A research note. *Australian Journal of Psychology,* 1966, **18,** 284–286.
71. Jurjevich, R. M. Interrelationships of anxiety indices of Wechsler intelligence scales and MMPI scales. *Journal of General Psychology,* 1963, **69,** 135–142.
72. Jurjevich, R. M. The regression toward the mean in MMPI, California Psychological Inventory and Symptom Check List. *Educational and Psychological Measurement,* 1966, **26,** 661–664.
73. L'Abate, L. The relationship between WAIS-derived indices of maladjustment and MMPI in deviant groups. *Journal of Consulting Psychology,* 1962, **26,** 441–445.
74. LaForge, R. A correlational study of two personality tests. *Journal of Consulting Psychology,* 1962, **26,** 402–411.
75. Lipsher, D. H. Consistency of clinicians' judgments based on MMPI, Rorschach, and TAT protocols. *Dissertation Abstracts,* 1962, **22,** 4409–4410.
76. Megargee, E. I. Estimation of CPI scores from MMPI protocols. *Journal of Clinical Psychology,* 1966, **22,** 457–458.
77. Murray, J. B., and Galvin, J. Correlational study of the MMPI and GZTS. *Journal of General Psychology,* 1963, **69,** 267–273.
78. Nash, C. B. Relation between ESP scoring level and the Minnesota Multiphasic Personality Inventory. *Journal of the American Society for Psychical Research,* 1966, **60,** 56–62.
79. Pool, D. A., and Brown, R. A. Kuder-Strong discrepancies and personality adjustment. *Journal of Counseling Psychology,* 1964, **11,** 63–71.
80. Quero, R., Caille, E. J. P., Boudon, R. C. P., and Lautman, J. F. La mesure de l'adaptabilité sociale à partir de l'Inventaire de Tempérament de Guilford-Zimmerman et du MMPI: Essai de construction d'un questionnaire d'adaptation sociale (The scale of social adaptability derived from the Guilford-Zimmerman Temperament Inventory and the MMPI: Attempt to construct a social adaptation questionnaire). In F. Geldard (Ed.), *Defense psychology,* London: Pergamon, 1962. Pp. 275–285.
81. Rodgers, D. A. Estimation of MMPI profiles from CPI data. *Journal of Consulting Psychology,* 1966, **30,** 89.
82. Schill, T. R. The effects of MMPI social introversion on WAIS *PA* performance. *Journal of Clinical Psychology,* 1966, **22,** 72–74.

Response Bias (General)

83. Branca, A. A., and Podolnick, E. E. Normal, hypnotically induced and feigned anxiety as reflected in and detected by the MMPI. *Journal of Consulting Psychology,* 1961, **25,** 165–170.
84. Cantor, J. M. All-or-none style of thinking as a source of test bias. *Psychological Reports,* 1964, **15,** 355–358.
85. Delay, J., Pichot, P., and Perse, J. La detection de la simulation a l'Inventaire Multiphasique de Personnalité du Minnesota. (The detection of simulation on the MMPI). *Revue de Psychologie Appliquée,* 1960, **10,** 249–262.
86. DeSoto, C. B., and Kuethe, J. L. The set to claim undesirable symptoms in personality inventories. *Journal of Consulting Psychology,* 1959, **23,** 496–500.
87. Devries, A. G. Demographic variables and MMPI responses. *Journal of Clinical Psychology,* 1966, **22,** 450–452.
88. Draguns, J. G. Response sets on the MMPI and in structuring ambiguous stimuli. *Psychological Reports,* 1963, **13,** 823–828.
89. Elvekrog, M. O. The development of measures on three response styles and their relationships to test and non-test variables. *Dissertation Abstracts,* 1965, **25,** 4814–4815.
90. Finney, J. C. Effects of response sets on new and old MMPI scales. *Psychological Reports,* 1965, **17,** 907–915.
91. Goldberg, P. A., and Miller, S. J. Structured personality tests and dissimulation. *Journal of Projective Techniques and Personality Assessment,* 1966, **30,** 452–455.
92. Lanyon, R. I. Simulation of normal and psychopathic MMPI personality patterns. *Journal of Consulting Psychology,* 1967, **31,** 94–97.
93. Liberty, P. G., Vitola, B. H., and Pierson, J. S. Set and content scores for personality scales and response styles in the MMPI. *Journal of Applied Psychology,* 1965, **49,** 326–331.
94. Miller, S. J. Structured personality tests and dissimulation. *Connecticut College Psychology Journal,* 1966, **3,** 20–24.
95. Mills, D. H., and Hannum, T. E. The transparency of the Taylor Scale of Manifest Anxiety in a college population. *Journal of Applied Psychology,* 1959, **43,** 8–11.
96. Weiss, R. L., and Moos, R. H. Response biases in the MMPI: A sequential analysis. *Psychological Bulletin,* 1965, **63,** 403–409.
97. Wiggins, J. S. Strategic, method, and stylistic variance in the MMPI. *Psychological Bulletin,* 1962, **59,** 224–242.
98. Wilcox, R., and Krasnoff, A. Influence of test-taking attitudes on personality inventory scores. *Journal of Consulting Psychology,* 1967, **31,** 188–194.
99. Young, R. C. Effects of differential instructions on the Minnesota Multiphasic Personality Inventories of state hospital patients. *Proceed-*

ings of the Seventy-third Annual Convention of the American Psychological Association, 1965, 281–282.

Social Desirability and Acquiescence

100. Boe, E. E. Social desirability considerations in separate acquiescence set and content scores. *Psychological Reports,* 1964, **15,** 699–702.
101. Boe, E. E., Gocka, E. F., and Kogan, W. S. A factor analysis of individual social desirability scale values. *Multivariate Behavioral Research,* 1966, **1,** 287–292.
102. Boe, E. E., and Kogan, W. S. Social desirability response set in the individual. *Journal of Consulting Psychology,* 1963, **27,** 369.
103. Boe, E. E., and Kogan, W. S. Effect of social desirability instructions on several MMPI measures of social desirability. *Journal of Consulting Psychology,* 1964, **28,** 248–251.
104. Boe, E. E., and Kogan, W. S. Social desirability in individual performance on thirteen MMPI scale. *British Journal of Psychiatry,* 1966, **57,** 161–170.
105. Buss, A. H. The effect of item style on social desirability and frequency of endorsement. *Journal of Consulting Psychology,* 1959, **23,** 510–513.
106. Couch, A., and Keniston, K. Agreeing response set and social desirability. *Journal of Abnormal and Social Psychology,* 1961, **62,** 175–179.
107. Crowne, D. P., and Marlowe, D. A. new scale of social desirability independent of psychopathology. *Journal of Consulting Psychology,* 1960, **24,** 349–354.
108. Dempsey, P. Overall performance on the MMPI as it relates to test-taking attitudes and clinical scale scores. *Journal of Clinical Psychology,* 1964, **20,** 154–156.
109. Dempsey, P. Depression or social desirability: Comments on Edwards' appraisal of the D_{30} scale. *Journal of Consulting Psychology,* 1965, **29**, 274–276.
110. Dicken, C. "Acquiescence" in the MMPI: A method variance artifact? *Psychological Reports,* 1967, **20,** 927–933.
111. Dicken, C., and Van Pelt, J. Further evidence concerning acquiescence and the MMPI. *Psychological Reports,* 1967, **20,** 935–941.
112. Dicken, C., and Wiggins, J. S. The social desirability scale is not a short form of the MMPI: A reply to Edwards and Walker. *Psychological Reports,* 1964, **14,** 711–714.
113. Edwards, A. L. Social desirability or acquiescence in the MMPI? A case study with the *SD* scale. *Journal of Abnormal and Social Psychology,* 1961, **63,** 351–359.

114. Edwards, A. L. Social desirability and expected means on MMPI scales. *Educational and Psychological Measurement*, 1962, **22**, 71–76.

115. Edwards, A. L. Prediction of mean scores on MMPI scales. *Journal of Consulting Psychology*, 1964, **28**, 183–185. (a)

116. Edwards, A. L. Social desirability and performance on the MMPI. *Psychometrika*, 1964, **29**, 295–308. (b)

117. Edwards, A. L. Correlation of "A unidimensional depression scale for the MMPI" with the *SD* scale. *Journal of Consulting Psychology*, 1965, **29**, 271–273.

118. Edwards, A. L. A comparison of 57 MMPI scales and 57 experimental scale matches with the MMPI scales in terms of item social desirability scale values and probabilities of endorsement. *Educational and Psychological Measurement*, 1966, **26**, 15–27.

119. Edwards, A. L., and Diers, C. J. Social desirability and the factorial interpretation of the MMPI. *Educational and Psychological Measurement*, 1962, **22**, 501–509.

120. Edwards, A. L., and Heathers, L. B. The first factor of the MMPI: Social desirability or ego strength? *Journal of Consulting Psychology*, 1962, **26**, 99–100.

121. Edwards, A. L., Heathers, L. B., and Fordyce, W. E. Correlations of new MMPI scales with Edwards' *SD* scale. *Journal of Clinical Psychology*, 1960, **16**, 26–29.

122. Edwards, A. L., and Walker, J. N. A note on the Couch and Keniston measure of agreement response set. *Journal of Abnormal and Social Psychology*, 1961, **62**, 173–174. (a)

123. Edwards, A. L., and Walker, J. N. A short form of the MMPI: The *SD* scale. *Psychological Reports*, 1961, **8**, 485–486. (b)

124. Edwards, A. L., and Walker, J. N. Social desirability and agreement response set. *Journal of Abnormal and Social Psychology*, 1961, **62**, 180–183. (c)

125. Elvekrog, M. O., and Vestre, N. D. The Edwards Social Desirability Scale as a short form of the MMPI. *Journal of Consulting Psychology*, 1963, **27**, 503–507.

126. Feldman, M. J., and Corah, N. L. Social desirability and the forced choice method. *Journal of Consulting Psychology*, 1960, **24**, 480–482.

127. Fischer, G. The performance of male prisoners on the Marlowe-Crowne social desirability scale: II. Differences as a function of age and crime. *Journal of Clinical Psychology*, 1967, **23**, 471–473.

128. Fox, J. Social desirability and the prediction of MMPI scores. *Journal of Consulting Psychology*, 1966, **30**, 460.

129. Fox, J. Social desirability, prediction equation, regression equations, and intrinsic response bias. *Psychological Bulletin*, 1967, **67**, 391–400.

130. Gloye, E. E. A note on the distinction between social desirability and acquiescent response styles as sources of variance in the MMPI. *Journal of Counseling Psychology*, 1964, **11**, 180–184.

131. Gocka, E. F. The introversion-extraversion factor and social desirability. *Journal of Clinical Psychology,* 1960, **16,** 380–383.
132. Gocka, E. F., and Burk, H. W. MMPI test taking time and social desirability. *Journal of Clinical Psychology,* 1963, **19,** 111–113.
133. Hanley, C. Social desirability and response bias in the MMPI. *Journal of Consulting Psychology,* 1961, **25,** 13–20.
134. Heilbrun, A. B. Social-learning theory, social desirability and the MMPI. *Psychological Bulletin,* 1964, **61,** 377–387.
135. Katkin, E. S. Sex differences and the relationship between the Marlowe-Crowne Social Desirability Scale and MMPI indexes of psychopathology. *Journal of Consulting Psychology,* 1966, **30,** 564.
136. Lebovits, B. Z., and Ostfeld, A. M. Note on the Edwards Social Desirability Scale. *Psychological Reports,* 1966, **19,** 1271–1277.
137. Lichtenstein, E., and Bryan, J. H. Acquiescence and the MMPI: An item reversal approach. *Journal of Abnormal Psychology,* 1965, **70,** 290–293.
138. Marlowe, D., and Crowne, D. P. Social desirability and response to perceived situational demands. *Journal of Consulting Psychology,* 1961, **25,** 109–115.
139. Marlowe, D., and Gottesman, I. I. The Edwards *SD* scale: A short form of the MMPI? *Journal of Consulting Psychology,* 1964, **28,** 181–182. (a)
140. Marlowe, D., and Gottesman, I. I. Prediction of mean scores on MMPI scales: A reply. *Journal of Consulting Psychology,* 1964, **28,** 185–186. (b)
141. Megargee, E. I. The Edwards *SD* Scale: A measure of adjustment or of dissimulation? *Journal of Consulting Psychology,* 1966, **30,** 566.
142. Messick, S., and Jackson, D. N. Acquiescence and desirability as response determinants on the MMPI. *Educational and Psychological Measurement,* 1961, **21,** 771–790. (a)
143. Messick, S., and Jackson, D. N. Acquiescence and the factorial interpretation of the MMPI. *Psychological Bulletin,* 1961, **58,** 299–304. (b)
144. Messick, S., and Jackson, D. N. Desirability scale values and dispersions for MMPI items. *Psychological Reports,* 1961, **8,** 409–414. (c)
145. Mukherjee, B. A cross-validation of the Marlowe-Crowne social desirability scale on an Indian sample. *Journal of Social Psychology,* 1967, **72,** 299–300.
146. Pumroy, D. K. Some counseling behavior correlates of the Social Desirability Scale. *Journal of Counseling Psychology,* 1961, **8,** 49–53.
147. Rorer, L. G., and Goldberg, L. R. Acquiescence in the MMPI? *Educational and Psychological Measurement,* 1965, **25,** 801–817. (a)

148. Rorer, L. G., and Goldberg, L. R. Acquiescence and the vanishing variance component. *Journal of Applied Psychology,* 1965, **49,** 422–430. (b)

149. Rosenthal, R., Persinger, G. W., and Fode, K. L. Experimenter bias, anxiety, and social desirability. *Perceptual and Motor Skills,* 1962, **15,** 73–74.

150. Schultz, C. B., Kogan, W. S., and Chapman, H. Favorability, unfavorability, and content considerations in *SD* scales. *Psychological Reports,* 1962, **10,** 619–622.

151. Sheldon, M. S. Conditions affecting the fakability of teacher-selection inventories. *Educational and Psychological Measurement,* 1959, **19,** 207–219.

152. Stone, L. A. Relationships between response to the Marlowe-Crowne Social Desirability Scale and MMPI scales. *Psychological Reports,* 1965, **17,** 179–182. (a)

153. Stone, L. A. Reliability estimate for favorability (social desirability) ratings of MMPI items. *Psychological Reports,* 1965, **16,** 720. (b)

154. Stone, L. A. Social desirability and order of item presentation in the MMPI. *Psychological Reports,* 1965, **17,** 518. (c)

155. Stone, L. A. Social desirability response bias and MMPI content categories. *Psychology,* 1965, **2,** 2–3. (d)

156. Stone, L. A. Subtle and obvious response on the MMPI as a function of acquiescence response style. *Psychological Reports,* 1965, **16,** 803–804. (e)

157. Stone, L. A. Corrected (for curtailment) correlations between the Marlowe-Crowne Social Desirability Scale and the MMPI. *Psychological Reports,* 1966, **19,** 103–106.

158. Taylor, J. B. Social desirability and the MMPI performance of schizophrenics. *Dissertation Abstracts,* 1959, **19,** 1828. (a)

159. Taylor, J. B. Social desirability and MMPI performance: The individual case. *Journal of Consulting Psychology,* 1959, **23,** 514–517. (b)

160. Wahler, H. J. Item popularity and social desirability in the MMPI. *Journal of Applied Psychology,* 1965, **49,** 439–449.

161. Walder, J. N. An examination of the role of the experimentally determined response set in evaluating Edwards' Social Desirability Scale. *Journal of Consulting Psychology,* 1962, **26,** 162–166.

162. Walker, J. N. An examination of the role of the experimentally determined response set in evaluating Edwards' Social Desirability Scale. *Dissertation Abstracts,* 1961, **22,** 1712–1713.

163. Wiggins, J. S. Interrelationships among MMPI measures of dissimulation under standard and social desirability instruction. *Journal of Consulting Psychology,* 1959, **23,** 419–427.

164. Wiggins, J. S. Social desirability under role playing instructions: A reply to Walker. *Journal of Consulting Psychology,* 1963, **27,** 107–111.

165. Wiggins, J. S. Social desirability estimation and "faking good" well.

Educational and Psychological Measurement, 1966, **26,** 329–341.

166. Wiggins, J. S., and Lovell, V. R. Communality and favorability as sources of method variance in the MMPI. *Educational and Psychological Measurement,* 1965, **25,** 399–412.

167. Wiggins, J. S., and Rumrill, C. Social desirability in the MMPI and Welsh's factor scales *A* and *R*. *Journal of Consulting Psychology,* 1959, **23,** 100–106.

168. Wiggins, N. Individual viewpoints of social desirability. *Psychological Bulletin,* 1966, **66,** 68–77.

Stability of the MMPI

169. Burns, N. M., and Ayers, F. W. MMPI profile changes during an eighteen day confinement study. *Perceptual and Motor Skills,* 1966, **23,** 877–878.

170. Dana, R. H., and Condry, J. C., Jr. MMPI retest results: Context, order, practice, and test-taking anxiety. *Psychological Reports,* 1963, **12,** 147–152.

171. Gloye, E. E., and Zimmerman, I. L. MMPI item changes by college students under ideal-self response set. *Journal of Projective Techniques and Personality Assessment,* 1967, **31,** 63–69.

172. Jurjevich, R. M. Short interval test-retest stability of MMPI, California Psychological Inventory, Cornell Index, and Symptom Check List. *Journal of General Psychology,* 1966, **74,** 301–306.

173. Lewinsohn, P. M. Dimensions of MMPI change. *Journal of Clinical Psychology,* 1965, **21,** 37–43.

174. Lichtenstein, E., and Bryan, J. H. Short-term stability of MMPI profiles. *Journal of Consulting Psychology,* 1966, **30,** 172–174.

175. Pauker, J. D. MMPI profile stability in a psychiatric, inpatient population. *Journal of Clinical Psychology,* 1965, **21,** 281–282.

176. Pauker, J. D. Stability of MMPI profiles of female psychiatric inpatients. *Journal of Clinical Psychology,* 1966, **22,** 209–212. (a)

177. Pauker, J. D. Stability of MMPI scales over five testings within a one-month period. *Educational and Psychological Measurement,* 1966, **26,** 1063–1067. (b)

178. Pepper, L. J. MMPI: Initial test predictions of retest changes. *Dissertation Abstracts,* 1965, **26,** 1780–1781.

179. Rosen, A. Stability of new MMPI scales and statistical procedures for evaluating changes and differences in psychiatric patients. *Journal of Consulting Psychology,* 1966, **30,** 142–145.

180. Sivanich, G. Test-retest changes during the course of hospitalization among some frequently occurring MMPI profiles. *Dissertation Abstracts,* 1961, **21,** 2787.

181. Stone, L. A. Test-retest stability of the MMPI scales. *Psychological Reports,* 1965, **16,** 619–620.

182. Weigel, R. G., and Phillips, M. An evaluation of the MMPI scoring accuracy by two national scoring agencies. *Journal of Clinical Psychology,* 1967, **23,** 102–103.

SPECIFIC RESEARCH AREAS

Achievement

183. Barger, B., and Hall, E. Personality patterns and achievement in college. *Educational and Psychological Measurement,* 1964, **24,** 339–346.
184. Boxhill, C. J. A special MMPI scale related to the retention and dismissal of freshman college students on academic probation. *Dissertation Abstracts,* 1966, **27,** 384.
185. DeSena, P. A. Comparison of consistent over-, under-, and normal-achieving college students on a Minnesota Multiphasic Personality Inventory special scale. *Psychology,* 1964, **1,** 8–12.
186. Drake, L. E. MMPI patterns predictive of under-achievement. *Journal of Counseling Psychology,* 1962, **9,** 164–167.
187. Finger, J. A., and Schlesser, G. E. Academic performance of public and private school students. *Journal of Educational Psychology,* 1963, **54,** 118–122.
188. Haun, K. W. A note on the prediction of academic performance from personality test scores. *Psychological Reports,* 1965, **16,** 294.
189. Himelstein, P. Validities and intercorrelations of MMPI subscales predictive of college achievement. *Educational and Psychological Measurement,* 1965, **25,** 1125–1128.
190. Kennedy, W. A., and Smith, A. H. A high performance MMPI scale for adolescents. *Psychological Reports,* 1962, **11,** 494.
191. Lebovits, B. Z., and Ostfeld, A. M. Personality, defensiveness, and educational achievement. *Journal of Personality and Social Psychology,* 1967, **6,** 381–390.
192. Lundin, R. W., and Kuhn, J. P. The relationship between scholarship achievement and changes in personality adjustment in men after four years of college attendance. *Journal of General Psychology,* 1960, **63,** 35–42.
193. McKenzie, J. D., Jr. An attempt to develop Minnesota Multiphasic Personality Inventory scales predictive of academic over- and underachievement. *Dissertation Abstracts,* 1961, **22,** 632.
194. McKenzie, J. D., Jr. The dynamics of deviant achievement. *Personnel and Guidance Journal,* 1964, **42,** 683–686.
195. Seegars, J. E., Jr. A further investigation of an MMPI scale for predicting college achievement. *Personnel and Guidance Journal,* 1962, **41,** 251–253.
196. Thurston, J. R., Brunclik, H. L., and Finn, P. A. The relation of MMPI

scores to personality and achievement levels of student nurses. *Journal of Psychological Studies,* 1961, **12,** 75–86.

197. Tryon, R. C. Person-clusters on intellectual abilities and on MMPI attributes. *Multivariate Behavioral Research,* 1967, **2,** 5–34.
198. Vaughan, R. P. Personality characteristics of exceptional college students. *Proceedings of the Seventy-fourth Annual Convention of the American Psychological Association,* 1966, 281–282.
199. Winkler, L. A study of Minnesota Multiphasic Personality Inventories of bright achievers, bright underachievers, and students with designated learning difficulties. *George Washington University Bulletin: Summaries of Doctoral Dissertations,* 1965, **65,** 140–146.

Aging

200. Aaronson, B. S. A dimension of personality change with aging. *Journal of Clinical Psychology,* 1960, **16,** 63–65.
201. Britton, P. G., and Savage, R. D. The MMPI and the aged: Some normative data from a community sample. *British Journal of Psychiatry,* 1966, **112,** 941–943.
202. Calden, G., and Hokanson, J. E. The influence of age on MMPI responses. *Journal of Clinical Psychology,* 1959, **15,** 194–195.
203. Canter, A., Day, C. W., Imboden, J. B., and Cluff, L. E. The influence of age and health status on the MMPI scores of a normal population. *Journal of Clinical Psychology,* 1962, **18,** 71–73.
204. Gynther, M. D., and Shimkunas, A. M. Age and MMPI performance. *Journal of Consulting Psychology,* 1966, **30,** 118–121.
205. Joshi, M. C., and Singh, B. Age-wise score constancy in MMPI. *Psychological Studies,* 1966, **11,** 110–114.
206. Pearson, J. S., Swenson, W. M., and Rome, H. P. Age and sex differences related to MMPI response frequency in 25,000 medical patients. *American Journal of Psychiatry,* 1965, **121,** 988–995.
207. Postema, L. J., and Schell, R. E. Aging and psychopathology: Some MMPI evidence for seemingly greater neurotic behavior among older people. *Journal of Clinical Psychology,* 1967, **23,** 140–143.
208. Swenson, W. M. Structured personality testing in the aged: An MMPI study of the gerontic population. *Journal of Clinical Psychology,* 1961, **17,** 302–304.

Anxiety and Stress

209. Eschenbach, A. E., and Dupree, L. The influence of stress on MMPI scale scores. *Journal of Clinical Psychology,* 1959, **15,** 42–45.

210. Fulkerson, S. C. Individual differences in reaction to failure-induced stress. *Journal of Abnormal and Social Psychology,* 1960, **60,** 136–139.

211. Javal, I., Riveng, F., and Voillaume, C. Quelques indications concemant la relaxation: Etude psychometrique réalisée a l'aide du MMPI (Some indications concerning relaxation: Psychometric study realized with the help of the MMPI). *Psychologie Française,* 1961, **6,** 67–70.

212. Kuethe, J. L. The interaction of personality and muscle tension in producing agreement on commonality of verbal associations. *Journal of Abnormal and Social Psychology,* 1961, **62,** 696–697.

213. Kraus, H. H., and Ruiz, R. A. Anxiety and temporal perspective. *Journal of Clinical Psychology,* 1967, **23,** 454–455.

214. Martin, B. The measurement of anxiety. *Journal of General Psychology,* 1959, **61,** 189–203.

215. Mendelsohn, G. A., and Griswold, B. B. Anxiety and repression as predictors of the use of incidental cues in problem solving. *Journal of Personality and Social Psychology,* 1967, **6,** 353–359.

216. Miller, N. B., Fisher, W. P., and Ladd, C. E. Psychometric and rated anxiety. *Psychological Reports,* 1967, **20,** 707–710.

217. Moss, C. S., and Waters, T. J. Intensive longitudinal investigation of anxiety in hospitalized juvenile patients. *Psychological Reports,* 1960, **7,** 379–380.

218. Nishisato, S. A factor analytic study of an anxiety scale. *Japanese Journal of Psychology,* 1960, **31,** 228–236.

219. Oetting, E. R. Examination anxiety: Prediction, physiological response and relation to scholastic performance. *Journal of Consulting Psychology,* 1966, **13,** 224–227.

220. Pichot, P., Gorceix, A., and Perse, J. L'appréciation de l'anxiété pathologique par la méthode des questionnaires (The estimation of pathological anxiety by means of questionnaires). *Revue de Psychologie Appliquée,* 1960, **10,** 263–279.

221. Pomeranz, D. M. The repression-sensitization dimension and reactions to stress. *Dissertation Abstracts,* 1963, **24,** 2605–2606.

222. Price, J. R. Relationship of the hysteria-psychasthenia dimension to stimulus generalization under stress. *Dissertation Abstracts,* 1963, **23,** 3480–3481.

223. Vaughan, R. P. The effect of stress on the MMPI scales *K* and *D*. *Journal of Clinical Psychology,* 1963, **19,** 432.

Drug Studies

224. Fiddleman, P. B. The prediction of behavior under lysergic acid diethylamide (LSD). *Dissertation Abstracts,* 1962, **22,** 2873–2874.

225. Haertzen, C. A., and Hill, H. E. Effects of morphine and pentobarbital

on differential MMPI profiles. *Journal of Clinical Psychology,* 1959, **15,** 434–437.
226. Hawkins, D. R., Pace, R., Pasternack, B., and Sandifer, M. G., Jr. A multivariant psychopharmacologic study in normals. *Psychosomatic Medicine,* 1961, **23,** 1–17.
227. Johannsen, W. J., Friedman, S. H., Feldman, E. I., and Negrete, A. A re-examination of the hippuric acid-anxiety relationship. *Psychosomatic Medicine,* 1962, **24,** 569–578.
228. Judson, A. J., and MacCasland, B. W. The effects of chlorpromazine on psychological test scores. *Journal of Consulting Psychology,* 1960, **24,** 192.
229. Keeler, M. H., and Doehne, E. F. Consistency of psilocybin induced changes in the Minnesota Multiphasic Personality Inventory. *Journal of Clinical Psychology,* 1965, **21,** 284.
230. Lebovits, B. Z., Visotsky, H. M., and Ostfeld, A. M. LSD and JB 318: A comparison of two hallucinogens. *AMA Archives of General Psychiatry,* 1960, **2,** 390–407.
231. Muller, B. P. Personality correlates of the placebo reaction. *Dissertation Abstracts,* 1961, **21,** 3855.

Family and Parent Studies

232. Adrian, R. J., Vacchiano, R. B., and Gilbart, T. E. Linear discriminant function classification of accepted and rejected adoptive applicants. *Journal of Clinical Psychology,* 1966, **22,** 251–254.
233. Butcher, J. N. Manifest aggression: MMPI correlates in normal boys and their parents. *Dissertation Abstracts,* 1965, **25,** 6755–6756.
234. Dunteman, G. H., and Wolking, W. D. Relationship between marital status and the personality of mothers of disturbed children. *Journal of Consulting Psychology,* 1967, **31,** 220.
235. Ferreira, A. J., and Winter, W. D. Stability of interactional variables in family decision-making. *Archives of General Psychiatry,* 1966, **14,** 352–355.
236. Goodstein, L. D., and Rowley, V. N. A further study of MMPI differences between parents of disturbed and nondisturbed children. *Journal of Consulting Psychology,* 1961, **25,** 460.
237. Gross, S. Z. A normative study and cross validation of MMPI subtle and obvious scales for parents seen at a child guidance clinic. *Psychology,* 1964, **1,** 5–7.
238. Hanvik, L. J., and Byrum, M. MMPI profiles of parents of child psychiatric patients. *Journal of Clinical Psychology,* 1959, **15,** 427–431.
239. L'Abate, L. The effect of paternal failure to participate during the referral of child psychiatric patients. *Journal of Clinical Psychology,* 1960, **16,** 407–408.

240. Lauterbach, C., London, P., and Bryan, J. MMPIs of parents of child guidance cases. *Journal of Clinical Psychology,* 1961, **17,** 151–154.
241. Lauterbach, C., Vogel, W., and Hart, J. Comparison of the MMPI's of the male problem adolescents and their parents. *Journal of Clinical Psychology,* 1962, **18,** 485–487.
242. Liverant, S. MMPI differences between parents of disturbed and non-disturbed children. *Journal of Consulting Psychology,* 1959, **23,** 256–260.
243. Loeb, J. The personality factor in divorce. *Journal of Consulting Psychology,* 1966, **30,** 562.
244. Loeb, J., and Price, J. R. Mother and child personality characteristics related to parental marital status in child guidance cases. *Journal of Consulting Psychology,* 1966, **30,** 112–117.
245. Marzolf, S. S. Parent behavior as reported by college students. *Journal of Clinical Psychology,* 1965, **21,** 360–366.
246. Murstein, B. I. The relationship of mental health to marital choice and courtship progress. *Journal of Marriage and the Family,* 1967, **29,** 447–451.
247. Neubeck, G., and Schletzer, V. M. A study of extramarital relationships. *Marriage and Family Living,* 1962, **24,** 279–281.
248. Stennett, R. G. Family Diagnosis: MMPI and CTP results. *Journal of Clinical Psychology,* 1966, **22,** 165–167.
249. Wolking, W. D., Dunteman, G. H., and Bailey, J. P., Jr. Multivariate analyses of parents' MMPI's based on the psychiatric diagnoses of their children. *Journal of Consulting Psychology,* 1967, **31,** 521–525.
250. Wolking, W. D., Quast, W., and Lawton, J. J., Jr. MMPI profiles of the parents of behaviorally disturbed children and parents from the general population. *Journal of Clinical Psychology,* 1966, **22,** 39–48.

Genetic Studies

251. Gottesman, I. I. Heritability of personality: A demonstration. *Psychological Monographs,* 1963, **77,** (9, Whole No. 572).
252. Gottesman, I. I. Personality and natural selection. In S. G. Vandenberg (Ed.), *Methods and goals in human behavior genetics.* New York: Academic Press, 1965. Pp. 63–80.
253. Gottesman, I. I., and Shields, J. Schizophrenia in twins: Sixteen years' consecutive admissions to a psychiatric clinic. *British Journal of Psychiatry,* 1966, **112,** 809–818. (a)
254. Gottesman, I. I., and Shields, J. Contributions of twin studies to perspectives on schizophrenia. In B. A. Maher (Ed.), *Progress in*

experimental personality research. Vol. 3. New York: Academic Press, 1966. Pp. 1–84. (b)

255. Gottesman, I. I., and Shields, J. In pursuit of the schizophrenic genotype. *Proceedings of the Second Invitational Conference on Human Behavioral Genetics.* Louisville, Ky., 1967.
256. Reznikoff, M., and Honeyman, M. S. MMPI profiles of monozygotic and dizygotic twin pairs. *Journal of Consulting Psychology,* 1967, **31,** 100.

Measurement of Control

257. Collins, D. J. Some dimensions of behavioral control and their relation to MMPI scales. *Dissertation Abstracts,* 1965, **25,** 4812.
258. Jurjevich, R. M. Hostility and anxiety indices on the Rorschach Content Test, Hostility Guilt Index, and the MMPI. *Psychological Reports,* 1967, **21,** 128.
259. Megargee, E. I., Cook, P. E., and Mendelsohn, G. A. Development and validation of an MMPI scale of assaultiveness in overcontrolled individuals. *Journal of Abnormal Psychology,* 1967, **72,** 519–528.
260. Megargee, E. I., and Mendelsohn, G. A. A cross-validation of twelve MMPI indices of hostility and control. *Journal of Abnormal and Social Psychology,* 1962, **65,** 431–438.
261. Nakamura, C. Y. Measures of over-controlled and under-controlled behavior: A validation. *Journal of Clinical Psychology,* 1960, **16,** 149–153.
262. Sivley, R. B., and Johnson, D. T. Psychopathology and locus of control. *Journal of Clinical Psychology,* 1965, **21,** 26.
263. Thomas, C. A. The "yell fire" response as an indicator of impaired impulse control. *Journal of Clinical Psychology,* 1966, **22,** 221–223.

Mothers of Illegitimate Children

264. Griswold, B. B., Wiltse, K. T., and Roberts, R. W. Some personality and intellectual correlates of repeated out-of-wedlock childbirth among welfare recipients. *Journal of Clinical Psychology,* 1966, **22,** 348–353.
265. Jacokes, L. E. MMPI prediction of the unwed mother's decision regarding child placement. *Journal of Clinical Psychology,* 1965, **21,** 280–281.
266. Malmquist, C. P., Kiresuk, T. J., and Spano, R. M. Personality characteristics of women with repeated illegitimacies: Descriptive as-

pects. *American Journal of Orthopsychiatry,* 1966, **36,** 476–484.
267. Malmquist, C. P. Kiresuk, T. J., and Spano, R. M. Mothers with multiple illegitimacies. *Psychiatric Quarterly,* 1967, **41,** 339–354.

Operant Conditioning

268. Bernard, J. L. Manipulation of verbal behavior without reinforcement. *Psychological Reports,* 1962, **11,** 390.
269. Brady, J. P., Pappas, N., Tausig, T. N., and Thornton, D. R. MMPI correlates of operant behavior. *Journal of Clinical Psychology,* 1962, **18,** 67–70.
270. Halberstam, J. L. Some personality correlates of conditioning generalization, and extinction. *Psychosomatic Medicine,* 1961, **23,** 67–76.
271. Oakes, W. F., and Droge, A. E. Operant conditioning of responses to social introversion scale items on the MMPI. *Psychological Reports,* 1960, **6,** 223–225.

Perception

272. Christensen, C. M. Use of design, texture, and color preference in assessment of personality characteristics. *Perceptual and Motor Skills,* 1961, **12,** 143–150.
273. Christensen, C. M. Dimensions and correlates of texture preferences. *Journal of Consulting Psychology,* 1962, **26,** 498–504.
274. Hull, J., and Zubek, J. P. Personality characteristics of successful and unsuccessful sensory isolation subjects. *Perceptual and Motor Skills,* 1962, **14,** 231–240.
275. Kidd, A. H., and Rivoire, J. L. The correlation between level of field-dependence and the elevation of MMPI scale scores. *Journal of Clinical Psychology,* 1964, **20,** 256–257.
276. Knapp, R. H., and Green, S. Preferences for styles of abstract art and their personality correlates. *Journal of Projective Techniques,* 1960, **24,** 396–402.
277. Liberty, P. G., Jr., Lunneborg, C. E., and Atkinson, G. C. Perceptual defense, dissimulation, and response styles. *Journal of Consulting Psychology,* 1964, **28,** 529–537.
278. McDonald, R. L., and Hendry, C. H. Repression-sensitization, field-dependence, and "adjustment." *Psychological Reports,* 1966, **19,** 558.
279. Meier, M. J. Interrelationships among personality variables, kinesthetic figure aftereffect, and reminiscence in motor learning. *Journal of Abnormal and Social Psychology,* 1961, **63,** 87–94.

280. Sappenfield, B. R. Perceptual conformity and ego strength. *Perceptual and Motor Skills,* 1965, **20,** 209–210.
281. Shultz, L. B. Personality and physical variables as related to refractive errors. *American Journal of Optometry,* 1960, **37,** 551–571.
282. Van de Castle, R. L. Perceptual immaturity and acquiescence among various developmental levels. *Journal of Consulting Psychology,* 1962, **26,** 167–171.
283. Wahba, M. A multivariate analysis of a figure preference personality test. *Dissertation Abstracts,* 1966, **26,** 4821–4822.
284. Zuckerman, M., and Buss, A. Perceptual defense and "prerecognition responsivity" in relation to hostility, anxiety, and impulsivity. *Journal of Clinical Psychology,* 1960, **16,** 45–50.

Physiological Responses

285. Collins, L. G., and Stone, L. A. Family structure and pain reactivity. *Journal of Clinical Psychology,* 1966, **22,** 33.
286. Gilberstadt, H., and Maley, M. GSR, clinical state and psychiatric diagnosis. *Journal of Clinical Psychology,* 1965, **21,** 235–238.
287. Greenfield, N. S., Katz, D., Alexander, A. A., and Roessler, R. The relationship between physiological and psychological responsivity: Depression and galvanic skin response. *Journal of Nervous and Mental Disease,* 1963, **136,** 535–539.
288. Halevy, A., Moos, R. H., and Soloman, G. F. A relationship between blood serotonin concentrations and behavior in psychiatric patients. *Journal of Psychiatric Research,* 1965, **3,** 1–10.
289. Kanfer, F. H. Verbal rate, eyeblink, and content in structured psychiatric interviews. *Journal of Abnormal and Social Psychology,* 1960, **61,** 341–347.
290. Loiselle, R. H., and Mollenauer, S. Galvanic skin response to sexual stimuli in a female population. *Journal of General Psychology,* 1965, **73,** 273–278.
291. McDuffie, F. C., and McGuire, F. L. Clinical and psychological patterns in auto-erythrocyte sensitivity. *Annals of Internal Medicine,* 1965, **63,** 255–265.

Profile Similarity

292. Beier, E. G., Rossi, A. M., and Garfield, R. L. Similarity plus dissimilarity of personality: Basis for friendship? *Psychological Reports,* 1961, **8,** 8.
293. Butcher, J. N., and Messick, D. Parent-child similarity and aggression: A preliminary study. *Psychological Reports,* 1966, **18,** 440–442.

Racial and Ethnic Differences and Cross-cultural Use

294. Abe, S. K. Nisei personality characteristics as measured by the Edwards Personal Preference Schedule and Minnesota Multiphasic Personality Inventory. *Dissertation Abstracts,* 1959, **19,** 2648.
295. Altus, W. D. "Jewish" names and MMPI items. *Psychological Reports,* 1964, **14,** 870.
296. Ball, J. C. Comparison of MMPI profile differences among Negro-white adolescents. *Journal of Clinical Psychology,* 1960, **16,** 304–307.
297. Burger, A. W. De validiteit van enkele MMPI-gestoord-heidsschalen (The validity of certain MMPI measures of psychopathology). *Nederlands Tijdschrift voor de Psychologie en haar Grensgebieden,* 1967, **22,** 55–61.
298. Butcher, J., Ball, B., and Ray, E. Effects of socioeconomic level on MMPI differences in Negro-white college students. *Journal of Counseling Psychology,* 1964, **11,** 83–87.
299. Comrey, A. L. Comparison of certain personality variables in American and Italian groups. *Educational and Psychological Measurement,* 1960, **20,** 541–550.
300. Comrey, A. L., and Nencini, R. Factors in MMPI responses of Italian students. *Educational and Psychological Measurement,* 1961, **21,** 657–662.
301. Devries, A. G. Demographic variables and MMPI responses. *Journal of Clinical Psychology,* 1966, **22,** 450–452.
302. Engelsmann, F. Nase zkusenosti s Minnesotskym dotaznikem (Our experiences with the Minnesota inventory). *Československá Psychiatrie,* 1959, **55,** 108–118.
303. Harrison, R. H., and Kass, E. H. Differences between Negro and white pregnant women on the MMPI. *Journal of Consulting Psychology,* 1967, **31,** 454–463.
304. Herreid, C. F., and Herreid, J. R. Differences in MMPI scores in native and non-native Alaskans. *Journal of Social Psychology,* 1966, **70,** 191–198.
305. Hokanson, J. E., and Calden, G. Negro-white differences on the MMPI. *Journal of Clinical Psychology,* 1960, **16,** 32–33.
306. Joshi, M. C., and Singh, B. Construct validity of some MMPI scales. *Indian Psychological Review,* 1966, **3,** 67–68. (a)
307. Joshi, M. C., and Singh, B. Influence of socioeconomic background on the scores of some MMPI scales. *Journal of Social Psychology,* 1966, **70,** 241–246. (b)
308. Joshi, M. C., and Singh, B. Sex difference on MMPI scores. *Indian Psychological Review,* 1966, **2,** 150–152. (c)
309. Leu, W., Ko, Y., and Chen, W. A preliminary report of the tryout of MMPI on the freshmen of National Taiwan University. *Acta Psychologica Taiwanica,* 1966, **8,** 79–84.

310. Levinson, B. M. The MMPI in a Jewish traditional setting. *Journal of Genetic Psychology,* 1962, **101,** 25–42.
311. McDonald, R. L., and Gynther, M. D. MMPI norms for southern adolescent Negros. *Journal of Social Psychology,* 1962, **58,** 277–282.
312. McDonald, R. L., and Gynther, M. D. MMPI differences associated with sex, race, and class in two adolescent samples. *Journal of Consulting Psychology,* 1963, **27,** 112–116.
313. Miller, C., Wertz, C., and Counts, S. Racial differences on the MMPI. *Journal of Clinical Psychology,* 1961, **17,** 154–161.
314. Rosen, E., and Rizzo, G. B. Preliminary standardization of the MMPI for use in Italy: A case study in inter-cultural and intra-cultural differences. *Educational and Psychological Measurements,* 1961, **21,** 629–636.
315. Singh, B. Development of some MMPI scales in Indian conditions: A preliminary report. *Indian Psychological Review,* 1964, **1,** 75–80.
316. Singh, B. Development of MMPI profiles for different academic groups. *Indian Psychological Review,* 1965, **2,** 69–73. (a)
317. Singh, B. Item-analysis of the Indian adaptation of some MMPI scales. *Psychological Studies,* 1965, **10,** 61–65. (b)
318. Singh, B. Development of some MMPI scales in Indian conditions. *Indian Psychological Review,* 1967, **3,** 151–153.
319. Spreen, O. The translation of personality scales and their adaptation for cross-cultural and clinical use. *Acta Psychologica, Amsterdam,* 1961, **18,** 337–341.
320. Spreen, O., and Spreen, G. The MMPI in a German speaking population: Standardization report and methodological problems of cross-cultural interpretations. *Acta Psychologica, Amsterdam,* 1963, **21,** 265–273.
321. Spreen, P. O. (Ed.) *MMPI Saarbrücken: Handbuch zur Deutschen Ausqabe des Minnesota Multiphasic Personality Inventory* (Guide to the German publication of the MMPI). Bern, Switzerland: Hans Huber, 1963. 104 pp.
322. Thomas, J. E. Diagnostic clinical tests. Unpublished doctoral thesis, University of Kerala trivandrum, India, 1967.
323. Yamada, A. MMPI oyobi Rorschach test ni yoru seishin shogaisha no ruikei shidan: Seishin bunretsubyo oyobi shinkeisho ni tsuite (A typological diagnosis of mentally disturbed persons by MMPI and Rorschach test: On schizophrenics and neurotics). *Japanese Journal of Educational Psychology,* 1960, **8,** 92–105.

Suicide

324. Devries, A. G. Methodological problems in the identification of suicidal behavior by means of two personality inventories. *Dissertation Abstracts,* 1964, **24,** 5541.

325. Devries, A. G. Identification of suicidal behavior by means of the MMPI. *Psychological Reports,* 1966, **19,** 415–419.
326. Devries, A. G. Control variables in the identification of suicidal behavior. *Psychological Reports,* 1967, **20,** 1131–1135.
327. Devries, A. G., and Farberow, N. L. A multivariate profile analysis of MMPI's of suicidal and non-suicidal neuropsychiatric hospital patients. *Journal of Projective Techniques and Personality Assessment,* 1967, **31,** 81–84.
328. Devries, A. G., and Shneidman, E. S. Multiple MMPI profiles of suicidal persons. *Psychological Reports,* 1967, **21,** 401–405.
329. Farberow, N. L., and Devries, A. G. An item differentiation analysis of MMPIs of suicidal neuropsychiatric hospital patients. *Psychological Reports,* 1967, **20,** 607–617.

DIAGNOSIS OF PSYCHOPATHOLOGY

General Diagnosis of Psychopathology

330. Cone, J. D., Jr. A note on Marks' and Seeman's rules for actuarially classifying psychiatric patients. *Journal of Clinical Psychology,* 1966, **22,** 270.
331. Cooke, J. K. The MMPI in diagnosing psychological disturbance among college males. *Dissertation Abstracts,* 1965, **26,** 1771.
332. Cooke, J. K. Clinicians' decisions as a basis for deriving actuarial formulae. *Journal of Clinical Psychology,* 1967, **23,** 232–233. (a)
333. Cooke, J. K. MMPI in actuarial diagnosis of psychological disturbance among college males. *Journal of Counseling Psychology,* 1967, **14,** 474–477. (b)
334. Danet, B. N. Prediction of mental illness in college students on the basis of "nonpsychiatric" MMPI profiles. *Journal of Consulting Psychology,* 1965, **29,** 577–580.
335. Donoghue, J. R. A consideration of Taulbee and Sisson's "Configurational Analysis of MMPI Profiles of Psychiatric Groups." *Journal of Clinical Psychology,* 1962, **18,** 309–312.
336. Eisenman, R. Psychopathology and sociometric choice. *Journal of Abnormal Psychology,* 1966, **71,** 256–259.
337. Garfield, S. L., and Sineps, J. An appraisal of Taulbee and Sisson's "Configurational Analysis of MMPI Profiles of Psychiatric Groups." *Journal of Consulting Psychology,* 1959, **23,** 333–335.
338. Goldberg, L. R. Diagnosticians vs. diagnostic signs: The diagnosis of psychosis vs. neurosis from the MMPI. *Psychological Monographs,* 1965, **79** (Whole No. 602), 29 pp.
339. Gorman, J. A. MMPI and demographic patterns for discriminating abnormal behavior. *Dissertation Abstracts,* 1965, **25,** 6759.

340. Gynther, M. D. A note on the Meehl-Dahlstrom rules for discriminating psychotic from neurotic MMPI profiles. *Journal of Clinical Psychology*, 1963, **19**, 226.
341. Heilbrun, A. B., Jr. Revision of the MMPI K correction procedure for improved detection of maladjustment in a normal college population. *Journal of Consulting Psychology*, 1963, **27**, 161–165.
342. Henrichs, T. Objective configural rules for discriminating MMPI profiles in a psychiatric population. *Journal of Clinical Psychology*, 1964, **20**, 157–159.
343. Jackson, D. N., and Messick, S. Response styles on the MMPI: Comparison of clinical and normal samples. *Journal of Abnormal and Social Psychology*, 1962, **65**, 285–299.
344. Kakkar, S. B. A diagnosis of abnormal personality patterns. *MANAS*, 1963, **10**, 57–63.
345. Klett, W. G., and Vestre, N. D. Demographic and prognostic characteristics of psychiatric patients classified by gross MMPI measures. *Proceedings of the Seventy-fifth Annual Convention of the American Psychological Association*, 1967, **2**, 205–206.
346. Laforge, R. Objective estimates of clinical judgments. *Journal of Consulting Psychology*, 1961, **25**, 360–361.
347. Little, K. B., and Shneidman, E. S. Congruencies among interpretations of psychological test and anamnestic data. *Psychological Monographs*, 1959, **73**, 42 pp.
348. Loy, D. L. The validity of the Taulbee-Sisson MMPI scale pairs in female psychiatric groups. *Journal of Clinical Psychology*, 1959, **15**, 306–307.
349. Lutzker, D. R. A validity study of Tamkin's "MMPI scale measuring severity of psychopathology." *Journal of Clinical Psychology*, 1961, **17**, 289–290.
350. Meehl, P. E., and Dahlstrom, W. G. Objective configural rules for discriminating psychotic from neurotic MMPI profiles. *Journal of Consulting Psychology*, 1960, **24**, 375–387.
351. Moos, R. H. Effects of training on students' test interpretations. *Journal of Projective Techniques*, 1962, **26**, 310–317.
352. Pauker, J. D. Identification of MMPI profile types in a female, inpatient, psychiatric setting using the Marks and Seeman rules. *Journal of Consulting Psychology*, 1966, **30**, 90.
353. Segal, B. E., and Phillips, D. L. Work, play, and emotional disturbance. *Archives of General Psychiatry*, 1967, **16**, 173–179.
354. Shaffer, J. W., Ota, K. Y., and Hanlon, T. E. The comparative validity of several MMPI indices of severity of psychopathology. *Journal of Clinical Psychology*, 1964, **20**, 467–473.
355. Silver, R. J., and Sines, L. K. Diagnostic efficiency of the MMPI with and without the *K* correction. *Journal of Clinical Psychology*, 1962, **18**, 312–314.
356. Tamkin, A. S. An MMPI scale measuring severity of psychopathology. *Journal of Clinical Psychology*, 1959, **15**, 56.

357. Vestre, N. D., and Lorei, T. W. Relationships between social history factors and psychiatric symptoms. *Journal of Abnormal Psychology,* 1967, **72,** 247–250.

Alcoholism and Drug Addiction

358. Ballard, R. G. The interrelatedness of alcoholism and marital conflict: III. The interaction between marital conflict and alcoholism as seen through MMPI's of marriage partners. Symposium, 1958, *American Journal of Orthopsychiatry,* 1959, **29,** 528–546.
359. Barry, J. R., Anderson, H. E., Jr., and Thomason, O. B. MMPI characteristics of alcoholic males who are well and poorly adjusted in marriage. *Journal of Clinical Psychology,* 1967, **23,** 355–360.
360. Ellinwood, E. H., Jr. Amphetamine psychosis: I. Description of the individuals and process. *Journal of Nervous and Mental Disease,* 1967, **144,** 273–283.
361. Gilbert, J. G., and Lombardi, D. N. Personality characteristics of young male narcotic addicts. *Journal of Consulting Psychology,* 1967, **31,** 536–538.
362. Hill, H. E., Haertzen, C. A., and Glaser, R. Personality characteristics of narcotic addicts as indicated by the MMPI. *Journal of General Psychology,* 1960, **62,** 127–139.
363. Kogan, K. L., and Jackson, J. K. Stress, personality and emotional disturbance in wives of alcoholics. *Quarterly Journal of Studies on Alcohol,* 1965, **26,** 486–495.
364. Korman, M. Two MMPI scales for alcoholism: What do they measure? *Journal of Clinical Psychology,* 1960, **16,** 296–298.
365. MacAndrew, C. The differentiation of male alcoholic outpatients from nonalcoholic psychiatric outpatients by means of the MMPI. *Quarterly Journal of Studies on Alcohol.* 1965, **26,** 238–246.
366. MacAndrew, C. Self-reports of male alcoholics: A dimensional analysis of certain differences from nonalcoholic male psychiatric outpatients. *Quarterly Journal of Studies on Alcohol.* 1967, **28,** 43–51.
367. McGinnis, C. A., and Ryan, C. W. The influence of age on MMPI scores of chronic alcoholics. *Journal of Clinical Psychology,* 1965, **21,** 271–272.
368. Muzekari, L. H. The MMPI in predicting treatment outcome in alcoholism. *Journal of Consulting Psychology,* 1965, **29,** 281.
369. Olson, R. W. MMPI sex differences in narcotic addicts. *Journal of General Psychology,* 1964, **71,** 257–266.
370. Palola, E. G., Jackson, J. K., and Kelleher, D. Defensiveness in alcoholics: Measures based on the Minnesota Multiphasic Personality Inventory. *Journal of Health and Human Behavior,* 1961, **2,** 185–189.

371. Rae, J. B., and Forbes, A. R. Clinical psychometric characteristics of the wives of alcoholics. *British Journal of Psychiatry,* 1966, **112,** 197–200.

372. Rotman, S. R., and Vestre, N. D. The use of the MMPI in identifying problem drinkers among psychiatric hospital admissions. *Journal of Clinical Psychology,* 1964, **20,** 526–530.

373. Sikes, M. P., Faibish, G., and Valles, J. Evaluation of an intensive alcoholic treatment program. *Proceedings of the Seventy-third Annual Convention of the American Psychological Association,* 1965, 275–276.

374. Sinnett, E. R. The prediction of irregular discharge among alcoholic patients. *Journal of Social Psychology,* 1961, **55,** 231–235.

375. Whisler, R. H., and Cantor, J. M. The MacAndrew Alcoholism Scale: A cross-validation in a domiciliary setting. *Journal of Clinical Psychology,* 1966, **22,** 311–312.

376. Zelen, S. L., Fox, J., Gould, E., and Olson, R. W. Sex-contingent differences between male and female alcoholics. *Journal of Clinical Psychology,* 1966, **22,** 160–165.

Brain Damage and Neurological Abnormalities

377. Costa, L. D., Cox, M., and Katzman, R. Relationship between MMPI variables and percentage and amplitude of EEG alpha activity. *Journal of Consulting Psychology,* 1965, **29,** 90.

378. Doehring, D. G., and Reitan, R. M. MMPI performance of aphasic and nonaphasic brain-damaged patients. *Journal of Clinical Psychology,* 1960, **16,** 307–309.

379. Hovey, H. B. Brain lesions and five MMPI items. *Journal of Consulting Psychology,* 1964, **28,** 78–79.

380. Hovey, H. B. Reply to Weingold, Dawson, and Kael. *Psychological Reports,* 1965, **16,** 1122.

381. Jortner, S. A test of Hovey's MMPI scale for CNS disorder. *Journal of Clinical Psychology,* 1965, **21,** 285.

382. Krug, R. S. MMPI response inconsistency of brain damaged individuals. *Journal of Clinical Psychology,* 1967, **23,** 366.

383. Meier, M. J., and French, L. A. Caudality scale changes following unilateral temporal lobectomy. *Journal of Clinical Psychology,* 1964, **20,** 464–467.

384. Meier, M. J., and French, L. A. Some personality correlates of unilateral and bilateral EEG abnormalities in psychomotor epileptics. *Journal of Clinical Psychology,* 1965, **21,** 3–9.

385. Shaw, D. J., and Matthews, C. G. Differential MMPI performance of brain-damaged vs. pseudo-neurologic groups. *Journal of Clinical Psychology,* 1965, **21,** 405–408.

386. Vogel, W. Some effects of brain lesions on MMPI profiles. *Journal of Consulting Psychology,* 1962, **26,** 412–415.
387. Weingold, H. P., Dawson, J. G., and Kael, H. C. Further examination of Hovey's "index" for identification of brain lesions: Validation study. *Psychological Reports,* 1965, **16,** 1098.
388. Zimmerman, I. L. Residual effects of brain damage and five MMPI items. *Journal of Consulting Psychology,* 1965, **29,** 394.

Computer Interpretation

389. Finney, J. C. Programmed interpretation of MMPI and CPI. *Archives of General Psychiatry,* 1966, **15,** 75–81.
390. Finney, J. C. Methodological problems in programmed composition of psychological test reports. *Behavioral Science,* 1967, **12,** 142–152.
391. Fowler, R. D., Jr. MMPI computer interpretation for college counseling. *Proceedings of the Seventy-fifth Annual Convention of the American Psychological Association,* 1967, **2,** 363–364.
392. Glueck, B. C., Jr., and Reznikoff, M. Comparison of computer-derived personality profile and projective psychological test findings. *American Journal of Psychiatry,* 1965, **121,** 1156–1161.
393. Gravitz, M. A. A new computerized method for the fully automated printout of MMPI graphic profiles. *Journal of Clinical Psychology,* 1967, **23,** 101–102.
394. Hovey, H. B., and Lewis, E. G. Semiautomatic interpretation of the MMPI. *Journal of Clinical Psychology,* 1967, **23,** (Monogr. Suppl.) **15,** 123–134.
395. Kleinmuntz, B. Personality test interpretation by digital computer. *Science,* 1963, **139,** 416–418.
396. Kleinmuntz, B. MMPI decision rules for the identification of college maladjustment: A digital computer approach. *Psychological Monographs,* 1964, **77,** (4, Whole No. 557), 1–22.
397. Kleinmuntz, B., and Alexander, L. B. Computer program for the Meehl-Dahlstrom MMPI profile rules. *Educational and Psychological Measurement,* 1962, **22,** 193–199.
398. Pearson, J. S., et al. Development of a computer system for scoring and interpretation of Minnesota Multiphasic Personality Inventories in a medical clinic. *Annals of the New York Academy of Sciences,* 1965, **126,** 684–692.
399. Rome, H. P., Swenson, W. M., Mataya, P., McCarthy, C. E., Pearson, J. S., Keating, F. R., Jr., and Hathaway, S. R. Symposium on automation techniques in personality assessment. *Proceedings of the staff meetings of the Mayo Clinic,* 1962, **37,** 61–82.
400. Swenson, W. M., Rome, H. P., Pearson, J. S., and Brannick, T. L. A totally automated psychological test. *Journal of the American Medical Association,* 1965, **191,** 925–927.

401. Wiggins, N., and Hoffman, P. J. Models for simulating clinical judgments of the MMPI. *Proceedings of the Seventy-fourth Annual Convention of the American Psychological Association,* 1966, 237–238.

Crime and Delinquency

402. Apfeldorf, M., Acheinker, J. L., and Whitman, G. I. MMPI responses of aged domiciled veterans with disciplinary records. *Journal of Consulting Psychology,* 1966, **30,** 362.
403. Ball, J. C. *Social deviancy and adolescent personality.* Lexington: University of Kentucky Press, 1962. 119 pp.
404. Beyer, A. Estudio controlado de algunas escalas del MMPI y rendimiento en conducta en un grupo de adolescentes (A controlled study of some MMPI scales and deportment in a group of adolescents). *Revista Interamericana de Psichologia,* 1967, **1,** 51–53.
405. Briggs, P. F., Johnson, R., and Wirt, R. D. Achievement among delinquency-prone adolescents. *Journal of Clinical Psychology,* 1962, **18,** 305–309.
406. Briggs, P. F., Wirt, R. D., and Johnson, R. An application of prediction tables to the study of delinquency. *Journal of Consulting Psychology,* 1961, **25,** 46–50.
407. Caditz, S. B. Effects of a forestry camp experience on the personality of delinquent boys. *Journal of Clinical Psychology,* 1961, **17,** 78–81.
408. Caldwell, M. G. Personality trends in the youthful male offender. *Journal of Criminal Law and Criminology,* 1959, **49,** 405–416.
409. Craddick, R. A. Selection of psychopathic from nonpsychopathic prisoners within a Canadian prison. *Psychological Reports,* 1962, **10,** 495–499.
410. Craddick, R. A. MMPI scatter of psychopathic and nonpsychopathic prisoners. *Psychological Reports,* 1963, **12,** 238.
411. Edwards, J. A. Rehabilitation potential in prison inmates as measured by the MMPI. *Journal of Criminal Law, Criminology and Police Science,* 1963, **54,** 181–185.
412. Erikson, R. V., and Roberts, A. H. An MMPI comparison of two groups of institutionalized delinquents. *Journal of Projective Techniques and Personality Assessment,* 1966, **30,** 163–166.
413. Gough, H. G., Wenk, E. A., and Rozynko, V. V. Parole outcome as predicted from the CPI, the MMPI, and a Base Expectancy table. *Journal of Abnormal Psychology,* 1965, **70,** 432–441.
414. Grant, T. F. Personality characteristics of youthful offenders expressing anxiety and not expressing anxiety in the MMPI and interview situations. *Dissertation Abstracts,* 1965, **25,** 7378.
415. Gynther, M. D., and McDonald, R. L. Personality characteristics of prisoners, psychiatric patients, and student nurses as depicted

by the Leary system. *Journal of General Psychology,* 1961, **64,** 387–395.

416. Hathaway, S. R., and Monachesi, E. D. *An atlas of juvenile MMPI profiles.* Minneapolis: University of Minnesota Press, 1961. 402 pp.

417. Hathaway, S. R., and Monachesi, E. D. *Adolescent personality and behavior.* Minneapolis: University of Minnesota Press, 1963.

418. Hathaway, S. R., Monachesi, E. D., and Erickson, M. L. Relationship of college attendance to personality characteristics and earlier delinquent behavior. *Sociological Quarterly,* 1960, **1,** 97–106.

419. Herzog, E. Juvenile delinquency: Facts and facets. Vol. 5. Identifying potential delinquents. Washington, D.C.: United States Children's Bureau, 1960. 6 pp.

420. Jurjevich, R. M. Normative data for the clinical and additional MMPI scales for a population of delinquent girls. *Journal of General Psychology,* 1963, **69,** 143–146.

421. Kanun, C., and Monachesi, E. D. Delinquency and the validating scales of the Minnesota Multiphasic Personality Inventory. *Journal of Criminal Law, Criminology and Police Science,* 1960, **50,** 525–534.

422. Kingsley, L. MMPI profiles of psychopaths and prisoners. *Journal of Clinical Psychology,* 1960, **16,** 302–304.

423. Lamb, H. W. A multitest approach to the analysis of personality patterns of delinquents. *Pennsylvania Psychiatric Quarterly,* 1966, **6,** 26–40.

424. Lawton, M. P., and Kleban, M. H. Prisoners' faking on the MMPI. *Journal of Clinical Psychology,* 1965, **21,** 269–271.

425. Lefkowitz, M. M. MMPI scores of juvenile delinquents adjusting to institutionalization. *Psychological Reports,* 1966, **19,** 911–914.

426. Mandel, N. G., and Barron, A. J. The MMPI and criminal recidivism. *Journal of Criminal Law, Criminology, and Police Science,* 1966, **57,** 35–38.

427. McKegney, F. P. An item analysis of the MMPI *F* scale in juvenile delinquents. *Journal of Clinical Psychology,* 1965, **21,** 201–205.

428. Morgan, P. K. Attitudes, attitude change, and group conformity in the psychopathic personality. *Dissertation Abstracts,* 1961, **21,** 2367–2368.

429. Murphree, H. B., Karabelas, M. J., and Bryan, L. L. Scores of inmates of a federal penitentiary on two scales of the MMPI. *Journal of Clinical Psychology,* 1962, **18,** 137–139.

430. Panton, J. H. The response of prison inmates to MMPI subscales. *Journal of Social Therapy,* 1959, **5,** 233–237. (a)

431. Panton, J. H. The response of prison inmates to seven new MMPI scales. *Journal of Clinical Psychology,* 1959, **15,** 196–197. (b)

432. Panton, J. H. MMPI code configurations as related to measures of

intelligence among a state prison population. *Journal of Social Psychology,* 1960, **51,** 403–407.

433. Panton, J. H. The identification of habitual criminalism with the MMPI. *Journal of Clinical Psychology,* 1962, **18,** 133–136.

434. Panton, J. H. Use of the MMPI as an index to a successful parole. *Journal of Criminal Law, Criminology and Police Science,* 1962, **53,** 484–488.

435. Persons, R. W. Psychological and behavioral change in delinquents following psychotherapy. *Journal of Clinical Psychology,* 1966, **22,** 337–340.

436. Randolph, M. H., Richardson, H., and Johnson, R. C. A comparison of social and solitary male delinquents. *Journal of Consulting Psychology,* 1961, **25,** 293–295.

437. Richardson, H., and Roebuck, J. Minnesota Multiphasic Personality Inventory and California Psychological Inventory differences between delinquents and their nondelinquent siblings. *Proceedings of the Seventy-third Annual Convention of the American Psychological Association,* 1965, 255–256.

438. Rosen, E., and Mink, S. H. Desirability of personality traits as perceived by prisoners. *Journal of Clinical Psychology,* 1961, **17,** 147–151.

439. Rowley, V. N., and Stone, F. B. MMPI differences between emotionally disturbed and delinquent adolescents. *Journal of Clinical Psychology,* 1962, **18,** 481–484.

440. Shinohara, M., and Jenkins, R. L. MMPI study of three types of delinquents. *Journal of Clinical Psychology,* 1967, **23,** 156–163.

441. Silver, A. W. TAT and MMPI Psychopath Deviant scale differences between delinquent and nondelinquent adolescents. *Journal of Consulting Psychology,* 1963, **27,** 370.

442. Steininger, E. H. Changes in the MMPI profiles of first prison offenders during their first year of imprisonment. *Dissertation Abstracts,* 1959, **19,** 3394–3395.

443. Stone, F. B., and Rowley, V. N. MMPI differences between emotionally disturbed and delinquent adolescent girls. *Journal of Clinical Psychology,* 1963, **19,** 227–230.

444. Volkman, A. P. A matched-group personality comparison of delinquent and non-delinquent juveniles. *Social Problems,* 1958–59, **6,** 238–245.

445. Watman, W. A. The relationship between acting out behavior and some psychological test indices in a prison population. *Journal of Clinical Psychology,* 1966, **22,** 279–280.

446. Wattron, J. B. A prison maladjustment scale for the MMPI. *Journal of Clinical Psychology,* 1963, **19,** 109–110.

447. Wirt, R. D., and Briggs, P. F. Personality and environmental factors in the development of delinquency. *Psychological Monographs,* 1959, **73,** (15, Whole No. 485), 47 pp.

Epilepsy

448. Aaronson, B. S. Hypochondriasis and somatic seizure auras. *Journal of Clinical Psychology,* 1959, **15,** 450–451.
449. Hovey, H. B., Kooi, K. A., and Thomas, M. H. MMPI profiles of epileptics. *Journal of Consulting Psychology,* 1959, **23,** 155–159.
450. Jordan, E. J., Jr. MMPI profiles of epileptics: A further evaluation. *Journal of Consulting Psychology,* 1963, **27,** 267–269.
451. Klove, H., and Doehring, D. G. MMPI in epileptic groups with differential etiology. *Journal of Clinical Psychology,* 1962, **18,** 149–153.

Neuroses

452. Blackburn, R. Emotionality, repression-sensitization, and maladjustment. *British Journal of Psychiatry,* 1965, **111,** 399–404.
453. Carr, J. E., Brownsberger, C. N., and Rutherford, R. C. Characteristics of symptom-matched psychogenic and "real" pain patients on the MMPI. *Proceedings of the Seventy-fourth Annual Convention of the American Psychological Association,* 1966, 215–216.
454. Corah, N. L. Neuroticism and extraversion in the MMPI empirical validation and exploration. *British Journal of Social and Clinical Psychology,* 1964, **3,** 168–174.
455. Dana, R. H., and Christiansen, K. Repression and psychopathology. *Journal of Projective Techniques,* 1959, **23,** 412–416.
456. Delay, J., Klotz, H. P., Pichot, P., Weil, F., and Perse, J. Tetanie et hysterie. (Tetany and hysteria). *Encephale,* 1961, **50,** 437–449.
457. Endicott, N. A., and Jortner, S. Correlates of somatic concern derived from psychological tests. *Journal of Nervous and Mental Disease,* 1967, **144,** 133–138.
458. Foulds, G. A., and Caine, T. M. Symptom clusters and personality types among psychoneurotic men compared with women. *Journal of Mental Science,* 1959, **105,** 469–475.
459. Gottesman, I. I. Differential inheritance of the psychoneuroses. *Eugenics Quarterly,* 1962, **9,** 223–227.
460. Grater, H. Impulse repression and emotional adjustment. *Journal of Consulting Psychology,* 1960, **24,** 144–149.
461. Kyriazis, P. W. The relation between measured hypochondriasis and semantic differential profiles (among college students). *George Washington University Bulletin, Summaries of Doctoral Dissertations,* 1965, **65,** 34–35.
462. Martin, D. V., and Caine, T. M. Personality change in the treatment of chronic neurosis in a therapeutic community. *British Journal of Psychiatry,* 1963, **109** (Whole No. 459), 267–272.
463. O'Connor, J. P., and Stefic, E. C. Some patterns of hypochondriasis.

Educational and Psychological Measurement, 1959, **19,** 363–371.
464. Popplestone, J. A. A scale to assess hyperchondriasis: The converse of hypochondriasis. *Psychological Record,* 1963, **13,** 32–38.
465. Tuthill, E. W., Overall, J. E., and Hollister, L. E. Subjective correlates of clinically manifested anxiety and depression. *Psychological Reports,* 1967, **20,** 535–542.

Physical Disorders

466. Archibald, H. C., Bell, D., Miller, C., and Thompson, C. W. Psychosomatic V. *Journal of Psychology,* 1961, **52,** 281–285.
467. Aronson, A. E., Peterson, H. W., Jr., and Litin, E. M. Psychiatric symptomatology in functional dysphonia and aphonia. *Journal of Speech and Hearing Disorders,* 1966, **31,** 115–127.
468. Blackman, S., and Goldstein, K. M. A comparison of MMPI's of enuretic with non-enuretic adults. *Journal of Clinical Psychology,* 1965, **21,** 282–283.
469. Crumpton, E., Wine, D. B., and Grott, H. MMPI profiles of obese men and six other diagnostic categories. *Psychological Reports,* 1966, **19,** 1110.
470. Davis, C. H., and Jenkins, C. D. Mental stress and oral disease. *Journal of Dental Research,* 1962, **41,** 1045–1049.
471. Feingold, B. F., Gorman, F. S., Singer, M. T., and Schlesinger, K. Psychological studies of allergic women. *Psychosomatic Medicine,* 1962, **24,** 193–202.
472. Fisher, J. Some MMPI dimensions of physical and psychological illness. *Journal of Clinical Psychology,* 1964, **20,** 369–375.
473. Freeman, E. H., Gorman, F. J., Singer, M. T., Affelder, M. T., and Feingold, B. F. Personality variables and allergic skin reactivity: A cross-validation study. *Psychosomatic Medicine,* 1967, **29,** 312–322.
474. Gilberstadt, H. A modal MMPI profile type in neurodermatitis. *Psychosomatic Medicine,* 1962, **24,** 471–476.
475. Gilberstadt, H., and Farkas, E. Another look at MMPI profile types in multiple sclerosis. *Journal of Consulting Psychology,* 1961, **25,** 440–444.
476. Gilberstadt, H., and Jancis, M. "Organic" vs. "functional" diagnoses from 1-3 MMPI profiles. *Journal of Clinical Psychology,* 1967, **23,** 480–483.
477. Gilberstadt, H., and Sako, Y. Intellectual and personality changes following open-heart surgery. *Archives of General Psychiatry,* 1967, **16,** 210–214.
478. Harris, J. G., Jr. Rorschach and MMPI responses in severe airsickness. *USN School of Aviation Medicine Research Report,* 1963. Proj. MR005. 13-5001, Subtask 1, Report No. 22, 13 pp.

479. Hooke, J. F., and Marks, P. A. MMPI characteristics of pregnancy. *Journal of Clinical Psychology,* 1962, **18,** 316–317.
480. Hovey, H. B. MMPI testing for multiple sclerosis. *Psychological Reports,* 1967, **21,** 599–600.
481. Imboden, J. B., Canter, A., Cluff, L. E., and Trever, R. W. Brucellosis: III. Psychologic aspects of delayed convalescence. *AMA Archives of Internal Medicine,* 1959, **103,** 406–414.
482. Kodman, F., Jr., and McDaniel, E. Further investigation of the reliability of an MMPI scale for auditory malingerers. *Journal of Clinical Psychology,* 1960, **16,** 451.
483. Kodman, F., Jr., Sedlacek, G., and McDaniel, E. Performance of suspected auditory malingerers on the subtle-obvious keys of MMPI. *Journal of Clinical Psychology,* 1960, **16,** 193–195.
484. Lair, C. V., and Trapp, E. P. The differential diagnostic value of MMPI with somatically disturbed patients. *Journal of Clinical Psychology,* 1962, **18,** 146–147.
485. Lanyon, R. I. The MMPI and prognosis in stuttering therapy. *Journal of Speech and Hearing Disorders,* 1966, **31,** 186–191.
486. Levitt, H., and Fellner, C. MMPI profiles of three obesity subgroups. *Journal of Consulting Psychology,* 1965, **29,** 91.
487. Ludy, E. D., Ware, J. G., Senf, R., and Frohman, C. E. Stress and the precipitation of acute intermittent porphyria. *Psychosomatic Medicine,* 1959, **21,** 34–39.
488. Lupton, D. E. A preliminary investigation of the personality of female temporomandibular joint dysfunction patients. *Psychotherapy and Psychosomatics,* 1966, **14,** 199–216.
489. Maier, L. R., and Abidin, R. R. Validation attempts of Hovey's five item MMPI index for CNS disorders. *Journal of Consulting Psychology,* 1967, **31,** 542.
490. Markwell, E. D., Jr. Autonomic nervous system measures and factor correlates with personality indices in a tuberculous population. *Journal of Consulting Psychology,* 1962, **26,** 194.
491. McCall, C. M., Jr., Szmyd, L., and Ritter, R. M. A study of personality characteristics in patients with temporomandibular joint symptoms. *USAF School of Aviation Medical Report,* 1960, No. 60-46, 8 pp.
492. Moos, R. H., and Solomon, G. F. Minnesota Multiphasic Personality Inventory response patterns in patients with rheumatoid arthritis. *Journal of Psychosomatic Research,* 1964, **8,** 17–27.
493. Ostfeld, A. M., Lebovits, B. Z., Shekelle, R. B., and Paul, O. A prospective study of the relationship between personality and coronary heart disease. *Journal of Chronic Diseases,* 1964, **17,** 265–276.
494. Schmale, A. H., Jr., and Iker, H. P. The affect of hopelessness and the development of cancer. *Psychosomatic Medicine,* 1966, **28,** 714–721.
495. Shekelle, R. B., and Ostfeld, A. M. Psychometric evaluations in cardio-

vascular epidemiology. *Annals of New York Academy of Sciences,* 1965, **126,** 696–705.
496. Smith, C. M., and Hamilton, J. Psychological factors in the narcolepsy-cataplexy syndrome. *Psychosomatic Medicine,* 1959, **21,** 40–49.
497. Smith, R. E. A Minnesota Multiphasic Personality Inventory profile of allergy. *Psychosomatic Medicine,* 1962, **24,** 203–209. (a)
498. Smith, R. E. A Minnesota Multiphasic Personality Inventory profile of allergy: II. Conscious conflict. *Psychosomatic Medicine,* 1962, **24,** 543–553. (b)
499. Werkman, S. L., and Greenberg, E. S. Personality and interest patterns in obese adolescent girls. *Psychosomatic Medicine,* 1967, **39,** 72–80.
500. Zimet, C. N., and Berger, A. S. Emotional factors in primary glaucoma. *Psychosomatic Medicine,* 1960, **22,** 391–399.

Psychoses

501. Adams, A., and Foulds, G. A. Personality and the paranoid depressive psychoses. *British Journal of Psychiatry,* 1963, **109** (Whole No. 459), 273–278.
502. Affleck, D. C., and Garfield, S. L. The prediction of psychosis with the MMPI. *Journal of Clinical Psychology,* 1960, **16,** 24–26.
503. Bhaskaran, K. Borderline schizophrenia. *Pratibha,* 1959, **2,** 8–13.
504. Dahlstrom, W. G., and Prange, A. J. Characteristics of depressive and paranoid schizophrenic reactions on the Minnesota Multiphasic Personality Inventory. *Journal of Nervous and Mental Disease,* 1960, **131,** 513–522.
505. Eichman, W. J. Discrimination of female schizophrenia with configural analysis of the MMPI profile. *Journal of Consulting Psychology,* 1959, **23,** 442–447.
506. Foulds, G. A., and Caine, T. M. The assessment of some symptoms and signs of depression in women. *Journal of Mental Science,* 1959, **105,** 182–189.
507. Gross, L. R. MMPI *L-F-K* relationships with criteria of behavioral disturbance and social adjustment in a schizophrenic population. *Journal of Consulting Psychology,* 1959, **23,** 319–323.
508. Hama, H. Evaluation of clinical depression by means of a Japanese translation of the Minnesota Multiphasic Personality Inventory. *Psychologia: An International Journal of Psychology in the Orient,* 1966, **9,** 165–176.
509. Havener, P. H., and Izard, C. E. Unrealistic self-enhancement in paranoid schizophrenics. *Journal of Consulting Psychology,* 1962, **26,** 65–68.
510. Higgins, J., Mednick, S. A., and Philip, E. J. The Schizophrenia scale of the MMPI and life adjustment in schizophrenia. *Psychology,* 1965, **2,** 26–27.

511. Holroyd, R. G. Prediction of defensive paranoid schizophrenics using the MMPI. *Dissertation Abstracts,* 1964, **25,** 2048–2049.

512. Kiresuk, T. J. The effect of test sophistication on the diagnostic validity of the Minnesota Multiphasic Personality Inventory and the Rorschach with paranoid schizophrenics. *Dissertation Abstracts,* 1962, **22,** 2875.

513. Kleinmuntz, B. Two types of paranoid schizophrenia. *Journal of Clinical Psychology,* 1960, **16,** 310–312.

514. Klett, W. G. The effect of historically based inferences on the behavior of withdrawn psychiatric patients, *Journal of Clinical Psychology,* 1966, **22,** 427–429.

515. Olden, G. W. The influence of context on the Depression scale of the MMPI in a psychotic population. *Journal of Consulting Psychology,* 1961, **25,** 178–179.

516. McKeever, W. F., May, P. R. A., and Tuma, A. H. Prognosis in schizophrenia: Prediction of length of hospitalization from psychological test variables. *Journal of Clinical Psychology,* 1965, **21,** 214–221.

517. Meehl, P. E. A comparison of clinicians with five statistical methods of identifying psychotic MMPI profiles. *Journal of Counseling Psychology,* 1959, **6,** 102–109.

518. Porer, K. D. A comparison of three methods for developing MMPI indicators of psychosis and an attempt to demonstrate a "Bootstraps Effect." *Dissertation Abstracts,* 1964, **24,** 5550.

519. Sines, L. K., and Silver, R. J. An index of psychopathology (*IP*) derived from clinicians' judgments of MMPI profiles. *Journal of Clinical Psychology,* 1963, **19,** 324–326.

520. Walton, D., Mather, M., and Black, D. A. The validity of the Meehl MMPI psychotic scale in the diagnosis of schizophrenia. *Journal of Mental Science,* 1959, **105,** 869–871.

521. Wilson, I. C., Alltop, L. B., and Buffaloe, W. J. Parental bereavement in childhood: MMPI profiles in a depressed population. *British Journal of Psychiatry,* 1967, **113,** 761–764.

522. Winter, W. D., and Stortroen, M. A. A comparison of several MMPI indices to differentiate psychotics from normals. *Journal of Clinical Psychology,* 1963, **19,** 220–223.

Sexual Deviation

523. Aaronson, B. S., and Grumpelt, H. R. Homosexuality and some MMPI measures of masculinity-femininity. *Journal of Clinical Psychology,* 1961, **17,** 245–247.

524. Blank, L., and Roth, R. H. Voyeurism and exhibitionism. *Proceedings of the Seventy-fourth Annual Convention of the American Psychological Association,* 1966, 225–226.

525. Cutter, F. Psychological changes in sexual psychopaths. *Psychological Newsletter,* New York University, 1959, **10,** 322–329.
526. Dean, R. B., and Richardson, H. Analysis of MMPI profiles of forty college-educated overt male homosexuals. *Journal of Consulting Psychology,* 1964, **28,** 483–486.
527. Dean, R. B., and Richardson, H. On MMPI high-point codes of homosexual versus heterosexual males. *Journal of Consulting Psychology,* 1966, **30,** 558–560.
528. Friberg, R. R. Measures of homosexuality: Cross-validation of two MMPI scales and implications for usage. *Journal of Consulting Psychology,* 1967, **31,** 88–91.
529. Krippner, S. The identification of male homosexuality with the MMPI. *Journal of Clinical Psychology,* 1964, **20,** 159–161.
530. Panton, J. R. A new MMPI scale for the identification of homosexuality. *Journal of Clinical Psychology,* 1960, **16,** 17–21.
531. Taylor, A. J. W., and MacLachlan, D. G. MMPI profiles of six transvestites. *Journal of Clinical Psychology,* 1963, **19,** 330–332.
532. Yamahiro, R. S., and Griffith, R. M. Validity of two indices of sexual deviancy. *Journal of Clinical Psychology,* 1960, **16,** 21–24.
533. Zucker, R. A., and Manosevitz, M. MMPI patterns of overt male homosexuals: Reinterpretation and comment on Dean and Richardson's study. *Journal of Consulting Psychology,* 1966, **30,** 555–557.

MMPI and Treatment

534. Borghi, J. H. An investigation of treatment attrition in psychotherapy. *Dissertation Abstracts,* 1965, **26,** 1770–1771.
535. Carson, R. C., and Heine, R. W. Similarity and success in therapeutic dyads. *Journal of Consulting Psychology,* 1962, **26,** 38–43.
536. Christensen, C. M., and MacDonald, J. Directed cognition and personality change. *Alberta Journal of Educational Research,* 1960, **6,** 211–217.
537. Forsyth, R. P., Jr. MMPI and demographic correlates of posthospital adjustment in neuropsychiatric patients. *Dissertation Abstracts,* 1961, **21,** 2783–2784.
538. Forsyth, R. P., Jr. MMPI and demographic correlates of posthospital adjustment in neuropsychiatric patients. *Psychological Reports,* 1965, **16,** 355–366.
539. Goldstein, A. P. Patients' expectancies and non-specific therapy as a basis for (un)spontaneous remission. *Journal of Clinical Psychology,* 1960, **16,** 399–403.
540. Hedstrom, L. J. Prediction of duration of psychothotherapy by the MMPI and ratings of initial interview behavior and socio-economic status. *Dissertation Abstracts,* 1966, **26,** 6848.
541. Johnston, R., and McNeal, B. F. Combined MMPI and demographic

data in predicting length of neuropsychiatric hospital stay. *Journal of Consulting Psychology,* 1964, **28,** 64–70.
542. Johnston, R., and McNeal, B. F. Residual psychopathology in released psychiatric patients and its relation to readmission. *Journal of Abnormal Psychology,* 1965, **70,** 337–342.
543. Sines, L. K., Silver, R. J., and Lucero, R. J. The effect of therapeutic intervention by untrained "therapists." *Journal of Clinical Psychology,* 1961, **17,** 394–396.
544. Wiener, D. N. Personality correlates of type of outpatient psychotherapy chosen. *American Journal of Orthopsychiatry,* 1960, **30,** 819–826.

GENERAL STUDIES

Additional Scale Development

545. Aaronson, B. S. A comparison of two MMPI measures of masculinity-femininity. *Journal of Clinical Psychology,* 1959, **15,** 48–50.
546. Anker, J. M. Chronicity of neuropsychiatric hospitalization: A predictive scale. *Journal of Consulting Psychology,* 1961, **25,** 425–432.
547. Astin, A. W. A factor study of the MMPI psychopathic deviate scale. *Journal of Consulting Psychology,* 1959, **23,** 550–554.
548. Astin, A. W. A note on the MMPI psychopathic deviate scale. *Educational and Psychological Measurement,* 1961, **21,** 895–897.
549. Baker, J. N. Effectiveness of certain MMPI dissimulation scales under "real-life" conditions. *Journal of Counseling Psychology,* 1967, **14,** 286–292.
550. Ball, J. C., and Carroll, D. Analysis of MMPI cannot say scores in an adolescent population. *Journal of Clinical Psychology,* 1960, **16,** 30–31.
551. Barrows, G. A., and Zuckerman, M. Construct validity of three masculinity-femininity tests. *Journal of Consulting Psychology,* 1960, **24,** 441–445.
552. Bendig, A. M. An inter-item factor analysis of two "lie" scales. *Psychological Newsletter,* New York University, 1959, **10,** 299–303.
553. Blazer, J. A. MMPI interpretation in outline: I. The ? scale. *Psychology,* 1965, **2,** (2), 23–24. (a)
554. Blazer, J. A. MMPI interpretation in outline: II. The *L* scale. *Psychology,* 1965, **2,** (3), 2–7. (b)
555. Blazer, J. A. MMPI interpretation in outline: III. The *F* scale. *Psychology,* 1965, **2,** (4), 2–9. (c)
556. Blazer, J. A. MMPI interpretation in outline: IV. The *K* scale. *Psychology,* 1966, **3,** 4–11.
557. Blumberg, S. MMPI *F* scale as an indicator of severity of psychopathology. *Journal of Clinical Psychology,* 1967, **23,** 96–99.

558. Briggs, P. F., and Tellegen, A. An abbreviation of the social introversion scale for 373-item MMPI. *Journal of Clinical Psychology,* 1967, **23,** 189–191.
559. Brown, R. A., and Goodstein, L. D. Adjective check list correlates of extreme scores on the MMPI depression scale. *Journal of Clinical Psychology,* 1962, **18,** 477–481.
560. Byrne, D. The Repression-Sensitization Scale: Rationale, reliability and validity. *Journal of Personality,* 1961, **29,** 334–349.
561. Byrne, D. Repression-Sensitization chapter. In B. Maher (Ed.), *Progress in experimental personality research.* Vol. 1. New York: Academic Press, 1964. Pp. 169–202.
562. Byrne, D., Barry, J., and Nelson, D. Relation of the revised Repression-Sensitization Scale to measures of self-description. *Psychological Reports,* 1963, **13,** 323–334.
563. Canter, A. A brief note on shortening Barron's Ego Strength scale. *Journal of Clinical Psychology,* 1965, **21,** 285–286.
564. Cooke, R. M. An "Internalization" scale based on the Minnesota Multiphasic Personality Inventory (MMPI) *Dissertation Abstracts,* 1964, **25,** 3105.
565. Costa, L. D., London, P., and Levita, E. A modification of the *F* scale of the MMPI. *Psychological Reports,* 1963, **12,** 427–433.
566. Coyle, F. A., Jr., and Heap, R. F. Interpreting the MMPI *L* scale. *Psychological Reports,* 1965, **17,** 722.
567. Craddick, R. A., and Stern, M. R. Note on the reliability of the MMPI scatter index. *Psychological Reports,* 1963, **13,** 380.
568. Crumpton, E., Cantor, J. M., and Batiste, C. A factor analytic study of Barron's Ego Strength scale. *Journal of Clinical Psychology,* 1960, **16,** 283–291.
569. Cutter, F. Self-rejection distress: A new MMPI scale. *Journal of Clinical Psychology,* 1964, **20,** 150–153.
570. Dempsey, P. A unidimensional depression scale for the MMPI. *Journal of Consulting Psychology,* 1964, **28,** 364–370.
571. Eaddy, M. L. An investigation of the Cannot Say scale of the group Minnesota Multiphasic Personality Inventory. *Dissertation Abstracts,* 1962, **23,** 1070–1071.
572. Edwards, A. L., Gocka, E. F., and Holloway, H. The development of an MMPI acquiescence scale. *Journal of Clinical Psychology,* 1964, **20,** 148–150.
573. Feder, C. Z. Relationship of repression-sensitization to adjustment status, social desirability, and acquiescence response set. *Journal of Consulting Psychology,* 1967, **31,** 401–406.
574. Finney, J. C. Development of a new set of MMPI scales. *Psychological Reports,* 1965, **17,** 707–713.
575. Finney, J. C. Relations and meaning of the new MMPI scales. *Psychological Reports,* 1966, **18,** 459–470.
576. Frank, G. H. A review of research with measures of ego strength derived

from the MMPI and the Rorschach. *Journal of General Psychology,* 1967, **77,** 183–206.

577. Gauron, E., Severson, R., and Englehart, R. MMPI *F* scores and psychiatric diagnosis. *Journal of Consulting Psychology,* 1962, **26,** 488.

578. Gocka, E. F., and Holloway, H. A composite MMPI introversion-extraversion scale. *Journal of Clinical Psychology,* 1962, **18,** 474–477.

579. Gold, S., DeLeon, P., and Swenson, C. Behavioral validation of a dominance-submission scale. *Psychological Reports,* 1966, **19,** 735–739.

580. Gottesman, I. I. More construct validation of the Ego Strength scale. *Journal of Consulting Psychology,* 1959, **23,** 342–346.

581. Grater, H. Impulse repression and emotional adjustment. *Journal of Consulting Psychology,* 1960, **24,** 144–149.

582. Gredt, F. H., and Downing, L. An extraversion scale for the MMPI. *Journal of Clinical Psychology,* **1961,** **17,** 156–159.

583. Griffith, A. V., and Fowler, R. D. Psychasthenic and Hypomanic scales of the MMPI and reaction to authority. *Journal of Counseling Psychology,* 1960, **7,** 146–147.

584. Gynther, M. D. The clinical utility of "invalid" MMPI *F* scores. *Journal of Consulting Psychology,* 1961, **25,** 540–542.

585. Gynther, M. D., and Petzel, T. P. Differential endorsement of MMPI *F* scale items by psychotics and behavior disorders. *Journal of Clinical Psychology,* 1967, **23,** 185–188.

586. Gynther, M. D., and Shimkunas, A. M. Age, intelligence, and MMPI *F* scores. *Journal of Consulting Psychology,* 1965, **29,** 383–388. (a)

587. Gynther, M. D., and Shimkunas, A. M. More data on MMPI *F* scores. *Journal of Clinical Psychology,* 1965, **21,** 275–277. (b)

588. Hawkinson, J. R. A study of the construct validity of Barron's Ego Strength scale with a state mental hospital population. *Dissertation Abstracts,* 4081.

589. Heilbrun, A. B., Jr. The psychological significance of the MMPI *K* scale in a normal population. *Journal of Consulting Psychology,* 1961, **25,** 486–491.

590. Himelstein, P., and Lubin, B. Relationship of the MMPI *K* scale and a measure of self-disclosure in a normal population. *Psychological Reports,* 1966, **19,** 166.

591. Himelstein, P., and Stoup, D. D. Correlation of three *MF* measures for males. *Journal of Clinical Psychology,* 1967, **23,** 189.

592. Holmes, D. S. Male-female differences in MMPI ego strength: An artifact. *Journal of Consulting Psychology,* 1967, **31,** 408–410.

593. Johnson, M. H., and Holmes, D. S. An attempt to develop a process-reactive scale for the MMPI. *Journal of Clinical Psychology,* 1967, **23,** 191.

594. Jurjevich, R. M. Relationships among the MMPI and HGI hostility scales. *Journal of General Psychology,* 1963, **69,** 131–133.
595. Kania, W. An investigation of the *K* scale of the MMPI as a measure of defensiveness in Protestant theological seminary students. *Dissertation Abstracts,* 1966, **26,** 6169–6170.
596. King, G. F., and Schiller, M. A research note on the *K* scale of the MMPI and "defensiveness." *Journal of Clinical Psychology,* 1959, **15,** 305–306.
597. Kleinmuntz, B. An extension of the construct validity of the Ego Strength scale. *Journal of Consulting Psychology,* 1960, **24,** 463–464. (a)
598. Kleinmuntz, B. Identification of maladjusted college students. *Journal of Counseling Psychology,* 1960, **7,** 209–211. (b)
599. Kleinmuntz, B. The college maladjustment scale (*Mt*): Norms and predictive validity. *Educational and Psychological Measurement,* 1961, **21,** 1029–1033.
600. Klopfer, W. G. Correlation of women's *Mf* scores on the MMPI and Strong VIB. *Journal of Clinical Psychology,* 1966, **22,** 216.
601. Knapp, R. R. A reevaluation of the validity of the MMPI scales of dominance and social responsibility. *Educational and Psychological Measurement,* 1960, **30,** 381–386.
602. Krippner, S. The relationship between MMPI and WAIS masculinity-femininity scores. *Personnel and Guidance Journal,* 1964, **42,** 695–698.
603. Kuethe, J. L. Acquiescent response set and the Psychasthenia scale: An analysis via the Aussage experiment. *Journal of Abnormal and Social Psychology,* 1960, **61,** 319–322.
604. L'Abate, L. MMPI scatter as a single index of maladjustment. *Journal of Clinical Psychology,* 1962, **18,** 142–143.
605. Lawton, M. P. Deliberate faking on the psychopathic deviate scale of the MMPI. *Journal of Clinical Psychology,* 1963, **19,** 327–330.
606. Lingoes, J. C. MMPI factors of the Harris and the Wiener subscales. *Journal of Consulting Psychology,* 1960, **24,** 74–83.
607. Maine, R. F., and Goodstein, L. D. Cross-validation of the Aaronson *Mf* index with a college population. *Psychological Reports,* 1966, **19,** 1141–1142.
608. Mosher, D. L. Some characteristics of high and low frequency "cannot say" items on the MMPI. *Journal of Consulting Psychology,* 1966, **30,** 177.
609. Murray, J. B. The *Mf* scale of the MMPI for college students. *Journal of Clinical Psychology,* 1963, **19,** 113–115.
610. Murray, J. B., Munley, M. J., and Gilbart, T. E. The *Pd* scale of the MMPI for college students. *Journal of Clinical Psychology,* 1965, **21,** 48–51.

611. Nakamura, C. Y. Validity of *K* scale (MMPI) in college counseling. *Journal of Counseling Psychology,* 1960, **7,** 108–115.
612. Pehle, J. W. Repression-sensitization and psychological adjustment. *Dissertation Abstracts,* 1966, **27,** 1628.
613. Ries, H. A. The MMPI *K* scale as a predictor of prognosis. *Journal of Clinical Psychology,* 1966, **22,** 212–213.
614. Rosen, A. Development of the MMPI scales based on a reference group of psychiatric patients. *Psychological Monographs,* 1962, **76,** (8, Whole No. 527), 25 pp.
615. Rosen, A. Diagnostic differentiation as a construct validity indicator for the MMPI ego strength scale. *Journal of General Psychology,* 1963, **69,** 293–297.
616. Ruch, F. L., and Ruch, W. W. The *K* factor as a (validity) suppressor variable in predicting success in selling. *Journal of Applied Psychology,* 1967, **51,** 201–204.
617. Salmon, P. Fould's punitiveness scales in relation to MMPI validation and diagnostic scales. *British Journal of Social and Clinical Psychology,* 1965, **4,** 207–213.
618. Shaffer, J. W. A new acquiescence scale for the MMPI. *Journal of Clinical Psychology,* 1963, **19,** 412–415.
619. Shipman, W. G. The validity of MMPI hostility scales. *Journal of Clinical Psychology,* 1965, **21,** 186–190.
620. Simmons, A. D. A comparison of repression-sensitization scores obtained by two different methods. *Journal of Clinical Psychology,* 1966, **22,** 465.
621. Sines, L. K., and Silver, R. J. An index of psychopathology (*Ip*) derived from clinicians' judgments of MMPI profiles. *Journal of Clinical Psychology,* 1963, **19,** 324–326.
622. Smith, E. E. Defensiveness, insight, and the *K* scale. *Journal of Consulting Psychology,* 1959, **23,** 275–277.
623. Steimel, R. J. Childhood experiences and masculinity-femininity scores. *Journal of Counseling Psychology,* 1960, **7,** 212–217.
624. Stone, L. A. Another note on the reliability of the MMPI Scatter Index. *Psychological Reports,* 1964, **15,** 445.
625. Stricker, G. A comparison of two MMPI prejudice scales. *Journal of Clinical Psychology,* 1961, **17,** 43.
626. Strickland, J. F., and Kuethe, J. L. An experimental investigation of the relationship between psychasthenia and ego strength. *Journal of General Psychology,* 1959, **60,** 245–252.
627. Ullmann, L. P. An empirically derived MMPI scale which measures facilitation-inhibition of recognition of threatening stimuli. *Journal of Clinical Psychology,* 1962, **18,** 127–132.
628. Vincent, N. M., Linsz, N. L., and Greene, M. I. The *L* scale of the MMPI as an index of falsification. *Journal of Clinical Psychology,* 1966, **22,** 214–215.

629. Vogel, J. L. Failure to validate the *Cr* and *Sm* scales of the MMPI. *Journal of Consulting Psychology,* 1963, **27,** 367.
630. Wohl, J., and Hyman, M. Relationship between measures of anxiety and constriction. *Journal of Clinical Psychology,* 1959, **15,** 54–55.
631. Yonge, G. D. Certain consequences of applying the *K* factor to MMPI scores. *Educational and Psychological Measurement,* 1966, **26,** 887–893.

MMPI with a Wide Range of Populations

632. Anastasio, M. M. The relationship of selected personality characteristics to the chronology of the menstrual cycle in women. *Dissertation Abstracts,* 1960, **20,** 3823.
633. Ashbrook, J. B., and Powell, R. K. Comparison of graduating and non-graduating theological students on the Minnesota Multiphasic Personality Inventory. *Journal of Counseling Psychology,* 1967, **14,** 171–174.
634. Ayer, M. J., Thoreson, R. W., and Butler, A. J. Predicting rehabilitation success with the MMPI and demographic data. *Personnel and Guidance Journal,* 1966, **44,** 631–637.
635. Baer, D. J., and Moynihan, J. F. Stepwise discriminant-function analysis of seminary-candidate MMPI scores. *Journal of Psychology,* 1964, **58,** 418–419.
636. Booth, E. G., Jr. Personality traits of athletes as measured by the MMPI: A rebuttal. *Research Quarterly of the American Association for Health, Physical Education, and Recreation,* 1961, **32,** 421–423.
637. Brown, P. L., and Berdie, R. F. Driver behavior and scores on the MMPI. *Journal of Applied Psychology,* 1960, **44,** 18–21.
638. Butterfield, E. C., and Warren, S. A. The use of the MMPI in the selection of hospital aides. *Journal of Applied Psychology,* 1962, **46,** 34–40.
639. Butterfield, E. C., and Warren, S. A. Prediction of attendant tenure. *Journal of Applied Psychology,* 1963, **47,** 101–103.
640. Chatterjee, B. B. Masculinity-femininity as predictor of job satisfaction of teachers. Psychologia: *International Journal of Psychology, Orient,* 1964, **7,** 223–232.
641. Clark, D. F. The psychometric characteristics of an adult class in psychology. *British Journal of Psychiatry,* 1965, **111,** 745–753.
642. Clark, D. L. Exploring behavior in men's residence halls using the MMPI. *Personnel and Guidance Journal,* 1964, **43,** 249–251.
643. Cole, D. L. The prediction of teaching performance. *Journal of Educational Research,* 1961, **54,** 345–348.

644. Cooke, M. K., and Kiesler, D. J. Prediction of college students who later require personal counseling. *Journal of Counseling Psychology,* 1967, **14,** 346–349.

645. Dempsey, P. The dimensionality of the MMPI clinical scales among normal subjects. *Journal of Consulting Psychology,* 1963, **27,** 492–497.

646. Ekman, P., Friesen, W. V., and Lutzker, D. R. Psychological reactions to infantry basic training. *Journal of Consulting Psychology,* 1962, **26,** 103–104.

647. Evans, R. R., Borgatta, E. F., and Bohrnstedt, G. W. Smoking and MMPI scores among entering freshmen. *Journal of Social Psychology,* 1967, **23,** 137–140.

648. Forsyth, R. P., and Smith, S. F. MMPI related behavior in a student nurse group. *Journal of Clinical Psychology,* 1967, **23,** 224–229.

649. Golden, J., Mandel, N., Glueck, B. C., Jr., and Feder, Z. A summary description of fifty "normal" white males. *American Journal of Psychiatry,* 1962, **119,** 48–56.

650. Gravitz, M. A. MMPI personality patterns for several semiskilled and unskilled occupational groups. *Psychological Reports,* 1966, **19,** 1315–1318.

651. Guthrie, G. M., and McKendry, M. S. Interest patterns of Peace Corps volunteers in a teaching project. *Journal of Educational Psychology,* 1963, **54,** 261–267.

652. Gynther, M. D., and Kempson, J. O. Seminarians and clinical pastorial training: A follow-up study. *Journal of Social Psychology,* 1962, **56,** 9–14.

653. Harder, D. F. Differentiation of curricular groups based upon responses to unique items of the MMPI. *Journal of Counseling Psychology,* 1959, **6,** 28–34.

654. Hathaway, S. R., Monachesi, E. D., and Young, L. A. Rural-urban adolescent personality. *Rural Sociology,* 1959, **24,** 331–346.

655. Heilbrun, A. B., Jr. Personality differences between adjusted and maladjusted college students. *Journal of Applied Psychology,* 1960, **44,** 341–346.

656. Hewitt, J. H., and Rosenberg, L. A. The MMPI as a screening device in an academic setting. *Educational and Psychological Measurement,* 1962, **22,** 129–137.

657. Hooke, J. F., and Marks, P. A. MMPI characteristics of pregnancy. *Journal of Clinical Psychology,* 1962, **18,** 316–317.

658. Johnson, R. W. Discrimination between diagnosed vocational and emotional counseling cases through a configural scoring of the MMPI and the graduation rate of diagnosed groups. *Dissertation Abstracts,* 1966, **27,** 957–958.

659. Kennedy, W. A. MMPI profiles of gifted adolescents. *Journal of Clinical Psychology,* 1962, **18,** 148–149.

660. King, B. T. Predicting submarine school attrition from the Minnesota Multiphasic Personality Inventory. *USN Medical Research Laboratory Report,* New London, 1959, **18** (Whole No. 313), 25 pp.

661. Knehr, C. A., and Kohl, R. N. MMPI screening of entering medical students. *Journal of Psychology,* 1959, **47,** 297–304.

662. Lowe, C. M. Prediction of post-hospital work adjustment by the use of psychological tests. *Journal of Counseling Psychology,* 1967, **14,** 248–252.

663. McDonald, R. L. Personality characteristics, cigarette smoking, and obstetric complications. *Journal of Psychology,* 1965, **60,** 129–134.

664. Murray, J. B., and Connolly, F. Follow-up of personality scores of seminarians seven years later. *Catholic Psychological Record,* 1966, **4,** 10–19.

665. Nyman, A. J., and LeMay, M. L. Differentiation of types of college misconduct offenses with MMPI subscales. *Journal of Clinical Psychology,* 1967, **23,** 99–100.

666. Roston, R. A. Some personality characteristics of male compulsive gamblers. *Proceedings of the Seventy-third Annual Convention of the American Psychological Association,* 1965, 263–264.

667. Sandness, D. G. The MMPI as a predictor in vocational rehabilitation. *Dissertation Abstracts,* 1967, **27,** 3681.

668. Schubert, D. S. P. Personality implications of cigarette smoking among college students. *Journal of Consulting Psychology,* 1959, **23,** 376.

669. Silver, R. J., and Sines, L. K. MMPI high point code frequencies in a state hospital population. *Journal of Clinical Psychology,* 1960, **16,** 298–300.

670. Silver, R. J., and Sines, L. K. MMPI characteristics of a state hospital population. *Journal of Clinical Psychology,* 1961, **17,** 142–146.

671. Sines, L. K., and Silver, R. J. MMPI correlates of ward placement among state hospital patients. *Journal of Clinical Psychology,* 1960, **16,** 404–406.

672. Slusher, H. S. Personality and intelligence characteristics of selected high school athletes and non-athletes. *Research Quarterly,* 1964, **35,** 539–545.

673. Spielberger, C. D., Weitz, H., and Denny, J. P. Group counseling and the academic performance of anxious college freshmen. *Journal of Counseling Psychology,* 1962, **9,** 195–204.

674. Swords, I. R. An investigation of personality variables associated with specified behaviors in men's residence halls. *Dissertation Abstracts,* 1966, **27,** 1275.

675. Thumin, F. J., and Wittenberg, A. Personality characteristics and non-payment of bills. *Journal of Clinical Psychology,* 1964, **20,** 234–235.

676. Vaughan, R. P. The influence of religious affiliation on the MMPI scales. *Journal of Clinical Psychology,* 1965, **21,** 416–417.
677. Wagner, E. E., and Dobbins, R. D. MMPI profiles of parishioners seeking pastoral counseling. *Journal of Consulting Psychology,* 1967, 31, 83–84.
678. Wright, M. W., Chylinski, J., Sisler, G. C., and Quarrington, B. Personality factors in the selection of civilians for isolated northern stations: A follow-up study. *Canadian Psychologist,* 1967, **8,** 23–31.
679. Wright, M. W., Sisler, G. C., and Chylinski, J. Personality factors in the selection of civilians for isolated northern stations. *Journal of Applied Psychology,* 1963, **47,** 24–29.
680. Yamamoto, J., and Seeman, W. A psychological study of castrated males. *Psychiatric Research Report,* 1960, **12,** 97–103.

Related Studies

681. Adams, D. K., and Horn, J. L. Nonoverlapping keys for the MMPI scales. *Journal of Consulting Psychology,* 1965, **29,** 284.
682. Altus, W. D. Inferring the sex of an author. *Journal of Psychology,* 1959, **48,** 215–218.
683. Amati, G., Ragozzino, D., and Procaccini, S. Rilievi e considerazion: sulla validita dell'impiego del Minnesota Multiphasic Personality Inventory (MMPI) nella pratica psichiatrico-forense (Notes and considerations on the validity for the use of the MMPI in psychiatric legal practice). *Archivio di Psicologia, Neurologia e Psichiatria,* 1962, **23,** 249–273.
684. Bergman, P., Malasky, C., and Zahn, T. P. Relation of sucking strength to personality variables. *Journal of Consulting Psychology,* 1967, **31,** 426–428.
685. Bottenberg, E. H., and Wehner, E. G. Mitteilung zur Zuverlassigkeit und Interkonsistenz der Standard-Skalen des MMPI Saarbrücken (Dependability and interconsistency of the standard scales of the MMPI Saarbrücken). *Diagnostica,* 1966, **12,** 85–86.
686. Chance, J. E. Personality differences and level of aspiration. *Journal of Consulting Psychology,* 1960, **24,** 111–115.
687. Clagett, A. F. Hathaway vs. Welsh on coding MMPI and a method proposed to reconcile differences of viewpoint. *Journal of Clinical Psychology,* 1961, **17,** 154–156.
688. Codking, D. Attitudes toward the imaginary: Their relationship to level of personality integration. *Dissertation Abstracts,* 1966, **27,** 1616–1617.
689. Dempsey, P. Score vs. performance on certain MMPI scales. *Journal of Clinical Psychology,* 1964, **20,** 254–255.
690. Devries, A. G. Chance expectancy, sample size, replacement and nonreplacement sampling. *Psychological Reports,* 1966, **18,** 843–850.

691. Dietze, D., Stotland, E., and Sparks, L. Experimental manipulation of sense of competence. *Perceptual and Motor Skills,* 1967, **24,** 785–786.
692. Dubno, P. Group effectiveness in relation to the interaction between decision time characteristics of leaders and task conditions. *Dissertation Abstracts,* 1961, **21,** 2390–2391.
693. Duker, J. The utility of the MMPI Atlas in the derivation of personality descriptions. *Dissertation Abstracts,* 1959, **19,** 3021.
694. Eisenman, R., and Taylor, R. E. Birth order and MMPI patterns. *Journal of Individual Psychology,* 1966, **22,** 208–211.
695. Eysenck, H. J. A note on "Impulse Repression and Emotional Adjustment." *Journal of Consulting Psychology,* 1961, **25,** 362–363.
696. Fauls, L. B. Measurements of interrelationships among selected suppression factors, anxiety, impulse expression, and ego strength. *Dissertation Abstracts,* 1966, **26,** (12, Pt. 1), 7446.
697. Fillenbaum, S. Some stylistic aspects of categorizing behavior. *Journal of Personality,* 1959, **27,** 187–195.
698. Fisher, J. The twisted pear and the prediction of behavior. *Journal of Consulting Psychology,* 1959, **23,** 400–405.
699. Fordyce, W. E., and Crow, W. R. Ego disjunction: A failure to replicate Trehub's results. *Journal of Abnormal and Social Psychology,* 1960, **60,** 446–448.
700. Foulds, G. A., Caine, T. M., and Creasy, M. A. Aspects of extra- and intro-punitive expression in mental illness. *Journal of Mental Science,* 1960, **106,** 599–610.
701. Frederiksen, N., and Gilbert, A. C. F. Replication of a study of differential predictability. *Educational and Psychological Measurement,* 1960, **20,** 759–767.
702. Freeman, D. An experimental investigation of the construct of self-cognition. *Dissertation Abstracts,* 1960, **20,** 4443.
703. Fulkerson, S. C. Individual differences in response validity. *Journal of Clinical Psychology,* 1959, **15,** 169–173.
704. Ghiselli, E. E. Moderating effects and differential reliability and validity. *Journal of Applied Psychology,* 1963, **47,** 81–86.
705. Gilberstadt, H., and Duker, J. Case history correlates of three MMPI profile types. *Journal of Consulting Psychology,* 1960, **24,** 361–367.
706. Goodstein, L. D., and Kirk, B. A. A six-year follow-up study of graduate students in public health education. *Journal of Applied Psychology,* 1961, **45,** 240–243.
707. Gowan, J. C., and Dible, I. Age effects on the test scores of women teaching candidates. *California Journal of Educational Research,* 1960, **11,** 37–38.
708. Gynther, M. D. Degree of agreement among three interpersonal system measures. *Journal of Consulting Psychology,* 1962, **26,** 107.
709. Haan, N. Coping and defense mechanisms related to personality inventories. *Journal of Consulting Psychology,* 1965, **29,** 373–378.

710. Harwood, B. T. Some intellectual correlates of schizoid indicators: WAIS and MMPI. *Journal of Consulting Psychology,* 1967, **31,** 218.
711. Henrichs, T. F. A note on the extension of the MMPI configural rules. *Journal of Clinical Psychology,* 1966, **22,** 51–52.
712. Hood, A. B. A study of the relationship between physique and personality variables measured by the MMPI. *Journal of Personality,* 1963, **31,** 97–107.
713. Huff, F. W. Use of actuarial description of abnormal personality in a mental hospital. *Psychological Reports,* 1965, **17,** 224.
714. Jenkins, T. N. The primary trait anatomy of the MMPI. *Journal of Psychology,* 1963, **55,** 49–61.
715. Joy, V. L. Repression-sensitization, personality, and interpersonal behavior. *Dissertation Abstracts,* 1964, **24,** 2976–2977.
716. Jurjevich, R. M. The regression toward the mean in MMPI, California Psychological Inventory, and the Symptom Checklist. *Educational and Psychological Measurement,* 1966, **26,** 661–664.
717. Kassarjian, H. H., and Kassarjian, W. M. Personality correlates of inner- and other-direction. *Journal of Social Psychology,* 1966, **70,** 281–285.
718. Kerr, M., Maki, B., and Ammons, R. B. Personality, values, and "intellectualism." *Proceedings of the Montana Academy of Sciences,* 1962, **21,** 132–136.
719. Kidd, A. H., and Rivoire, J. L. Personality variables and attitudes toward traditional cultural fantasy. *Journal of Clinical Psychology,* 1965, **21,** 377–380.
720. Kleinmuntz, B. Screening: Identification or prediction? *Journal of Counseling Psychology,* 1961, **8,** 279–280.
721. Kreitman, N. Psychiatric orientation: A study of attitudes among psychiatrists. *Journal of Mental Science,* 1962, **108** (Whole No. 454), 317–328.
722. Kuethe, J. L., and Hulse, S. H. Pessimism as a determinant of the tendency to claim undesirable symptoms on personality inventories. *Psychological Reports,* 1960, **7,** 435–438.
723. Lerea, L., and Goldberg, A. The effects of socialization upon group behavior. *Speech Monographs,* 1961, **28,** 60–64.
724. Levitan, S., Goldfarb, J., and Jacobs, A. The relationship between an actuarial and a clinical analysis of MMPI profiles. *Psychological Newsletter,* New York University, 1959, **10,** 295–298.
725. Logue, P. E. Concurrent validation of two counselor selection inventories. *Dissertation Abstracts,* 1966, **26,** 6170–6171.
726. Lykken, D. T., and Rose, R. Psychological prediction from actuarial tables. *Journal of Clinical Psychology,* 1963, **19,** 139–151.
727. MacKinnon, D. W. Fostering creativity in students of engineering. *Journal of Engineering Education,* 1961, **52,** 129–142.
728. McDonald, R. L. Ego control patterns and attribution of hostility to self, parents, and others. *Perceptual and Motor Skills,* 1965, **21,** 340–348.

729. Madden, J. E. Semantic differential rating of self and of self-reported personal characteristics. *Journal of Consulting Psychology,* 1961, **25,** 183.

730. Mann, N. A. The relationship between defense preference and response to free association. *Journal of Projective Techniques and Personality Assessment,* 1967, **31,** 59–61.

731. Meehl, P. E. The cognitive activity of the clinician. *American Psychologist,* 1960, **15,** 19–27.

732. Mehlman, B., and Rand, M. E. Face validity of the MMPI. *Journal of General Psychology,* 1960, **63,** 171–178.

733. Oskamp, S. Clinical Judgments from the MMPI: Simple or complex? *Journal of Clinical Psychology,* 1967, **23,** 411–415.

734. Palem, R. M. Le clinicien devant le MMPI (The clinician before the MMPI). *Annales Médico-psychologiques,* 1966, **2,** 35–37.

735. Parker, C. A. The predictive use of the MMPI in a college counseling center. *Journal of Counseling Psychology,* 1961, **18,** 154–158.

736. Peek, R. M., and Olson, G. W. *Organization and internal structure of the MMPI.* (2nd ed.) Hastings, Minn.: Hastings State Hospital, 1959, 66 pp.

737. Peskin, H. Unity of science begins at home: A study of regional factionalism in clinical psychology. *American Psychologist,* 1963, **18,** 96–100.

738. Pichot, P., Perse, J., and Zimbaca, N. Etude sur la fidélité de l'Inventaire Multiphasique de Personnalité du Minnesota (MMPI) par la méthode du partage par moitié (Study of the reliability of the MMPI by the split-half method). *Revue de Psychologie Appliquée,* 1961, **11,** 297–301.

739. Rees, M. E., and Goldman, M. Some relationships between creativity and personality. *Journal of General Psychology,* 1961, **65,** 145–161.

740. Rogers, A. H., and Walsh, T. M. Defensiveness and unwitting self-evaluation. *Journal of Clinical Psychology,* 1959, **15,** 302–304.

741. Rosman, R. R., Barry, S. M., and Gibeau, P. J. Problems in Atlas classification of MMPI profiles. *Journal of Clinical Psychology,* 1966, **22,** 308–310.

742. Schulman, R. E., and London, P. Hypnotic susceptibility and MMPI profiles. *Journal of Consulting Psychology,* 1963, **27,** 157–160.

743. Sheldon, M. S., Coale, J. M., and Copple, R. Concurrent validity of the "warm teacher scale." *Journal of Educational Psychology,* 1959, **50,** 37–40.

744. Shupe, D. R., and Bramwell, P. F. Prediction of escape from MMPI data. *Journal of Clinical Psychology,* 1963, **19,** 223–226.

745. Singer, J. L., and Schonbar, R. A. Correlates of day-dreaming: A dimension of self-awareness. *Journal of Consulting Psychology,* 1961, **25,** 1–6.

746. Steiner, I. D. Sex differences in the resolution of A-B-X conflicts. *Journal of Personality,* 1960, **28,** 118–128.

747. Stone, L. A., and Margoshes, A. Verbal embellishment responses on the MMPI. *Journal of Clinical Psychology*, 1965, **21**, 278–279.

748. Taggart, M. Characteristics of participants and nonparticipants in individual test-interpretation interviews. *Journal of Consulting Psychology*, 1967, **31**, 213–215.

749. Tart, C. T. Frequency of dream recall and some personality measures. *Journal of Consulting Psychology*, 1962, **26**, 467–470.

750. Terwilliger, R. F. Sensitivity and recall. *Psychological Reports*, **14**, 217–218.

751. Wagner, R. F., and Williams, J. E. An analysis of speech behavior in groups differing in achievement imagery and defensiveness. *Journal of Personality*, 1961, **29**, 1–9.

752. Wallach, M. S., and Schooff, K. Reliability of degree of disturbance ratings. *Journal of Clinical Psychology*, 1965, **21**, 273–275.

753. Weisgerber, C. A. Comparison of normalized and linear *T* scores in the MMPI. *Journal of Clinical Psychology*, 1965, **21**, 412–415.

754. Wilke, M. M. Experimentally induced "repression" as a function of personality variables. *Dissertation Abstracts*, 1961, **22**, 655–656.

755. Young, R. C. Some parameters of personality description with the MMPI in a state hospital population. *Dissertation Abstracts*, 1963, **24**, 2129.

756. Zuckerman, M., and Oltean, M. Some relationships between maternal attitude factors and authoritarianism, personality needs, psychopathology, and self-acceptance. *Child Development*, 1959, **30**, 27–36.

NAME INDEX

SUBJECT INDEX